THE SILVER FORK]

In the early nineteenth century there was a sudden vogue for novels centring on the glamour of aristocratic social and political life. Such novels, attractive as they were to middle-class readers, were condemned by contemporary critics as dangerously seductive, crassly commercial, designed for the 'masses' and utterly unworthy of regard. Until recently, silver fork novels have eluded serious consideration and been overshadowed by authors such as Jane Austen. They were influenced by Austen at their very deepest levels, but were paradoxically drummed out of history by the very canon-makers who were using Austen's name to establish their own legitimacy. This first modern full-length study of the silver fork novel argues that these novels were in fact tools of persuasion, novels deliberately aimed at bringing the British middle classes into an alliance with an aristocratic programme of political reform.

EDWARD COPELAND is Emeritus Professor of English at Pomona College, Claremont, California.

CAMBRIDGE STUDIES IN NINETEENTH-CENTURY
LITERATURE AND CULTURE

General editor
Gillian Beer, *University of Cambridge*

Nineteenth-century British literature and culture have been rich fields for interdisciplinary studies. Since the turn of the twentieth century, scholars and critics have tracked the intersections and tensions between Victorian literature and the visual arts, politics, social organization, economic life, technical innovations, scientific thought – in short, culture in its broadest sense. In recent years, theoretical challenges and historiographical shifts have unsettled the assumptions of previous scholarly synthesis and called into question the terms of older debates. Whereas the tendency in much past literary critical interpretation was to use the metaphor of culture as 'background', feminist, Foucauldian and other analyses have employed more dynamic models that raise questions of power and of circulation. Such developments have reanimated the field. This series aims to accommodate and promote the most interesting work being undertaken on the frontiers of the field of nineteenth-century literary studies: work which intersects fruitfully with other fields of study such as history, or literary theory, or the history of science. Comparative as well as interdisciplinary approaches are welcomed.

A complete list of titles published will be found at the end of the book.

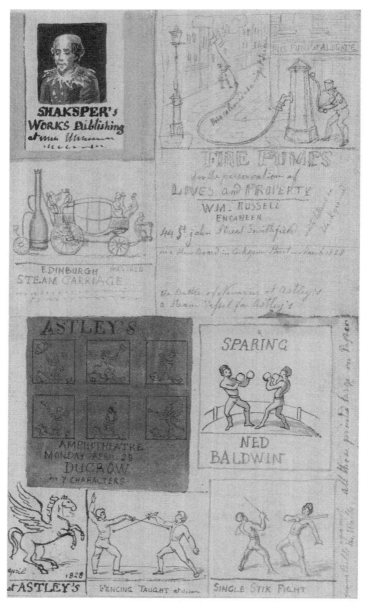

Frontispiece: 'Flyposters (1828)', by George Scharf. Courtesy of the British Museum.

THE SILVER FORK NOVEL

Fashionable Fiction in the Age of Reform

EDWARD COPELAND

CAMBRIDGE
UNIVERSITY PRESS

CAMBRIDGE
UNIVERSITY PRESS

University Printing House, Cambridge CB2 8BS, United Kingdom

Cambridge University Press is part of the University of Cambridge.

It furthers the University's mission by disseminating knowledge in the pursuit of education, learning and research at the highest international levels of excellence.

www.cambridge.org
Information on this title: www.cambridge.org/9781107507661

© Edward Copeland 2012

First published 2012
First paperback edition 2015

A catalogue record for this publication is available from the British Library

Library of Congress Cataloguing in Publication data
Copeland, Edward.
The silver fork novel : fashionable fiction in the age of reform / Edward Copeland.
pages   cm. – (Cambridge studies in nineteenth-century literature and culture ; 81)
Includes bibliographical references and index.
ISBN 978-0-521-51333-3
1. English fiction–19th century–History and criticism.   2. Great Britain–Social life and customs–19th century.   3. Fashion in literature.   I. Title.
PR868.S615C66   2012
823′.809–dc23
2012011695

ISBN 978-0-521-51333-3 Hardback
ISBN 978-1-107-50766-1 Paperback

Contents

Figures

Acknowledgements

This study began quite a few years ago and has inevitably brought on many debts to the kindness of strangers and the tolerance of friends and relations. My appreciation for institutional support goes first to Pomona College for its never-failing generosity in providing financial support and leaves of absence for research. For recent financial support towards the completion of this project, I am grateful to the Andrew W. Mellon Foundation for making a year of work at The British Library in 2008–9 possible. To Robert Folkenflik at the University of California, Irvine, and to Anne Mellor at the University of California, Los Angeles, I am grateful for opportunities to present my ideas to their colleagues for advice that has been most useful. In the early stages of the project, I met hospitality and assistance of the same kind from Emma Clery and her colleagues at the University of Sheffield. To the Austen Society, UK, and to JASNA, the Jane Austen Society of North America, I can express my gratitude again for the repeated kindness of Society members in listening to talks at various stages in this study's progress. To the Chawton House Library, Hampshire, I would like to express my gratitude for asking me to speak as the project was nearing completion, a memorable opportunity to draw things together.

I would like to acknowledge the research done by scholars in the field of silver fork studies whose work I have called on, particularly Winifred Hughes, who set the pattern for present-day studies, and recent essays by Andrea Hibbard, April Kendra, Patrick Leary, Margaret Linley, Nicholas Mason, Marie Mulvey-Roberts, Rebecca Newman and Tamara Wagner, to mention only a few. Muireann O'Cinneide's excellent *Aristocratic Women and the Literary Nation, 1832–1867* (2008) and a recent 'Special Issue: Silver Fork Fiction' in the journal *Women's Writing* (August 2009), edited by Tamara Wagner, have been sources of inspiration and information. This study would have been impossible without the work done in recent years by theorists of Regency and late-Regency literature who have taken on the task of reintegrating it into its contemporary contexts. My thanks go to them, to Claudia Johnson, Deidre Lynch, Clara Tuite, Kathryn Sutherland, Jocelyn Harris and Clifford Siskin in particular, but to the many other scholars in the field whose work has been most helpful. I have relied heavily on historians of the period and am only concerned that I have internalized so much of their work that I have not given proper credit when and where it is due – to the work of Arthur Aspinall, David Cannadine, Linda Colley, Eric Evans, Norman Gash, Peter Jupp, Leslie Mitchell, Frank O'Gorman, Donald Southgate and Dror Wahrman. For the courtesies and assistance given me by librarians at the University of California, Los Angeles, the Huntington Library in San Marino, California, the Honnold Library in Claremont, California, and The British Library in London, I am deeply appreciative.

I am indebted to Michèle Cohen for reading the chapter 'Reform and the Silver Fork Heroine' and giving me useful advice on revisions, and to Linda Bree and my Cambridge University Press readers who have guided me in shaping and organizing the study. I would like to express my thanks to the editors of *Eighteenth-Century Life* for permission to draw on my essay entitled 'Crossing Oxford Street: Silver Fork Geopolitics', 25 (Spring 2001), pp. 116–34, for material in Chapter 5 of this study. To Jane Austen friends who have listened to my obsession with silver fork novels, Deirdre Le Faye, Helen Lefroy, David Selwyn, Juliet McMaster, Kathryn Sutherland and Jocelyn Harris, I say thank you. For indispensable help with computer challenges I am grateful to Philip Copeland and to Denise Ostman Copeland. To my wife, Margaret Mathies, who read every word many times, listened to my lectures, laughed at the right times, and whose editorial skills made the book possible, I am grateful beyond thanks.

Introduction

The first sounding for this project, a study of late-Regency novels of fashionable life, came in a telephone call from the Regency Club of Southern California. Could I do a lecture, a brief one please, for the Regency Club gala? I could talk during dinner, perhaps while people were eating dessert, after which the members of the Club could get on with what they came for, Regency dancing. As the speaker I would not need to wear a Regency costume (unless I wanted to), but everyone else would be in Regency dress. The topic, 'something about food or wine', would be ideal. This happened a long time ago, and I missed my chance. I had to tell the chairman that I did not know a thing about the Regency – what *I* did was Jane Austen. Today it seems strange to remember such a restricted world of literary studies. Nevertheless, the Regency Club chairman put me to rethinking the issue – that, first, I really ought to know something about the Regency and, second, that the Regency must have something more interesting going for it than dancing and smart costumes.

In the 1970s there seemed to be two Regencies, the one that was respectable to study, Jane Austen for the most part, and then its bedraggled shadow, the Regency of ripped bodices, Georgette Heyer and Harlequin romances. Today Regency studies do much better, with Byron, Jane Austen, Walter Scott, Anna Laetitia Barbauld, Maria Edgeworth, Frances Burney and Susan Ferrier, all solid and respectable enough to be included in anybody's doctoral dissertation. But these authors, Byron excluded, have little to say about the seductive, glamorous Regency that the party-minded Regency Club had in mind. Besides, the careers of these early Regency authors (Scott's an exception) were done and dusted considerably before the close of the 'long' Regency in 1837, when Victoria's Regency-era uncle died and everyone became a Victorian.

Until recently, the second half of the 'long' Regency, the reign of George IV, 1820 to 1830, and that of his younger brother William IV, 1830 to 1837, has been a missing piece in the history of the novel. Fresh studies of the novels of the period, the 1820s and 1830s, only began to appear in the 1990s. The exceptions to this, of course, are Matthew Whiting Rosa's *The Silver-Fork School: Novels of Fashion Preceding* Vanity Fair (1936), Alison Adburgham's *Silver Fork Society: Fashionable Life and Literature from 1814 to 1840* (1983) and Ellen Moers' brilliant study, *The Dandy: from Brummell to Beerbohm* (1960). Matthew Rosa's study, however, belongs to a period of formalist criticism of the 1930s, a style of criticism which takes novels of fashionable life, at best, as slightly embarrassing precursors to 'great literature', i.e. Thackeray. Alison Adburgham, a former journalist and newspaper writer, captures the point of fashionable-life novels far better, celebrating their close attachment to consumerism, celebrity news, insider social information and the wider world of power and politics, but she unintentionally offers a reprise of the silver fork novel at its most anarchic: a display of facts and insights that defy organization, with enough scandal, gossip and surprising information, not all of it accurate, to please Henry Colburn himself, the contemporary publisher of silver fork novels.

At present there is no general framework for identifying 'the silver fork school' in the outlines of its historical and literary contexts. Rosa's study suggests that the task is not worth doing and Adburgham's that it may not be possible. Neither is the case. The number of authors writing silver fork novels, for example, is not difficult to determine – around eight significant authors, four men and four women, with a few extras tucked in around the edges. The period of time in which novels of fashionable life flourished, 1825 to 1841, is limited on both ends by the span of the Reform era, beginning in 1825 as the winds of political change began to whisper, and closing in 1841 with the defeat of Lord Melbourne's post-Reform Whig government. The significant role of silver fork novels in the political and social debates of the Reform era cannot be overestimated. This is a period, historians remind us, in which Britain came closest to violent revolution since the seventeenth century. Novels of fashionable life were novels about power, who has it and who doesn't. Reform produced the issues that silver fork authors engaged, the renegotiation of traditional systems of power, including the shifts in social relationships and status that come along with such momentous change.

Thus far it is simple enough to mark out the boundaries and political significance of the 'school'. However, a truly off-kilter fact – that silver fork novels were more or less expunged from literary history – complicates our ability to look at them dispassionately. The black hole in literary history between Jane Austen and Charlotte Brontë remains. Reasons for the disappearance of silver fork novels are not hard to understand. First of all, the materials of modern life that made them exciting to contemporaries – social rivalries, political manoeuvring, fashion, newspapers, ephemeral print culture in general – make them difficult to experience the same way again. Once the excitement was over, later generations were bound to find a diminishing interest in them. Second and far more effective in sending them off-stage, however, was the effort of a nascent, self-defining literary establishment of the 1830s to sink these novels as non-canonical, low, commercial and not worthy to be included in the company of Literature. The programme was motivated in some cases by personal animosity towards a specific writer, but more generally by the lofty notion that Authorship was a Profession, and that novels conceived and marketed solely for profit were definitely downmarket, not Literature, and an embarrassment to the status aspirations of real Authors. A third reason for their disappearance, one not usually considered, is that silver fork novels were a political embarrassment to the next generation, both to liberal-leaning and to conservative Victorians. With only a few exceptions, silver fork novels had supported the liberalizing Whig Party policies of social and political reform that led to the Reform Bill. The Whig programme, in its most general terms, aimed to unite in a reformed Parliament the traditional ruling classes with the newly enfranchised middle classes. The future government of Great Britain would then consist of responsible aristocratic overseers generously guiding an enlarged middle-class electorate – an essential buffer against more troubling political demands from radicals and the working classes. From 1825 until the passage of the Reform Bill in 1832, this had been the leading liberal position in Great Britain. After Reform, however, this Whig vision of political reform began to look more and more unsatisfactory, largely because the aristocracy did not adapt to the changes in the political climate, but continued to govern in the same old ways. To contemporaries the supremely aristocratic Whig governments of Lord Grey and later Lord Melbourne seemed little different from any other pre-Reform governments they had known. Gratitude for the significant achievements of Whig liberalism, for the urgent compromises, the high ideals and the courage that it had taken to get their Reform Bill all the way to the King's signature, was in short supply. There was now another game in town, organized partisan politics that saw no reason to encourage sentimental notions of aristocratic power. As a consequence, the very novels that had helped to prepare the way for Reform became a political embarrassment, particularly to male middle-class Authors, some of whom had their own ambitions for political careers in the new world of party politics. Disraeli and Bulwer, once Whig liberals themselves, prudently altered later editions of their pre-Reform novels to mitigate the offence.

Another reason for the low visibility of silver fork novels today is that they are truly eccentric to present-day readers who expect to find in them the conventions of the realist novel. They can seem irresponsibly giddy in their acceptance of surfaces, of print culture, advertisements and fashion as ways of knowing, which is Matthew Whiting Rosa's main objection to them. Their plots seem to twist and turn disturbingly with little reference to the psychological forces that move the realist fictions of Jane Austen, for example. The suspicion arises that there must be something else in the wider culture propelling these narratives. For contemporaries in the Reform era, there was little more exciting, or distressing, than the sense that their lives were literally 'passing before their eyes'. Parliamentary debates in the newspapers, fire-breathing editorials from the political left and right, an aristocracy eager to flaunt and display its power were not distant phenomena for the reading public. They were quite literally 'street' knowledge. Novels that could package such knowledge as a way of knowing the world were highly marketable – enough to make their publishers, if not their authors, very rich indeed. Today, allusions in these novels to an unfamiliar political and social history can tempt a modern reader to slide by them for the easier attractions of well-turned plots and finely probed characters.

In constructing an ordered map of the 'silver fork school', two plans suggest themselves: first, an author-by-author trip through the novels to package the material and make it conveniently accessible. To accomplish this aim, an Appendix to this study lists the authors alphabetically, with brief biographical information, followed by the author's works arranged chronologically by publication date, each work accompanied by a plot summary and by an explanatory comment, if appropriate.

The second approach, the one chosen for the body of the study, attempts to explain how contemporary readers might have experienced these novels. A consideration of the political and social issues that attracted readers is of course an important task, but an examination of the print culture in which the novels found their place is equally revealing. The great flourishing of visual knowledge in the 1820s and '30s – advertisements, newspapers, museums, scientific demonstrations, panoramas – was essential to the experience of reading silver fork novels. See the Frontispiece, *Flyposters* (1828).

Chapter 1, 'Cultural contexts', addresses the reading practices of a society flooded with such an abundance of information. How, for example, new ways of reading could make silver fork novels, each three volumes in length and consisting of more than three hundred pages per volume, delightful enough to bring readers back to the circulating library for the next novel and the next author. The reading skills of speed, the fast return and hurry-up that lending libraries demanded of their readers, inevitably produced different expectations of what a novel should be and how it should be read. Chapter 2, 'The woman's tradition: Edgeworth, Burney and Austen', turns the tables on new reading styles for a consideration of an earlier women's literature. It explores how this familiar heritage gave authors and readers of silver fork fiction useful signposts for interpreting the contemporary moral, social and political issues at stake. Paradoxically, silver fork novels cast a light backwards on the significance of the older tradition, sifting it for powers that were perhaps never envisioned by the earlier writers.

The political history of the period, of course, demands attention, the task that occupies Chapter 3, 'Reform and the silver fork novel'. It would be hard to overestimate the attachment of these novels to the politics of reform, not merely general, but in specifics. Year by year silver fork novels follow the political and social developments, responding to each – the elections, the change of government from Tories to Whigs, the propaganda of the parties, representations of the best-known political players – not just to sell novels, but as attempts to lever power, to bring about the major changes in attitude necessary to make an effective union of the middle classes and the traditional ruling classes. The next chapter, Chapter 4, on 'Newspapers and the silver fork novel', delves into the awareness in the novels of a union of classes already well under way. Silver fork novelists exploit the power of newspapers to bear witness to a shared commercial culture of classes.

Chapter 5, 'The topography of silver fork London' brings attention to the politics of the urban landscape in silver fork novels, particularly the political fictions governing the topographic importance of Oxford Street in separating the aspiring residents of Marylebone, to the north of the street, from elegant, aristocratic and politically powerful Mayfair, on the south side of the street. The political design of Regent Street, which provides a convenient conduit to Westminster, the seat of government, through both of these power neighbourhoods, Marylebone and Mayfair, plays a large role for characters in the novels, but also for the social and political imaginations of contemporary Londoners. The Colosseum, a Marylebone entertainment venue situated at the southern end of Regent's Park, provides contemporary witness to the contested political imagination that governs the topography of silver fork novels.

The last chapter, 'Reform and the silver fork heroine', takes into account the fate of aristocratic women in silver fork novels. The traditional skills of 'polite discourse' that gave heroines an essential role in the display of aristocratic power simply disappear as an essential element of political life after 1832. They had begun to diminish in their significance years before, as Elizabeth Bennet's rejection of Mr Darcy's notions of 'an accomplished woman' reminds us. But silver fork novelists give 'accomplishments', understood as 'politeness discourse', a last chance to convey their literary and political powers into Reform. It's a story of mixed triumph and defeat, but an aristocratic heroine's accomplishments provide a remarkably poignant conclusion to the silver fork genre and the fatal loss of its political basis for existence.

Silver fork novels are so intimately attached to the political and cultural issues of the Reform years that they can scarcely be understood, much less appreciated, outside that context. The danger for present-day scholars is to underestimate these novels, to let them become confused with the novels George Eliot pillories in 'Silly Novels by Lady Novelists' (1856), works written twenty years later, divorced from the cultural upheavals that gave silver fork novels their reason for being. 'Fashion', the running trope of silver fork novels, is under review at all times, not as mindless 'millinery', but as the drapery of power – in social occasions, political poses, dress, shopping, architecture, reading and manners. The ephemeral conditions of fashion, in fact, give it its strength. In novels driven by the consciousness of moving time, 'fashion' becomes the novelist's deliberate instrument of choice – the perfect trope for a nation, as it seemed to contemporaries, rushing pell-mell towards an uncertain, ambivalent future.

So, we are back to the Regency Club and my invited lecture, which has turned out to be rather longer than requested, not a brief talk suitable for presenting over dessert and coffee. On the other hand, the Regency Club diners would have found readings from the novels absolutely delightful. I have taken the opportunity in this study, in fact, to include liberal citations from the novels in order to give present-day readers a sense of the wit and sharp observation that contemporary readers would have appreciated.

Some novels appear more than once, in one chapter and then another, for the richness of their source material. The focus of each chapter is an attempt take the silver fork genre a step beyond Rosa's and Adburgham's studies by situating the novels in the literary and political history that brought them into being, both as reporters and as active participants in contemporary struggles for Reform.

Cultural contexts

There is a wonderful power in words, formed into regular propos-
itions, and printed in capital letters, to draw assent after them.

William Hazlitt[1]

NEW CONTEXTS

The most telling mark of the late Regency is its vast culture of flourishing
print, with 'print' understood, paradoxically, as Clifford Siskin describes
'writing', a shorthand for the 'entire configuration of writing, print, and
silent reading'.[2] Novels of fashionable life embrace this culture vigorously
to present, in Walter Benjamin's perceptive term, 'moral dioramas ... of
unscrupulous multiplicity'.[3] Alexander Zevin suggests that 'the question
of representation, of how ideologies, institutions, names and images are
codified' is exactly the task of such panoramic literature – to bring prints,
maps, guides, caricatures, pamphlets, posters, advertisements, journals,
magazines into their purview. Their joint 'obsession' to codify, he writes,
was one in which 'newspapers and novels were *concomitant* with panoramic literature'.[4] As the *Westminster Review* remarked in 1829, 'The daily
press ... has an omnipresent vision—there is nothing too high for its
grasp—nothing too minute for its attention. It occupies itself with all
public affairs—and with all private concerns as soon as they come within
the circle of public interest.'[5]

Benjamin's 'unscrupulous multiplicity' of print creates a reality of its
own, as Clifford Siskin argues, citing the physicist David Deutsch for
confirmation: 'in our planetariums, books, films, and computer memories, and in our brains – there are images of physical reality at large,
images not just of the appearance of objects, but of the structure of reality'. Deutsch argues, 'To the extent that [they] are true – that is, they
resemble in appropriate respects the concrete or abstract things they refer

to – their existence gives reality a new sort of self-similarity, the self-similarity we call knowledge.'[6]

In the early years of the nineteenth century, the novel had become 'the vehicle of almost every kind of knowledge', writes Siskin. 'The reform-minded public of 1832 wanted "facts" and fiction was now valued as a practical way of meeting the demand' – which is to say, argues Siskin, 'Novels began to become "information systems".'[7] Bulwer's remark in the 'Introduction' to *Paul Clifford* (1830) makes a similar point: 'Readers now look into fiction for facts, as Voltaire, in his witty philosophy, looked among facts for fiction.'[8] The 'information systems' of the silver fork novel, however, were perceived almost exclusively in exhibitionary forms, not in the organizational systems that would become the characterizing feature of later, Victorian literature.

The culture of silver fork novels rests on surfaces – dioramas, panoramas, the spectacles of urban life perceived as transparent conveyors of knowledge.[9] Letitia Landon confesses in her novel *Romance and Reality* (1831), 'One great reason why we believe so devoutly in the beauty of Italy, is that we chiefly know it from plates.' She then proceeds to recall seeing a print that mystified her:

I remember seeing an architectural view—on one side stood a noble old house, the spire and roof of a church, a mass of fine-looking buildings, a distant view of a colonnade, and a broad open space with an equestrian statue. I did not at first believe it could be Charing Cross whose effect was so imposing; and it was not till Northumberland House and St. Martin's Church were identified, that my confession was fairly extorted, of how little justice one does to the beauty of London. (II, 265)

The visual technologies of popular London culture, the Panorama in Leicester Square,[10] the Colosseum in Regent's Park,[11] the Cosmorama in Regent Street,[12] the Diorama near Regent's Park and Madame Tussaud's in Baker Street offered Londoners an epistemology of the world. For the Diorama, the spectators sat on benches in the dark to face a painting apparently set in a frame, but actually placed in a perspective tunnel.[13] The painting, done in translucent and opaque pigments, had natural light on it manipulated from above by a system of screens and shutters to produce a show lasting for ten to fifteen minutes, one of the most popular being a ruined abbey emerging from the dim illumination of starlight and moonlight into the opening rays of morning and full day.[14] 'There is no effect that cannot be produced in this admirable establishment', marvelled contemporaries: 'Sunrise and sunset; dawn and twilight, moonlight; the obscuration of the sun by a passing cloud ... are all faithfully delineated, and without anything like theatrical effect.'[15] Henry Lister borrowed a representation of this technology for an early morning view of Oxford Street in his novel *Granby* (1826):

The whole extent of that long vista, unclouded by the mid-day smoke, was distinctly visible to his eye at once. The houses shrunk to half their span, while the few visible spires of the adjacent churches seemed to rise less distant than before, gaily tipped with early sunshine, and much diminished in apparent size, but heightened in distinctness and in beauty. Had it not been for the cool grey tint which slightly mingled with every object, the brightness was almost that of noon. But the life, the bustle, the busy din, the flowing tide of human existence, were all wanting to complete the similitude. (1, 298)

The visual information of print (in its widest sense) turns London into 'an endless promotion of surfaces', a fresh way of knowing the world.[16] The frontispiece of this book, for example, shows *Flyposters* (1828), George Scharf's sketch of a London wall offering a comically wide range of poster enticements: 'Shakesper's Works', 'Fire Pumps', 'The Edinburgh Steam Carriage', 'Single Stick Fighting', 'Sparing Ned Baldwin', 'Fencing Taught' and 'DUCROW' (the famous equestrian performer) appearing on 'Monday, April 28, in 7 Characters', six individually illustrated. Timeliness and surface immediacy are the expectation. A diorama of *The Burning of the Houses of Parliament* was painted, mounted and available for viewing within a week of the event.[17] Anna Jameson's novel *Diary of an Ennuyée* (1826) demonstrates the extent of public interest in the power of such 'virtual presence'. After travelling to see Lake Geneva for herself, the heroine of the novel reports:

The Panorama exhibited in London just before I left it, is wonderfully correct, with one pardonable exception; the artist did not venture to make the waters of the lake of the intense ultramarine tinged with violet as I now see them before me; 'So darkly, deeply, beautifully blue.' It would have shocked English eyes as an exaggeration, or rather impossibility. (37)

Urban life in fashionable novels rests on a reader's familiarity with a wide variety of such urban representations produced by popular culture. As the advertising puff for Catherine Gore's novel *Women as They Are* claimed in the *Morning Post*, 11 February 1830, 'Altogether this Work forms a *moving panorama* of the manners of the day.' In his study *Imagining the Middle Class* Dror Wahrman describes the 1820s as being 'strangely quiet', as if the mammoth upheaval of the great Reform Bill, like the blast of an unexpected storm, appeared with no preparation. In fact, during the ten years prior to the shock of September 1831, when Lord Grey actually introduced a bill for parliamentary reform, a long stream of ephemeral productions – woodcuts, engravings, lithographs, city guides, newspapers, novels, magazines, journals, annuals – had been documenting the changing face of the nation with obsessive attention, particularly to material changes that readers could see in the streets. The effects of fashion threatened new attitudes to rank and station, with spruce new clothing in the lower ranks, and rafts of other observable *things* that were simply not as they used to be. The inflamed resistance of conservatives to change, social and political, was in part a response to what everyone else could see daily around them. As an elderly aristocrat in Lady Bury's novel *The Separation* (1830) claims, 'Oh! I always thought what the improvements would bring us to—steam, and gas, and the march of intellect—I always prophesied it—now, my lord, you will see that steam, and gas, and intellect, will ruin us at last' (I, 37–8).

Long before the constitutional strife of Catholic Emancipation and the Reform Bill arrived to capture public attention in the mid 1820s and early 1830s, a popular scrutiny of the aristocracy and the middle classes had been common in the press, mostly formulaic, with frowns directed towards the extravagance of the aristocracy and mocking laughter towards pretensions to fashion in the middle classes. The early silver fork novelists of the mid 1820s recycle Frances Burney's Branghton family from *Evelina* (1778), but greatly bumped-up in wealth and increasingly at the head of the social parade, flaunting money, consumer flash and an aggressive new attitude towards their social advancement. 'What constituted the bone of contention' in the new representations of class, claims Wahrman in his discussion of social concerns in the mid 1820s, 'was the existence, the relevance and the consequences of a social *middle*.'[18] And *who*, in another way of picking this bone, was willing to bear the onus of *that* designation?

Lady Blessington's *The Magic Lantern* (1822), her first attempt in 'fashionable life' publications, suggests that this particular issue had become pressing by the early 1820s.[19] Blessington takes her readers to a series of well-known public sites, including two socially iconic ones: Hyde Park Corner for the Sunday parade of fashionable carriages – a 'motley crowd', she says – and the Italian Opera, where aristocrats could enjoy their airs and graces in better company. *The Magic Lantern* revisits the familiar formulas of London types, but there is a new and subtle difference in their presentation. Blessington, by placing her figures in specific public settings where any reader could match observations with her, shows the instincts of a modern fashion reporter with a strong penchant for malice

and an eye for the telling detail.[20] Her scenes of fashionable life move
the reader towards consideration of social status, political responsibility
and the destabilizing effects of a money economy. Lady Blessington forces
'Fashionable Life' out of the society columns onto the more combustible
pages of public opinion.

Describing the parade of carriages in Hyde Park, for example, she
writes, 'Next follows the gaudy, but ill appointed coach of some citizen,
crowded almost to suffocation with his fat and flashy wife.' The 'bon-
nets' of his 'rosy cheeked smiling daughters' look 'like beds of tulips' that
blossom, she implies, in very much the wrong part of town (pp. 21–2). In
pointed contrast, 'The elegant curricle, driven by its more elegant owner,
the beautiful Lady F***, now follows, and attracts all eyes, while this
lovely female *Phaeton*, enveloped in capes and veils, scarcely deigns to
shew a portion of those beauteous features, that have never been seen
without exciting admiration' (p. 24). At the Italian Opera, she observes
confidently, those people who do *not* belong there are always 'found out'
by those people who *do*: 'A frequenter of the Opera will soon distinguish
the casual occupiers of a box from the owners ... Those who hire a box for
the night, enter it with an appearance of *mauvaise honte* ... and their over
dressed heads shew how much trouble they have taken to adorn themselves for the unusual exhibition' (p. 65).

In a nod to fairness, Lady Blessington exposes the persistent moral
failings of her aristocrats and, worse, the careless display of their class's
moral failings in public. She initially marvels, for example, to see so much
'conjugal happiness' in the shady walks of Hyde Park: 'I was delighted
at finding so many instances of domestic felicity in the higher classes of
society; but, alas!', she cries, 'a knowing acquaintance', whom she meets
by chance, awakens her to the truth of this misleading picture, saying:

It is too bad; it really is too bad ... That couple who are this moment turning so
abruptly from us, are the sixth pair of lovers that I have seen within the last ten
minutes.—The ladies are all married, and mothers; their husbands, good, honourable, unsuspecting men, who believe their worthless partners to be, at this
moment, at evening service, or occupied in paying friendly visits.

This revelation of specific and very public misbehaviour holds more power
than the despairing sigh or contemptuous shrug of traditional complaints. That such scandalous behaviour in the Park can be verified by
public report makes the difference: 'My friend then mentioned the names
of some of the parties, and I was shocked at finding the delinquents to
belong to some of the most respectable families in the kingdom', that is,
the traditional governing families of Great Britain (pp. 31–3).

Aristocratic misbehaviour at the Opera provides Lady Blessington with another opportunity to show 'private' misbehaviour as a public offence. She explains exactly how the familiar old business is managed in this elegant setting:

> In many a box may be seen ladies who go to the Opera to meet their lovers; this is generally arranged by two ladies who have a perfect understanding of each others views, but who either affect ignorance, or else with well bred ease, mutually accommodate each other; they have a partnership in the box, and by this means a very delectable quartette is formed, each lady being solely occupied by her own part in the performance; and each giving by her presence the appearance, at least, of propriety to the arrangement, as a *tête à tête* might occasion remarks, and would shock their ideas of decorum. (p. 62)

The passage catches the rhythm of news reporting at its most immediate, scandal-sheet best, a private view, the 'delectable quartette' exposed, the perversity of aristocratic 'performance' laid bare, morality and 'decorum' in the higher classes left in tattered confusion.

At the same time, the middle classes are making their own observations of aristocratic behaviour, most notably in Pierce Egan's wildly popular publication in 1821, *Life in London*.[21] This boisterous tour of London, an exposure of London vice that includes excursions to the fashionable West End and to criminal purlieus in the East End, was the great print success of its year, inspiring a play, an opera and numerous imitations. Egan's *Life in London* is, in fact, not very different from Blessington's *Magic Lantern* in its exposé of a morally lax aristocracy, but it offers a cast of characters drawn from the middle classes who are only too eager to join in aristocratic pleasures – City clerks, artisans, tradesmen and, of course, the country gentry and blooming families of the newly rich.

An anonymous imitation of Egan's *Life in London*, called *Real Life in London* (1821–2), gets even nearer to the quick of middle-class life.[22] The unknown author focuses on the economy as the source of a general rush of all classes to dissipation. Fashionable Bond Street, with its 'magic splendour', claims Tom, the perceptive middle-class narrator of *Real Life in London*, 'has very peculiar properties. It makes the tradesman forget— while he is cheating a lovely and smiling Duchess—that in all probability her ladyship is endeavouring to cheat him' (1, 104). As Tom suggests, consumer society is completely democratic in its dangers: 'When the glittering of London pleasures first meets the eye of a young man placed upon the road of mercantile life', he adds, 'or when he enters any of the multifarious departments in the machine of society', the tradesman and the 'smiling Duchess' are equally caught in the maw of the same 'machine' and share the same perils.

Onto this stage emerged a new group of writers, novelists of fashionable life. The writers were young, glamorous, largely from the genteel middle classes, and eager to cultivate their own celebrity in print, which they did with handsomely engraved, widely distributed portraits of themselves displayed in the frontispieces to their novels and in contemporary print shops. Publication of a new novel of fashionable life was a decidedly public event. Two ladies in Mrs Burdett's *At Home* (1828) compete to be first to get the latest. Each 'frequently contrived to anticipate her [competitor] in a new novel, and always knew "from the *best* authority," not only the real name of the author, but also those of his fictitious personages' (II, 42). The market demanded that these novelists have the glitter of fashionable life sprinkled around them. Lord Normanby carried stardust in his title. Henry Lister married into the aristocracy. Edward Bulwer paraded his gentry-based claims in London society.[23] Disraeli found an introduction to 'aspiring dandies, writers, and politicians' through Bulwer, which he followed up by the cultivation of notable ladies, Lady Cork and Lady Jersey among them, and later Lady Londonderry.[24] Theodore Hook achieved early fame through comic writing and some highly publicized practical jokes, but most prominently for his editorship of the Tory journal *John Bull*, an irresistibly amusing, if scabrous, effort to counter Whig support for Queen Caroline during the divorce crisis of 1820.

Women authors courted their public image by pressing against traditional cultural boundaries for women. Their engraved portraits were presented to the public in journals, annuals, the print shops and in an occasional frontispiece to one of their novels. Lady Blessington's famous political and literary salon at Seamore Place and later, in 1835, at Gore House, Kensington, was enriched by her attendance at the Opera seated in a box situated in the most prominent spot in the house, directly across from Wellington's.[25] Lady Charlotte Bury had the social distinction of being the youngest child of the fifth Duke of Argyll, but she achieved public celebrity through her position in Queen Caroline's household during the 'Delicate Investigation' into Queen Caroline's adulteries. Forced to testify in public in the Queen's defence, she made profit of it later through a sensational account of her time in Caroline's court.[26] Catherine Gore was described by Disraeli as 'a very sumptuous personage, looking like a full-blown rose'.[27] In Paris, where Mrs Gore lived with her husband during his years there as a diplomat, she maintained a lively literary salon.[28] Letitia Landon achieved literary fame as the poet L. E. L., but when poetry suffered a downturn in the market in the mid 1820s, her novel *Romance and Reality* (1831) and her editorship of two annuals brought her into the publishing machine of fashionable literature.[29] Disraeli saw her at a soirée at the Bulwers' London house and reported, 'I avoided L. E. L., who looked the very personification of Brompton—pink satin dress and white satin shoes, red cheeks, snub nose, and her hair *à la Sappho*.'[30] An unfair judgement of a woman hard put to afford suitable clothes for social engagements, not unexpected in the competitive literary world of silver fork writers, but simply her reward for courting commercial success without apology.[31] Gossips, however, did not hesitate to offer invidious comparisons of authorial incomes. 'Lady Blessington's novels', writes Nathaniel Parker Willis, 'sell for a hundred pounds more than any other author's except Bulwer's. Bulwer gets £1400; Lady Blessington, £400; Mrs Norton, £250 ... and most other authors below this. D'Israeli cannot sell a book *at all*, I hear. Is that not odd? I would give more for one of his books than for forty of the common saleable things about town.'[32] Sydney Owenson, it was said, waited until her husband-to-be, a physician, had a title, so that she could publish more profitably as *Lady* Morgan.[33]

The contract that all authors of fashionable novels held with their readers was the claim that they knew exclusive society as active participants. Most of the leading silver fork novelists, as we have seen, had relatively limited access to London's most exclusive society. With the exception of Lord Normanby, most authors had their strongest cultural ties to the upper middle classes or the genteel professional classes. It must be admitted that all of them worked to place themselves as near as possible to the company of the privileged 'three hundred' members of exclusive society. In other words, though they were not the intimates of exclusive company, most of the authors managed an occasional ride in the carriage. As the hero of Bulwer's 'dandy' novel *Pelham* (1828) boasts, 'We ... entered the carriage ... and *went off* with the rapidity of a novel upon "fashionable life"' (II, 5).

NEW READERS, THE ADVERTISING IMPULSE

The potential reach of the new print culture, especially the daily papers, into the lower ranks of the British population fuelled concern among the ruling classes. In 1829, the *Westminster Review*, a utilitarian journal, commented on the reading habits of the working classes. In the past, claims the journal, when working men met at coffee houses, 'their object then was, to smoke and to drink, but now no man, or no man who can read (and how few are there who go to coffee-shops who cannot read), thinks of calling for his cup of coffee without at the same time asking for a newspaper'.[34] Henry Colburn, the primary publisher of silver fork novels, outraged contemporaries by placing advertisements into the columns of the daily newspapers disguised as news, an unheard of practice.[35] Notices of the publication of Lord Normanby's *Matilda* (1825) for example could appear salted in among the estate sales – 'It is long since we have read any novel so piquant, so pleasant, so racy, as this production of Lord Normanby.'[36] 'Time and again', reports John Sutherland, 'one finds the allegation that Henry Colburn's use of advertisement to promote and publicize his books is, somehow, against the rules of the game.'[37] Michael Sadleir notes with scarcely suppressed disapproval that Colburn 'revolutionised publishing in every aspect'.[38] John Chapman, a contemporary publisher, reckoned that Colburn spent £27,000 in advertising his firm's publications between 1829 and 1832, an astonishing sum, if true.[39]

Colburn's claim that his novels were written by social exclusives, people of the highest fashion, was an ingenious hook to bring in readers. Colburn's novels were in fact offering a much more compelling product – a fictional *back story* for all those bits in the newspapers that everybody was reading about at the breakfast table or the coffee house: the stock market, bankruptcies, the occasional 'matrimonial fracas' in high life, political speeches and, not least, classified advertisements, estate sales and auctions. Moreover, Colburn did not depend on the patronage of social exclusives for his literary profits. Instead, as Sutherland reports, Colburn sold his wares for huge profits at the elegantly high price of 31s. 6d., about twice the going price of novels, to the nation's circulating libraries, the major access to novels for a much wider reading public.[40] These profit-seeking institutions were responding to a reader-demand created by Colburn's new advertising strategies. According to Matthew Whiting Rosa, 'Hardly any books of the day except the cheapest tracts surpassed in circulation the guinea or guinea-and-a-half, three volume Colburn novels.'[41]

Edward Bulwer's observation that novels of fashionable life were 'read by all classes, in every town, in every village', that is, by anyone who could read a newspaper, would appear to confirm the success of Colburn's self-interested advertising.[42] As Jonathan Mulrooney notes in a recent essay, 'even more than the narration of public events, advertisements were the daily newspaper's most prominent textual sign'.[43] Romantic-period commercial daily newspapers, he writes, 'engendered' a set of reading practices which amounted to *'intimate commercialism'*, a combination of advertising and informational reporting, private and national at the same time, that conjured up 'the idea of "Britain" as a network of social interactions'.[44]

Jennifer Wicke's broad definition of advertising in her study *Advertising Fictions* – 'physical activities, performances, written artefacts, lights, mechanical reproductions, and all occurrences that exhibit the advertising impulse' – describes an epistemology that had been extended to readers of every sort in the post-Napoleonic period, regardless of class or status.[45] In his essay on panoramic literature in 1830s Paris, Alexander Zevin suggests that the arbitrary divisions between 'high culture', the claim of realist novels and journals, as against the popular culture of advertisements, newspapers and mass entertainments, has been a false one, and that, on the contrary, markets for newspapers, caricatures, satires and political diatribes fold into one another and into the modern urban novel. 'These genres', says Zevin, 'were inscribed not only within each other, but within a wider marketplace in which speed, volume and price were king.' French 'panoramic literature', for example, 'contains elements of realist novels, newspapers, lithographic broadsheets, all as they develop in a miasma of popular culture', thus making the urban novel 'a fundamentally hybrid' genre.[46] Disraeli's 'receipt' for a modern novel in *The Young Duke* (1831) suggests that much the same set of conditions ran current in English novels of fashionable life: 'Take a pair of pistols and a pack of cards, a cookery-book and a set of new quadrilles; mix them up with half an intrigue and a whole marriage, and divide them into three equal portions' (II, 22).

The daily newspaper, for example, is simply assumed in silver fork novels to belong to the routine of daily life. The first paragraph of Lady Blessington's novel *The Governess* (1839), for example, begins with a newspaper advertisement: '"Read this advertisement, my dear Clara," said Mrs. Waller to her niece; "perhaps it may suit you. I have only looked at the two first lines, so read it aloud." Clara complied' (I, I). In Lord Normanby's *Yes and No* (1828), a house-party entertainment includes, among the usual charades and musical entertainments, a group exercise in the 'critical analysis of poor Mr. Medium's advertisement; where, to be sure ... some sentences were cruelly burdened with a "dead weight" of adverbs and adjectives: and pronouns were arbitrarily entrusted with authority over considerable portions of the address, which are usually supposed in such a case to be themselves governed by a verb' (I, 183–4).

In the years after Waterloo, market advertising had become an expression of British national identity, an observable fact, as the hero of Bulwer's *Pelham* (1828) remarks in comparing the roads that lead into London with those of other great European cities:

We are now—at the distance of five miles—arrived at the extremity of one of those straggling, crablike claws, with which London fixes its brick-and-mortar grasp upon the country!—Instead of the corn fields and vineyards which spread their salubrious vacuum under the walls of Paris or Vienna ... behold the assurance of 'droves taken in,' and 'table beer,' in all its varieties of *ex*-cellence;—or a general invitation to 'use Turner's Blacking,' as if we were a nation of *décrotteurs*. Instead of 'Reeling with grapes, red waggons in the way,' behold drays, and dust carts, and anti-phil-animalite two-horse coaches! (III, 44–5)

Table beer and Turner's Blacking now stand in for the nation, a significant metonymy that, as Foucault argues, is 'not of a consensus but of the materiality of power operating on the very bodies of individuals'.[47] Advertising not only entangles the fashionable novel through Colburn's aggressive promotional activity, but it also gives novelists access to contemporary life with intimate involvement of the reader guaranteed. As Jennifer Wicke argues, advertising is the 'shadow partner' of 'high art', having its own 'codes', 'cultural structure', and 'roots in myriad discourses ... as a lexicon, an idiom, a display, a site for the reading of our culture'. Moreover, she concludes, it is not even 'isolable to any one central function—not even "selling products"'.[48] The silver fork novel, which sells many things – itself, celebrity, publicity and politics, only to begin the list – drinks deeply of advertising's intoxicating draught.

The visual seductions of advertising, 'the magic of print', as Robert Montgomery calls it in the 'Introductory Epistle' to his mock-epic *The Puffiad* (1828), puts the rational mind on hold. 'There is ... no species of dulness', he writes, 'which may not find a critic ready to fire away his triumphant Puffs in its support; and such is the magic of print, that ... the common reader is caught, and the splendid volume must be purchased.'[49] A contemporary reviewer of Mrs Gore's novel *Pin Money* (1831) likened her novel to 'a sort of London Directory', and wondered slyly whether 'the authoress ... has made any bargain with her tradespeople'.[50] In the novel's world of surface meanings, commodities are irresistible attractions for novelists and their readers – houses, gardens, furniture, hats, dresses, jewellery, china, plate. William Hazlitt in *The Examiner*, 18 November 1827, responds sharply to the advertising shadow of fashionable novels: 'You dip into an Essay or a Novel, and may fancy yourself reading a collection of quack or fashionable advertisements:—Macassar Oil, Eau de

Cologne, Hock and Seltzer Water, Otto of Roses, *Pomade Divine* glance through the page in inextricable confusion and make your head giddy.'[51] Advertising, as Richard Salmon argues in his revealing essay on James' *The Ambassadors*, 'The Secret of the Spectacle', 'usurps' the normative binary model of surface and depth to produce, as Hazlitt observes of the fashionable novel, a 'giddy' parade of surfaces, pure publicity as it were, surface and depth collapsed into 'inextricable confusion'. [52] On the other hand, this advertising shadow conceals a surprising paradox, the unlimited power that novelists have at their disposal to catalogue contemporary society. Novelists tap into advertising's only logic, its power to organize society through appropriations of consumer status.

Although silver fork novels themselves are promoted as revealing the fashions of aristocratic London, they specialize, as Simon During sensibly observes, 'in representations of Society for a middle-class readership'.[53] The consumer goods of silver fork fiction are poised in a relationship between an elite, aristocratic consumer world and a middle-class readership invested in its own priorities. If anything, the cataloguing and organizing of the middle classes by consumer goods becomes the more pressing and frequent task of silver fork fiction. As During writes, the 1820s were 'a period of in-betweenness in British history, an interstice between deference and duty'.[54]

The publishing industry of the period was keen to profit from such ambiguities. Gift books for the Christmas holidays, the 'annuals', were shuffled into the machine of an aggressive market eager to bridge social gaps in consumer identification. These volumes were designed for drawing-room display, gilt-edged, colourful, frequently encased in ornate covers of silk or embossed leather bindings. An enormously profitable enterprise, many of them were edited and written by silver fork novelists themselves – most prominently Lady Blessington, Caroline Norton, Letitia Landon and Catherine Gore. Poetry and prose came with the package, of course, but it was their handsome steel engravings that made them truly desirable, somewhere between ten and thirty plates depending on the publisher, with engravings of titled ladies, world-famous paintings and topographical sites holding special claims to beauty or historical significance. The grander annuals could be expensive, strictly for the carriage trade, costing 'as high as a guinea', but cheaper versions could be found 'in the ten to twelve shilling range', as Margaret Linley observes, well within a middle-class person's buying power and 'less expensive than a year's subscription to a quarterly'. Linley also reports that the marketing of annuals 'was fiercely competitive, with sixty-three gift books making an appearance in 1832 and more than two hundred by the end of the decade'.[55] 'If journals', argues Linley, 'attempted to establish how a middle-class person should think, annuals laboured to establish the *look* of middle-class leisure.'[56]

Newspaper advertisements of the Christmas annuals commenced as early as October. Their omnipresent advertising in the daily papers ironically made them 'presentable' to a much larger sweep of society than their ostentatious elegance tried to suggest. A character in Catherine Gore's *Women as They Are* (1830) marks their inevitable trip down the social ladder: 'What have we here?—Annuals, annuals,—annuals! ... after exhibiting their gilding and morocco for a week on the drawing-room table, they are degraded to the ante-room, for the amusement of any sentimental *valet de chambre* who may have a taste for "stanzas on the last rose," or "lines to an early swallow"' (II, 231).

Discussions of commodity consumption in silver fork novels are always coded with suppressed anxiety about their social implications. In Lister's *Granby* (1826), an acquaintance asks the hero, 'And the heir is a gentleman of fashion?' Granby hesitates, 'Um—fashion?—I hardly know what to say to that. A good many people will tell you he is ... Of course he derives his distinction through the medium of his trades-people;—a spurious kind of fashion, but it goes down with some people. In fact, fashion is not so aristocratic as many imagine', he concludes, 'it may be bought, like most other things. We, who had great grandfathers, ought to wish it were otherwise' (I, 256–7). Letitia Landon observes a polyglot, trickle-down of patrician artistic tastes in *Romance and Reality* (1831): 'What are the casts which enjoy most plaster-of-Paris popularity? Napoleon in his cocked hat—the Duke of Wellington—Tam-o-Shanter and Souter Johnny—though even these yielded in attraction to china Madame Vestris or Liston as broom-girls' (III, 179).

Wolfgang Iser's famous observation holds: it is 'the "unwritten" part of a text ... which endows it with its reality'.[57] The unwritten 'reality' of silver fork novels is the cognitive map of contemporary commercial culture that the novels shared with their readers. Such a mental map introduces boundaries of 'categorization and the hierarchization of categories', claims Richard Bjornson, for which 'there is no precedent in the object world'.[58] Silver fork novelists patrol the social borders of their novels for *admissible* aspects of market culture against threats of *inadmissible* social intrusions into the realms of exclusivism. A classified advertisement in the daily papers, for example, can exclude a product from patronage by the novel's social exclusives. The village surgeon in Mrs C. D. Burdett's

At Home (1828) is the only person to shine his boots with 'all the glory of Warren's Blacking' (I, 6). The hero of Bulwer's *Pelham* (1828) shudders to bathe his hands in 'that vile composition entitled, Windsor soap' (II, 285). Rich arrivistes, like the Hobsons in Lord Normanby's *Matilda* (1825), take their 'Harvey's sauce' with them to France (I, 111). Even a fashionable and expensive object such as a Brequet watch is too well known among the hoi polloi to be admissible in Bulwer's *Pelham*: '"Pray, Mr. Pelham," said Miss Paulding, turning to me, "have you got one of Brequet's watches yet?" "Watch!" said I: "*do* you think *I* could ever wear a watch? I know of nothing so plebeian; what can any one, but a man of business, who has nine hours for his counting-house and one for his dinner, ever possibly want to know the time for?"' (I, 62–3).

Lady Birmingham, a rich parvenue in Marianne Hudson's *Almack's* (1826), dresses flamboyantly, knows the price of everything, collects Colburn's novels, even to building a special set of shelves for them. She is always in motion, directing servants, shopping, seeing to a better carriage, but when she pauses it is for a tableau, a kind of dressed-out shop window, an advertisement of her economic power and her aspirations to social power:

Her morning attire was rich in the extreme; her watch chain, her bracelets, her rings, were all outrageously fine and massive. The table was covered with notes and cards: her ladyship was writing, but laying down her pen, the stick of which was of ivory inlaid with precious stones; she pushed from her a most superb gold inkstand richly chased, as well as a splendidly gilt Russia blotting-book. (II, 265)

Such a scene holds kinship with the 'theatre of self-display' that William Gleenslade finds to be a sign of the advertising impulse in James' *The Ambassadors*, where the furnishings of Chad Newsome's private rooms in Paris demonstrate 'an intuitive understanding of how to produce a medium in which he can appropriate the subjectivity of others'.[59] Chad, we learn, is preparing himself to take over the advertising department of his family's business. Similarly, the reader looks for clues in Lady Birmingham's scene and finds them on the lady's richly furnished desk. It is from this power base that the parvenue Lady Birmingham commands the reluctant, grumbling deference of London exclusives, bidding them to attend the grand opening of her richly furnished new Regent Street house – which they most certainly do. The reader's subjectivity, captured by this carefully managed display, is not misled. Lady Birmingham's self-confident social power comes exactly 'as advertised'.

The editor Daniel Stuart boasted of the power of first-page advertisements to catch buyers for his paper, the *Morning Post*, the same paper that published 'Fashionable World', a column devoted to news of the most exclusive society. He explains why he favoured placing the small, personal advertisements on the front page of the newspaper instead of grander advertisements for the opera, the theatre and musical performances, which he consigned to the second page:

I encouraged the small miscellaneous advertisements in the front page, preferring them to any others, upon the rule that the more numerous the customers, the more independent and permanent the custom. Besides; numerous and various advertisements interest numerous and various readers, looking out for employment, servants, sales, and purchases, &c., &c. Advertisements act and re-act. They attract readers, promote circulation, and circulation attracts advertisements. [60]

The strategy was a great success. A clerk in the anonymous author's *Real Life in London* announces to his travelling mates in a coach, 'I'll have you to know, Sir, that that there hat was bought of Lloyd, in Newgate Street, only last Thursday and cost eighteen shillings; and if you look at the book in his window on hats, dedicated to the head, you'll find that this here hat is a real *Exquisite*' (1, 18). Mr Lloyd's hats, of course, make regular appearances in the front-page advertisements of *The Times* (and other papers) as any contemporary reader would know.[61] Moreover, Mr Lloyd himself is the author of that 'book in his window', *A Treatise on Hats*, with twenty-four engravings and 'now in its fourth edition', so we have two advertisements in one. Lloyd's customers, explains *Real Life in London*, 'have only to refer to the engravings in Mr. Lloyd's work, where every possible variety [of hat] is clearly defined, and to order such as may suit the rank in life they either possess or *wish to assume*' [emphasis added] (1, 18). In short, in the daily papers and in Mr Lloyd's book 'dedicated to the head', 'all the senses are tantalized with profusion, and the eye is dazzled with temptation, for no other reason', says the author, 'than because it is the constant business of a fashionable life—not to live in, but out of self' (1, 104).

John Vernon argues in *Money and Fiction* that the paper money issued to help fund the French wars made it much easier to conceive of living 'out of self'. Wealth was no longer considered 'in terms of the security of a landed estate, but in terms of personal ambitions associated with expanding capital'. With the first appearance in fiction of commodities with price tags, claims Vernon, 'visions of reality' danced in the heads of readers 'as an unredeemed physical surplus'.[62] 'Paper money', he asserts, 'became not only a medium of exchange but an object of imagination and desire—indeed a "human fiction" and "collective hallucination"', and in addition, 'a leveller and a key to social power, the thing', he writes, 'that made people equal and unequal.'[63] When Lady Birmingham in Marianne Hudson's *Almack's* (1826) opens her grand new house in Regent Street, its costs are the real news of the day, its grandeur a second attraction to Lady Birmingham's power of funding it: 'The new furniture shone out to the greatest advantage, rich scarlet damask set off with the most splendid gilding; each chair cost thirty guineas, as Lady Birmingham took an early opportunity of informing her friends, and it served as a very agreeable subject of conversation' (III, 59).

The specific and comparative price of all commodities, of every *thing*, had become public conversation through the press. Statistics suggest the scope of the influence of paper money on the economy and, in particular, on print culture.[64] Newspapers increased in number from sixty papers published in England in 1760 to 135 in 1821 and to 248 in 1833.[65] An 'energetic bill-sticker could put up between four hundred and four hundred and fifty bills in a day', reports *Grant's London Journal* in 1840.[66] 'To live out of self' became the goal and condition of life in the new world of easily moveable capital. It was a world, as Simon During claims, with a 'commingled sense of fearfulness, unpredictability, opportunity and weightlessness'.[67]

Before *Persuasion* and *Sanditon*, writes Vernon, 'money in Jane Austen is what it had been for centuries, a medium of exchange, not capital'. But beginning in *Persuasion*, Mr Elliot considers Kellynch as no more than a commodity, a resource to be auctioned off to supply his fashionable way of life.[68] In *Sanditon*, before the narrative even begins, Mr Parker has mortgaged his estate to wager its capital on the commercial success of Sanditon, the fragile seaside resort in which he is heavily invested. The action of the piece commences with a newspaper advertisement, information which leads Mr Parker on a fool's errand to a wrecked carriage and a sprained ankle – an ominous beginning for his investment career. Waterloo and Trafalgar, two of the greatest events in British history, are for Mr Parker nothing more than advertising fodder for his speculative venture: 'Trafalgar House—which, by the bye, I almost wish I had not named Trafalgar—for Waterloo is more the thing now'.[69] In *Persuasion*, Captain Wentworth jokes that his life is worth no more than its value in newsprint. He relates his ship's escape from a Channel storm to the admiring Musgrove girls: 'Four-and-twenty hours later, and I should only have been a gallant Captain Wentworth, in a small paragraph at one corner of the newspapers; and being lost in only a sloop, nobody would have thought about me.'[70]

The going opinion of literary historians until only recently has been that readers of Colburn's novels of fashionable life were comfortably well-off members of society – exclusives themselves, nouveau riche aspirers to fashion or the landed gentry and polite professionals able to visit provincial resorts such as Cheltenham, Bath and Brighton. Recent scholarship, however, has suggested that the readership of novels in the circulating libraries dips much further down the social scale than previously thought. Romantic-period newspapers, as Jonathan Mulrooney demonstrates, nourished a readership with an insatiable appetite for 'miscellaneous matter and informational reporting' that demanded 'a daily dose of text that rendered the public world—in all its commercial and political dimensions—completely intelligible, and consumable *as text*'.[71] Silver fork novelists positioned themselves to take advantage of this public craving for 'informational reporting' by exploiting the crossover tastes of daily newspaper readers.[72] Silver fork novels, like contemporary newspapers, 'defined by the continual intersection of multiple strains of information', commanded new practices of reading.[73]

Charles Lamb's revealing experience of reading the daily papers suggests a paradoxical intimacy embedded in this way of knowing the public world. In a letter to Wordsworth sympathizing with him for his 'decaying sight', Lamb is struck with Wordsworth's loss of 'the pleasure of reading a London newspaper'. Living in Enfield for the sake of economy, Lamb candidly confesses to Wordsworth, 'A newspaper is the single gleam of comfort I receive here; it comes from rich Cathay with tidings of mankind.' He admits that newspaper reading calls for a different state of consciousness and a different way of reading: 'the light paragraphs must be glid over by the proper eye, mouthing mumbles their gossamery substance', he writes. Nevertheless, ''Tis these trifles I should mourn in fading sight.' Such reading, he confesses, does not suit 'the poets' or 'any thing high', which, he claims, 'must be read out' aloud. For Lamb, and later for F. R. Leavis and his followers, literature or 'any thing high' had to be speech-based.[74] The daily newspapers' 'tidings of mankind' belong to a different sort of communication, admits Lamb, which, though he prizes it as 'a gleam of comfort', he understands it as a silent, private pleasure: 'Yet I could not attend to it read out by the most beloved voice.'[75]

The circulating libraries that stocked Henry Colburn's lengthy three-volume novels expected the same silent, gliding eye of their customers as a condition of lending novels. In the service of profits, a speedy practice of returning the volumes was the first demand of the circulating library on its customers.[76] Barbara Benedict's essay, 'Sensibility by the Numbers: Austen's Work as Regency Popular Fiction', analyzes the effect of the libraries on contemporary reading practice. In return for complying with short turnaround schedules for book returns, in some cases less than a week, library patrons expected to find the convenience of repeated formulas and familiar titles attached to traditional plots that could be spotted easily as their eyes 'glid' over the library's catalogue.[77] Austen's *Sense and Sensibility* and *Pride and Prejudice*, for example, participate in this strategy by giving the library reader a distinct hint from their titles of the sort of novel to be found within. In turn, the libraries expected the novelists to place plot hooks at the end of each volume in order to bring borrowers back to the library to rent the next one. As Benedict notes perceptively, the novels favoured by circulating libraries were 'interchangeable rather than unique', predictable even in their 'marble, sky-blue, or rose-coloured paper bindings'. Library borrowers could choose a novel in the full expectation that they would encounter intertextual allusions to other novels in their choice, a welcome practice that would assist them in reading efficiently and also provide them with the comfortable sense that they were taking part in a shared fictional conversation. Circulating library novels were to be enjoyed, Benedict argues, first, as 'mere novels' by time-pressed library patrons reading them at speed. An elite readership with more money and time could treat them as 'literature' if they pleased. It all depended 'on the reader's own context'.[78]

By the late 1820s, according to David Allan in *A Nation of Readers: The Lending Library in Georgian England*, circulating libraries in smaller, humbler towns were charging subscription rates set low enough for persons of quite modest means to take advantage of their services. Allan considers former estimates of the number of circulating libraries to be far below those that we now know to be in operation in the early nineteenth century – 'at least eighty-eight' in Liverpool, in 'Bristol a minimum of seventy-eight', in Manchester 'forty-one libraries that have so far been identified; Birmingham forty-six; Leeds twenty-four'.[79] Industrial towns make a surprising addition to our estimates of a new reading public. According to Allan, the records of Waters' library at Kettering, a boot-manufacturing centre, show the library charging subscribers 'fourteen shillings per annum as a single charge or four shillings per quarter', and for non-subscribers 'a price of two pence per duodecimo and three pence per octavo' for a week's borrowing period, evidence, says Allan, in 'the absence of unit prices for larger books … that this particular collection overwhelmingly comprised novels'.[80] Wilson's library at Nottingham, also 'strongly novel-centred', charged only eight shillings for an annual subscription. R. C. Tomlinson's Circulating Library in Stoke-on-Trent in 1833 was requiring 'one pound from the annual subscriber, or, alternatively, six pence for a week's loan of a quarto, three pence for an octavo and two for a duodecimo for less well-off patrons'.[81] In the great resort towns of Bath, Cheltenham and Brighton, libraries were considerably more expensive, but these institutions were known to lower their rates in the offseason to bring in customers with smaller incomes. As Allan suggests, it may be that among these readers 'rather than among the clergy, the nobility, the gentry or the official classes, that the circulating libraries often registered their most dramatic and most lasting impact'.[82]

This is certainly the fear expressed by Lady Morgan in a series of essays for *The Athenæum*, 1839–40, in which she couches her objections to fashionable fiction in just these terms.[83] She deplores the supposition that their 'authors take their tone from their readers, instead of giving it; and … write down to the mediocrity of the purchasing multitude'.[84] Worse, she writes, the publisher, 'from the returns of his ledger … collects with statistical accuracy the sort of book which is wanting', and then dictates to authors what they must write.[85] The result, she concludes, is that 'the demand for books having descended to the masses, has rendered an inferior literature not merely tolerable, but acceptable'.[86]

The supply of cheap books, as Lady Morgan complained, begets in the reader 'a diseased passion for novelty' and the 'habit of reading without judgment'.[87] Silent surface-reading, words 'glid over by the proper eye', is a highly subversive practice for those literary critics promoting high culture, such as Lady Morgan. It belongs, I suggest, to Colin Campbell's famous consumer category of 'autonomous, self-illusory hedonism', a mental state that Campbell argues to be the key to 'the modern mode of consumption'.[88] 'Modern hedonism', as opposed to the hedonism of traditional morality, says Campbell, demands a gliding eye, like Lamb's, where the reader can allow his or her eye to skim over the material – advertisements, for example, or the commodity-rich texts of silver fork novels – in 'day-dreaming of pleasures associated with novel products and experiences [that] are necessarily unknown'. Such a state of suspended discernment, says Campbell, makes it possible 'to believe that they might resemble those more perfect pleasures already experienced in imagination'.[89] As a consequence, the social and political potential of a fiction of surfaces can hardly be overestimated.

As all exclusives know, a little newspaper attention nourishes celebrity, an addition to the 'self' that Gore's hero in *Cecil* (1841) admits is a highly desirable acquisition for exclusive life. 'My name was mentioned with honour in the despatches', Cecil reports of his war service, 'and even at one's last gasp one is never sorry to see oneself in print' (II, 277). Such an appetite for publicity, advertising in its broadest sense, signifies a major reshaping of public discourse. For Jürgen Habermas, the 'bourgeois public sphere' demands a distinction between private and public worlds. Richard Salmon touches on the public–private dilemma in Henry James' long quarrel with modern publicity: 'Whereas, previously, publicity had functioned as a principle of critical public scrutiny', writes Salmon, 'it is now ... an asymmetrical form of social display. In the modern sense of the word, publicity is represented before a public rather than being constituted by it.'[90]

The gliding eye that roves over the morning paper takes in a dialectic of 'news' and advertising, writes Jennifer Wicke, that informs them both.[91] The 'Macassar Oil, Eau de Cologne, Hock and Seltzer Water, Otto of Roses, *Pomade Divine*' that William Hazlitt objects to in novels of fashionable life may have offended Hazlitt's literary tastes, but it also alerted him to the dangers posed by the relationship of novels and advertising. As Wicke explains, the cultural discourse embedded in advertising (and novels) can 'theatricalize the conditions of politics, gender, class, and race—by neutralizing their conflicts'.[92] Such 'neutralizing' lies at the heart of Hazlitt's angry condemnation of Theodore Hook's novels of fashionable life: 'he ... informs you that the quality eat fish with silver forks ... It is so new to him and he is so delighted with it, that provided a few select persons eat fish with silver forks, he considers it a circumstance of no consequence if a whole country starves: ... that *they eat their fish with a silver fork*.'[93] Ironically, Hazlitt's angry derogation, 'silver fork', has given these novels of fashionable life their familiar name.[94]

Richard Salmon's analysis of 'commodity aesthetics' suggests that Hazlitt had good reason for worry about the advertising impulse that was implicit in novels of fashionable life. Hazlitt feared that the seductions of luxury goods would lead middle-class readers to an admiration of privileged commodities and, next, to an acceptance of their owners as the natural, rightful governors of the country. 'Commodity aesthetics', writes Salmon, 'channels the cultural meaning attached to the sign, in order to channel it back on the object of desire.' In other words, as he explains, 'commodity aesthetics functions primarily in a retroactive mode such that it may refashion the individual's "life-planning and identity process" within the moment of consumption'.[95] Such a 'community', Salmon warns, is not a harmless, illusory cultural space, but a condition of altered consciousness, where 'space comes to be perceived as a virtual effect of time'. The effect of such a 'virtual' space-time relationship, even though experienced only at the moment of consumption, still possesses the power to produce an unmediated communal space for rhetorical forces to operate in real time.[96] Dickens has such a consumer community in mind with the silver fork novel 'The Lady Flabella' which he embeds in *Nicholas Nickleby* (1838–9), a notional fiction that prompts Mrs Wititterly's 'uncritical veneration for the patrician inhabitants of the beau monde', according to Winifred Hughes.[97]

Mrs Gore's protagonist in *Cecil: or the Adventures of a Coxcomb* (1841) catches the contemporary lust for such imaginative engagement with surfaces in the description of the lasting satisfaction Lady Ormington, his mother, holds for the newspaper fame she achieved as a celebrity consumer in her youth:

> But if fashionable notoriety constituted the object of her desires, the ambition was gratified. There was an Ormington *pouf*, and an Ormington *vis-à-vis*; and Ormington green and an Ormington minuet. In those unfettered times Annuals were not: but the languishing portrait, limned by Cosway, was charmingly engraved by Bartolozzi; and the Right Hon. Lady Ormington, leaning on a demi-column, with 'Sacred to friendship' engraven on the plinth, a stormy sunset in the background, and a bantam-legged silken spaniel staring its eyes out in the foreground, figured in all the printsellers' windows. (I, 6)

Lady Ormington is equally gratified to find on her return to Paris a quarter of a century after the Revolution that her portrait is still seen: 'Among these [older women] Lady Ormington was an idol. They had worn her in their heart of hearts; and the old Cosway print, deepened in its tints by a quarter of a century's smoke and smut, was still extant in more than one hotel of the Rue de Grenelle' (II, 151). The melancholy irony of Cecil's memory of his mother's personal vanity turns into a general lament, first, for a decadent aristocracy passing into history, and second, for the futility of its aspirations, couched in Lady Ormington's mind as 'fashion'.

As Deidre Lynch suggests, the practice of reading for surfaces 'invites readers to implement the piecemeal procedures that were elicited by the blazons and the verbal portraits of the seventeenth-century character book'.[98] Her richly suggestive word 'blazon' alludes not only to the 'war shield' and 'coats of arms' of an earlier literature, but brings these associations to Dr Johnson's more contemporary definition of 'blazon' as 'show, divulgation, publication', to 'blazon forth'.[99] Cecil's recital of his mother's fashion trophies invokes one kind of blazon, but Letitia Landon introduces another with a startlingly different purpose, to express her distress at the failure of the Whig Party's Poor Laws of 1834. Landon's narrator stands before a pawnbroker's shop in *Romance and Reality* (1831):

The glass cases on the counter still sent forth a sort of dull glitter; they were filled with various ornaments, some pretty, though mostly tarnished by time, but each telling some little history of a happier hour ... There were cords passed along the ceiling, from whence hung articles of wearing apparel of the most common description, things that spoke of every-day use, and there was one whole line of little children's frocks; moreover, in one corner appeared, piled up, a large heap of blankets. (III, 276)

Characters and settings in silver fork novels operate with the power allegory possesses in an older literature, carrying the iconic signs of virtue, hypocrisy and vanity for everyone to see, a practice in these novels reminiscent of political propaganda in its simplest terms. Edward Bulwer in *England and the English* (1833) recognizes this as an unexpected power of silver fork fiction:

Few writers ever produced so great an effect on the political spirit of their generation as some of these novelists, who, without any other merit, unconsciously exposed the falsehood, the hypocrisy, the arrogant and vulgar insolence of patrician life. Read by all classes, in every town, in every village, these works, as I have before stated, could not but engender a mingled indignation and disgust at the parade of frivolity, the ridiculous disdain of truth, nature, and mankind, the self-consequence and absurdity, which, falsely or truly, these novels exhibited as a picture of aristocratic society. The Utilitarians railed against them, and they were effecting with unspeakable rapidity the very purposes the Utilitarians desired. (252)

Silver fork novels engage in a game of a 'manipulative publicity' very much like that of advertising itself, the very danger acknowledged by Richard Salmon's analysis of 'commodity aesthetics'.[100]

The fashionable novel's obsessive interest in social status and commodity display is not a delight in the snobbishness of fashion for its own satisfactions and pleasures, but constitutes an exploration of social status generated by the Reform years. The range of 'the middle classes' covers in its rhetorical vagueness an especially controversial tract of the social landscape – from the landed country gentry, downwards to genteel professionals in the army, the navy and the Church, or from bankers, stockbrokers, factory owners, great merchants, downwards to small tradesmen and artisans – all of these parties burning to secure a rung on the ladder of social and political power. Silver fork novels are completely obsessed with power – who has it and who does not, who can be included in the feast and who can be dismissed or, alas, perhaps not.[101]

The relationship of advertising and novels brought fierce attacks from the political left, as seen in Hazlitt's criticism, and from the political right in the editorial politics of *Fraser's* and *Blackwood's*.[102] The levelling of hierarchical distinctions in a consumer culture could pose a threat to either end of the political spectrum. Moreover, most silver fork novels were actively 'selling' their readers a Whig version of reform, which was by no means intended to be understood as democratic. Margaret Linley's keen description of the politics of fashionable annuals, the luxury gift books, could be applied with equal justice to the politics of Whig-oriented silver fork novels as they balance precariously between liberal impulse and aristocratic constraint. This conflicting duality could mislead even the best readers. 'Coded in the polite tones of chivalry', says Linley, 'middle-class competition gains a semblance of aristocratic disinterest while aristocratic privilege is recast, renewed and subsumed within middle-class notions of merit and virtue.'[103]

THE ISSUES

A close look at silver fork novels brings them into the focus of the major issues of the day. Catherine Gore's novel of 1830, *Women as They Are: or, The Manners of the Day*, is one of the first to address the relationship between social status and consumer goods with reflective attention to their effects on class differences. At the commencement of the story, Helen Mordaunt, eighteen years of age, succumbs to pressure from her ambitious family (of mere baronet rank) to marry Lord Willersdale, forty years of age, rich, an aristocrat and the prime minister as well. Helen is confused, feels none of the traditional feelings of 'love', does not much like how delighted her parents are to get rid of her to the highest bidder, and cannot rejoice in their happiness at her future material prosperity. Lord Willersdale, the best of men, though deeply solicitous for Helen's happiness, is reserved. He wants Helen to love him for himself, not for his riches or his position. Neither one of these two people has the slightest idea about how to effect a connection of heart and mind.

Willersdale first takes Helen to his villa on the Thames at Richmond. His provincial bride is puzzled as to how she should respond. '"If I mark too strong an interest in this beautiful villa," thought Helen, "he will think me interested;—If I acknowledge how much I am delighted by these exquisite conservatories—this aviary—he will be shocked by childishness".' She decides to not comment at all: ' "No! I will leave him to find out, by time and patience, the humility and sincerity with which I am desirous of meriting his good opinion, and justifying his rash choice. Pray Heaven it be not already secretly repented!"' Helen acts with the best of intentions, but, 'the bridegroom, meanwhile, grieved and surprised by Helen's increasing reserve ... began to form suspicions the most painful and perplexing' (1, 24). Willersdale tries again. They go to London where he presents Helen with his late mother's most treasured possessions. Helen is again bewildered: 'But how was Helen to dream of this affectionate condescension?—how to imagine the pains and the time he had devoted to the supposed gratifications of her fancy?—satisfied that the vases of Sevres or Dresden, the bijouteries of or-moulu [*sic*], and malachite, and mother-of-pearl, had courted the London dust in the very position they actually occupied, since the days of the late Lady Willersdale', she affects a cool disinterest (1, 34–5). When Helen sees that her husband is again disappointed, she responds with an over-reaction of pleasure when he presents her, next, with an opera box and, then, with 'a suit of diamonds ... in which Rundell had done his best for the advantage of a collection of gems of unequalled beauty'. 'She suddenly burst forth', writes Mrs Gore, 'into an enthusiasm of applause and delight, which could be interpreted into nothing better than the expression and idle triumph of a selfish, personal vanity!' (1, 35–6)[104]

It is like a fairy tale where the princess gets three questions and gives the wrong answer to each one. But how is Helen to know Baudrillard's dictum, that 'An object is not an object of consumption unless it is released from its psychic determinations as an object of consumption'?[105] Helen must negotiate a proper response to an aristocrat's gifts of houses, land and, most puzzling, the dusty furniture and personal belongings of his late mother. Any lessons from her middle-class (that's what baronets are in aristocratic novels) parents would have taught her to gauge such objects solely for their commodity value. Her aristocratic husband, on the other hand, offers his gifts to her as symbols of love and intimacy. Aware that she is out of her cultural depths, Helen initially chooses the response she thinks is the safest, not to react at all. When this does not work, she feigns pleasure over gifts that, unfortunately, possess the least personal symbolic value, but the most éclat as commodities, the opera box and the diamonds, expressly from Rundell, supplier to the king. The progress of the novel follows Helen's re-education into a code of symbolic consumption that must, by definition, be kept at arm's length from the commodity world of her parents.

In the best of the silver fork 'shopping' novels, Mrs Gore's *Pin Money* (1831), the simple relationship between surface and meaning, that of Lady Birmingham's possessions in Hudson's *Almack's* (1826), becomes increasingly difficult to sustain. Three tales meander their way through the serpentine plot of *Pin Money*, each one with its social edges blurred in an effort to bring a middle-class reading audience into sympathetic identification with aristocratic consumer dilemmas.[106] In the primary story, the heroine, Frederica Launceston, is in her first year of marriage to Sir Brooke Rawleigh and in possession of an independent £400 per year income of 'pin money'. Sir Brooke disapproves of 'pin money' as an 'aristocratic' measure, but is forced to go along with the proposal by Frederica's insistent aunt, Lady Olivia. Frederica mismanages the money, mostly by being too obliging to a scheming friend, and complications ensue.

Second there is *Pin Money*'s Waddlestone story. Leonora Waddlestone, the beautiful daughter of a 'soapboiler', is heiress to an immense fortune from trade. Her father, who has legitimate claims to gentleman status, has married into a City fortune, exchanged his genteel name of Beverly for his wife's family name, Waddlestone, along with her soap factory and fortune. Mr Waddlestone, formerly Mr Beverly, retains his social position only by removing himself and his daughter to Rome, educating her there and cultivating his own entrance into the highest cultural circles of artists, collectors and musicians in the foreign city. But the wife and mother, Mrs Waddlestone, massively vulgar and a pushy arriviste, becomes a social embarrassment to the culturally enriched father and daughter on their return to London. The rumour that Leonora Waddlestone may be 'engaged' to her brother, Lord Launceston, strikes Frederica with horror. This is not truly the case. Launceston is part of an elaborate ruse designed to allow his friend Colonel Rhyse, engaged to Leonora, to visit the girl with Lord Launceston when he calls on the Waddlestones. Mrs Waddlestone will only allow her daughter to marry 'a Lord'.

Finally, there is Launceston's own story. He has been a spendthrift, and though supposedly reformed, is still short of money and in love with his mother's 'poor companion', Lucy Elbany. Lady Olivia, his aristocratic aunt, is mortified, believing the girl to have insinuated herself into the family through a newspaper advertisement: 'a *clergyman's daughter*. My dear, that is a regular companion-and-governess trap!' (I, 233). In this much contrived subplot, 'Lucy' is actually the high-born cousin Launceston was engaged to in his infancy by their parents. Launceston refuses to honour the 'engagement' as an infringement on his freedom, so it is arranged by his mother that the cousin, Lady Mary Trevelyan, should arrive in London disguised as 'Lucy Elbany', the 'poor companion'. Lady Mary has been away for so many years in Italy that Launceston doesn't recognize her. Launceston falls in love with the 'as advertised' companion, the impoverished 'Lucy'. At the conclusion, 'Lucy' is revealed to be none other than Lady Mary, a pure-gold aristocrat. *Caveat emptor.*

Of these three plots, the cultural negotiation that most directly touches the vacillating heart of silver fork exclusivism is that of Leonora Waddlestone, the 'soapboiler' heiress. Frederica's first impression of the girl is disbelief, not unlike Darcy's in *Pride and Prejudice* in his searching remark to Elizabeth, '*You* cannot have been always at Longbourn' (II, ch. 9). 'Charming, indeed!', says Frederica to her brother, 'but no Leonora *Waddlestone* I am persuaded. She must have been changed in her cradle by a fairy or an Irish nurse' (I, 99–100). Curious to know more, she accompanies her aunt to the Waddlestone house in Kensington Gore, a sufficient distance from Mayfair to shield Leonora from social slights. Frederica enters the house to be 'startled by the profusion and selection of the objects of *virtù* which met her eye on every side ... and the vestibule through which they passed into the drawing-room, was ornamented by fine copies of ... the Dying Gladiator, and by an original Diana with a greyhound, from the classical chisel of Schadoff.—The soapboiler was evidently a patron of the arts' (I, 109). The saloon into which she is shown, boasts 'five *chef d'oeuvres* from the hands of Claude, Hobbima, Ruysdael, Salvator Rosa, and Vandyke' (I, 110). She meets Leonora, the very image of a plate from the best of the annuals, in the conservatory, 'as Leonora stood with her slight figure and silken curls, leaning against a marble vase, in the shadowy coolness of a trelliced walk covered with flowering acacias' (I, 117). Here is cultural capital in abundance. The question, of course, is whether or not an aristocrat can accept a connection to the Waddlestone establishment with only cultural capital to set in the balance with a soap factory.

Leonora understands the problem: '"You know," said Leonora, blushing deeply, and shaking away the curls from her deep blue eyes with a smile of proud humility, "we are but *parvenus*; a fact which *here* [in Kensington Gore] I can easily forget; but which is incessantly recalled to me in a London ball-room, either by the want of refinement of our equals, or by the contemptuous bearing of our superiors"' (I, 118–19). Pierre Bourdieu helps unravel Frederica's dilemma. 'Symbolic goods are a two-faced reality', writes Bourdieu, 'a commodity and a symbolic object', a conundrum

Frederica prefers to resolve temporarily by referring to Mr Waddlestone as 'a patron of the arts'. What Frederica cannot handle is Bourdieu's next step, the commercial truth of it: 'It follows that those "inventions" of Romanticism—the representation of culture as a kind of superior reality, irreducible to the vulgar demands of economics ... appear to be just so many reactions to the pressures of an anonymous market.'[107] Launceston, who is not about to marry Miss Waddlestone, enjoys teasing Frederica with the same economic truth: '"Think, my dear Fred., think how proud you will be when, in washing your fair hands, you detect beneath the intaglio of Windsor-castle on your soap, the names of Waddlestone and Co.;—or Waddlestone, Launceston, and Co.! ... My father used to make an annual speech on the amelioration of the manufacturing classes;—and how can we amend them more satisfactorily than by a mutual exchange of our superfluous commodities—rank and wealth?"' (I, 188).

Frederica remains deeply unconvinced as to whether works of art can 'sanction' or 'reinforce' the Waddlestone establishment by their 'cultural consecration' since no matter how you represent it, these beautiful objects are, after all, fruits of a soapboiler's fortune. Her aristocratic aunt, however, has no such doubts. '"But tell me, my dear aunt"', Frederica asks Lady Olivia, '""what can you see to enchant you in his union with—"'. Her aunt interrupts her: 'The heiress of one of the wealthiest men in England?—Every thing!—You will find my dear Fred. that in this *nation boutiquière*, a little city gold becomes necessary once in a century to assist in emblazoning the escutcheon, where there is neither a coal-pit nor a lead-mine on the family estate, to pay off the fortunes of the younger children, and the jointures of dowagers.' 'But there are heiresses who are not daughters to soapboilers', objects Frederica. Lady Olivia closes the conversation with decision: 'Not such heiresses as Miss Waddlestone; who has a hundred thousand pounds in ready money, and five hundred thousand more on the death of her father' (I, 236–7).[108]

In the tale of Frederica's pin money, her mismanagement of it causes the heroine profound grief. 'No one indeed thought less of money than Frederica,—because no one could have been placed more completely beyond its need; nor till she found herself threatened with an empty purse, had a pecuniary care ever intruded on her mind' (III, 5). The economic realities of commercial life intrude as the recommended corrective. 'Every single knock at the door seemed annunciatory of some trifling bill peculiarly addressed to her "separate maintenance,"—some milliner's or shoemaker's, or haberdasher's, or bookseller's "small account"' (III, 5). One afternoon she discovers 'three letters lying on the hall-table, closed in all the commercial odium of waferhood ... At any other time they would have been mechanically opened and thrown aside; but now, a cold dew moistened her brow as the horrors of an unpaid and unpayable bill first occurred to her imagination.' Trembling, she opens them to discover three separate advertisements begging her patronage for goods and services:

> The first of these wafered envelopes contained a lithographic address from a ready-money tailor,—setting forth peculiar inducements of thrift in the purchase of livery-coats and velveteens;—the second was a satin-paper circular from a fashionable library, professing to circulate all the new works on the day of publication, or in other words, to supply three hundred copies of every idle novel to its three hundred grateful subscribers;—the third contained a card from Messrs. Stubble and Bubble, hosiers, drapers, silk-mercers, and haberdashers, thanking her ladyship for the liberality of her past favours, (which she had very unwittingly bestowed,) and soliciting her further attention to their new stock, on their new premises, 16, William-street, Clerkenwell. (III, 222–3)

Gore structures the episode as comic relief – 'Clerkenwell' is a distinctly lower-class address. But the condition of mind the advertisement intends to promote, the 'aura' of uninhibited desire it seeks to cast, is exposed for the commercial seduction it exerts on all classes of society. The next day's mail brings a more ominous letter, 'which while emanating from a more humanized district than Clerkenwell, emulated all its partnership in dignity of address. But instead of adding to their thanks for past favours and solicitation for new ones, the Bond-street haberdashers subjoined to the expression of their gratitude a "full account, which being the close of the season, or Midsummer half-year they conceived it might be agreeable to her ladyship to look over and settle previously to leaving town"' (III, 266). *Pin Money* affirms a thoroughly middle-class bottom line at the conclusion, affirming the kinship and alliance of the middle classes and aristocracy in a market economy.

Frederica's self-recognition through reading – here, comically, advertisements for consumer goods and bills demanding payment for them – places Frederica in that half-way condition of 'round' and 'flat' characters that Deidre Lynch claims mark the 'history of material and affective practices, a history in which changes in the retailing of novels and changes in what novel readers *did* with characters, play as important a role as democratic ideals'.[109] On the one hand, Frederica is a 'characteristic' figure, the blazon of a ruling class ripe for moral and political reform. On the other, she is a delightful, charming young woman, very much in love with her husband, resentful of his time away from her, attracted by the urban pleasures of London life and driven onto the mercies of a false friend to fill her idle time.

Historians of the novel in the twentieth century, as Claudia Johnson observes, have ruled that 'novels are narratives of private life, that they turn inward, forming subjectivities that occlude or mystify the political'.[110] Silver fork novels tell us otherwise. Instead of looking for psychological realism or 'virtual subjectivity' in silver fork novels, argues Deidre Lynch, we would do better 'to conceive of an institutionalized instability within the cultural field that the romantic-period reinventions of literariness, literacy, and reading relations brought into being'.[111] The urgent demand for surface-reading made by silver fork novels arises from such instabilities, particularly social and political changes that at the time appeared massive, even revolutionary. Contemporary critics beating the drum for a high-culture literature of reflective reading, as Lady Morgan does in her *Athenæum* reviews, distinguish between 'good' reading and 'bad' reading very much on the grounds that Frederic Jameson suggests in *The Political Unconscious* that the politics of 'high culture' depends upon the defining of 'mass culture'.[112] The problem, as Lynch sees it, is that high-culture definitions of 'good' reading, those novels that enable a reader to 'explore her inner life' by sharing sympathies with a literary character, have 'made it hard to find anything worthwhile to say about nineteenth-century writers' recapitulation of the impersonal perspectives of characteristic writing or nineteenth-century writers' fascination with remarkable characters'.[113]

My own experience in reading silver fork novels tells me that it is not always as easy to determine *good* reading from *bad* reading as you might think. *Bad* reading as 'an act of the body', a practice exactly opposed to *proper* reading, 'an act of the mind', has much to recommend it, especially in novels of fashionable life.[114] I would suggest that *bad* reading is the ideal form for capturing a world in flux. Silver fork characters traverse a landscape and cityscape made visual through a world driven by print information, an experience which is surprisingly analogous to watching the television evening news where the moving images, the announcer's voice describing the event, and captions of print chasing along the bottom of the screen simultaneously give us our version of the changing world. The 'exhibitionary forms' in silver fork novels make their 'characters, classes, locales, and bodies adamantly visible', as Deidre Lynch maintains.[115] I suggest that they can do the same for the Reform era itself.

CHAPTER 2

The woman's tradition: Edgeworth, Burney and Austen

I hope you like nothing of Miss Edgeworth's or Miss Austen's. They are full of commonplace people, that one recognises at once.

Lady Harriet, in *Granby* (1826)[1]

Silver fork novels certainly find their lifeblood, their speed and dash, in the heady excitements of commodity culture, a burgeoning print industry and a world in which newspapers, advertisements and novels feed on the same commercial energies. On the other hand, there is the steadying hand of women's fiction to keep the silver fork carriage from running off the road. The traditions of the woman's novel, particularly as represented by Frances Burney, Maria Edgeworth and Jane Austen, are there to apply the brakes, to keep the reader focused on a plot and to provide the all-important conclusion to the tale. In the doing of these tasks, however, the older traditions of women's fiction find themselves much altered by their fashionable new contexts.

First of all, it must be obvious that when the eye 'glides' over the surface of a three-volume silver fork novel it is going to encounter a problem that a single page of the daily paper does not present. The 'gossamery substance' of its imagined commodities and consumer delights can stretch the plot past breaking. 'The general plotlessness of the silver fork mode', as Winifred Hughes calls it in her foundational essay, 'Elegies for the Regency', troubled contemporaries from the beginning.[2] Disraeli in *The Young Duke* (1831) attributes the problem to the dullness of aristocratic society itself: 'And so your novelist twists his golden thread with some substantial silver cord, for use, and works up, with the light dance, and the heavy dinner, some secret marriage or some shrouded murder. And thus,' he concludes, 'by English plots and German mysteries, the page trots on, or jolts, till, in the end, Justice will have her way,—and the three volumes are completed' (III, 16). A writer for the *Quarterly Review* (1832) more soberly complains that the plot of a novel of fashionable life simply provides '*separating links*' for those 'descriptions, however faithful and minute, which have no connexion with any object that we much care to contemplate, and which contribute to the construction of nothing'.[3] I would argue that the plot structures, these '*separating links*' borrowed by silver fork novelists from the traditions of women's fiction, are road signs that provided readers of fashionable novels with directions for interpreting the flood of contemporary culture – material, political and social – that gave these novels their immediacy.

Early silver fork novels, between 1825 and 1831, those in which youth and optimism drive their consumer display – such as Marianne Hudson's *Almack's* (1826), Lister's *Granby* (1826), Bulwer's *Pelham* (1828) or Catherine Gore's *Pin Money* (1831) – could offer rich rewards for readers willing to dispense with the need for a strong plot. The seductive attraction of an 'imagination cut free from the imprisoning source of economic dependence', like Lambert Strether's blithe experience in the glamorous Paris of James' *The Ambassadors*, could be irresistible.[4] The experience of Colin Campbell's 'modern hedonism' or Strether's 'purified' consumption may well be tentative, impermanent and, finally, 'self-illusory', but, as Richard Salmon concludes in 'The Secret of the Spectacle', 'James paradoxically locates the "secret" of Strether's desire ... at the level of the "inessential", the superficially present.'[5]

Keenly aware of the charges levelled against their works, authors of fashionable novels defend them with spirit. 'Novels,—especially such as affect to treat fashionable life,—are born to such an inheritance of shame', writes Mrs Gore, who interrupts the plot of *Pin Money* to complain of the critics, '[I]t is so much the custom of dull or silly people of all ages and sexes to reprobate them with a sentence of contempt as the most frivolous, flighty, useless, and condemnable productions of the press ... that it becomes necessary from time to time to throw a heavy lump of marl on the surface', something dull and tedious, 'in order to deceive the dunces into a belief that some mysterious process of improvement is carrying on for their advantage' (II, 53–4). In a letter to Bulwer in which she complains of a perceived bias in his criticism of her novels, Gore cites a distinguished tradition of fiction that deals with fashionable life: 'I leave it to *Grandison*, *Clarissa*, *Belinda*, *Ennui*, *The Absentee*, *Vivian Grey*, etc. to plead their cause, and intrench myself in the obstinacy of a woman's opinion that every picture of passing manners, if accurate, is valuable from the drawing-room to the ale house, and that every writer does best who paints the scene more immediately before him.'[6] The narrator of Bulwer's *The Disowned* (1828) boasts of the genre with comic defensiveness: 'A fashionable novel (that intellectual libertine of literature), requires *no* rules. It bursts on the admiring world, as did the accomplished Lady Blarney on the bewildered circle of the Vicar of Wakefield, carrying every earthly perfection *in its title*, and bearing in the *"living jingos"* of its phraseology only additional proofs of its superior breeding' (I, xx).

Bulwer addresses the troublesome issue of passing fashion in the 'Preface' to *Godolphin* (1833) by taking refuge in the historian's task, claiming that he is simply a 'compiler' whose task it has been, 'from a Memoir to construct a Romance'. Disraeli's heroine in *Henrietta Temple* (1837), however, confesses herself uneasy at the division that she senses between the 'reporting' of contemporary life and the plot structure of the novel she is reading. 'I like the lively parts', she tells a companion, 'but not the serious ones ... the author has observed, but he has not felt.' Fashionable novelists fail, she concludes, because, 'they accept as a principal that which is only an insignificant accessory; and they make existence a succession of frivolities, when even the career for the most frivolous has its profounder moments' (III, 136–7).[7]

The supposed 'author' of Bulwer's 'Preface' to *The Disowned* (1828) offers an imagined novelist some canny advice on the demands of the three-volume fashionable novel:

I have paid great attention to the art of popular novel-writing, and will favour you with some hints. *Imprimis*:—A first volume is like the first *debut* of a beauty; you must sacrifice every thing to give it *éclat!* In the second volume, and half the third, you may be as dull as you like: you please from the pleasure you have already given; but in the last, your work must (like the beauty still) make every exertion to secure a glittering termination to its career, and end, amidst a blaze of literary gems and diamonds, in a fortunate marriage!—(I, xviii)

His listener, the potential 'novelist', admires Bulwer's formula, especially its conclusion in a 'fortunate marriage', but declares concern that this courtship narrative could well lead a novelist 'into a very suburban set ... respectable people in their way—but you will allow, more respectable than interesting' (I, xx).

EDGEWORTH AND BURNEY

The origin of such a 'respectable', less interesting 'set' is addressed by Letitia Landon in *Romance and Reality* (1831). 'One does not easily forget the impressions of our youth,' says Mr Morland, the author's spokesperson, 'and mine passed in the reign of female authorship.' Mr Morland remembers reading Minerva novels with pleasure in his youth, but claims the better company of Mary Robinson, Ann Radcliffe and Charlotte Smith as early 'companions'.[8] He recollects Maria Edgeworth's novels as coming later, 'A school of common sense and real life. Miss Edgeworth only wanted imagination to have secured her the very highest place in novel-writing.' Edward Lorraine, Mr Morland's companion in the conversation, adds his own memories of early reading, 'I never liked Miss Burney. Her pages are a succession of caricatures' (II, 192–4). Mr Morland agrees, 'I prefer Miss Austen's: they are the truest pictures of country life, whose little schemes, hopes, scandals, &c. are detected with a woman's tact, and told with a woman's vivacity.' 'Yes, they are amusing to a degree', says Lorraine, 'but her pen is like a pair of skates—it glides over the surface … Pride and Prejudice is her best work; but I cannot forgive Elizabeth for her independence … Mr Darcie [*sic*] is just a stiff family portrait, come down from its frame to be condescending.' Here Landon places a tardy footnote at the bottom of the page: 'I had not read Persuasion when the above was written. Persuasion in my very humble opinion, is one of the most touching and beautiful tales in our language' (II, 195–6).[9]

The sweep of women's fiction represented in the novels of Robinson, Radcliffe and Smith, even the popular Minerva tradition, can regularly be felt in the plots of silver fork novels, especially through their 'conclusions in marriage', but even more profoundly in their business-like accounts of fortunes and competences that continue to characterize the traditions of women's fiction.[10] But it is the triumvirate of Edgeworth, Burney and Austen that Landon considers to be the main precursors of contemporary fashionable novels. Edgeworth's novels, frequently noted by contemporaries as less amenable to silver fork tastes than Burney's or Austen's, offer the novelists of fashionable life an admonitory benchmark, as a discussion in Bulwer's *Pelham* (1828) suggests. '"Speaking of morals," said Lady Roseville, "do you not think every novel should have its distinct *but*, and inculcate, throughout, some one peculiar moral, such as many of Marmontel's and Miss Edgeworth's?"' Bulwer's spokesperson responds with a firm, 'No! … every good novel has one great end— the same in all—*viz*: the increasing our knowledge of the human heart … *This* great and universal end, I am led to imagine, is rather crippled than extended by the rigorous attention to the *one* isolated moral you mention' (I, 143–4). Instead, he says, 'an acute, active, and vigilant observer of men and manners' is more appropriate to the modern novel (II, 145). Henry Lister contributes a guarded respect for Edgeworth's moral achievements, suggesting that, 'the desirableness of adapting a fictitious tale to the illustration of some one particular point of conduct, may perhaps be questioned; but never has this difficult task been executed with such clearness, directness and apparent ease, as by Miss Edgeworth'.[11]

Catherine Gore incurs a somewhat more practical debt to Edgeworth's *Belinda* (1801) for help in resolving the conclusion of *Pin Money* (1831) with *Belinda*'s trope of a 'dénouement' painting that resolves all difficulties of the plot when it is dramatically exposed at the conclusion of *Belinda* by drawing a 'green curtain'. In *Pin Money*, 'folding-doors into the drawing-room' are thrown open for the same purpose, to expose a *tableau vivant* that resolves, like Edgeworth's painting, a case of mistaken identities.[12] Gore also makes use of Lady Delacour's bitter competition with Mrs Luttridge in *Belinda* to model the political differences that consume Lady Danvers and Lady Alberville in *Women as They Are* (1830).[13]

Echoes of Fanny Burney's novels are found far more frequently than Edgeworth's in silver fork novels. In Lister's *Herbert Lacy* (1828), the Branghtons from Burney's *Evelina* (1778) supply a model for the Bagshawes, who, exactly like Burney's irrepressible middle-class clowns, attend the opera only to note that the price of tickets to the opera 'have *ris* of late', and to wish Madame Pasta would not 'stick to her Italian' and would sing a 'right good English song ... "God save the King," and "Rule Britannia"' (III, 107).[14] The Branghtons also put in a guest appearance in Lord Normanby's *Matilda* (1825) as the Hobsons, where the family travels to France with English supplies tucked away in the carriage: 'Cocoa paste, essence of coffee, &c. were not very serviceable at dinner, but some Harvey's sauce was hailed with great glee; though, as there was not fish, there arose some difficulty whether to apply it to *fricandeau, fricassé, pâté, mêlée*, or *poulet rôti*' (I, 111). Burney's *Cecilia* (1782) supplies Catherine Gore with the trope of a faithful dog used as the icebreaker to restore communication between the hero and heroine in the tale 'The Separate Maintenance' from *The Fair of Mayfair* (1832). The heroine's dog in Gore's tale, 'old Tartar', like Cecilia's dog in Burney's novel, follows the hero to London from the heroine's home in the suburbs (Putney), thus providing an opportunity to return the dog and open a conversation that will resolve all difficulties (II, 166–7).

A more substantive contribution comes from Burney's complex character of Elinor Joddrell in *The Wanderer* (1814) made use of by Marianne Hudson to form Lady Anne Norbury in *Almack's* (1826), a character with equally plainspoken ideas that challenge the hegemonic pieties of the heroine. Lady Anne, like Burney's Elinor, becomes a spokesperson for many unwelcome truths, remarking of Barbara Birmingham, the manufacturing-class heroine, for example, that 'she will probably be one of the greatest heiresses, if not the greatest, in the kingdom; and who do you think will care whether her money came by a shoeblack or a Jew? ... Whoever hears of love now?' (I, 335).[15] For the same novel, Hudson also makes use of another Burney character, her ranting doomsayer Mr Albany from *Cecilia*: "'Ah!" said the stranger ... "Who would be a politician in these days? ... who, that had a spark of fire or soul left? What an absurd nation we are! We worship a set of chimeras we have raised up ourselves—the very shadow of shades! And then, like madmen, we rail at those who see and would expose our delusions!"' (III, 179).

Lady Blessington's *The Governess* (1839) makes extensive use of Burney's employment trope from *The Wanderer* (1814). Blessington's genteel heroine Clara, 'the only child and orphan of a merchant' (I, 3), answers a newspaper advertisement for a governess only to be launched onto a career of unsatisfactory employments, losing each situation exactly as Burney's 'Wanderer' does, through the petty jealousies and envious mistreatment of other women. Mrs Williamson, Clara's first employer, dismisses her because she suspects that Mr Williamson has taken a liking to the pretty new governess. The heroine's next employer, Mrs Robinson, a dead ringer for Madame Duval in *Evelina*, treats the heroine to a night at the opera every bit the equal of Evelina's miserable evening. 'Look at the painted old Jezebel', says one onlooker in Blessington's novel. 'Vy, hang me, if that ere pretty gal aint ashamed to be seen with that old wixen', says another (II, 1). As in Burney's *Evelina*, Blessington's heroine is mortified by the old woman's loud talk about the price of the tickets, the surprised glances of genteel patrons and her desperate embarrassment, as in the *Evelina* model, when she must seek a coach when the opera is ended. Lord Normanby's novel *Yes and No* (1828) is another of the silver fork novels to make use of *The Wanderer*'s employment motif, borrowing the London humiliations of Burney's heroine as a seamstress in a shop and her failed efforts at doing piecework at home (*The Wanderer* IV, chapters 17–20). The heroines of both Burney's and Normanby's works are doomed by the same reason, the universal male conviction that no woman employed to work with her hands can be virtuous. Helen, Normanby's heroine, must take her piecework in the early morning to a shopkeeper in a London bazaar (II, 140–50; 154–73). Gentlemen revellers, drunk from their night's celebrations, chase her through the streets on the way back to her humble lodgings: 'Helen meanwhile rushed up stairs to her own apartment, threw herself upon the sofa, crouching like a hunted hare; and whilst her heart beat violently against her breast, listened anxiously for the dreaded sounds of pursuit' (II, 143–4).

AUSTEN

Jane Austen's novels are a different matter altogether in the extent of their influence on silver fork fiction. In less than ten years from the publication of Austen's last works, *Northanger Abbey* and *Persuasion* in 1818, all six of her novels were dressing out silver fork novels with choice bits and pieces taken from Austen's dialogues, characters and plots. The standard tale of literary historians has always been that Jane Austen remained 'a relatively select coterie writer, a critic's and a novelist's novelist', and that Jane Austen's popular reputation lay quietly sleeping until 1870, when the fairy touch of her nephew James Edward Austen-Leigh's *Memoirs* awakened it for posterity.[16] As Deidre Lynch observes in the 'Introduction' to *Janeites: Austen's Disciples and Devotees*, 'Over the last century and a half much has been invested in the premise that the appreciation of Austen's excellence is a minority taste.'[17]

Repeated attempts to readjust the timeline of Austen's popular reputation have had nothing to say about her relationship with silver fork fiction. A recent account of Austen's influence on the nineteenth-century novel cites Mrs Gaskell's *North and South* (1854–5) as Austen's 'earliest literary legacy'. Two other studies mark *Jane Eyre* (1846) as the earliest of novels to reference Austen.[18] Charles Beecher Hogan's essay, 'Jane Austen and her Early Public', cites praise of Austen in the 1820s and 1830s, as well as allusions to Austen's novels in contemporary journals and letters, but nothing about the response of silver fork fiction.[19] Brian Southam's *Jane Austen: The Critical Heritage* offers examples largely of professional critical response.[20] Annika Bautz's study *The Reception of Jane Austen and Walter Scott* argues that the appearance of Austen's novels in a collected edition in 1832–3 shows popular interest in Austen's novels climbing steadily.[21] Bautz also observes that the catalogues of lending libraries show that interest in Austen's novels increased through the 1820s and 1830s, and that, like Scott's novels, they remained continuously on the shelves of existing libraries and were added to the fresh holdings of new libraries. In consequence, Austen's reading public, says Bautz, grew steadily 'as new cohorts joined the libraries'.[22]

Catherine Gore drew public attention to Jane Austen's influence on her silver fork novel *Pin Money*, published in 1831, acknowledging in the 'Preface' that her novel had simply been, 'an attempt to transfer the

familiar narrative of Miss Austin [*sic*] to a higher sphere of society', that
is to elevate the gentry society of Highbury to the aristocratic precincts
of Mayfair. Edward Bulwer many years later, remembering the fashionable novels of the 1830s, affirmed the linkage of Austen and Gore in the
minds of contemporaries by yoking these two authors together, praising
them for 'their familiar images that you may cut out of an oak tree'.[23]
Henry Lister's novel *Granby* (1826) praises Austen with one of the finest backhanded compliments ever devised, the epigram of this chapter:
'I hope you like nothing of Miss Edgeworth's or Miss Austen's', says the
scatterbrained Lady Harriet, 'They are full of commonplace people, that
one recognises at once' (I, 148).[24] Lister's opinion, without the irony of
Lady Harriet's aristocratic dismissal, followed in the *Edinburgh Review*,
30 July 1830: '[Austen's] forte lay ... in drawing characters; and in this she
stands almost alone ... We feel as if we had lived among them.'[25] Walter
Scott also associated silver fork novels with Austen's work in his notes on
Granby (1825–6): 'The women do this better—Edgeworth, Ferriar [*sic*],
Austen have all had their portraits of real society, far superior to any thing
Man, vain Man, has produced of a like nature.'[26]

In fact, by the 1830s it was assumed that Jane Austen's novels and silver fork novels belonged in the same basket, so much so that the editor of the 1833 Bentley edition of *Sense and Sensibility* announced, 'Miss
Austen is the founder of a school of novelists; and her followers are not
confined to her own sex, but comprise in their number some male writers of considerable merit', presumably a reference in this year to Edward
Bulwer, T. H. Lister, Lord Normanby and perhaps Benjamin Disraeli,
the leading male authors of fashionable novels and all known admirers of Austen's work.[27] It may also have been an attempt on Bentley's
part to raise Austen's fiction to the prestige of male authorship, as Clara
Tuite argues in *Romantic Austen: Sexual Politics and the Literary Canon*,
in recognition of the fact that the canon was becoming male dominated.
As early as Whately's critique of Austen in the *Quarterly* (Jan. 1821), the
practice had begun of setting Austen apart from 'the female-identified
novel genre' of sentimental fiction.[28]

Jane Austen's novels might well have seemed to contemporaries more
suited to the modes of fashionable fiction than, say, Edgeworth's or
Burney's. First of all, the London points of social-topographical reference in her novels dovetail with those of silver fork fashionable life. In
Pride and Prejudice, for example, the snobbish Miss Bingley has the joy
of boasting an address in Grosvenor Street, Mayfair, only venturing out
of this charmed neighbourhood once, to pay a chilly courtesy call on

Jane Bennet who is staying in Gracechurch Street in the City, of all the unfashionable places, with her aunt and uncle, the Gardiners. In *Sense and Sensibility* Elinor and Marianne Dashwood stay with Mrs Jennings on Upper Berkeley Street, a Mayfair neighbourhood by courtesy, near Portman Square. Jane Austen herself lived on Upper Berkeley Street when her brother Henry took a house there in 1801, at Number 24.[29] As for Austen's Mayfair characters, Willoughby takes rooms on Bond Street, the main commercial street in Mayfair, after abandoning Marianne for a richer woman. Colonel Brandon has rooms in St James' Street, a more solid, respectable address in Westminster. Elinor and Marianne stroll through Mayfair with their brother John to the Middletons' house in Conduit Street after meeting John unexpectedly at Mr Gray's shop in Sackville Street, also in Mayfair. John Dashwood's report to his wife of the Middletons' Mayfair address in Conduit Street so moves her that she makes a social call on the fortunate family the very next morning (11, ch. 11). John and Fanny, sadly, must lay their heads outside Mayfair, in Harley Street, Marylebone, a neighbourhood notorious to contemporaries as the home of small gentry and City parvenus lusting for more fashionable society. In short, Jane Austen understood Mayfair exactly like silver fork novelists, well enough to incorporate its snobberies and subtleties of street address into the fabric of her novels.

Moreover, Jane Austen, like everyone else in her class, watched the daily newspapers for celebrity gossip. 'Mrs Welby has been singing Duetts with the Prince of Wales', Austen writes, 14–16 January 1801; 'the Duchess of Orleans, the paper says, drinks at my pump', she writes Cassandra, reporting on 4 September 1816 the news from Cheltenham where Austen had just spent a holiday.[30] Newspapers in Jane Austen's novels become a fashion trope to themselves, from the regulation announcement in *Sense and Sensibility* of the birth of the Palmers' baby in the London papers to the scandal of Mrs Rushworth and Mr Crawford's little slip from virtue in *Mansfield Park*. In Lister's *Granby* (1826), the hero uses his newspaper as a plausible screen from view, very like Edmund Bertram uses his newspaper in *Mansfield Park*, even to the rhythms of Austen's text, reading 'over again the "Fashionable arrangements", advertisements for the sale of "seasoned hunters", and "cabinet bijoux", the undoubted property of an eminent connoisseur, returned from the continent' (11, 168–9).[31] Such material trivia as this, writes William Galperin, made 'Austen's fiction initially perceived as anarchic and even surreal' to her contemporaries. It was the Victorians, he argues, who reinvented her as the mother of 'normative regulatory realism'.[32]

The terms Jane Austen's contemporaries used to describe her novels bring into focus the kinship later novelists would find in her works. Mrs Pole's comments on *Mansfield Park*, which Austen copied into her personal collection of 'Opinions of *Mansfield Park*', catch exactly the values that Austen's silver fork followers would identify as their own:

They are so evidently written by a Gentlewoman ... most Novellists fail & betray themselves in attempting to describe familiar scenes in high Life, some little vulgarism escapes & shews that they are not experimentally acquainted with what they describe, but here it is quite different. Everything is natural, & the situations & incidents are told in a manner which clearly evinces the Writer to *belong* to the Society whose Manners she ably delineates.[33]

A reviewer for the *British Critic*, March 1818, concurs, writing, 'She seems to be describing such people as meet together every night, in every respectable house in London ... And yet, by a singular good judgment, almost every individual represents a class ... one of those classes to which we ourselves, and every acquaintance we have, in all probability belong.'[34]

This is the significant lens through which silver fork novelists viewed Jane Austen, through her reputation for catching the nuances of social station.[35] In the turbulent years preceding and following the Reform Bill such distinctions of station were the driving force of reform politics and of the fashionable novel. A gentleman in Bulwer's novel *Pelham* (1828) offers this cautionary advice to an aspiring novelist of fashionable life: 'There is only one rule necessary for a clever writer who wishes to delineate the *beau monde*. It is this: let him consider that "dukes, and lords, and noble princes," eat, drink, talk, move, exactly the same as any other class of civilized people—nay, the very subjects in conversation are, for the most part, the same in all sets' (III, 49–50). T. H. Lister adds the final blessing to Austen's silver fork reputation for social accuracy in the *Edinburgh Review* of 1830, 'In dialogue she also excelled. Her conversations are never *bookish*—they are just what might have been said.'[36]

We shouldn't wonder then that novels of the silver fork school draw frequently on Austen's novels.[37] Even a casual remark in one of these novels can show Austen's hand. Lady Charlotte Bury's *The Devoted* (1836) gives us, 'What sort of person is she? I am curious to know, for hitherto I have only heard of her as a woman whom everybody praises, but nobody seems to care for' (II, 180), the very expression Willoughby uses to disparage Colonel Brandon in *Sense and Sensibility*: 'Colonel Brandon is just the kind of man ... whom every body speaks well of, and nobody cares about' (I, ch. 10). A verbal echo of *Mansfield Park* appears in Catherine Gore's novel *Mothers and Daughters* (1831) that brings Fanny Price to mind at once: 'Cousin Mary—surrounded by her books, her work, her music, her easel, her flowers, her birds! … sufficing to her own amusement—yet ever ready to lay aside her favourite pursuits and preoccupations in order to contribute to the happiness of others' (III, 32). It is as if we have stumbled into a Biedermeier reconstruction of Fanny's east room at Mansfield Park (see Figure 1). 'Her plants, her books—of which she had been a collector, from the first hour of her commanding a shilling—her writing desk, and her works of charity and ingenuity, were all within her reach … Every thing was a friend, or bore her thoughts to a friend' (I, ch. 16).

Austen's works frequently operate as a storeroom of characters, plots and dialogue to be hauled out by silver fork novelists for use as needed. Mr Collins shows up in Lord Normanby's *Matilda* (1825) as Sir James Dornton, married to the heroine in this novel and causing her humiliating pain by his rendition of Mr Collins' self-introduction to Mr Darcy. Sir James also shares Mr Rushworth's stupidity in dinner table conversation (I, 17–18). In Mrs Gore's novel *The Opera* (1832), an indignant version of Elizabeth Bennet appears long enough to refuse a marriage proposal from the Duke of Cardigan (III, 312–13), more melodramatic than Elizabeth's refusal, but echoing the same rhythms and rhetorical gestures: '"You say you love me;—you would prove it by outraging, for my sake, all the bonds of family union, all the claims of state and station, the prejudices of society, the pride of your own heart … Infatuated, miserable man!—listen to my reply.—I loathe you!—There is not an atom of dust lying at my feet more worthless in my sight than yourself' (III, 312). Elizabeth's refusal of Darcy also gets an outing in Gore's *The Cabinet Minister* (1839), where Bessy Grenfell, a Fanny Price-figure with Elizabeth Bennet's rhetorical skills, rejects an arrogant marriage proposal from Lord Warkworth: 'Your incivility, my lord, justifies me in declaring what delicacy would have otherwise prompted me to conceal, that were Lord Warkworth King of England instead of Lord Teviot's heir, I should still have disliked his society too much to accept him as a companion for life' (II, 46–7).

Like Fanny Price, Bessy Grenfell must endure the consequences of her refusal of Lord Warkworth's unwelcome proposal in the violent reproaches of her termagant aunt, who is a fine combination of Mrs Norris and Sir Thomas Bertram: 'What right had she to refuse such a connection?—I only ask you what right Miss Grenfell had to reject a marriage so advantageous to the whole family? … the niece, to whom I have shown such marked and uniform kindness, to defeat my plans for her brilliant establishment in life, by petulance and folly' (II, 47). Lady Bertram's sleepy

Figure 1 *The Maiden's Chamber*, by A. E. Chalon

habits surface in Hudson's *Almack's* (1826), 'One morning, during break-fast, Lady Norbury observed in her usual soft, sleepy tone, as she sat balancing her tea-spoon on the edge of her cup … ' (II, 135). Her letter-writing skills descend to another character in that novel, who writes in Lady Bertram's best style: 'In the first place she writes a very running hand … yet altogether it is very flowing and elegant-looking, only one word will sometimes fill up a whole line:—"So inexpressibly obliged for Lady Norbury's gratifying attention, which has been most gratefully received; such a pleasing mark of decided friendship, displayed with such good sense and judgment, that it found its way at once to a heart over-flowingly alive to kindness"' (II, 140–1).

Jane Fairfax's trips to the post-office, as well as Mr John Knightley's kind sentiments, reappear in Hudson's *Almack's*: '"I fancy, when your ladyship is a little older," said the Duke, smiling, "you will find your nerves not quite so easily excited: none but very young ladies ever receive such exquisitely interesting letters."' Miss Bates' praise of Jane Fairfax's 'crossed' letters may inspire Lord George's remark to Louisa in *Almack's*: 'I have often wondered what the deuce women can find to write about: such crossed sheets! One ought to be paid for deciphering their chequer-work' (II, 137). Mr Woodhouse, still averse to sudden noises, appears in female guise in the same novel: '"I am not fond of young men," said Lady Norbury, yawning; "they make such a noise in the house with their boots, and they clap the doors so after them"' (I, 193). In Lister's *Herbert Lacy* (1828), Mr John Knightley's opinions on travelling to dine with his coun-try neighbours reappear as Sir William Lacy's: 'Conceive, if you can, a spectacle more delightful, than that of a whole family going, in the worst of weather, six miles out and back again, actuated and supported only by a noble determination to do as other people do' (I, 285).

Sometimes a novel will start with an Austen evocation, a bit like the author clearing her throat. Catherine Gore's *Mothers and Daughters* (1831) commences with an anti-heroine who 'was neither handsome, clever, nor amiable' (I, 3), an implied comparison to 'Emma Woodhouse, handsome, clever, and rich', and sufficient to alert the reader to a story of mistaken judgements and moral error. Letitia Landon's novel *Lady Anne Granard* (1842) begins with a Mr Granard and his silly ambitious wife about to launch into familiar Austen territory: 'For five years every thing went on exceedingly well, excepting that every year a daughter made its appear-ance, a fact which astonished no one so much as it did Lady Anne herself … Moreover it was a son they wanted, as a male heir was necessary before any settlement could be made of the property' (I, 11). The most casual reader of *Pride and Prejudice* would recall that, 'When first Mr Bennet had married, economy was held to be perfectly useless; for, of course, they were to have a son. This son was to join in cutting off the entail ... Five daughters successively entered the world, but yet the son was to come; and Mrs Bennet ... had been certain that he would' (III, ch. 8). When Landon's Mr Granard dies, his wife is much annoyed in the manner of Mrs Bennet: 'What did people mean by having heirs-at-law? Why were she and her children to be impoverished for a stranger?' (I, 15). The plot that follows takes off on another track altogether, but it was Jane Austen who got the author going.

The canniest thing silver fork novelists ever did was to steal from Jane Austen. Their thefts lift the 'Do Not Resuscitate' order stamped on the spines of their novels. Moreover, they refresh Jane Austen's political significance for the Reform era. Fashionable novels claiming to 'get the manners right', Austen's acknowledged legacy to silver fork novelists, mark their pages just as Austen's do, 'as a site for the dramatization of the acute class consciousness that characterized England' during the Reform era.[38] Austen's signal reputation for discriminating social accuracy made her plots and characters easily the weaponry of choice for fashionable novelists engaged in their own battles for parliamentary reform.

Norman Gash explains the specific political context that would lead these writers to mine Austen's novels. Aristocratic reform politicians, writes Gash, were eager 'to rally middle-class support round the aristocratic system', to employ any strategy available for detaching 'the middle classes from a dangerous alliance with the lower classes'.[39] Donald Southgate, in his history of the Whig Party, emphasizes the urgency of the task: 'The prospect of ... mass discontent, made it all the more necessary to rally to the régime the classes to whom wealth gave a claim to power which the constitution did not recognise.[40]

In a sense, silver fork novelists act as fifth columnists for this liberalizing political programme. It was their mission, as it were, to infiltrate both the middle classes and the aristocracy, and once having established their credentials and novelistic characters among the aristocratic fashionables of Mayfair and the middle-class un-fashionables of Marylebone, to persuade each group to accept a useful new social mythology, one in which the middle classes are joined with the aristocracy to constitute a new governing class. The peculiar circumstances of politics in the 1820s and 1830s made working both sides of the street a necessity for them. Silver fork novels are thus designed to worry the middle classes into *gentility* and to urge the aristocrats into *respectability*. Their ultimate political aim was 'to redraw the dividing line of society', as M. L. Bush writes, to make a new political elite, 'a compound of aristocracy and bourgeoisie', that explicitly marked off the 'gentility from the working people'.⁴¹

Bush's political insight exposes the astringent edge in William Hazlitt's dislike of Theodore Hook's novels of fashionable life cited earlier, in which 'silver forks' are used to mock Hook's conservative politics.⁴² Like Hazlitt, Norman Gash also views the paradox of reform politics with distinct irony, remarking that middle-class enfranchisement, limited as it most certainly was, was possible only with the cooperation of the aristocracy: 'In effect, the whole purpose of national agitation in 1832', writes Gash, 'was to support one aristocratic faction against another.'⁴³ It was the leading principle of Whig politics that as aristocratic guardians of the Revolution of 1688, the Whig Party was to guarantee political stability to the nation by guiding adjustments to the constitution to suit changing conditions. The time for the enfranchisement of the middle classes had come. Jane Austen's legacy, her language of the *genteel* middle classes, 'just what might have been said', as T. H. Lister observes, becomes the social idiom that silver fork novelists take from Austen as political strategy.

Most Austen echoes in silver fork novels, however, are responses to a writer's practical need at the moment of composition. It is as if familiarity with Austen's work is so complete that an author can take a colour or trope, as in a box of crayons, and use it at will. The momentous year of 1832, for example, produced two politically oriented variations on Austen's home theatricals in *Mansfield Park*: Catherine Gore's *The Opera* and Henry Lister's *Arlington*, each novel redeploying Austen's theatricals to explore the threat that 'performing' Reform could hold for the social fabric. The *Mansfield Park* theatre trope appears again later, in post-Reform circumstances, in Lady Bury's *The Devoted* of 1836, a novel that includes a remarkable Fanny Price lookalike, Ethel Delamere, coerced into taking the part of Nurse in the novel's play. Lady Bury uses her theatricals to express her anger in this novel at the failed 'performance' of aristocrats in the post-Reform Parliament, 1832–6. In 1839, Catherine Gore's *The Cabinet Minister* employs a remarkably close adaptation of *Mansfield Park*, with most of Austen's cast of characters in the same positions they occupy in Austen's novel, but adapting Austen's tale to protest Tory encroachments on the struggling Whig government of 1836–8.⁴⁴

DEEP STRUCTURE

Katie Trumpener in her essay 'The Virago Jane Austen' writes of 'the deep structure' of Austen's influence, drawing attention to twentieth-century women writers' attraction to *Mansfield Park* because of 'their interest in female agency'.[45] At the silver fork novelists' best, the influence of 'the deep structure' of an Austen novel can enter one of their novels of fashionable life, sometimes only briefly, but when it happens it transforms the emotional resonance. Where Austen's work enters the 'deep structure' it can bring Austen's strengths and the silver fork novel's politically informed goals into startling confluence. Three of these 'deep structure' adaptations deserve exploration – Lord Normanby's *Matilda* (1825) which uses *Persuasion* for its model, Catherine Gore's extension of *Sense and Sensibility* in *The Hamiltons* (1834), and a disturbing post-Reform re-visioning of *Mansfield Park* in Gore's *Stokeshill Place* (1837).

In Lord Normanby's *Matilda* (1825) the society columns of the daily papers open the plot: 'It was early in the month of July, when that most valuable department of the daily press, which is headed "Fashionable Arrangements," contained, among many other pieces of information ... "Lord Ormsby (late the Honourable Augustus Arlingford) is arrived at Mivart's Hotel, after an absence of two years on the Continent"' (1, 1). Augustus Arlingford, now Lord Ormsby, has returned to England like *Persuasion*'s Captain Wentworth, no longer as a penniless suitor, but rich and deeply resentful that his fiancée Lady Matilda, unlike Jane Austen's faithful Anne Elliot, has married another.

This catastrophe is the consequence of a false report in a newspaper, the scandalous Tory paper the *John Bull*, a paper that Lord Normanby calls 'the most infamous publication that ever disgraced the press', ultra-conservative and devoted to printing scandal about its political enemies, Whigs, liberals and radicals. This paper has published false information about Augustus, the liberal-minded hero, claiming that he is involved in a foreign love affair. 'It was in this veracious record of passing events that there appeared, in its usual style of vulgar ribaldry, the most unfounded reports of a supposed intrigue between Augustus Arlingford [Ormsby] and a distinguished female resident in Rome, whom to see is to admire' (1, 29). Lady Matilda unwisely accepts the truth of the newspaper report, giving up Augustus and succumbing to her guardian's self-interested choice of a husband for her. The guardian has embezzled her fortune, but can recuperate his losses if he 'sells' her to the wealthy, newly rich and newly titled Sir James Dornton. The newspaper report of Augustus' Roman 'affair' helps change the heroine's intentions, but there is also the encouragement of Matilda's oldest female friend, who like Austen's Lady Russell, favours the supposedly eligible match. 'Is it to be wondered at', concludes the narrator, 'that, alternately threatened and cajoled by her natural guardian, artfully persuaded by her only friend, apparently abandoned by her former lover … she at last consented to give her hand to Sir James Dornton?' (1, 34–5).

The pleasure for readers familiar with Austen's *Persuasion*, but also with *Pride and Prejudice* and *Mansfield Park*, is to watch the Austen pennies drop into place so resoundingly. The first painful meeting of Matilda and Lord Ormsby after his return from abroad takes place at a dinner party at Lord Eatington's house in Grosvenor Square, where Matilda's new husband Sir James' display of self-importance chimes painfully with Mr Collins' embarrassing self-introduction to Mr Darcy at the Netherfield ball in *Pride and Prejudice*:

[I]t was with horror that Lady Matilda observed him, with ostentatious punctilio, moving up the whole length of the room, with a sort of jerking strut, to make his excuses to Lady Eatington … his slight rotundity of form well harmonizing with a singular obtuseness of features. But when a rigmarole unnecessary apology, beginning with—'Your Ladyship will excuse'—'Parliamentary duties,' &c. ended with something about—'my better half'—she thought that she should have sunk into the ground, at the idea of Augustus having lived to hear her called *better half*. (1, 16–17)

Elizabeth Bennet's silent distress and Charlotte Lucas' more dismal fate as Mr Collins' 'better half' are poignant enough reminders of Austen's story, but Sir James, who is a political idiot and a Tory, has more Austenian humiliations in store for the heroine.[46] When he is asked about politics at the dinner table, echoes of Mr Rushworth's memorable performance in *Mansfield Park* provide the thumbscrew to Matilda's sensibilities:

The inquisitive gentleman now applied himself to Sir James, who readily undertook to explain, but soon got bewildered—amongst—'Equalization of duties'—'spirit of innovation'—'proper source of influence of the Crown,' &c.; and when the more frequent application of spoonfuls of soup had become inadequate to fill up the interstices of his ideas, and just as Lady Matilda, in a furtive glance at Lord Ormsby, perceived the dreaded curl of his lip, the Baronet was most providentially rescued by a prudent pensioner opposite [with an offer of wine …] (1, 18)

Here, Sir James' confusion and his rescue by an opportune offer of wine, in addition to the Austen reader's recollections of Anne Elliot's anxious attention to Wentworth's facial expressions in *Persuasion* (1, ch. 8) touch the 'deep structure' of Austen's work with unerring success. Lord Normanby's reworking of Austen's tropes discovers that the heroine's loss of Augustus burns into her soul. The problem, ironically, for present-day readers of Lord Normanby's *Matilda* and for contemporary readers, is the very insistence of *Persuasion*'s felt presence in this novel. Even when Lord

Normanby's tale dawdles along with the lax plot of a typical circulating library novel, *Persuasion* is always lurking in the background. A contemporary reviewer accurately describes the disturbing effect: 'Perhaps there is a want of keeping in the grouping and colouring, so to speak, which has arisen from an anxiety on the part of the author to introduce variety and contrasts into his scenes. But the charm and the value of the work consist in the masterly description, which it exhibits of the fatal progress and issue of a passion.'[47] Lord Normanby's comic-relief Hobsons, the Branghton-like characters who inhabit the same novel, are amusing pre-1832 middle-class boors that frequent fashionable novels before passage of the Reform Bill, but they and the other comic characters in the novel are very much out of 'keeping in the grouping and colouring', as the critic says. Although front-loaded with *Persuasion*'s plot and characters, *Matilda* diverts the Austen tale from its course and scatters the plot in wasted directions.

The writer for the *Quarterly Review* who had suggested that plots provide only *'separating links'* for the silver fork novel, neglects the power these 'separating links' possess as plot enforcers, policemen of the hegemony that refuse to go away even when their structures are thin on the ground. When Santelmo, an Italian patriot, meets Matilda miserably honeymooning with Dornton in Italy, Santelmo's description of Italian 'liberty' in terms of a woman's body arrives just at the moment when the perilous state of Matilda's own body is in anxious negotiation. Dornton, we find, is a wife-beater. Matilda and Ormsby meet by chance in Italy and recognize that they are still in love with one another, but know also that they cannot act on their feelings. Santelmo in instructing Matilda in contemporary Italian history unknowingly draws a comparison with the political state of his homeland that mirrors Matilda's condition as an unhappy wife: 'What a change in her [Italy's] situation … she sank at once into the purchased slave of mean and sordid natures; kept as the mere servile instrument of their pleasure; pillaged, insulted, despised, and brutalized! Then it was that I felt all the infamy of her degraded state—the prostitution of her beauties by boorish strangers' (1, 162). Matilda's earnestly engaged response to Santelmo's picture of Italian politics produces an unintended, candid response to the dilemma that she and Augustus face in this *Persuasion*-beset novel: '"But why view only the gloomy side of the question?" said Matilda; "the spirit of the age is now working in your favour; the wishes of the good and liberal, of every country, are enlisted on your side; and long days of happiness and independence are yet in store for Italy"' (1, 160). No ameliorating 'spirit of the age', however, awaits Matilda in her unhappy marriage. Lord Normanby concludes the novel by having her elope with Augustus – he has witnessed Dornton strike Matilda – followed by Matilda's death in childbirth, miserably oppressed with guilt for having left her husband. Augustus leaves to fight for the Greeks with Matilda's image, says the narrator, 'never absent from his solitary pillow' (II, 379). 'As a story, it is fraught with the deepest interest', claims the *Monthly Review* (Aug. 1825), 'and at the same time forms one of the most eloquent lessons of morality that we have ever perused.' Meanwhile the reader's memory of the final happiness of *Persuasion*'s Anne Elliot and Captain Wentworth haunts Lord Normanby's novel, his heroine and hero defrauded by political lies, cheated by aristocratic greed and crushed by middle-class sensibilities.

Catherine Gore's extension of the plot of *Sense and Sensibility* in her novel *The Hamiltons* (1834) employs the 'separating links' of Austen's two-sister plot for an equally disturbing relationship with its Austen source. *The Hamiltons*, published in 1834 and set in the recent past of 1829 to 1832, arrived on the scene as a defence of a post-Reform Whig government that in 1834 had fallen under siege by defections, irresolution of leadership and, finally, a peremptory dismissal by William IV at the end of the year.[48] In *The Hamiltons* Mrs Gore's ostensible political goal is to remind her readers of how lucky they are to have an honest, reforming Whig Party in the seat of power instead of a reactionary, corrupt Tory Party, and that there had been fifty years, mind you, of Tory misrule before Lord Grey's new Whig government had been allowed to bless the nation with Progress and a 'New Aera', which is, in fact, the secondary title of *The Hamiltons: or The NewÆra*.

Gore's sensitive understanding of Austen, however, gains the upper hand over her political campaign and gives birth to a small masterpiece of silver fork writing. *The Hamiltons* begins in the usual Austen way, in a country village, Laxington, 'some ten miles N. N. E. of Northampton', a village taking pride, says Mrs Gore wryly, in its universal reputation for 'gentility'. The rumoured arrival of new residents, as in Austen's *Pride and Prejudice*, agitates the neighbourhood with excitement. Weald Park is to be let at last, a political family, the Hamiltons, are moving in – the father a high government minister, *Tory* of course – the number in the party uncertain, but at least one marriageable gentleman, the son, young Augustus Hamilton will be coming, that much is certain. The Berkely sisters, Marcia and her younger sister Susan, live in Laxington in reduced circumstances with their widowed mother, Lady Berkely, a 'staunch Whig' who has decidedly mixed feelings about the arrival of this new family, the Hamiltons – 'What should you know about exclusivism?' says she to the ladies of Laxington, '—the truth is, these Hamiltons are mere government people;—*parvenus* probably,—like most of the Tory party' (I, 20).

Handsome young Augustus Hamilton, though a Tory, with his good manners and unmistakable admiration of her younger daughter Susan, wins Lady Berkely's affections and, of course, Susan's love. Augustus' main leisure activity in Laxington has been his attempted seduction of young Susan Berkely with Willoughby's old ploys from *Sense and Sensibility* – favourite duets and like tastes in poetry. Marcia, however, the Elinor-like older sister in the novel, mistrusts Augustus for his 'fashionable' morals and his Tory family, and wishes he would simply go away, which he does – suddenly, like Austen's Willoughby, and with no intention of coming back. His father has removed the entire Hamilton family to London. Susan's heart is broken. She goes into a serious, Marianne-like decline.

Meanwhile, Marcia Berkely, the Elinor-like sister, finds herself in love with a local gentleman, Bernard Forbes, 'ungainly' and 'gloomy of temper', two unappealing traits that he shares with Edward Ferrars. Bernard, also like Edward Ferrars, struggles with an unsatisfactory previous engagement to a young woman of light principles, the Lucy Steele of the piece. Marcia, setting aside her own personal grief over Bernard Forbes' unfortunate engagement, exerts herself to console Susan for her loss of Augustus, employing the same unhelpful advice that Elinor gives to Marianne: '"Do not expect me to encourage you in regretting him," said she to Susan, in quiet sisterly confidence. "He is unworthy of you; an egotist,—a sloth,—a being incapable of those domestic affections so indispensable to your happiness"' (I, 105). As for Susan's response to Marcia's well-meant words, those readers familiar with *Sense and Sensibility* are prepared: 'The poor girl uttered not a word of complaint; but her spirits were gone,—her beauty going,—she rested not by night,—she smiled not by day—she was an altered being!' (I, 115).

The Lucy Steele figure in Gore's novel follows the pattern set by Austen's Lucy in *Sense and Sensibility* by unexpectedly abandoning her engagement to Bernard Forbes, with his relatively meagre income of £1,600 a year, for a Mr Cadogan, a man-about-town with a more generous £8,000 a year. Bernard's unexpected delivery from this entanglement brings Marcia her full 'measure of happiness'. As Mrs Gore writes, 'the affection, so long and blindly withheld from her, was lavished, at last, without limit or reservation' (II, 149–50). They move to Bloomsbury.

Here is the point where Jane Austen's *Sense and Sensibility* is revealed as a richer source for Mrs Gore than simply a convenient model for a plot. Mrs Gore extends the plot of *Sense and Sensibility* in order to take the lives of Elinor and Marianne, as Marcia and Susan, into their imagined futures in marriage. *The Hamiltons*, miraculously and very much to its good, stays closely tethered to Austen's conceptions of the two sisters' characters. We follow the sympathetic extensions of Elinor and Marianne Dashwood through the crucial choices that the women must make in their married lives during the social and political turbulence of reform, a period Gore uses to refine the identity of each of the two sisters. The male characters in *The Hamiltons* are identified solely by their relation to contemporary political reform, their parties and loyalties; the women are known by the success with which they navigate the lives demanded of them by the politics of their men.

Marcia, now Mrs Bernard Forbes, goes through the Reform years vacillating, very much as Elinor Dashwood does, between her deeply felt attraction to social convention and her equally powerful desire to resist it. These inner demons make Marcia no more warm or approachable in *The Hamiltons* than they do Elinor in *Sense and Sensibility*, but they are a tribute to Mrs Gore's feeling for her source. Marcia's relationship with Bernard Forbes' politics illustrates the point. On the one hand, Marcia relishes Bernard's radical attacks on the aristocratic system. 'When he spoke, her whole attention was employed', reports Mrs Gore, 'when he ceased speaking, her eye wandered furtively round the room ... her cheek flushed with excitement.' She considers herself to be an equal partner in her husband's career. 'There was no need to descend to the level of frivolous female companionship', says Mrs Gore, concluding, 'It was impossible to see a happier or better assorted couple' (II, 149–50). Susan's Tory husband Augustus expresses a rather more astringent version of Marcia's happiness: 'She will place herself at the head of a *bureau d'esprit* somewhere in the parish of Bloomsbury; set up for a Madame Neckar, and be the greatest, as well as the happiest, woman in the *pays Latin*' (II, 39).

Social problems arise for Marcia when the aristocratic Lady Leighton comes calling from Mayfair. Lady Leighton takes one look around Marcia's Bloomsbury neighbourhood and says, with well-intended kindness, 'But tell me, my dear Mrs Forbes, do you never intend to emerge from this funereal quarter of the town, and appear in society?' Marcia is instantly on the defensive. 'It is the quarter inhabited by most persons of my husband's profession', she says curtly, '—by *all* who make it their profession in earnest. With respect to society, your ladyship's compassion is quite superfluous. I associate familiarly with many of the first people of the day' (II, 265). You may not like Mrs Gore's version of a married Elinor Dashwood, snobbish, stiff-necked and churlish, but you do have to consider the possibility that Elinor, as Mrs Edward Ferrars, the vicar's wife, situated in a very modest vicarage herself, might also have the occasional need to assert her dignity in the parish.

On the other hand, Susan's more harrowing pilgrimage to maturity lifts Mrs Gore's novel into something approaching brilliance as the author engages Marcia's younger sister's struggle towards self-knowledge. Augustus, having more or less forgotten Susan Berkely, drops by Laxington again. He encounters the still-grieving Susan and is smitten once again by her beauty and simplicity. Impulsively he persuades his father, the Tory cabinet minister, to accept Susan as his daughter-in-law, reasoning that Susan will be a useful accessory to his father's social duties. Susan gets her heart's desire, marriage to Augustus, and is thus tied for life to the millstone of Augustus Hamilton, who is Gore's powerfully evocative version of Jane Austen's Mr Willoughby, now the heroine's husband but as selfish and feckless as ever.

The couple make their home with Augustus' father, Mr Hamilton (later to become Lord Laxington), in Spring Gardens, a government neighbourhood near Trafalgar Square and at an easy distance from Downing Street and Parliament. Unhappily Susan finds that the public role her husband intends her to serve has nothing that can give her fulfilment. 'Should we not be happier, poor and independent, than in splendid bondage such as this?' she asks Augustus plaintively. Susan also takes stock of the financial corruption she witnesses in her father-in-law's Tory household: 'So little was Mrs Hamilton habituated to the details of public service, that she could not help attaching an idea of shabbiness to the prodigality with which public money and public agents were rendered subservient to the rise and convenience of those who are themselves the servants of the public, in a higher capacity' (I, 214–15). There is worse to come. Augustus removes Susan from the protection of her father-in-law's London house to take a courtier's place in George IV's morally infamous establishment at Windsor (II, 199).

Re-enter the Lucy Steele figure, whose name is now Caroline Cadogan, having married the £8,000 a year Mr Cadogan. Austen's Lucy, we remember, abandoned her engagement to Edward Ferrars to marry his richer brother Robert, and in Mrs Gore's parallel version, Caroline has abandoned Bernard Forbes to marry the wealthy Mr Cadogan. Sadly, Caroline discovers that she has made a bad bargain. She is bored with her marriage 'to a frigid egoist' and tired of her only other occupation, the dissipation of Mayfair society. 'Education had done nothing to enlarge her mind', says Mrs Gore, recalling Elinor Dashwood's analysis of Lucy Steele's weakness, 'and it contracted at last', writes Gore, 'in quintessential malignity, into the poison-drop that yields destruction to others' (II, 297).

Here Mrs Gore introduces a variation on the Austen plot and a significant political extension of the predatory range enjoyed by Lucy Steele in *Sense and Sensibility*. Caroline Cadogan embarks on the seduction of Susan's husband Augustus Hamilton, now a much-favoured courtier. In order to screen her clandestine liaison with Augustus, Caroline treacherously engages Susan as her best friend. Susan's gradual discovery of her husband's affair with Caroline spins out in revelations that directly attach themselves to events that mark the 'political free-fall' of the Tory Party from 1829 to 1832.

Susan first suspects that something is amiss when Augustus snatches a letter from her hands before she can read it. It is from her sister Marcia warning her to be on her guard against Caroline, the gist of which Augustus recognizes just as he hands the letter over to Susan. In the scuffle, Susan falls to the floor causing her to give birth prematurely to Augustus' son and heir, a sickly weak child who dies on the same day as George IV, 4 June 1830, the beginning of the end for the Tory Party.

During Susan's period of mourning, she calls on Caroline, supposedly her best friend, who has herself just given birth to a handsome healthy son. When Susan catches a brief glimpse of Caroline's baby, which Caroline hurriedly rushes forward to shield from view, Susan experiences a 'sickening' sense of recognition, 'Her own lost child seemed to rise before her eyes' – in plain language, she recognizes Augustus' features. In that summer of 1830, writes Mrs Gore, 'Few suffered ... as the gentle Susan Hamilton.' Her political world as well as her personal world turns upside-down. On 2 November, in that autumn of 1830, Wellington makes his calamitous declaration in Parliament against reform. On 9 November, the King's visit to the Guildhall is cancelled for fear of pro-Reform mob violence. Susan, alarmed for Augustus' safety, goes to her husband's desk that afternoon to check his calendar for his whereabouts and finds a letter lying open from Caroline Cadogan. She reads it. 'She found herself an object of hatred and derision to both:—to the husband she loved—to the friend who had pretended to love her' (III, 61). She falls into a fever. When she returns to consciousness on 16 November, she awakens to find that Wellington's Tory government has fallen that very day, the Whigs have come to power, her Tory father-in-law is out of office, and she must leave her home in Spring Gardens.

The personal tragedy, however, is more than the scandal. Susan and Augustus actually love one another, but they don't always know it and certainly have no conception of how to communicate their feelings. Their intentions, good or otherwise, sail past each other with no recognition on either side. After Susan's discovery of his affair with Caroline Cadogan, Augustus watches from the opera stalls as Susan sits 'grey and frozen' in her opera box. Augustus knows that he loves her, but is trapped in the catastrophe of his careless life.

Following some months in this stalemate, Augustus arrives at his father's house, knowing exactly the time when he can safely find Susan alone, very like Darcy's unexpected visit to Elizabeth Bennet at the Collins' cottage. Susan of course does not know that Augustus is at this very moment on his way to meet Caroline's betrayed husband for the inevitable duel. 'As we may not meet each other for some time', he says to Susan tenderly, he asks if he may kiss her. Susan first, and correctly, believes he is affirming his love for her. Then suddenly she thinks it must be his way of announcing that he is going off with Caroline Cadogan. 'I would sooner throw myself at once upon the stones below, than receive from you the slightest token of tenderness', she tells him in righteous indignation. '"As you please!" said he, vexed into the assumption of his usual petulance' (III, 151). And off he goes to meet his death at the hands of Mr Cadogan. Mrs Gore, once again, takes her inspiration from Austen, the Darcy and Elizabeth first-proposal confrontation in *Pride and Prejudice*. Like Gore's Susan-Augustus crisis, the moment is an unwelcome intimacy for Elizabeth and an occasion of offence for Darcy. Even the rhetorical violence of Susan's response to Augustus is prefigured in the furious excess of Elizabeth's reply to Darcy: 'You could not have made me an offer of your hand in any possible way', says Elizabeth, 'that would have tempted me to accept it ... I had not known you a month before I felt that you were the last man in the world whom I could ever be prevailed on to marry.' Darcy's retort is also a prime match for Augustus' petulant 'As you please!' 'You have said quite enough, madam', says Darcy, '"Forgive me for having taken up so much of your time" ... and with these words he hastily left the room ... and quit the house' (II, ch. II). The two scenes have much in common – missed communications, total surprise – shock, anger, revenge, petulance and, what makes them electric, the missed potential for mutual self-knowledge.

Mrs Gore also provides a Colonel Brandon figure in the novel to rescue Susan Hamilton from her grief. He is not exactly parachuted in – he
has been hanging about as a minor presence throughout the novel – Lord
Claneustace, ideally well-suited for the job. He has a clear £70,000 a year,
a great estate many miles around and has embraced liberal politics under
the influence of Bernard Forbes, Marcia's radical husband. As confirmation of his high principles, he abandons the Tory Party for the Whigs.
Following Augustus' death, Lord Claneustace presents Susan's Tory
father-in-law, his former guardian, with a small estate to live on, where
Susan, who remains loyal to the old man, is to be seen nursing him in his
last days. Claneustace visits his former guardian regularly, and ever more
frequently as he falls in love with the pale but beautiful Susan Hamilton,
who has been much strengthened in spirit and character by her suffering.
He proposes marriage.

It is worth remembering that in all of Jane Austen's novels marriages
resolve power relations between ranks and classes. The marriage of Susan
and Claneustace picks up the trope, but in specifically Whiggish political terms. Significantly, the marriage takes place at the conclusion of
the novel, in 1832, just post-Reform and at the beginning of the New
Aera. Susan, like her sister Marcia in Bloomsbury, becomes a participating partner in her husband's career. 'At Claneustace Court', writes Mrs
Gore, 'where the larger portion of their life is passed, they are constantly
together, reading, riding, walking, planning improvements, visiting the
happy tenantry committed to their charge, and adopting, in the legislation of their estate, the moral system suggested on a yet wider scale by
Bernard Forbes, for the enlightenment of the country' (III, 317–18). In a
sentimental novel, Susan Hamilton would have remained a widow at the
conclusion, but she doesn't. Like Anne Elliot in *Persuasion*, Susan chooses
her husband for his generous spirit and for political principles that she can
respect. If we smile at Mrs Gore's exalted description of the Claneustaces'
partnership of political and domestic happiness – 'the Marchioness has
not only her own happiness to attribute to the love and protection of
her husband, but indulges in the heartfelt joy of knowing the welfare of
thousands to be secured by his interposition' – we have to acknowledge
that the last words of Gore's novel are a ringing echo of the happiness
of *Persuasion*'s Anne Elliot – 'She gloried in being a sailor's wife, but she
must pay the tax of quick alarm for belonging to that profession which is,
if possible, more distinguished in its domestic virtues than in its national
importance' (II, ch. 12).

As a final, if less expansive, example of emotional resonance garnered from Austen's works by Mrs Gore, there is her redeployment of *Mansfield Park*'s plot in *Stokeshill Place* (1837), a dark story featuring a lawyer's daughter, Margaret Barnsley as the Fanny Price-like heroine. Margaret becomes a house guest in a family of local aristocrats and is treated more or less in the same humbling ways that Fanny suffers in the Bertram family. Gore's plot quotation of Austen's novel goes along smoothly enough, if mechanically, rather like T. H. Lister's reuse of the *Mansfield Park* theatricals in his novel *Arlington* (1832). Such a device has its pleasures for Austen readers then and now, but for a long while the echoes of *Mansfield Park* in *Stokeshill Place* produce no special resonance of power for Gore's novel like she harnessed in *The Hamiltons*.

We first see Margaret Barnsley, as we do Fanny Price, newly arrived in a household much above her own, as the guest and companion of the Drewe sisters, the aristocratic daughters of the house. 'Inexperienced in the magic of operas and concerts, she was enchanted by the perfection of their musical accomplishments; and after being introduced to their easels and embroidery frames, their Spanish, German and Italian libraries, the poor girl shrank from the contemplation of her comparative incapacity. She allowed nothing for difference of tuition. She only felt that she was a dunce' (I, 102–3). The Drewe sisters, however, are as arbitrarily kind and as casually cruel as Maria and Julia Bertram: 'The Drewes were tall, handsome, high-bred girls', writes Gore, 'with no worse disqualification than the selfishness into which their excellent disposition had been cramped by the fond indulgence of their mother. All without was bright and polished,—and all within hollow and unprofitable.' As for the treatment of their new humble companion, they match the Bertram sisters point for point: 'Rivalship with such a person was out of the question; and instead of treating her want of connection with the scorn it would have provoked from some country baronet's daughter, they were fascinated by her unassuming gentleness, and amused by her *naïveté*' (I, 101). There are no home theatricals for poor Margaret to negotiate in this novel, but there is a much-heralded ball which places her in the humiliating position of having to ask advice from the sisters on a proper dress. In addition, as in *Mansfield Park*, the man for whom the heroine holds a secret passion is in love with the only woman in the novel who is ever kind to her. Austen's *Mansfield Park* plot keeps putting up old, familiar signs, but the intervening links, the story of Margaret's banker father and his destructive attempts to insert himself in the political and class privileges of his aristocratic neighbourhood, achieve little Austenian connection until the great ball held by her aristocratic hosts, the Drewes. Margaret, dressed in white, compelled by her father to wear opals instead of the more modest pearls she had asked for, and like Fanny Price more beautiful than ever with her raised complexion, retires from the ball a great social success, feverish, but not with happiness. Scarlet fever is the source of her raised complexion (I, 210–11). The Mansfield Park ball morphs into a symbolically poisonous event in Gore's *Stokeshill Place*, an obvious link to her father's mad, obsessive desire to achieve political and social equality with his aristocratic neighbours. 'Little as she knew of worldly distinctions, Margaret could not but discern the truth;—that she was living among people of a rank superior to her own; and that Lord Shoreham regarded the daughters of Lord Tynemouth and the niece of Lord Brereton in a different light from the daughter of Mr Barnsley of Stokeshill;—an attorney bred, and born of parents, the existence of whose progenitors was proved only by the immutable laws of physiological nature' (I, 207).

The resonance of Gore's *Mansfield Park* quotation falls into place, finally. Margaret returns home weakened by illness, bereft of love – the hero has married her friend and rival – and profoundly shaken to learn of her father's destructive excesses, his mental instability and his financial extravagance in an election that has drained his fortune. The upper servants can see that 'their sweet young missus was wasted to a shadow. They discerned not that a far more wonderful transformation had taken place;—that the timid girl had become a feeling woman!' (II, 2). As her governess leads her through her old schoolroom, Margaret looks about to experience a revised version of Fanny Price's east room, now a heartbreaking scene of emptiness and loss: '*There* stood the piano, awaiting her with its figures and concertos,—the drawing-box with its chalks,— the eternal tapestry-frame with its worsteads and floss-silk;—while Blair, Chapone, Graham, Trimmer, Hannah More, Fordyce, Gisborne, and a few other female classics, displayed their well-worn tomes on the shelves of her limited bookcase (see Figure 1). Nothing in Margaret's education has prepared her for modern life. 'All was as it had been from her childhood,—formal, dry and unexciting. But from these few objects, endeared to her by a thousand early associations, she turned to the depths of her own heart; where a thousand emotions were already in action, like the troubles fermenting beneath the tranquil oliveyards and vineyards of Vesuvius' (II, 3).

We have become accustomed to hearing about the politics of Jane Austen's novels, beginning with Marilyn Butler's groundbreaking study, *Jane Austen and the War of Ideas* right through to Jocelyn Harris' recent

A Revolution Almost Beyond Expression. Jane Austen's novels, as well as the novels of Burney and Edgeworth, have everything to do with the politics of power, a fundamental source of their attraction to the Reform generation. Power in Austen's novels especially is always a present concern – whether from class, land, money, gender or inheritance. Power is the 'interest' in Austen's novels that runs society, ranging from the grand affairs of marriages to the trivial ones of shopping, walking, riding, visiting, dressing and eating. As Andrea Hibbard perceptively observes of Austen's novels, domestic realism that 'gets the manners, in particular, right'[49] creates a pattern for delineating power. Edward Neill's vigorous argument for Austen's subversive resistance to 'ruling-class ideology' in his study *The Politics of Jane Austen* offers a clue to Mrs Gore's expressions of ambivalence about power, especially in her novels *The Hamiltons, Mrs. Armytage* and *Stokeshill Place*.[50] It should come as no surprise that the 1820s and 1830s novels of fashionable life drew on this subversive tradition to explore Reform, the greatest power struggle of the age.

CHAPTER 3

Reform and the silver fork novel

They mutually agreed that ambition was the only passion worthy the
mind of man, and politics the only science deserving his attention.
Mrs C. D. Burdett, *At Home* (1828)[1]

In August 1832, almost two months after the passage of the Reform Act,
a C. J. Grant cartoon appeared in response to the cultural shock of the
event.[2] In May the Reform Bill had appeared doomed and the nation's
frustration seemed to be inclining dangerously towards revolution, but
after the passage of the Bill and the King's signature on 7 June, political news in the daily papers had been unnaturally subdued. It was as if
the nation itself needed time to absorb the news. Grant's caricature opera
(Figure 2), 'The LAST SCENE of the TRIUMPH OF REFORM,
or the FALL of the BORO'MONGERS', comes like a burst of laughter, relief from the stress of the past three years.[3]

Grant's cartoon scarcely exaggerates the political melodrama that had
culminated in the King's signature, reluctantly given. The Tory leader
Wellington lies prostrate at stage right, 'As Arthur lived, so he Died.' Peel,
Wellington's Home Secretary, kneels nearby with his 'Poison' chalice:
'Ye Gods above avenge our Cause.' The Duke of Cumberland, an ultra-
Tory royal, arms upraised at stage centre cries, 'Die All die nobly.' The
chorus bear banners celebrating the Whig victory: 'THE PEOPLE',
'REFORM', 'LIBERTY of the PRESS', 'THE UNIONS',
'OUR KING AND COUNTRY', 'CIVIL AND RELIGIOUS
LIBERTY'. In the audience, the newly enfranchised middle classes
rejoice in the upper balcony with cries of 'Throw 'em Over', 'Turn them
Tories out'. The aristocratic boxes applaud with a bevy of 'Bravos', while
the genteel middle classes with seats in the stalls, connoisseurs of this
particular opera, join the aristocrats in their 'Bravos'. No wonder such
applause greets the last scene of 'The Fall of the Boro'mongers'. Revolution,
the threat that had haunted all politics for the past three years, had been

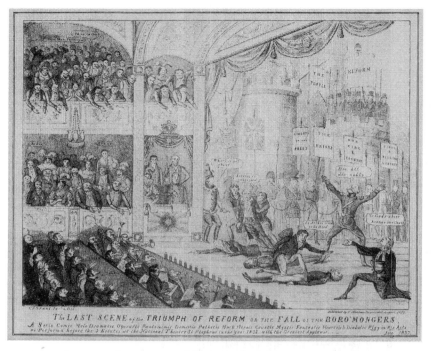

Figure 2 *The Last Scene of the Triumph of Reform*, by C. J. Grant

averted, just. Most surprising of all, only a very few years before, even in 1830, reform had been considered by Whig and Tory a most unlikely event, a political liability and waste of time, very much a dead political issue.

WHIGS AND TORIES

The big story of 1827, for example, was not parliamentary reform, but the sudden divisive breakup of the Tory Party with the stroke and resignation of the Tory prime minister, Lord Liverpool. His loss exposed a long-simmering crisis in parliamentary politics – a general sense that the two traditional political parties, the Tories and the Whigs, had been in a declining state for years. The Tory Party had held the reins of government for almost half a century with only three years of interruption and was to remain in power for three more years. But the vacuum created by the loss of the Tory leader allowed fractious energies within the Tories to throw not only the party itself into serious disarray, but also to set confusion among the Whigs as well.[4] Lord Holland, a leading Whig, took note of the weakness of both parties in 1826 and gave his opinion that 'party government' based on 'attachments to different systems of policy or adherence to opposite leaders in the State' had finally collapsed.[5] The next year, 1827, Henry Brougham, the radical Whig politician, complained bitterly that the Whig Party had 'ceased to act as a party'.[6] The old political division between Whigs and Tories appeared to be antiquated, inadequate and fast fading.[7]

Historians, however, are not in agreement. Frank O'Gorman argues in *The Long Eighteenth Century* that the two parties, the Whigs and the Tories, dominated the decade before the Reform Act, noting that even before 1812, 'party' MPs were a clear majority in the House of Commons. He also notes that during Liverpool's ministry, 'only about 10–15 per cent of MPs wavered in their loyalties to government or opposition by voting for both [parties]', and that in a single session, 'only about 5 per cent of MPs would vote on both sides'.[8]

Eric J. Evans, much more cautious in his *The Forging of the Modern State*, suggests that party identity is not always reliable as a guide to actual voting patterns, given the 'fluid condition of party allegiance and the continuing strength of independent MPs'.[9] Party strength also fluctuated from lack of attendance rather than from measurable shifts of opinion, since only committed politicians came to London at the beginning of a given parliamentary session or stayed until it was over, and on particular issues such as taxation and expenditure the opposition (the Whigs) and independents could combine to embarrass the Tory government. Moreover, 'the distinction', he observes, 'between administration supporters and independents or uncommitted was hazy'.[10] Peter Jupp, equally cautious in *British Politics on the Eve of Reform*, estimates that 'even on the most optimistic evaluations, barely half the 658 MPs of post-Union parliaments voted consistently for either government or opposition', and that 'most notably ... the country gentlemen who prided themselves on being independent of parties of government and opposition' contributed to a marked looseness in a system that defies modern notions of party allegiance.[11]

Novels of fashionable life get their start in this contemporary muddle of party identity. The ambiguities produced an opportunity for novelists to explore the social confusions of a new political scene. Theodore Hook, a Tory journalist, held both parties in equal contempt in his novel *Sayings and Doings* (1824).[12] The concluding scene of Hook's tale 'Danvers' from the second series of *Sayings and Doings* (1825) exposes corrupt electioneering as the way of the world. The hero loses his contested election and his £30,000 fortune, all inclusive, for necessary bribes, entertainment, food, lodging and transportation for the electors (1, 131–2).

Robert Plumer Ward's novel *Tremaine*, published in 1825, places the 'independent gentleman', the man who votes his conscience as opposed to the man who votes by party discipline, at centre stage. Ward's Tremaine, a haughty young Whig aristocrat on a tour of his northern estates, visits his mentor and old friend Mr Evelyn in Yorkshire. As a local landowner himself with a moderate income (£2,000 a year), Mr Evelyn instructs Tremaine in the importance of compromise and political adjustment. As Mr Evelyn tells his old pupil, it is 'men, not measures' (i.e. pragmatism, not theories) that should guide a man's actions in the small and the great political world. Tremaine, however, has been accustomed to take the opposite position, 'measures, not men', a principle he has imbibed from Whiggish reading in abstract philosophy (1, 51).[13] Evelyn pointedly reminds Tremaine of the obvious electoral limitations of such thinking, 'It is long since Whigs have been in office!' Tremaine smiles with some bitterness at the implication, writes Ward, but Mr Evelyn presses the lesson home: 'I, who am neither Whig nor Tory, am at least content with our own men' (1, 109).

Ward's *Tremaine* is set during the historical Regency when the Whigs of 1811–12 were staggering from the Regent's unexpected turn to a conservative-led government, a political disappointment which explains young Tremaine's self-rustication to Yorkshire. The historical reference, however, is finely tuned to match more recent disappointments of the Whig Party in the 1820s, specifically the party's repeated failures to advance its most cherished measures, Catholic emancipation and the reform of parliamentary representation. The vicar teaches Tremaine, a Whig, to prepare himself for political cooperation with Tories. He first, however, lets his young grandee learn how to meet his more humble Yorkshire neighbours in political compromise – farmers, tradesmen, lawyers, small landowners, including a crusty yeoman who aggressively attacks Tremaine with ultra-Tory opinions that the young Whig aristocrat must hear out with patience and civility. For Ward, political cooperation, not party allegiance, is certain to be the future of parliamentary government.

As things developed, he could not have been more mistaken, although it was a useful and common political posture in the 1820s. In 1825, the independent country gentleman must have seemed an especially apt emblem for what most people supposed to be the future, a non-party government for Great Britain. The tradition of a candidate's 'independence' from partisan politics was a standard campaign posture that lasted well into the 1830s, one with a strong mythic resonance going back to the eighteenth century.[14] Despite this rhetoric of 'independence', as Eric Evans observes, 'Within ten years on either side of the Reform Act the independent MP, such an important factor in eighteenth-century politics, became a rarity, squeezed out by polarization on issues, the increased size of the electorate to which he had to appeal and by the ever wider political ground occupied by new party organizations.'[15] By 1832, according to *Fraser's Magazine*, the political climate had become violently partisan: 'This man is a fierce Whig or Tory, without knowing any thing of party creeds, because he was reared one ... that man devoutly believes in every thing Whigs or Tories utter, because he is a churchman and landowner, or a dissenter and manufacturer.' The present situation, concludes *Fraser's*, is 'that if we analyze society, we can scarcely find one party man who has chosen his party from a careful examination of its creed, or who judges impartially of public measures as they come before him.'[16] The 'independent' member, however, seemed important enough to the Whigs to frame their measures accordingly, recommending parliamentary reform as to 'remove at once, and for ever, all rational grounds for complaint from the minds of the intelligent and *independent* portion of the community' (emphasis added).[17]

Vivian Grey, Disraeli's first novel, published in April 1826, stands in marked contrast to the cheerful tone of Ward's *Tremaine* (1825), but rests on Ward's assumption that the two traditional parties were in a state of permanent decline. The publication of Disraeli's novel coincided with the condition of Lord Liverpool's Tory cabinet in 1825–6, a party obviously adrift, fragmented among conservative ultra-Tories and fractious 'liberal' Tories over the issue of Catholic emancipation. 'The real dividing line', writes Arthur Aspinall, 'was now not between those in and those out of office, but between the Liberals and the Illiberals.'[18] *Vivian Grey* bubbles up from the same political pot as *Tremaine*, but the plot of Disraeli's tale follows a strikingly different path.

Vivian, as a youngster, says Disraeli, 'stumbled upon a branch of study certainly the most delightful in the world,—but ... certainly the most pernicious—THE STUDY OF POLITICS' (1, 53). Middle-class and an opportunist, the young protagonist determines to satisfy his political ambitions by forming himself into a dandy, calculating exactly how his every act, word and gesture can be exploited for maximum political effect: 'Oh, yes! to *rule* men, we must be weak', Vivian confesses to the reader, 'to prove that we are giants, we must be dwarfs ... Our wisdom must be concealed under folly, and our constancy under caprice' (1, 56–7). In the contemporary vacuum of traditional party loyalties in 1825, Vivian starts his own party and, as Ellen Moers succinctly describes it, 'successively charms, flatters, beguiles, cheats and betrays a covey of visiting lords, millionaires, widows and virgins', failing in the end, however, to achieve success, 'betrayed by treachery and by his own over-confident, indecent machinations'.[19] Nevertheless, Vivian's approach to politics is a devastating indictment of the contemporary political world: 'A SMILE FOR A FRIEND, AND A SNEER FOR THE WORLD, is the way to govern mankind', he says, 'and such is the motto of Vivian Grey' (1, 108). His spectacular personal failure contains its own baleful revelation. As events spin out of control, Vivian discovers with horror that he is himself merely a disposable pawn in a much larger game of political intrigue, one that remains hidden even from his keen eyes.

As Gary Kelly observes in *English Fiction of the Romantic Period, 1789–1830*, the professional author, middle-class by definition, attempts 'to forge a new image of the social leader as gentleman', but must engage an aristocratic power elite undergoing its own uncertain process of redefinition. In hindsight, says Kelly, 'the new image would turn out to be the Victorian image of the gentleman; but in the late 1820s and the 1830s there was still much uncertainty as to how to form this new image, and the uncertainty shows up as a major concern in novels of fashionable life'.[20] The project of silver fork novels is to feel out the possibilities of this new and highly significant image still hidden in the future.

The characters that form the dramatis persona of silver fork novels belong, significantly, to the same genteel ranks that furnished over three-quarters of the MPs in the Commons, including the members of the civil service and the officers of the army and navy as well, all of whom had the right to put their leg forward with their more privileged kin in the upper aristocracy.[21] Aristocrats and gentry in 1828 simply assumed that status and rank mattered in politics, and their own especially. To all practical purposes 'status elite' and 'power elite' were the same thing, the House of Commons being hardly more than an extension of the peerage by both patronage and kinship.[22] The grand game of national policy had always belonged to a very small group of Tory and Whig politicians from the highest levels of the aristocracy, but lesser aristocrats and politically thrusting country gentry now found their opinions suddenly elevated to national importance by issues of reform.

The stumbling, divided Tory government and the stock market collapse of 1825–6 become the dual catastrophes of T. H. Lister's fashionable novel *Granby* (1826). The hero, Henry Granby, who has been orphaned and then rendered penniless by the market collapse, is forbidden by his uncle and guardian, General Granby, to enter a profession. This is inexplicable to Granby, who has only his allowance from the General, but the General possesses a secret, one with a certain current significance as political symbolism, that the present holder of the Malton title and estate, a Tory, is illegitimate and that Granby, a Whig, is the rightful heir. The political plot centres on Tory incompetence, a narrative played out through the tale of young Granby's love for Caroline Jermyn whose father is Sir Thomas Jermyn, a fatuous, pretentious Tory MP from the borough of Rottentown. Sir Thomas has forbidden Granby's courtship of his daughter on the grounds of Granby's limited income.

In describing Sir Thomas' politics, Lister opens the novel to the reader's reflection on Whig principles of political change, particularly the need for the reform of a patently flawed system of parliamentary representation, one embodied in the person and position of Sir Thomas Jermyn: 'Rottentown was a government borough, and, *therefore*, his politics were ministerial. In fact, his politics had long wavered ... yet, as most of his connections were on the ministerial side, and a comfortable borough was opportunely offered him from that quarter, saddled only with the obligation of uniformly voting for measures of which, after all, he could not see the great atrocity—under these circumstances he thought it as advisable to as it was easy, to range himself under the banners of the administration' (1, 53–4). As for the sacred Anglican constitution, the cry of all ultra-Tory politicians, Sir Thomas is not averse to joining the pack when it suits his selfish needs: he 'thought religion was a good thing, and ought to be kept up, and that, like cheap soup, it was "excellent for the poor" ... if it made his tenants pull off their hats and pay their rents, it was at any rate worth encouraging in them' (1, 54). Sir Thomas' insouciant corruption drifts comically through the sentimental narrative of his daughter's and poor Granby's frustrated courtship.

There is, however, a more dangerous figure in Lister's novel, a political dandy, a Mr Trebeck, with no responsible principles of government at all. He freely mocks Sir Thomas' all too obvious political fatuity – 'Politics, politics; I won his heart by calling him a Radical; and he brought out all his best common-places to prove that he was not' (1, 213). Trebeck's plot to marry Sir Thomas' heiress daughter only falters when Granby is revealed to be massively rich and the new Lord Malton. Her father enthusiastically consents to Granby's prompt proposal of marriage: 'Sir Thomas chuckled in anticipating the frequent instances in which his young and wealthy son-in-law, oppressed with the cares of his novel situation, would doubtless apply for the aid of his experience, and flattered himself that Henry's political proceedings in the Upper House, would be regulated upon the model of his father-in-law's judicious conduct in the Lower' (III, 326–7). The elevation of Granby, a Whig, to a position of political power is an early signal of the close relationship of silver fork novels with Whig political programmes.

CATHOLIC EMANCIPATION, 1829

By 1828, national partisan politics had become the running motif of Lord Normanby's novel *Yes and No*. Normanby's novel of that year reflects the rapidity of the development of an increasingly agitated, divided political society. Three highly political young gentlemen meet one another at a country inn – Oakley, a chilly, rank-conscious Whig aristocrat, his cousin Germain, vaguely liberal in politics and a novice man-about-town, and Germain's ostensible friend Fitzalbert, a dandy, a gambler and a Tory. As the three gentlemen part to go their ways, Oakley cautions Germain, who plans to continue the excursion with his Tory 'friend', Fitzalbert: '"Grouse-shooting?" asked Oakley;—"well, remember that Fitzalbert is sometimes supposed a—a pretty good long shot at a pigeon, that's all"' (I, 24).

In the year of its publication (1828), *Yes and No* is set at the leading edge of political turbulence, the Catholic question, which was the most divisive issue of the late 1820s, and the one that brought new life to partisan politics. 'Almost all Whigs supported emancipation', writes O'Gorman, 'while a majority of Tories opposed it.'[23] There had been numerous Whig attempts at the inclusion of Catholics within the body politic – in 1805, 1819, 1821 and 1825, each one with growing success in Parliament, but always ending in failure. 'In intellectual terms', writes Linda Colley, 'a majority of British MPs had accepted that Catholics must be admitted to civil rights.'[24] In fact a Catholic relief bill submitted by the radical Whig Sir Francis Burdett in 1825 passed in the Commons by a majority of 21 votes, only to be defeated in the Upper House the following week by the 'Protestant' Lords.[25]

Liberal Tory sympathy for Catholic emancipation had been the rock upon which the Tory Party split in 1827. Lord Normanby saw a chance to make his novel *Yes and No* a platform to encourage a renewal of Whig Party strength by supporting a new push for Catholic emancipation. Earnest Oakley, Normanby's Whig protagonist, represents, however, an old-style of Whig politics, of maintaining an aristocratic distance from the 'People' and a mistrust of the middle classes, a frame of mind that Normanby suggests Oakley must give up if the Whig Party's bid for political power is to have any chance of success. The contrast between the stiff-necked Oakley and his affable young cousin Germain, mildly political and 'independent', shows itself when the two cousins argue over the right and the wrong way to discuss politics. Oakley lectures his liberal cousin, 'it is sincere regard for you which induces me to tell you, once again, Germain, that, in over anxiety for other people's approbation, you will soon forfeit your own'. Germain responds, 'perhaps that very quality which you call facility, (meaning weakness,) and which I call candour, predisposes me whilst I am listening to you, to acknowledge there is some truth in what you are saying, and your firmness of character which some might mistake for obstinacy, prevents your ever yielding a tittle' (1, 6–7). Any Whig politician who picked up *Yes and No* for a leisurely read would immediately understand this as a preview of the dire consequences of Oakley's old-style Whiggery:

'There,' said Germain, 'as you have interrupted me, I must interrupt you. Look! you have put out the fire with your violence; that is what I complain that you do in society, which you enter, as stiff and as cold as a poker, and attempt to carry all by storm. Now I should have insinuated myself gently, and have soon been received with reviving warmth, and partaken of its influence. Much as you know, you have yet to learn the magic of manner.'

'The gilding that makes falsehood and folly pass current,' muttered Oakley, as the entrance of the landlady herself with the first dish prevented further reply. (1, 8–9)

In marked contrast to Oakley's dour approach, Germain's false friend Fitzalbert, the untrustworthy, 'fashionable' London dandy, has substantial gifts of the 'magic of manner'. Very like Disraeli's Vivian Grey, Fitzalbert uses these skills for his own personal advantage, regardless of principle, wherever he meets money or power. Fitzalbert, writes Normanby, had an 'acute and calculating character [that] would enable him to foresee advantages to himself from trifles, which a more enlarged mind or a more careless disposition would alike have overlooked'. This selfish and manipulating dandy represents a serious danger in this year of two-party redefinition – 'All his [Fitzalbert's] qualities as an agreeable member of society, were crowned by an easy off-hand manner, which most people avowedly (and probably all) really prefer to the Grandison, Gold-Stick sort of address' (I, 26–7).

Fitzalbert plies his charms at the country house of Lord Boreton and Lady Boreton, a female 'fire-brand' of the Whig persuasion. The Whig Boretons are hosting the local Tory magnates, Lord and Lady Latimer, for an annual visit held 'to preserve the political peace of the county, which was only maintained by a compromise between these two great rival interests' (I, 140). Lord Latimer, a politically moderate Tory, cares little for governing – he leaves it to other gentlemen of good recommendation to advise him, hence providing a splendid opening for Fitzalbert's malicious political interference.

The two couples, the Boretons and the Latimers, discuss what to do about a successor to 'their' Mr Medium, MP, who as an 'independent gentleman' is to retire at the end of the present Parliament. Mr Medium, writes Normanby, had been, 'for thirty years received as an oracle by both parties, principally from his own indecision of character ... Such as he was ... his general leaning to Tory principles had satisfied Lord Latimer, who was not an eager politician, and his occasional effective opposition to ministers [Tory] had almost consoled Lady Boreton, who was a red-hot liberal' (I, 141).

Meanwhile Oakley inherits the estate of his reclusive uncle, Lord Rockington, a Whig grandee who, feeling himself mistreated by the newspapers and by the government, had shut himself away from all public affairs. His ancient castle, the very image of Whig political history, bears 'in different parts the distinguishing marks of each succeeding century except the present; for it had fortunately escaped the mongrel patch-work of modern improvements' (I, 70). Earnest Oakley enters with alacrity upon this inheritance of old-style aristocratic Whig exclusiveness, closing the castle to visitors and insulting the middle-class lawyer who comes to welcome him, which is a grave mistake since the lawyer will take revenge when Oakley seeks political office.

The wily, meddling Fitzalbert persuades Lady Boreton to propose young Earnest Oakley as her Whig candidate for MP. Fitzalbert likewise manipulates Lord Latimer into putting up Germain, Oakley's cousin, as the liberal Tory opponent. Meanwhile the sitting MP for the county, Mr Stedman, an ultra-Tory, unexpectedly offers himself for re-election, making the affair a three-way race in which only two can be chosen. It will become expedient to arrange a coalition between two of them in order to defeat the third – the national dilemma writ small.

Germain's old tutor, the parish clergyman, Mr Dormer, supports Stedman's rigorous 'Ultra' principles, and, as Normanby observes wearily, 'If he seriously believed that it was the intention of half the government, and one branch of the legislature, to establish the Pope at Lambeth, it was an opinion which he shared with many who had more opportunities of knowing better' (1, 55–6). When Germain visits Mr Dormer to solicit his vote, his old tutor gives him a conservative earful on the dangers of Catholic enfranchisement. 'After folding in an important manner the newspaper he held in his hand, he began':

'Pray, Mr.Germain, might I ask whether in those popish parts you have lately visited, you were ever unfortunate enough to be present at any of those sacrifices to superstition—those auto-da-fès [*sic*]—those burnings of heretics?'

'No, indeed,' replied Germain, rather surprised: 'nor was I aware that any events of the kind had taken place within the memory of man. This is the first I ever heard of it.'

'I am sorry, my young friend,' rejoined Mr.Dormer, with an air of reproach, 'to find that you have made so little use of your time—that you have not been a more observant traveller.'

Then again unfolding the county paper, he read aloud, with earnest emphasis, the words in italics.

'*Characteristics of Catholicism—Burning of a Jew.* It is, we are proud to say, not a little owing to *our* unceasing efforts in the *good Protestant cause*, that these burning piles are seen only as a warning beacon from afar—that the flames are not now kindled in Smithfield, or the crackling faggots heard in the market-place beneath our own office-window. For if such is the treatment of the papists towards an unoffending *Israelite*, what might we expect, if they had the power, towards the objects of their unceasing detestation—the *loyal Protestants* of these most *religious realms*? Yet there are amongst us those infatuated enough to wish to open wide our doors to them. What doors? and to whom?—why the very doors of those two houses of parliament which, never let it be forgotten, they conspired to blow to atoms with their hellish popish plot.'

Germain attempts to talk reason, asking him, 'Do you think, sir, the Catholics would be so much more likely to blow up the parliament, if they had seats in it themselves?' 'God forbid we should ever try!' exclaims the Revd Mr Dormer (1, 107–08).

Oakley, always passionate in the Whig cause, has significant difficulties with forwarding his candidacy. His problems stand as Normanby's coded commentary on internal divisions that are plaguing the Whig Party in the year of the novel. When the aristocratic Oakley appeals to voters in a town near Goldsborough, his newly inherited estate, the narrator laments, 'his public speech revelled in those abstract theories of philanthropy and patriotism upon which liberal ideas in politics are founded—but what availed these general doctrines, when he sought in vain for an individual link of sympathy which might connect him with his kind' (1, 247). That evening at the inn where Oakley stops for dinner, he gets a hint of the day's success from his waiter. The talkative waiter, who though he may never vote himself, is more than happy to express an opinion, a recent state of public involvement that Oakley, and all other old-style Whig aristocrats by implication, would much prefer to ignore:

'Lord, sur, there's not a man, woman, or choild in all the country round, but has made a bit of a favourite of one of them; and as for our house, we're no two of a moind there. There's Betty Chambermaid all for Germain, because his colours are prattyest for to look on. Cook's all for ould Squire Stedman, because he's most against the Pope's roasting-alive consarn. As for me, from what I sees in the papers of Squire Oakley's talk, I conceits him the most, only I doubt its all gammon he says.'

'Why so?' enquired Oakley.

'Why, you see, he talks a deal about liberty and natural rights, and that all property is only in trust for the public;—well, he's gotten a mortal foine place, and park, and gardens, such as there's not the loike in the county, and he wont let a living soul get a soight of it ... Then, as to economy which he preaches, I doubt he practices that better: it's nothing to me that for certain, for the more as don't dine with him the more may come here. But I am tould that neither man, woman, nor choild, have ever had their trotters under his mahogany.'

'Get me some more mutton-chops,' said Oakley, whose pleasure in the conversation had quite ceased. (1, 250)

In contrast, Oakley's cousin Germain, who has been put up by Lord and Lady Latimer as their liberal Tory, is a born campaigner. Untroubled by aristocratic pride or abstract concepts, Germain 'proceeded prosperously with his canvass; to go through all the various duties of this busy time was to him much less of an effort than to Oakley', even if his motives are hardly lofty. 'Some amused him, others gratified his vanity', but he is effective, 'as they all were the source of active occupation and excitement, he never felt happier than whilst engaged in them, which feeling enabled him to perform them more easily, more effectually than if he had considered them as a drudgery.' Germain, says Normanby:

was moreover an excellent listener, a first-rate qualification in a candidate; and during the allotted period of each visit, he could sit with a face of intense interest whilst the topics that had been got up for his reception were regularly gone through. It was the same to him whether the subject matter was foreign or domestic—there he sat in silent acquiescence.

He had moreover a ready eye for any thing purposely put to be admired, whether of furniture or family; and no one had ever the mortification of reflecting after he went away, that any thing done to attract his attention had failed in its object. (I, 259–60)

Such an approach does not necessarily compromise Germain's moral principles, as Oakley has earlier maintained. Germain registers genuine shock when he is asked by his party manager (Tory) to embellish his campaign with anti-Catholic slogans. 'It is a pity, Mr Germain, that you and Lord Latimer could not have made up your mind to some sort of vague "no popery phrases" in your address; you would have been quite safe then, and I would have undertaken to have so worded it that it need not hereafter have been inconvenient under other circumstances.' Germain scarcely refrains from giving Mr Macdeed more than a prudent brush-off: 'It is just as well', he replies curtly, 'as it is' (I, 262).

Yes and No provides a serious assessment of political prospects for the Whigs in late 1828 and a public sounding of the party's uncertain future. As Normanby understands, the People had developed opinions of their own that must be heard with courtesy, possibly buttered by a little flattery. 'Whiggery always bore the stamp of aristocracy', as Donald Southgate observes, and if they wished to serve the public, they needed to invent a new relationship with it.[26] Germain, as the liberal Tory, gains the contested seat, but at the cost of forming an extremely unwelcome alliance with that 'live log' the ultra-Tory Stedman. Later in the novel Normanby withdraws sympathy from Germain, who, he says dismissively, 'executed the business of his constituents faithfully and punctually … but it was by no means an occupation of first-rate interest to him' (II, 107).

Oakley gains his Whig seat in another borough, but at a heavy personal cost. The middle-class lawyer he had insulted earlier forces him into unpalatable concessions. Nevertheless, as a committed Whig, 'to him the House was all in all … The earnest sincerity with which he spoke had never failed to win attention, though some of his opinions were reckoned rather extraordinary, or what in party slang is called *crotchetty* [*sic*]' (II, 109). Whig governance, however, remains, when all is said and done, a remote prospect in Normanby's *Yes and No*. 'When the parliamentary session [of 1830] began', writes Henry Brougham's biographer, 'only a handful of men believed that the institution of party, even in the rudimentary forms which it then took, still existed.'[27]

ELECTORAL REFORM

The parliamentary and political abuses cited in novels of the 1820s are, for
the most part, standard complaints, their authors' satire on an immoveable
status quo, a repeated trope in silver fork novels of those early years. The
protagonist of Disraeli's *Vivian Grey* (1826) operates in a political world of
corruption and incompetence with the sole aim of profiting from it. Lord
Normanby's three young men in *Yes and No* are trapped in an unchanging stalemate of business as usual. The hero in Bulwer's *Pelham* in 1828
gratefully accepts a seat from his uncle's proprietary borough of 'Buyemall'
(i, 82). In Charles White's *Almack's Revisited* of the same year, a seat in
Parliament trades hands as a gambling debt (i, 204). The Rottentown
constituency of Sir Thomas Jermyn in Lister's *Granby* (1826) amounts to
'sweet fifteen, *not* one *vote* more' (i, 53). In Catherine Gore's *Women as They
Are* (1830), Mr Forsyth, a wealthy 'slop seller' from the City, purchases his
seat for the 'borough of Catspaw' (iii, 136). 'Lord Snugborough', a corrupt office holder in Lord Normanby's novel *Matilda* (1825), 'continues, to
this day', Normanby reports laconically, 'in the undisturbed possession of
many well-earned dignities and emoluments' (i, 36).

There had been regular Whig motions for electoral reform for years, all
of them failures – in 1790, 1804, 1809, 1810, 1812, and in 1819, ominously
only a month prior to the massacre at Peterloo.[28] In more recent memory,
Lord John Russell in 1822 had introduced a bill to disfranchise two parliamentary seats held by 'a hundred of the smallest, and most corrupt,
parliamentary boroughs' in order to redistribute them to the new industrial and commercial towns and counties with no representation, another
failed attempt.[29] The cause of electoral reform seemed to be completely
defunct. The Whig leader Lord Grey advised his heir, Lord Howick, in
February 1830 not to 'hamper' himself with the question.[30]

The death of George IV in June 1830 changed all that. The election that
followed in July–August 1830, brought a genuine surprise. 'Although the
general election left the government with a theoretical majority of MPs',
writes Peter Jupp, 'it was clear that the elections in many open constitu-
encies had been won by supporters of parliamentary reform.'[31] The Whigs
suddenly found themselves in a position of almost completely unexpected political power.[32] The Tory liberal, Lord Sandon, professed himself
'astounded' that reform was now the demand of even 'the most sober and
peaceable classes'.[33] Wellington's catastrophically misjudged pronouncement on 2 November 1830 – that he could under no circumstances agree
to any measure of parliamentary reform – led to radical demonstrations

in London, the cancellation of a royal visit to the Guildhall for reasons of the King's safety, and the swift defeat of Wellington's Tory government on 14 November. A Whig-led government pledged to parliamentary reform took over under Lord Grey. The Whig backbencher Sir Robert Heron could only marvel, 'Two years ago, I thought Reform of Parliament almost hopeless. I now believe it to be certain and approaching.'[34]

The rest of Great Britain was not so certain or so sanguine about the prospect. The threat of parliamentary reform appeared to many people as, 'the greatest change possible short of violent revolution'.[35] 'My Lords', cried the aged Lord Eldon, 'sacrifice one atom of our glorious constitution and the rest is gone.'[36] 'There are two great antagonistic principles at the root of all government', claimed John Wilson Croker, a passionate Tory, 'stability and experiment. The former is Tory, and the latter Whig.'[37] 'The difference', said Palmerston, the Whig, sounding like a reverse image of Croker, is in 'those who hold liberal opinions and those whose prejudices are opposed to all innovation.'[38] The Tories feared any reform of representation as 'a disastrous opening up of politics to mob rule'.[39] Wellington had no doubt of it: 'If it is God's will that this great country should be destroyed, and that mankind should be deprived of this last asylum of peace and happiness, be it so!'[40]

The Whigs in principle held government to be 'a managed process of change'.[41] Even so, the Whig politician, Lord Fitzwilliam in 1840, looking back on the dangerous political turbulence that had accompanied reform, recalled the period as having seen a change of the greatest magnitude: 'We have been through one revolution, for now that we can speak of these events historically, it is idle to call by any other name the events of 1830, 31 and 32.'[42] Linda Colley in *Britons: Forging the Nation, 1707–1837* finds herself in agreement, emphasizing the size of the cliff to be scaled: 'What the Whigs did between their coming to power in November 1830 and the passage of the Reform Act in June 1832 was politically perilous and felt by them and their opponents to be so. Moreover, they very nearly failed to get away with it. Lord Grey and his supporters', she reminds her readers, 'were, after all, embarking on the first major reconstruction of the British representative system since Oliver Cromwell's rule in the 1650s.'[43]

THE MIDDLE CLASSES

Novels of fashionable life entered the Reform battle on a great wave of aristocratic anxiety over the possibility of a future of diminished power.

Parliamentary reform could portend ruptures in the great chain of social exclusivity. As Sydney Smith lamented in December 1829, 'My next door neighbour is dead, so much the better … but he has left his estate', he explains, 'to a little linen draper … and they are all coming to live here. What can this be but a visitation of Providence for my Whig principles?' He added a concern he shared with most of his rank, 'This is indeed a severe dose of the People.[44] The aristocratic hero of Edward Bulwer's *The Disowned* (1829) also receives a 'severe dose' from his aptly named land-lady in Highgate, Mrs Copperas: 'You are desirous, Sir', she questions Clarence, the hero, 'of entering into the bosom of my family? We pos-sess accommodations of a most elegant description—accustomed to the genteelest circles … you will find our retreat no less eligible than unique' (1, 109–10). The hero's brief stay in the Copperas 'bosom' is, sadly, no less unique than painful. As Clarence laments, 'this base, pretending, noisy, scarlet vulgarity of the middle ranks, which has all the rudeness of its inferiors, with all the arrogance and heartlessness of its betters—this pounds and pence patchwork, of the worst and most tawdry shreds and rags of manners, is alike sickening to one's love of human nature, and one's refinement of taste' (1, 136). But, a wise and experienced eld-erly gentleman from across the way advises him to moderate his dislike, to hold back on his ruffled temper for future political advantage. '"You will find your host and hostess", said the old gentleman, "certainly of a different order to the persons with whom it is easy to see you have asso-ciated; but, at your happy age, a year or two may be very well thrown away upon observing the manners and customs of those whom, in later life, you may often be called upon to conciliate, or perhaps to control"' (1, 142–3).

The sticking point in exclusive society and of course in high politics as well is the entrance of the 'middle classes' onto proprietary terrain. Who are these people and what are they doing here?[45] Reform was not intended as democratic change by any means. As Norman Gash explains it, 'The primary purpose of the Reform Bill introduced by Russell in March 1831 was to rally middle-class support round the aristocratic sys-tem to detach the middle classes from a dangerous alliance with the lower classes, founded on common dissatisfaction with the aristocratic sys-tem.[46] Lord Grey, the new Whig prime minister, however, had no inten-tion of giving away the power of the governing elite to *anybody*. The lavish display of rhetorical palm branches necessary to smooth the way of the middle classes into alliance with their social betters caused much con-sternation in exclusive quarters. It had to be unnerving for the genteel residents of Mayfair to hear Lord Grey calling the middle classes, 'the real and efficient mass of public opinion without whom the power of the gentry is nothing'.[47] David Cannadine's argument that hierarchical societies choose to describe themselves historically at one time as *dyadic* – 'upper and lower' – and at other times as *triadic* – 'upper, middle and lower' – marks the uncomfortable new 'triadic' redefinition that was making itself felt so keenly among the 'upper' orders.[48] Flattery of the middle classes was to be the order of the day for Whig politicians.

Prior to the awakening of public opinion to the possibility of political reform, earlier novelists had known exactly how to treat these encroaching new people. A long and satisfying tradition of ridicule and contempt was there for the taking, from Frances Burney's Branghtons to Jane Austen's Mrs Elton, and beyond. Lady Blessington's *The Magic Lantern* (1822) had described middle-class interlopers at the Hyde Park Sunday procession of carriages with casual contempt: 'The Lord Mayor's coach, with all the paraphernalia of mayoralty finery, next fills up the line, while the smug faces of my Lord and Lady, with their offspring, the embryo Lord Mayor or Lady Mayoress, form a group that might be painted as a personification of—"Oh, the roast beef of Old England!"—so visible are its nutritious effects on their countenances.[49]

Lord Normanby's novel *Matilda* (1825) includes a manufacturer, a Mr Hobson, the owner of 'the largest extent of staring brick front in Manchester', who herds his Branghton-like family through Europe with a talent for discovering other middle-class Englishmen just like themselves – a Mr Woodhead, for example, 'a fine fat-headed home-brewed young fellow, who, if he could stand the vulgar test of knowing chalk from cheese, it was almost the only thing he did know' (I, 160). Mrs Hobson's warm memories of Peterloo prompt future hopes for her son Jem: '"Who knows but, in time, Jem may live to be a—what was that great gentleman, who so civilly wrote to thank our people for killing the Radicals?"—"A Secretary of State, Mamma," said Miss Hobson' (I, 57).

Jane Austen's Mrs Elton is reborn in Marianne Hudson's novel *Almacks'* (1826) as Lady Birmingham: '"I think, my dear," said Lady Birmingham to her spouse, "you had better go in the donkey curricle ... Or suppose we were all to walk down to the bridge, the barouche landau with four horses could meet us there." The last plan was thought the best, so the barouche and four was ordered' (I, 189).

A noticeable shift in the political world marks the significance of such consumer posturing. In 1826, Lady Cowper, from real life, expressed her surprise to learn the results of that year's election: 'People think this new

Parliament will be a curious one', she wrote, 'such strange things have turned out. There are three stock-brokers in it, which was never the case ... before.' [50] Two middle-class gentlemen, a Mr Botts and a Mr Wrangle, are flies in the electoral ointment in Charles White's Tory novel *Almack's Revisited* (1828). Mr Botts plots his candidacy on a platform of radical reform, but, the author grumbles, 'he scarcely understood the real meaning of Whig or Tory, and would as gladly have jumped into a rotten borough as any one of the most shackled members in the House' (II, 176). White, an enthusiastic Tory, condemns Mr Wrangle, the other usurping contender, for burdening an honest baronet with unexpected and massive expenses in the election (III, 176–7).

Anxious tremors spread to Mayfair. An elderly aristocrat in Lady Bury's novel *The Separation* (1830) is shocked to the marrow to see a rich Mr Lawrence of Russell Square, Bloomsbury, introduced to 'the duke and the duchess': '"It is a sad thing," observed the old dowager Marchioness of Chelmsford, on beholding this presentation take place; "It is a sad thing to see how people let themselves down in these days ... But it is no wonder, when there is nobody whose business it is to look after society, and who has a decided right to keep every one in his proper sphere—till there is, we shall never see the end of this confusion"' (I, 37–8).

The 'social middle' with an emphasis on *middle*, writes Dror Wahrman in *Imagining the Middle Class*, becomes the definition that counts in contemporary political life.[51] Considered in sociological terms the middle classes in the 1820s and 1830s could embrace 'not only the industrialists and prosperous merchants ... stretching down to the vulnerable shopkeeper', says Eric Evans, but also another line of claimants, including professionals such as 'lawyers, doctors, apothecaries, civil engineers and architects'.[52] John Walsh, a Tory politician adamantly opposed to reform, argued that the *gentry* were the rightful 'middle class', with the learned professions included as an extension. Whig aristocrats and Tory traditionalists simply did not trust the commercial middle classes. During the French Revolution, these were the people thought to have instigated the troubles across the Channel. Years later Lord Melbourne, as the Whig prime minister, also confessed, 'I don't like the middle classes ... I like what is tranquil and stable.' In 1827, Robert Southey claimed, writes David Cannadine, 'that the new industrial middle classes represented the most dangerous threat to the established order, on account of their numbers and ambitions'.[53] 'What was going on', Cannadine concludes, 'was an unprecedentedly agitated discussion of social structure that ebbed and flowed.' 'During the passing of the Great Reform Act', he continues, 'this discussion was to become even more agitated.'[54]

As a general strategy for Whig presentation of the party's policies, Francis Jeffrey wrote to Lord Russell, 'It is of the utmost importance to associate the middle with the higher orders of society in the love and support of the institutions and government of the country.'[55] Historians are agreed that at least through the 1820s the middle classes had no real political or cultural coherence, but, as Dror Wahrman argues, they did not need to gather it themselves since aristocratic political strategies were to give them both. A mischievous paradox might suggest that the '*respectable* middle classes' were, to all intents and purposes, the creation of a calculating late Regency aristocracy, a strategic ploy for keeping the reins of political power in their own safe hands.

As Winifred Hughes suggests, neither the readers nor writers of silver fork novels were immune to a 'massive and internalised' complex of social insecurities that afflicted both the middle classes and the aristocracy. The position of silver fork novelists, Hughes writes, is not one of simple hypocrisy, much as it may be tempting to think so, but comes laden with serious political implications. The silver fork author becomes judge and disposer of a new order of society, redrawing 'the dividing lines of society', producing a fictional manufacture of society, as Hughes' amusing simile has it, 'like so many elegant yard goods',[56] or in the more weighty language of the historian M. L. Bush, 'the aristocratisation of the bourgeoisie combined with the eventual *embourgeoisement* of the aristocracy'.[57] Silver fork novelists constantly test the boundaries and borders of this imagined new social amalgam. In these novels of fashionable life, 'collisions' of rank, a matter of satiric comedy, devolve into 'collusions' of class, a more serious thing altogether.[58] As authors of fashionable novels look to construct gentility as 'a compound of aristocracy and bourgeoisie', they also aim at uniting this compound of classes in a single political objective, that of reform.[59]

Dror Wahrman argues that the middle classes become so contentious a subject because the process of their creation 'opens up new spaces and new configurations, often rapidly and unexpectedly; and then confronts its participants with the pressing need to renegotiate their positions *vis-à-vis* these new configurations'.[60] Lady Bury's novel *Flirtation* (1827) has a knowledgeable older lady point out such an unexpected new configuration. She spies a group of rather too well-dressed women in their box at the Italian Opera: 'I never saw any corps de ballet more perfect than they are in their parts', she says to Lady Emily, the heroine of the novel: 'It makes me die of laughing; but, notwithstanding all that, people remember who they were, and say every now and then—"But why has the barber's grand-daughter, or the fishmonger's, or the perfumer's, a right to do so and so?" It is beyond belief, when their backs are turned, how their dear friends pull them to pieces' (II, 282).

T. H. Lister's novel *Herbert Lacy* (1828) addresses the alliance of the aristocracy and the middle classes with greater subtlety and more plausible moral lubricants than Lady Bury's *Flirtation*, but even so the combination makes an uneasy tale. Mr Morton, father of the heroine, devotes his commercial inheritance from his old father who was 'in the iron trade' to covering its origins with expensive consumer luxuries. Sir William Lacy, the hero's patrician father, is a country baronet with an Elizabethan house, a solid fortune, and a massive fund of contempt for Mr Morton and his parvenu pretensions. The Morton family possesses, unfortunately, some embarrassing merchant cousins from the Bagshawe side whose recollections of good times at the Colosseum in Rome are strongly reminiscent of Burney's Branghtons at Vauxhall: 'Eliza', cries one of the younger Bagshawes, 'do you remember Mr Sharp carrying off a bottle of soda water into one of the dark passages, and making the cork fly, and groaning, to make us think that somebody had shot himself?' (III, 101–2). Such bumptious figures are easily packed off to social oblivion, but the new heroine of 1828, Agnes Morton, unlike Burney's Evelina in 1778, must defend her Bagshawe cousins to the hero, who has just witnessed an absolutely toe-curling display of their exuberance. '"To be honest," said she, "there are circumstances under which I feel very strongly the awkwardness of the association; but this is only when they are taken out of the sphere which best suits them. Place me with them in their domestic circle, where everything was natural and unconstrained, and, as a painter would say, "in keeping," and I could enter easily, and … take a pleasure in their company".' Agnes concludes her modest apologia with a remark that applies equally well to her own father's reckless social ambition: 'People are seldom ridiculous, unless when taken out of their proper station, or when their vanity makes them strive to appear what they are not.' Herbert, deeply impressed by Agnes' reclamation of the middle classes and their respectability, 'assented to her opinion, and regarded her with a look of admiration' (I, 134–5).

The real nettle in Lister's *Herbert Lacy* is not the Bagshawe embarrassment, nor even Mr Morton's extravagance, but Mr Sackville, a cunning young lawyer and property speculator, a new-style gentleman who displays a dangerous mix of aristocratic and middle-class signals. The furnishings of his private apartment suggest the dubious set of moral values residing in this new power-seeking class:

The place, a room somewhat too spacious and elegant for the antiquated name of study, yet to which those of library or drawing room would be equally inapplicable. It presented to the eye various insignia, alike of business and of literary leisure; and the spectator, like Hercules, pressed to make his choice, stood perplexed among the various inducements to exertion and to indolence. A solemn, business-like inkstand, of large dimensions, was opposed to the last contrivance for easy reading, a chair, ostensibly for study, but more truly calculated for sleep. (III, 4–5)

The 'solemn, business-like inkstand' is the giveaway, revealing the intrusion of the backroom furniture of a money lender's office into the study of a so-called gentleman. The inkstand has an operative function, too. Herbert Lacy, elected to Parliament, arrives at Westminster only to discover that Mr Sackville is widely known to be, if not directly involved in high corruption, prevented from it solely by his calculating 'prudence'. 'There was an absence of high-mindedness in Sackville ... With him, to gull and overreach, were by no means a discreditable exercise of ability. He sympathized with the triumphs of successful chicanery, and never betrayed indignation or sorrow, on seeing honourable simplicity borne down by the efforts of a dexterous knave' (III, 67–8).

At the conclusion of his novel, Lister restores the traditional social order in the plot, but not without wringing a concession from the proud old baronet, Sir William Lacy, Herbert's father. Sir William confesses to his son that he had been mistaken about Mr Morton all along. 'I once did him less than justice', he says. 'It shocked my aristocratical prejudices to perceive that a man, with less ostensible pretensions, was more courted than myself; and those prejudices were fostered by [my] seclusion.' With finely parsed condescension, he reassures his son, 'I have learned to shake off some portion of my former exclusiveness, and to applaud the liberal spirit of these times, which presents no insurmountable barrier to any species of ambition' (III, 282–3).[61]

With the commencement of a national push for parliamentary reform in 1830, mockery of the middle classes becomes a serious embarrassment to the silver fork school. Letitia Landon's literary friend, Edward Bulwer, then identifying himself as a political radical, takes the occasion of reviewing Landon's new novel *Romance and Reality* (1831) to deplore her mockery of a few middle-class characters. *Romance and Reality* includes the Higgses, vulgar and completely interchangeable with Lister's Bagshawes in *Herbert Lacy* three years earlier, but no longer welcome in novels of fashionable life. Landon's novel also includes an aristocratic heroine, who again, exactly like Lister's, displays the same generous tolerance for the Higgses' embarrassing, but essentially well-meant offers of friendship. Bulwer, however, reflects the changes in the political wind by objecting that Landon 'sullies her wings' by mocking the middle-class tastes of the male Higgses for 'such harmless vulgarities', he says, 'as "blue coats and brass buttons"'.[62] It should be noted that 'blue coats and brass buttons' were not so 'harmless' three years earlier in Bulwer's own novel *Pelham* (1828), in which the hero and his friend Vincent mercilessly mock the 'blue frock-coat' of the provincial Cheltenham dandy Mr Ritson, 'a most happy mixture of native coarseness and artificial decoration', they agree, and 'a made dish in Bloomsbury Square, garnished with cut carrots', that is, brass buttons, 'by way of adornment' (II, 38–9).

T. H. Lister, who had himself created the Bagshawes in *Herbert Lacy* (1828), nimbly climbs on the middle-class bandwagon in the *Edinburgh Review* (July 1830) to complain of Mrs Gore's mockery of a middle-class woman in *Women as They Are* (1830): 'Readers will not be slow to observe that she frequently exalts the character of those whose chief pursuit is pleasure, while she lowers those whose time is more usefully employed.' The truth of the matter is that Gore treats aristocrats, country gentry and the wealthy middle classes with equal measures of contempt in *Women as They Are*. She uses the opportunity to expose a weak governing class, an enervated aristocracy, a mean-spirited gentry and a range of behaviour in the middle classes that runs morally downwards, everyone maddened by snobbery and consumer ambition.

The passage referred to by Lister concerns a country baronet's family whose self-cancelling social pretensions both to aristocratic fashion and to middle-class rectitude fall under Gore's keen satiric eye. Gore is specifically interested in the 'new spaces and new configurations' that Wahrman marks out as the challenge of change in the Reform era.[63] 'Lady Lilfield', an aspiring member of the country gentry, writes Gore, as she skewers her for middle-class meanness, 'knew with the utmost accuracy of domestic arithmetic—to the fraction of a course or an *entrée*—the number of dinners which Beech Park was indebted to its neighbourhood … nor procrastinated by half a second the simultaneous bobs of her ostentatious Sunday-school, as she sailed majestically along the aisle towards her tall, stately, pharisaical, squire-archical pew' (I, 50). Aiming her withering irony at the middle-class idiom of Lady Lilfield's rectitude, Gore concludes ironically, 'All went well at Beech Park … for Lady Lilfield was the "excellent wife," of "a good sort of man!"' (I, 50).[64]

The country gentry, understood as Tory and reactionary, are meat for Mrs Gore's satiric grinder.[65] Sir Stephen Mordaunt, the heroine's father in *Women as They Are*, greets the arranged marriage of his daughter to the prime minister Lord Willersdale, a man twice her age, with the happy effusion, 'Next to the Chancellor's, there is no patronage like Lord Willersdale's;—we really are too fortunate!' (1, 14). Lady Mordaunt, a few months after her daughter's wedding, accuses the girl of inexcusable slackness in trawling the public pond for her brothers: 'I think you might have contrived that something should be done for your brothers before this', she writes. 'There is poor Jack, with his money lodged for a Company these four months—and nothing done. There is William grumbling at his curacy, with every chimney in the glebe-house smoking, and half his parishioners gone over to the meeting house—and nothing done.' Gore's 'excellent woman' is unstoppable: 'Poor Anna-Maria', the heroine's sister, 'assures me she wrote to you several times about getting her nurse's husband into the Customs; and Sir Herbert Gray's tutor only wanted a word from Lord Willersdale to get made chaplain to the infirmary at Sierra Leone—yet nothing has been done for either' (1, 164). As one might expect, the aristocratic Lord Willersdale finds that 'The very name of Beech Park', the symbolic home of the Tory gentry, 'was nauseous in his ears' (1, 126).

But as Lister recognizes, Mrs Gore scores a major triumph in *Women as They Are* with her introduction of a family of City parvenus, the Forsyth clan, a set of fully imagined bourgeois figures completely new to British fiction. As opposed to the Bagshawes and Higgses, the Forsyths possess demonstrable social and political weight, unwelcome certainly, but now an undeniable presence in modern society. In this novel Mrs Gore stays away from open mockery of such new people, a significant measure of restraint, and leaves her satiric asides to one of her best minor characters, an envious niece, the sharp-tongued Mrs Lucy Willis from a less fortunate branch of the Forsyth family. Helen, the heroine of the novel, wife of Lord Willersdale and the only member of the Mordaunt family with genuine aristocratic rank, defends her right to visit these middle-class arrivals to power. 'I am prouder meanwhile than even yourself', she says, rebuking an aristocratic friend who has advised her to keep clear of the Forsyths, 'for my *fiérté* tells me that I am wholly above the fear of contamination by dining in any house from Park Lane to Finsbury Square' (III, 123).

Helen calls at the elder Forsyths' Harley Street establishment to offer her congratulations on the family's most recent social triumph, the happy

elevation of the father of the clan, Mr James Forsyth, to the baronetage.
She finds her own mother Lady Mordaunt and her sister Jane present in
the gratified group. The Forsyth's lesser kinswoman Mrs Willis (Lucy)
joins the company, but solely to bait the more fortunate branch of her
family with poisoned congratulations. Our heroine Helen begins the conversation with a gracious compliment to her sister Jane, who is about to
marry one of the Forsyth sons:

'Let me wish you joy, Jane! [says Helen] since I conclude it is an event regarded
as desirable by the family in general.'
    'How can it be otherwise!' exclaimed Mrs. Willis, with affected rapture. 'He
will figure in the list with two physicians and an Irish apothecary; a Scotch
banker, a super-annuated Welch judge, and a discarded governor who was
shouldered by the late administration out of the dignities of some yellow-fever
colony.'
    'A baronetcy is a distinction, Ma'am, which no association can deteriorate,'
observed Lady Mordaunt, with a glance of pompous indignation.
    'My dear madam,—you are dating its value from the reign of Charles or
James; you are thinking of those well-worn honours which, like a military ban-
ner, we reverence in proportion to their ragged and poverty-struck antiquity.'
Again poor Jane assumed a deeper jaundice,—no longer for the Forsyths but for
the Mordaunts!

Lucy, having now insulted *two* families present in the room, commences
to celebrate the political advantages and interests that will come with
Mr Forsyth's new honours:

'We hear so much,' resumed the shrew, 'of throwing the landed interest into
the Peerage,—as a sort of weight I conclude, to balance its levity,—that we
cannot be surprised when our ministers—(I beg your ladyship's pardon,) complete the equipoize by patching up the baronetage with the ingots of the Royal
Exchange.
            Qui sert sa patrie n'a pas besoin d'aieux,[66]
and who so serviceable to the land as those whose pineries and armourial
bearings,—whose chariots and horsemen, augment the tax revenue, and diminish the poor's rates? I conceive my uncle, Sir James (ahem!) to be as valuable to
the state, as if he had fought at Waterloo.' (III, 304–6)

Satisfied, the victorious Mrs Willis, Lucy, sweeps from the room having
made her point, that an alliance with the middle classes is a bitter bolus
that the upper classes will have to choke down as best they can.
    Mothers and Daughters, published by Gore in 1831, moves towards a
more negotiated relationship of the new hierarchy of political and social
order. The Forsyth clan, from having been the butt of Lucy Willis'

unrelenting satire in *Women as They Are* (1830), have become the worthy Westland clan in *Mothers and Daughters*. The ambivalent social position of the Westlands puzzles two predatory young aristocrats who would like to get a fair shot at the Westland wealth through the daughters: 'But there is another; a Sir Westland Somebody—or Sir Somebody Westland;—one of our commercial upstarts—as rich as the Bank, and as vulgar as Oxford-street', says one of them to the other, complaining bitterly, 'You have no conception of the difficulty of getting into those monied, dinner-giving, regular houses!' On the other hand, in aristocratic society, he continues, 'All one's acquaintance are acquainted with Prince A__ or the Duke of B.__ *Almack's* and Parliament have their definitive and well-understood modes of entrance;—but who the deuce knows any thing about a parcel of ledgermen in Broadstreet or Great St. Helen's?' (III, 195–7).

Minnie, or Miss De Vesci, the heroine of *Mothers and Daughters*, visits this worthy banking family, the Westlands, because her late uncle had 'a very high respect' for them. She meets a room full of overdressed women, but that's to be expected. What she actually discovers is a culture differ-ent from her own, but one that she has to admit is quite admirable. Gore gives a brief account of the gathering:

At tables such as the Westlands, there exists so little of the coterie-intercommu-nication distinguishing the gossipry of the fashionable world, that the newspaper publicities of operas and plays, exhibitions and executions, levees, and draw-ing-rooms, and parliamentary debates, generally provision the commissariate department for the war of words. More than one member of the Westland fam-ily, indeed, was seated in that honourable House, whose verbal war is virtually the *property* of the public; and Miss De Vesci—albeit little of a politician, and at present most femininely indifferent to the state of the nation—found herself obliged to swallow her patés and cutlets in daily audience of the recapitulated debates of the preceding night. In these, and throughout all similar discussions, the name of her cousin Charles found honourable mention. (III, 52–3)

'Cousin Charles' is a secret kept in Minnie's heart of hearts in the very manner of Fanny Price's love for Edmund Bertram, necessary because Cousin Charles is 'in love', or so he thinks, with his own version of Miss Crawford, Minnie's cousin Eleanor, a title-seeker in the marriage market. Eleanor, like Miss Crawford, dumps Charles, a younger son, on the cal-culation that some richer, elder son will come her way. Any news at all of Cousin Charles is for Minnie the sweetest of news – and to hear it in such an unexpected company of newspaper readers and people who follow the parliamentary debates makes this the first time that Minnie grasps that there is a unity of political purpose between the middle classes and the aristocracy, that is to say between Cousin Charles and her own well-born self. More than that, in listening to the conversation of the Westland women, she gets her first lesson in the sort of conversation that she must learn in order to make her fit to be Charles' wife, which of course will be her happy destiny. She reminds herself that, 'the lady Duchesses and Countesses, the chosen friends of her elder sisters' might be more elegant than the Westland ladies, 'but then their Graces and Ladyships had little to say touching the "meeting of the friends to free trade at the Freemason's Hall," or the "general views of the City upon the abolition of Colonial Slavery!"' (III, 55). Politics is now most decidedly *everybody's* business.

THE BILL ITSELF

The mood of the nation the following year, 1832, the year of the Reform Bill, can only be described as one of national hysteria. The rhetoric from all shades of the political world can scarcely be equalled for extravagance. Six months before passage of the Bill the *Commercialist & Weekly Advertiser*, a thoroughly middle-class paper, asserted in an editorial, 'There are some of their lordships, we have occasion to know, who would prefer seeing the country struggling beneath the blood and flame of revolution, to quietly relinquishing their own unjust and detestable privileges at the indignant call of their inferiors in rank ... the "middle classes".'[67] The radical paper the *Examiner* on Sunday, 25 March 1832, frets at Lord Grey's delay in pushing the Bill, 'While starving industry waited for bread, the aristocrat continued to enjoy the fullness of self-complacency.' Blasts of equal violence issue from the conservative dailies. The ultra-Tory *Morning Post* of 12 May 1832, erupts in capital letters: 'Are Earl GREY and his colleagues to be the dictators, the CROMWELLS ... the ROBESPIERRES of England?' The screed ends with ominous prospects: 'This has now become the plain alternative—the Dictator GREY or the constitutional Sovereign WILLIAM the Fourth.'

Novelists of fashionable life are happy to profit from the public excitement. Catherine Gore's *The Opera* (1832), Lord Normanby's *The Contrast* (1832) and T. H. Lister's *Arlington* (1832) find occasion to represent a surprisingly wide range of the going opinions concerning the threat or promise of social change. Gore's novel *The Opera* (1832) is probably the most successful of the three in catching the note of public hysteria. In *The Opera*, Gore turns the Italian opera house, the glittering showcase of aristocratic social power, into a site for exploring a world turned upside-down by the prospect of political change.[68] The sickly, aristocratic heroine, who hardly appears in the novel, is displaced by the brilliant and malevolent presence of Gore's anti-heroine, La Silvestra, an internationally famous opera star who arrives in London on a mission of revenge. La Silvestra, we discover, is actually Stephanine Haslinger, a peasant girl and the former lover of Adrian Maldyn, son and heir of Count Maldyn, Lord Abbotscourt. Years earlier, when Lord Abbotscourt discovered their youthful affair, he had peremptorily separated the two, packing Stephanine off to Italy and his son to university. Stephanine's reappearance in London, known only as the celebrated 'La Silvestra', guides the plot of the novel as the former peasant girl lays waste to an aristocracy that tyrannized her in her youth and would shun her now if her origins were known.

Lord Normanby's novel of this momentous year, *The Contrast* (1832), also banks on the reading public's intense interest in the potential of such a social-political reverse. An advertising puff in the *Morning Chronicle* for 19 April 1832 accentuates the current political significance of Normanby's new novel: 'The promise of ... "the Contrast," has, we understand, caused more inquiries at the circulating libraries than has been known for a considerable time', reads the advert, 'and all are anxious to see the contrast afforded by the *Peasant Countess* transplanted from her humble sphere to the salons of the great in London, and the all-accomplished highly-bred woman of fashion, both of whom are rivals in the love of the same man' (p. 4). Lord Normanby's '*Peasant Countess*', unlike Mrs Gore's peasant diva, hails from Lancashire, much closer to home.

Lord Normanby's novel opens with a house party of aristocrats enjoying a day's excursion to explore the delights of Morden Bay. During a pause for their noon repast, the newspapers arrive, 'and as the newspaper of that day contained the account of the long-expected demise of one of the oldest supporters of the party to which they belonged, they found ample food for conversation, not in lamenting his loss, but in discussing the various pretensions of the probable claimants for his Government, his Garter, his Regiment, and his Sinecure' (I, 33). A group of happy peasants interrupts their political conversation as a welcome interlude, and one of them, Lucy Darnell, a local farm girl, attracts the attention of the handsome young Lord Castleton – the perfect occasion for testing the honourable intentions of a reform-minded aristocracy.

Lucy has formerly been harbouring a prepossession for her humble cousin George, who certainly loves her and provides her with a match within her own rank, but she is swept off her feet by Lord Castleton's unexpected declaration of love. They marry. The 'contrast' of the novel's title is Lady Gayland, a beautiful, witty aristocrat who loves Lord

Castleton and for whom Lord Castleton discovers a passion, but, alas, too late. When Lord Castleton takes Lucy, the new countess, to London, their cultural differences become a public embarrassment at the aristocratic Italian Opera: 'Every thing was a matter of bewilderment to Lucy, from the very first crash of the overture, which, except the war of the winter waves, was the loudest sound she had ever heard.' Lady Gayland, who is fond of Lucy, kindly explains the proceedings, but even Pasta's fine singing, which puts Lady Gayland and Lord Castleton into 'an exstasy', falls on ignorant ears with Lucy (III, 52). And when the great ballerina Taglioni comes onstage to do her famous *pirouette*, her legs 'rather *au naturel*', notes Lord Normanby, Lucy cries out in distress, '"O that is too bad! I cannot stay to see that!" and she turned her head away, blushing deeply' (III, 61).[69]

As soon as Lucy and Lord Castleton are in private, he tells her she must get used to new customs, that in her father's humble home there are things that 'disgust' him, too, and that in his society there are, likewise, some things that may shock her sensibilities. As the two address this delicate topic, they blunder into a far more serious social divide. 'I don't want to preach to any body', says Lucy, 'and you know how much it fashes me to contend with you', she says. 'Don't say FASHES, say distresses, or annoys, not *fashes*, for heaven's sake, my dear Lucy', Castleton impatiently replies. 'Oh dear, it was very stupid of me to forget it', Lucy returns. 'That was one of the first things you taught me, and it is many days since I said it last' (III, 68).

As Castleton sadly explains to Lady Gayland, it had been his distrust of aristocratic women in the courtship rituals of heartless, fashionable London that sent him to Lancashire: 'I sought, therefore, in another rank of life a perfect contrast. All that I could, in common reason, have expected in such an experiment, I have obtained: and with it every tie of honour obliges me to be satisfied—and so I will', adding, 'Go, dearest Lady Gayland, where prudence calls you' (III, 223).

Lady Gayland flees to the safety of the continent. Lucy goes to Lancashire to visit her relations, but drowns in a shipwreck on the way. 'As to Castleton himself', writes Normanby, temporarily postponing the union of Castleton and Lady Gayland, 'I have too much respect for the intensity of his present grief ... to anticipate the date when that elasticity of spirit ... shall, with the assistance of time, have triumphed over mortal sorrow', a conclusion eerily echoing Austen's postponement of the inevitable in *Mansfield Park*: 'I purposely abstain from dates on this occasion, that every one may be at liberty to fix their own, aware that the cure of unconquerable passions, and the transfer of unchanging attachments, must vary much as to time in different people' (III, ch. 17). In contrast to Fanny Price's powerful influence on Austen's baronet family in 1814, Lucy Darnell's old-fashioned farmhouse pieties cannot touch the aristocracy in 1832. Lady Gayland provides the modern alternative, with her middle-class moral rectitude and aristocratic culture conjoined, a happy substitution for Lucy's naivety and country ignorance. The reviewer from *Bell's New Weekly Messenger* (22 April 1832) does not buy it. 'Is it possible for any thing to be more *la la* than this? An innocent country girl is married by a dashing nobleman.—she is taken to the opera, where her unsophisticated sensibilities are shocked at the sight of Taglioni's legs, and then the dialogue ensues.' The reviewer suspects moral proselytisers from the radical East End of London to have been at work and concludes that 'had it not proceeded from the pen of a *lord*, we should have imagined it to be drawn rather from the "East," than from the high-born and highly-educated "West"'.

Henry Lister's *Arlington* (1832) omits the peasants of Gore's and Normanby's works for his Reform-year novel, but he introduces a radical merchant, Mr Baxter, who stirs the social pot with fears of revolution. 'I am in favour of doing general good to the whole body of my countrymen', the merchant tells the aristocratic hero, Lord Arlington, 'to see aristocracy in this country abolished altogether.' 'I hold', he continues, 'the whole system of aristocracy ... whether invested with legislative powers or without them, to be alike debasing, unjust, unnatural, and artificial' (III, 210). Lord Arlington denies this 'entirely', of course, arguing for the social stability of inheritance and for the House of Lords as 'a mediator between the antagonist principles of monarchy and democracy' (III, 212). Nevertheless, Mr Baxter's radical challenge is profoundly felt by the aristocratic hero. 'I am confident', Arlington rather apprehensively tells his friend Hargrave, 'that our class has only to "*marche avec leur siècle*," to maintain themselves usefully and honourably in their present station,' though he must admit, he confesses, to serious past failures of his class: 'It is to be regretted that they have exhibited too much supineness, and too little liberality.' Only re-education can correct that, he argues: 'I never was educated with any view to the functions which I would soon be called upon to perform. I have regretted it, and many probably will say the same' (III, 213).

Revolution was a fear for both the Whigs and Tories in 1832.[70] The well-known political cartoon, *Four Weighty Authorities on Reform*, published the year before, in 1831, suggests the public anxiety. In this piece,

C. J. Grant presents four contemporary political figures standing next to each other who each articulate a position for or against a Reform Bill. 'Reform is absolutely necessary to avoid Revolution', says the Whig.[71] 'I do maintain that Reform means nothing else than Revolution', returns the Tory. The Liberal waffles, 'A leetle Reform is wanting, but fiddlededee about Revolution.' The Radical pontificates ominously, 'I Say if we don't have a Real Radical Reform we'll have a Revolution.' The threat featured in Mr Baxter's radical opinions in *Arlington* hovers equally over Mrs Gore's peasant diva and Lord Normanby's '*Peasant Countess*'. 'The system, the present vile system, must be altered', says Lister's Mr Baxter, 'Mark my words, there is a storm brewing—we shall have a violent change by and bye' (III, 188). As John Wilson Croker, an ultra-Tory writer and politician warned, 'The reform Bill is a stepping stone in England to a republic. The Bill once passed, goodnight to the Monarchy and the Lords and the Church.'[72] Nor could anyone fail to remember that the recent French Revolution of 1830 had been cheered loudly in the British press, even in the ultra-conservative *Morning Post*. 'If the great mass of the middle class are bent upon that method of enforcing their views', Lord Holland told Lord Grey at the time, 'there is not in the nature of society any real force that can prevent them.'[73]

AFTER THE BILL

In early May 1832 the Reform Bill appeared to have met with complete blockage in the House of Lords. Fears of a revolution rose to combustible levels in the weeks known as the Days of May. Grey tendered his resignation, Wellington contemplated forming a government. As *The Times* reported, 12 May, 'The accounts from every quarter of the metropolis and of England are awful ... Birmingham refuses to pay taxes, Manchester refuses to pay taxes, Westminster and London, there is reason to believe, will not pay taxes until the Reform Bill—the *unmutilated* Bill—shall have passed.' Francis Place's call to withdraw private funds from the banks, 'To stop the Duke, go for gold!', remains the most memorable moment in the Days of May crisis, but public meetings, anti-Tory petitions, threats of tax strikes by petty shopkeepers as well as pro-reform land owners and, of course, the ever-present fear of violence kept public opinion at the boil. When Wellington failed to form a new ministry, parliamentary opposition melted, and on 4 June only twenty-two peers voted against the third reading of the Bill. The King gave his signed assent three days later.[74]

The newspapers, following two years of the most flaming rhetorical excess, had very little, almost nothing, to say about the passage of the Bill. It was over. The *Sunday Times* for 10 June catches the finality of the occasion:

The Reform Bill has now become a part of the law of the land … At this time of day to descant on the merits and probable effects of the new law, would be work of surplusage [*sic*]. Already we remark, with satisfaction, its fiercest opponents begin to contemplate the possibility of governing the nation in peace under its provisions, and profess themselves resolved to do their best to falsify their own predictions. This is wise and manly, and if the resolve be steadily acted upon, the best results may be looked for. (3)

Even the *Morning Post*, perhaps the most virulent of the opposition papers, greets the Bill with grudging but quiet acquiescence on 8 June:

The Bill has thus unhappily become part and parcel of the law of the land; and therefore, without indulging in any unnecessary forebodings in regard to its final results, we shall for the present content ourselves with imploring the protecting hand of Heaven against the manifold evils which, earlier or later, threaten to befall this once happy land. (3)

It would take years to work out what the Reform Bill actually meant, but novels of fashionable life, always sensitive to the smallest shifts in society, sensed that something profound had taken place even if the same peers and their allies still sat in the same parliamentary seats. 'Fashionable Exclusivity' was no longer to be the public face of political power, not even its tarnished face. It was universally felt that the middle classes had achieved a major triumph. Both political parties were eager to court them.[75] Exclusive life as a pressing issue of any sort, as silver fork novelists could plainly see, was a dead issue.

Edward Bulwer considered the fashionable novels of his generation to have been important movers and shakers in political life. 'Few writers ever produced so great an effect on the political spirit of their generation as some of these novelists', he writes in his *England and the English* (1833), 'who … exposed the falsehood, the hypocrisy, the arrogant and vulgar insolence of patrician life.'[76] The problem, as he recognized, was that novels about aristocratic, fashionable life after the Reform Bill were no longer relevant to contemporary politics. 'A description of the mere frivolities of fashion is no longer coveted', he says, 'for the public mind, once settled towards an examination of the aristocracy, has pierced from the surface to the depth; it has *probed* the wound, and it now desires to cure.'[77]

The new politics called for a new social posture. Exclusivism was out as a political gesture. 'I breakfasted the other day with M__' reports Bulwer in *England and the English*, 'you recollect that two years ago he was one of the super-eminent of the Dandies; silent, constrained, and insolent.' '*Now*' marvels Bulwer, 'his soul is no longer in his clothes ... *Now* he looks round him with a cordial air ... and seems mortally afraid lest he should by chance overlook some passing acquaintance.' The reason: 'All this is very strange! What can possibly have wrought such a miracle in M__? I will tell you; M__ HAS NOW GOT CONSTITUENTS.'[78] London had been the centre of urban political life in pre-1832 novels, but now trips to the country to cultivate voters are in store for the readers of silver fork novels. Life in novels, Bulwer recognizes with certainty, is going to become much more middle-class: 'less fine gentlemanship than formerly ... A graver aspect settles on the face of society'.[79]

Lady Bury's *The Disinherited* of 1834 offers a good example. The heroine, once rich but now poor, has moved to Sydenham. She takes the public coach to Elephant and Castle to find a hackney cab to take her to Lincoln's Inn Field: 'As she was in the act of crossing to walk to a stand on the opposite side of the road, a figure, too well imprinted on the tablets of her memory not to be immediately recognised, was at the very moment passing her.' She is recognized, 'not withstanding a large bonnet and a thick veil', by an aristocratic admirer of earlier, more prosperous days: 'Alfred Montagu started, and bending forward as he caught her hand, in the joy of gladness of the moment exclaimed—"Honoria, dear Honoria! and do we meet once more!"' (II, 15). Suburban life, less-fashionable streets, a bonnet and thick veil, and a 'graver face' – Bulwer was right.

The novel with Mrs Gore's most striking title, *Mrs. Armytage: or, Female Domination* (1836), attempts to map a new vision of the political nation by defining two kinds of country-establishment Whigs. The Mrs Armytage of the title represents old-style Whig political arrogance. The new-style, socially liberal face of Whiggism is represented by her son Arthur, together with a neighbouring family of liberal Whig aristocrats. The plot takes off when young Arthur, a new Whig, marries Marian Baltimore, a middle-class girl from unfashionable Baker Street in London, a person who is an anathema to his mother, the tyrannical, proud, 'Old Whig' Mrs Armytage. As for the Tories in the novel, they operate as invasive aggressors on the political map of Mrs Armytage's Whig neighbourhood – impudent village lawyers, small property holders, and a vile American, Mr Leonidas Lomax, a South Carolina slave owner and social climber, an aspirant to distinction among the local Tory powers. 'You inform me, Sir', says the slave-owning Leonidas Lomax, a Tory sympathizer, to a Whig neighbour, 'that under the operation of the Reform Bill, Thoroton has become a free and independent borough; and the inhabitants, I perceive, arrogate to themselves the privileges of independence, by holding meetings of a political tendency; by drinking Radical toasts, and venting free opinions upon the very parliament which has endowed them with a political existence' (I, 115–16). Only after Mrs Armytage has caused enough grief to her son and her much-abused daughter-in-law does the eventual discovery of a codicil to Arthur's grandfather's will dethrone Mrs Armytage and establish the new owner, her son Arthur, as the heir to Holywell. Arthur, now Sir Arthur, together with his middle-class wife Marian, initiates a reign of peace and plenty at Holywell. Marian's middle-class London relatives, 'the Baltimores and Robseys ... esteem it [Holywell] the Eden of the United Kingdom; the rich applaud its sayings and doings; the poor throng in cheerful confidence to its gates; all uniting to bless the now popular name of Mrs Armytage', that is to say, Marian, the *new* Mrs Armytage (III, 355).

WHIG DECLINE

The progress of the Whig Party, however, does not follow so promising a course in real life. As Eric Evans suggests, the party's 'growing unpopularity owed less to their incompetence than to the logic of the new political world'.[80] A conservative electorate leaned towards an aversion to further change, which is what the Whigs had to offer. And the Whig leadership, as that great friend to the Whig Party, Lord Holland, commented, 'was fast assuming the fatal character of Mediocrity and narrowness of views', concluding, 'I perceive a want of energy, boldness, and decision.'[81] Finally, the severe economic depression of 1837, a four-year-long disaster, had its effect on voters. Mrs Gore addresses each of these conditions of Whig decline, but the overarching feeling in her novels in the years before the defeat of the Whigs in 1841 is a dispirited sense of the end of an era.

By 1841, the year of Gore's novel, *Cecil: or the Adventures of a Coxcomb*, the Whigs had exhausted their friends and the public in general. Bulwer, a former supporter of Whig policies, attacked the aristocratic leaders of the party in 1833 in his *England and the English*: 'what son—what brother—what nephew—what cousin—what remote and unconjectured relative in the Genesis of the Greys, has not fastened his limpet to the rock of the national expenditure'.[82] Disraeli, also an early supporter, attacked the Whigs in 1835 in his *Vindication of the English Constitution*: 'In order to accomplish their object of ... concentrating the government of the state in the hands of a few great families, the Whigs are compelled to declare war against all those great national institutions ... which make us a nation.'[83] As William Hazlitt put it memorably, both parties were like 'Tweedledum and Tweedledee', and 'the distinction between a great Whig lord and a Tory lord is laughable'.[84]

Cecil, Mrs Gore's final silver fork novel, addresses the decline directly. *Cecil* is a splendid valediction to fashionable life that features an ageing dandy, Cecil Danby, as the narrator who compares the glory days of his youth with the dwindling circumstances of life in the post-Reform society in which he now lives. It is a brilliant scheme that allows Mrs Gore to explore 'Old Corruption' from the point of view of a character who is quite comfortable, thank you, with its pleasures, but also as a reflective character who regrets the loss of past glamour – 'The mast of the Victory has been carved into snuff-boxes' (I, 296) – and, at the same time, recognizes that the self-destructive seeds of aristocratic failure were there all the time. As for the political life of the nation, both contemporary and past, Cecil's cynical deprecation of it begins the novel in his recollection of the ritual remark his father's valet employed to send his master off for evening sessions of Parliament: 'every evening, as the under-nurse was hushing us off to sleep, the rumble of wheels from the door of our house in Hanover Square used to be hailed with a remark of—"There he goes to the 'ouse;—much good may it do 'em—"'(I, 7). Politics holds no interest for Cecil. Whenever politicians are to dine with his father, he leaves for his club: 'As a matter of taste, politics delighted me not, nor politicians neither. At a dinner-party, they are crammed down one's throat by one's neighbours, as fish sauces are forced upon one by the butler' (I, 196).

The political plot of the novel, which is of course always in the air, is a melancholy one. It rides on the contrast between Cecil's career as a Regency exclusive and dandy, and his elder brother John's career as a Whig politician and writer: 'Danby marched with the times, or, rather, marched with the pioneers who clear the way for the progress of the times', writes his younger brother, 'He was a scholar, and a ripe one' (I, 303). As Cecil admits ruefully, '*his* intellectual horizon was illimitable; while I, carrying with me wherever I wandered, the littleness of my own soul, had scarcely elbow-room for thought, so bounded was the compass of my views' (II, 251–2). Failure for both men, for Cecil, the dandy, and for John, the Whig politician, haunts the end of the novel. Looking back over the first half of the century, Cecil remembers early hints of decline:

'As coming events cast their shadows before them, one felt already, even in the early part of the reign of George IV a weary chill of mind and body, foreshowing the age of utilitarianism' (III, 168).

Cecil's sister Julia marries a colleague of Cecil's from Downing Street, now a civil servant, where they had both been clerks in early life. Julia's husband is a self-made man, a 'new' man as Cecil calls him (II, 26). His brother John leaves Mayfair for Connaught Place, scarcely more than a hundred yards from Mayfair, but a symbolic distance away from the old neighbourhood of power. As his mother Lady Ormington complains: 'Danby has a house in Connaught Place; just like him, (isn't it?) to go and settle at the extremity of the world!' (II, 102). Post-Reform Mayfair is a much-diminished thing: 'There was no cordiality between Lady Ormington and Julia,—who was now so completely an integral part of the ministerial circles, that she seemed scarcely to know herself when thrown by chance into general society. As to Danby', writes Cecil, 'his existence throughout the Session lay in the House of Commons; and, at any other period of the year, in his library at Forest Lodge', a house on the edges of Windsor Forest. Even Cecil stays away from Mayfair: 'Not one of the three entertained any really filial sympathy with that dreary old house in Hanover Square, now as dumb and dingy as a London sparrow. I seldom wore down my spirits by entering the door' (III, 158). His life in fashionable society rings hollow even to the ears of Lady Ormington, his fashionable, indulgent mother: 'In vain did I assure her that I was one of the finest gentlemen about town;—that I ate the best dinners in the best houses, day after day, from January till July; that my *bons mots* were recited at the Clubs ... She only shrugged her shoulders at my boastings' (III, 159).

In *Cecil* Mrs Gore mourns the loss of the cultural and political promise of the 1820s and 1830s, the great wave of high spirits that carried novels of fashionable life along with it. The new generation of Victorians, however, could only sigh with relief that the old days of aristocratic domination were happily done and dusted.[85] Silver fork novels were viewed in a very different light by the Victorians, exactly as Cecil cruelly describes the much-decayed 'older woman' who had introduced him to the pleasures of fashionable life in his days of youth: 'Everything about her now, was *postiche* [*sic*];—bandeaux, teeth, bloom, shape, lips, eyebrows, *all* as per advertisement!' (III, 161).

CHAPTER 4

Newspapers and the silver fork novel

My name was mentioned with honour in the despatches; and even
at one's last gasp one is never sorry to see oneself in print.

Cecil Danby, in *Cecil* (1841)[1]

Benjamin Haydon's *Gentleman Waiting for The Times* (1831), Figure 3, features two men in a coffee house. A gentleman seated to the right with elegant coat, fine hat, gloved hands, fawn trousers and furled umbrella looks pointedly at a much less decorous and less well-dressed man on the left with rough brown trousers, gloveless hands and scuffed shoes, his body sprawled over the chair and the adjacent table, a person obviously in full control of the coffee house's single edition of *The Times*.[2]

A better-known painting, David Wilkie's *Chelsea Pensioners* (1822), helps unlock the political and social significance of *Gentleman Waiting for The Times*.[3] *Chelsea Pensioners* was commissioned by the Duke of Wellington to celebrate Britain's victory at the Battle of Waterloo. It features an old man, a military pensioner, who stands outside a Chelsea pub reading to a crowd a newspaper, the official *Gazette*, announcing the first news of the great British victory at Waterloo. Wilkie termed the newspaper in the centre of his work 'the eye of the painting'.[4] Similarly *The Times* in the centre of Haydon's painting has its own great national event to announce and, exactly as in Wilkie's painting, the newspaper is made to stand in for the nation itself. Haydon's *Gentleman Waiting for The Times* announces a momentous event in British history, perhaps a rival to Waterloo, the impending approach of Reform, that renegotiation of parliamentary representation that was to permanently alter the social and political order of the nation. The well-dressed gentleman on the right waits, as he must, at the convenience of the middle-class person on the left for his turn at *The Times*.

Both Wilkie and Haydon break aesthetic ground by invoking contemporary events to record 'real solemn history' (the sort of history Jane Austen's Catherine Morland avoids)[5] as an 'imagined community' of

Figure 3 *Gentleman Waiting for The Times* (1831), by Benjamin Robert Haydon

national life. Haydon's fashionably dressed gentleman and his middle-
class antagonist represent a divided nation, with the newspaper, *The
Times*, 'moving steadily down (or up) history', as Benedict Anderson
describes the task of newspapers.[6] Brian Winkenweder, the art historian, imagines that the crowd in Wilkie's *Chelsea Pensioners* 'cheers' at
the exact moment they hear Wellington's words: 'The attack succeeded
in every point; the enemy was forced from his position on the heights
and fled in the utmost confusion.'[7] The impatient gaze of Haydon's fine
gentleman likewise pins the Reform Bill's reordering of social and political classes to a single moment. Haydon's newspaper, like Wilkie's,
becomes the 'eye' that construes the nation, says Anderson, as a great
'sociological organism moving calendrically through homogeneous,
empty time'.[8] The *Westminster Review* for July 1824, confirms Anderson's
insight, claiming that 'The instruction is conveyed, not by the direct
inculcation of opinions, but by the habit of looking beyond the narrow circle of one's personal observation to the results of a more enlarged

observation ... A newspaper is, in fact, the instrument which enables an individual to avail himself of the experience of the whole community.'[9] Even the King, William IV, reads the daily papers, as a contemporary records with amusement: 'After breakfast he reads *The Times* and *Morning Post*, commenting aloud on what he reads in very plain terms, and sometimes they hear "That's a damned lie," or some such remark, without knowing to what it applies.'[10]

Like Wilkie and Haydon, silver fork novelists enact the political and economic life of the nation in dramatic gestures equally suitable for framing. Whether these novelists set their narratives in an historic past, frequently in the earlier, official Regency, or in the immediate world of the 1820s and 1830s, there is a strong consciousness of contemporary history pressing against the lives of the characters they depict. Mikhail Bakhtin's *chronotope*, 'the place where the knots of narrative are tied and untied', illuminates the relationship between newsprint and historical time in silver fork novels. In the *chronotope*, writes Bakhtin, 'Time becomes, in effect, palpable and visible.' 'The chronotope', he claims, 'makes narrative events concrete, makes them take on flesh, causes blood to flow in their veins.'[11] A flood of print ephemera enters silver fork novels like the blood of Bakhtin's *chronotope*, carrying national life along on the heartbeat of advertisements, annuals, calendars, guides, travel literature and, above all, newspapers.

Newspapers mark the 'philological change' from a *medieval* concept of time, 'in which simultaneity is ... marked by temporal coincidence', writes Anderson, to *modern* time, where a conception of the 'meanwhile' rules and is 'measured by clock and calendar'.[12] In 'modern time', Anderson observes, an individual on one side of the globe may go about his business not knowing any persons on the other side, but 'with complete confidence in their steady, anonymous, simultaneous activity' – the very 'meanwhile' that newspapers (and novels) rely on. Readers are assured of the 'sociological reality' of their own lives, 'even as people and events appear and reappear in their newspaper, but never really disappear—just as they do in novels'.[13] Nathaniel Parker Willis provides a vivid example of this new world in the newsboys he records seeing at the Elephant and Castle coach stop in autumn, 1834: 'Noospipper, sir! Buy the morning pippers, sir! *Times, Herald, Chrinnicle,* and *Munning Post,* sir—contains Lud Brum's entire innihalation of Lud Nommanby—Ledy Flor 'Estings' murder by Lud Melbun and the Maids of Honour—debate on the Croolty-Hannimals Bill, and a fatil catastrophy in conskens of loosfer matches! Sixpence, only sixpence!'[14]

Catherine Gore features the spread of newspaper culture in her silver fork novel *Stokeshill Place* (1837), where Mr Heaphy, a small-businessman from Clapton, is characterized as, 'one of that peculiar class of the easy-circumstance order of Englishmen, who read nothing but the Holy Scriptures and the unholy newspapers ... Between parliamentary reports and law reports, the money markets and foreign intelligence, great letters and small, he managed to know all that had been passing in the world for the last twenty years, from the Black Sea to Rosamond's Pond.' As for the 'measured' time of newspapers through the eyes of this character, 'Not an inconsistency in any official career, but was noted down in the tablets of John Heaphy's brain' (III, 127–8).

The daily newspaper with its power to make time 'palpable and visible' through its obsession with commerce, fashion, society and politics is the silver fork novel's bridge to history – a global trade in news that contemporary novelists join with enthusiasm. The novelists may occasionally set their plots in the early Regency, twenty years in the past, but the real, undergirding time is that of the present, always ticking along in the 'meanwhile' of the daily newspaper. Aled Jones in his study *Powers of the Press* reflects on the pervasive force of the daily papers in early nineteenth-century culture, observing that 'newspapers were superlatively successful in generating public interest and enthusiasm, not so much for social or political causes as for newspapers themselves'. Moreover, he observes, 'the symbiotic relationship that existed between journalism and literature' was such that 'newspapers were not only read, they were also read about in popular fiction'.[15]

True enough. Silver fork novelists inevitably furnish their fashionable characters with breakfast and a morning newspaper, or barring that, a comfortable library for reading it later. Catherine Gore's *Mrs. Armytage: or, Female Domination* (1836), commences with a newspaper: '"The post is late this morning!" said Mrs. Armytage, having finished her second cup of tea, and pushed away a plate disordered with chippings of egg-shell and French roll' (I, 1–2). Lord Norbury, the pompous host to a mixed party of Tories and Whigs in Marianne Hudson's *Almack's* (1826), supplies his houseguests with a choice of the day's papers, properly ironed: 'Lord Norbury ... first distributed the newspapers. "My Lord Duke, here is the Courier and the Morning Chronicle; but of course your Grace will choose the former: will you pass the other to Lord Glenmore. Ladies, the Morning Post and the Herald"' (II, 146–7).[16]

The experience of reading a silver fork novel, as contemporaries recognized, is scarcely different from that of reading a newspaper. It is simply a turnaround of Benedict Anderson's delightfully perceptive insight, 'Reading a newspaper is like reading a novel whose author has abandoned any thought of a coherent plot.'[17] Present time becomes the brass ring for novelists of fashionable life. Speed has its own value. Catherine Gore calls her own fiction 'my little ormolu railroad' in a nod to modernity.[18] W. H. Smith, the newsagent, greets his customers in the *Morning Post* of 31 December 1831, a year of major reform agitation, with a renewed promise of speed in the delivery of the newspapers: 'W. H. Smith returns his grateful thanks for the great patronage he has received, and as the ensuing Session of Parliament will be most important the greatest exertions will be made to ensure a punctual supply to all his customers.'[19]

Silver fork novelists absorbed this world of print ephemera as the air they breathed.[20] 'Who has not seen a happy party dispersed round a library, all devouring news, public and private?' asks the narrator of Marianne Hudson's *Almack's* (1826), 'the gentlemen immersed in politics; the ladies deep in "births, deaths, and marriages." Who has not experienced the happiness of receiving a folio sheet of fashionable gossip, from the best possible authority?' (II, 147). The power of fashionable novels, like that of the newspapers, handbills, advertisements and city guides with which they shared their print world, lay in the assumption that *information* confirms existence.[21] The technological explosion of print in the Romantic period brought about a new sense of reality. 'There is no disguising it', the *Edinburgh Review* noted in 1843, 'we live and move and have our being in print.'[22] Even the social calling card, as the hero of Lister's *Granby* (1826) complains, has become 'the periodical certificate of one's being still alive' (I, 238).

What we experience 'is a virtual-reality rendering, conveniently generated for us by our unconscious minds'.[23] In a poignant example of the 'virtual reality' of newsprint, the hero's father in Catherine Gore's novel *Cecil* (1841), grief-maddened at the loss of his infant grandson, or more to the point, his last hope for the continuation of his bloodline, resorts to newspapers for solace and comfort in his grief: 'Morning papers, evening papers, weekly papers, monthly summaries, nay, even the Annual Register, of that disastrous year, were placed apart in his private room, tied up with mourning-strings and bindings, to be perused and re-perused' (III, 152).

The newspapers, as Jonathan Mulrooney asserts, produced 'a daily dose of text that rendered the world public'.[24] 'In this perspective', Anderson writes, 'the newspaper itself is merely an "extreme form" of the book ... May we say: one-day best-sellers?'[25] If we understand fashionable novels to be extensions or continuations of fictions already 'imagined' for the public by the larger world of contemporary print, especially through the daily newspapers, then the silver fork novel comes into an historically more expansive frame. *Blackwood's Magazine* (Sept. 1834), thoroughly disapproving this trend of things, would agree: 'Generally speaking, the press is decidedly democratic; and this is proved to demonstration', the author asserts, by the 'immense circulation' of 'those lighter productions which attract and are alone read by the multitude—newspapers, magazines, reviews, novels, superficial travels.'[26] The publishing history of Disraeli's first novel provides a revealing example of the phenomenon. When *Vivian Grey* was published, 22 April 1826, Henry Colburn, its publisher-promoter, had been talking up his new novel with the booksellers for some time as 'by a man of high fashion—very high—keeps the first society'.[27] It was not. Benjamin Disraeli, its twenty-two-year-old author, had, as Ellen Moers writes, nothing in his background but 'a Jewish childhood, an uncomfortable schooling, an exaggerated personal dandyism and glimpses of the Jewish, the literary and the professional men of the middle class'.[28] Colburn, however, promised in the *New Monthly Magazine*, 'A very singular novel of the satirical kind is on the eve of publication, to be called "Vivian Grey" ... We understand [that] nearly all the individuals at present figuring in fashionable society, are made to flourish, with different degrees of honour, in the pages of this new work.'[29]

The fact that the young Disraeli's complete fabrication of the fashionable world succeeded to the extent of three editions of the novel in its first year of publication makes sense only in terms of Anderson's 'imagined community' – a world already available and mutually confirming, both for the young author and his readers through the contemporary print world. In a very real sense, the omnibus of the daily newspaper makes the world go round in novels of fashionable life. The daily papers are never far from the minds of the characters or the narrator. Those most frequently cited are the three largest London dailies: the *Morning Post*, an ultra-Tory paper with regular coverage of national news and its all-important social column of aristocratic society, 'The Fashionable World'; the *Morning Chronicle*, Whiggish in politics with parliamentary news as its primary focus; and *The Times*, with especially strong financial news and a steady liberal political bias. A fourth newspaper, the *Morning Herald*, finds mention in the novels, usually in regard to its lively crime reports. This choice of papers represents the spread of opinions under review in the novels themselves. Yearly publication numbers may suggest the comparative political dimensions of their readerships:

the *Morning Post*, 318,000; the *Morning Chronicle*, 772,000; *The Times*, 1,779,000.[30] Opposed ideologically as these newspapers are, they do not sit uncomfortably together on the library tables of silver fork novels, each newspaper usefully offering its own politically nuanced presence.[31] In addition, as Aled Jones observes, the 'political identity' of the different newspapers was 'complicated by the multiplicity of discourses embodied' in their texts.[32] Mrs C. D. Burdett describes the up-to-date library of the local vicar in her novel *At Home* (1828): 'Its tables were covered with newspapers and other ephemeral productions', she notes approvingly. The village apothecary, as he waits for the vicar's attention, checks the vicar's papers for dates: 'He took up and laid down every newspaper in turn; ascertained that his new army-list was fifteen months older than that of Mr Fielding' (I, 7–8).

The most important contribution of the newspapers to the silver fork novel, however, was the construction of a national society in their pages, with each page possessing a distinct, formal function. *Page one* presented advertisements of domestic goods, entertainments, personal services, schools, horses, carriages, musical instruments, books, clothing, soaps, patent medicines, dental and hair products, and so on. During sessions of Parliament when all the newspapers commandeered the first page to report parliamentary debates, classified advertisements spilled over into the following pages as necessary. *Page two* presented national news, foreign news, editorials, letters to the editor, bankruptcies and a miscellany of domestic news from other British cities and towns. *Page three* was given over to reports of fashionable society in the *Morning Post* where the 'Fashionable World' could be found with its subheadings of 'Arrangements', 'Arrivals', 'Departures', with accounts of private concerts and balls (the guests listed in order of rank) with detailed notes on the caterer, the musical offerings, the decorations and, for very grand affairs, descriptions of the dresses worn by the women of rank. Also to be found on *page three* were advertisements for the opera, with times and performances, play reviews, charity appeals, notes of fashionable life in provincial watering places and advertisements of genteel interest, puffs for recent novels and, if possible, a sordid 'We regret to report' scandal from high life. *The Times* rejected news of fashionable life, on principle, to report foreign news and financial analysis on the third page. *Page four* (the back page) was the place in all the newspapers for business and legal news – shipping, stock market reports, criminal reports, advertisements for the rental and sale of houses and land, the contents of estate auctions and a small section devoted to genteel domestic services – servants, governesses, lady's companions, private tutors and the like. Marriages and births could also appear on *page four*, but such happy occasions for the upper orders usually graced the more elegant columns of *page three*.

Vivian Grey (1826) reveals just how the young Disraeli was able to construct his novel from the straw and clay of the daily papers:

Page one: classified advertisements. The action of the novel commences with an advertisement: '"I am told, my dear," observed Mrs. Grey … "that Dr. Flummery's would do very well for Vivian. Nothing can exceed the attention which is paid to the pupils. There are sixteen young ladies, all the daughters of clergymen, merely to attend to the morals and the linen—terms very moderate—100 guineas per annum, for all under six years of age, and few extras, only for fencing, pure milk, and the guitar"' (1, 4–5). The 'gothic' story concocted by Disraeli's hero to amuse the heroine calls on their shared familiarity with the 'classifieds': 'Sounds of strange music attract my attention to a part of the castle which I have not before frequented. There I shall distinctly hear a female voice chaunting the "Bridesmaids Chorus," with Erard's double pedal accompaniment', a regular *page one* advertisement featuring the firm's most expensive harp (III, 316–17).

Page two: political, financial and domestic news. Political gossip in the *Morning Post* tempts a nobleman to enter politics: 'We are informed that some alteration of the present administration is in contemplation; Lord Past Century, it is said, will retire; Mr. Liberal Principles will have the ___; and Mr. Charlatan Gas the __' (1, 87). The stock market crash of September 1825, an event of immediate contemporary interest, finds a prominent place in the narrative: 'A fall in stocks! And halt! to "the spread of knowledge!" and "the progress of liberal principles"' (II, 161–2).

Page three: news of 'the fashionable world'. A parodic version of the *Morning Post's* 'Fashionable Changes' informs the reader of Vivian's plan for the holidays: 'Christmas was to be passed by the Carabas family, the Beaconsfields, the Scropes, and the Clevelands, at Lord Courtown's villa at Richmond; at which place the Viscount had determined *to make out* the holidays, notwithstanding the Thames entered his kitchen windows, and the Dona del Lago was to be acted in the theatre with real water—Cynthia Courtown performing Elena, paddling in a punt' (II, 147–8).

Page four: business and legal news: sales, auctions, births and deaths. A lawyer's acquisition of a country house from a bankrupt nobleman is reported in the style of newspaper estate sales: 'He "took it off the hands" of a "distressed client", says Vivian wryly, 'merely to convenience him.' '"Attorneys," as Bustle the auctioneer says, "have *such* opportunities!"' (I, 208).

William Jerdan, the contemporary critic and editor of the *Literary Gazette*, was early to suspect the 'fashionable' muse of *Vivian Grey*. Its author, wrote Jerdan, appeared too familiar with books, about which, 'the mere man of fashion knows little and cares less'.[33] There is indeed a great deal of talk in *Vivian Grey* about what is and is not fashionable to read: De Quincy, Southey ('All his works … are alike political pamphlets'), Wordsworth, Tom Moore, Sir Walter Scott and Byron (II, 102 ff.), including a casual skewering of more easy targets: 'There is every probability of Madam de Genlis writing more volumes than ever', says Vivian. 'I called on the old lady, and was quite amused with the enthusiasm of her imbecility' (II, 139). Today's literature, says Vivian with pronounced distaste, is simply 'a fungus production' of the recent financial bubble, 'the mere creature of imaginary wealth'.[34] 'Every body being very rich has afforded every body to be very literary', he claims, 'books being considered a luxury almost as elegant and necessary as Ottomans, bonbons, and pier-glasses' (II, 160–1). Jean Baudrillard's claim that 'Everywhere prestige haunts our industrial societies, whose bourgeois culture is never more than the phantom of aristocratic values' seems a pale echo of Disraeli's more vibrant linking of social status and the commercial status of literature.[35] In the consumer world, literature along with politics, fashion, finance, society and the press are all engaged in separate, but 'homologous' efforts, as Bourdieu argues, for the 'maximising of material or symbolic profit'.[36] Patrolling an ever-changing frontier of signs that represent their society, the novels of fashionable life inevitably mark the cultural and political boundaries of a world in awkward transition.

In politics, for example, if one could imagine the primary movers for political change, the aristocratic Whigs, placing an advertisement in the daily papers, their paradoxical, hard-to-reconcile political goal might read as follows: *'Aristocratic Party seeks Alliance with Middle Classes for Constitutional Change—**OBJECT**, to Prolong the Power of the Aristocracy.'* In return, one could imagine the wealthy middle classes posting an advertisement with a different, but equally awkward object of desire: '*Respectable Classes seeking Aristocratic Prestige—Ready* **MONEY** *for Suitable Accommodation.*' This latter group, however, the 'advanceable classes', as Baudrillard so aptly names them, faced a frustrating law that no amount of money could repeal. 'It is known that an essential problem in these mobile strata', writes Baudrillard, 'is the disparity between intentional mobility aspirations and real mobility (objective chances of social promotion) … Past a certain threshold of mobility they do not even exist: there is absolute resignation.'[37] The fashionable novel, and this is the case in every one of them, runs its plot as a test of Baudrillard's pessimistic pronouncement. Each silver fork novel obsessively replays the 'absolute resignation' of this social conundrum as comedy or tragedy, and nowhere more keenly than in the competitive race of the middle classes to take on signs of aristocratic status.

Marianne Hudson in *Almack's* (1826) briskly confirms Baudrillard's observation, writing, 'the few at the height of *ton* looking down with contempt on their servile followers; those half-way up the ladder pushing down the steps by which they mounted; and the greater part at the bottom affecting philosophic contempt of the eminence to which one and all are alike endeavouring to attain' (II, 113). As Lady Anne Norbury, a character in the novel remarks, 'The Birminghams may be very rich, and all that sort of thing, but they can never be one of us' (II, 159). Like the canary in the mine, the meeting of commerce and exclusivity sets alarms ringing in every direction, both for exclusives and 'advanceables'.

The separation of the first page's classified commercial advertisements from the third page's fashionable parade may be a line in the sand drawn by newspaper editors, but in silver fork novels these two contrary pages are thrown into active, challenging relationships. The balancing of two opposed moralities of consumption, as Baudrillard describes them – an aristocratic morality of '*otium*' and a 'puritan work ethic' – appears in silver fork novels as a comic struggle between aristocrats who are hard-pressed to hang on to the privileges of '*otium*' and parvenus who are only too anxious to shake the dust of the 'puritan work ethic' from their heels.[38] This is the running joke in early novels of fashionable life, from 1825 to 1830. In later years, after passage of the great Reform Bill in 1832, aristocrats and the middle classes find their positions reversed in the silver fork novel. After Reform, it is 'puritan ethics' that wields a mighty rod over the feckless body of aristocratic '*otium*'.

THE SILVER FORK NOVEL AND THE PRESS, 1825 TO 1830

Before Reform, from 1825 to 1830, fashionable novels were more likely to measure social achievement in calibrations of public celebrity than in degrees of public rectitude. That newspapers exist for social manipulation is a basic understanding among the silver fork fashionables and, of course, among those seeking to join their company. 'For many succeeding years, Sir Gilbert existed for the duty of … giving dinners to the aristocratic kinsmen of his wife and daughter and getting them duly advertised in the newspapers', Catherine Gore notes in her story 'My Grand-daughter', from *The Fair of Mayfair* (1832) (III, 159). Pelham's ambitious 'lady mother' in Bulwer's novel *Pelham* (1828) staunchly defends the practice of reporting dinners in the press: 'He not only gives the best dinners in town', she says of an acquaintance, 'but the best account of them, in the Morning Post, afterwards; which I think is very properly upholding the dignity of our order' (III, 100). A striving parvenue, 'Poor Mrs Luttrell', in Gore's *Pin Money* (1831), decides to enhance the newspaper report of her entertainment by inviting the aristocracy, 'and had already made up her mind that … the name of the Honourable Lady Rawleigh should grace her Morning Post advertisement on the morrow,—in company with "Messrs. Rosin's incomparable band, and Messrs. Gunter's delicacies of the season"' (I, 95).

The high premium placed on newspaper celebrity is one of the earliest hallmarks of silver fork fiction, appearing in Lord Normanby's *Matilda* (1825), Marianne Hudson's *Almack's* (1826), T. H. Lister's *Granby* (1826) and Disraeli's *Vivian Grey* (1826). A second tranche of fashionable novels, were more wary of its dangers: Edward Bulwer's *Pelham* (1828), Lady Charlotte Bury's *Flirtation* (1827), Lady Caroline Lucy Scott's *A Marriage in High Life* (1828), Charles White's *Almack's Revisited* (1828), a second novel by T. H. Lister, *Herbert Lacy* (1828) and a second by Disraeli, *The Young Duke* (1831). The excitement of urban London links them all, each one paradoxically embracing print celebrity as the pivot of exclusive life. As one dandy confesses anxiously in *The Young Duke*, 'I never now stand still in the street, lest my portrait be caught for a lithograph; I never venture to a strange dinner, lest I should stumble upon a fashionable novelist' (II, 115).

Lady Birmingham, an 'advanceable' in Hudson's *Almack's* (1826), plots the social campaign for her daughter with regular notices directed to the editors of the *Morning Post*'s 'Fashionable World'. The account of her grand new London house, for example, figures in the Baron de Wallenstein's recital of the *Morning Post*'s fashionable news to his wife:

Then we have—'Birmingham House. This greatly to be admired residence is now completed, and its unequalled decorations, both exterior and interior, we may venture to pronounce, are decidedly unique, both for design and execution. The fashionable Lady Birmingham will after Easter open her splendid suite of rooms to the *haut ton*, for the purpose of introducing her daughter, the lovely and accomplished Miss Birmingham. This young lady, it is presumed, will be the general magnet of attraction, as fame speaks largely of the amount of her expectations.' (II, 250)

As an ignorant foreigner, the Baron remains unaware that the *Morning Post* depends upon its 'news' of the fashionable world for voluntary contributions from its readers. Innocent of all guile, he expresses shock at the *Post*'s allusion to Barbara's wealth: 'The idea of puffing off a young heiress, as an itinerant hawker would do his goods! it is really preposterous; but these newspapers appear to make free with everything'. The reader knows well enough the Lady who sent this 'news' to the paper.

In a passage that truly escapes parody, Hudson provides an account of the opening of Lady Birmingham's new London house in the best style of the *Morning Post*'s 'Fashionable World':

On Tuesday, the 1st of May, about eleven o'clock, the carriages began to arrive: they continued setting down, without intermission, till past midnight; and then what a glorious assemblage of grandees were collected together! The house was magnificent beyond description, and illuminated in the most brilliant style. Five grand apartments were open *en suite*, and terminated in a beautiful conservatory, filled with rare plants from the Abbey, whose rich perfume added another charm to this enchanting Elysium. Wind-instruments were played at intervals to relieve Collinet's inspiring band ... The richly embossed gold plate was all displayed. It was massive in the extreme. (III, 344)

With wealth and celebrity as her standard bearers, Lady Birmingham arrays herself in an over-the-top dress to accompany her daughter to her royal presentation at Carleton House – 'her train of gold tissue, her robe of the finest blonde, her immense plume of feathers, and her splendid tiara of diamonds'. The author notes smugly, however, that, 'the tout ensemble failed in its general effect; yet it answered every end, for she was the glory of her maid—the boast of her milliner—the *chef-d'oeuvre* of her hair-dresser—the wonder of all the newspapers, and', she adds, 'the amusement of the *distingués* at the drawing-room' (III, 296). Those who are gratified by the display, however, the maid, the milliner and the hairdresser, celebrate Lady Birmingham as a walking advertisement, a veritable billboard display of their talents.

In contrast, Lady Birmingham's daughter Barbara 'had with much difficulty obtained permission to follow the bent of her own unassuming taste', says Hudson: 'The simple elegance of her appearance formed a happy contrast to her mother's gaudy attire. Her dress was white crape, ornamented with bouquets of lily of the valley mixed with rose-buds; the same in her hair; and, for the first time, she wore the beautiful pearls which her father had given her on her birthday' (III, 296–7). Taste and sentiment make the difference, or so it would seem.[39] But Barbara's white crêpe, rosebuds, lilies of the valley and her father's birthday pearls – all of these equally fashion fodder for the newspapers along with her mother's diamonds – transform her into a proper candidate for aristocratic marriage, not to mention her handsome £20,000-a-year inheritance, a sum, which for the sake of comparison, amounts to twice that of Darcy's ample income in *Pride and Prejudice*.

As Jonathan Mulrooney suggests, stories in the daily papers provide a 'continual intersection of multiple strains of information: reporting of political and national events', and, he argues, 'sensationalist accounts of domestic troubles and gossip' as competitive items in their spread of consumer offerings.[40] The *Westminster Review* observes this newspaper penchant for the yoking of private and public life as early as 1829: 'the daily press ... occupies itself with all public affairs—and with all private concerns as soon as they come within its circle of public interest'.[41] Henry Lister's novel *Granby* (1826) explores the comic consequences of such a mix of the trivial and significant. Lady Jermyn brings a passage from the morning newspaper to her friend Mr Duncan for elucidation. Mr Duncan suggests a few names that he thinks might help Lady Jermyn fill the blanks in her imagination, but he gets everything wrong as the reader knows. Lady Jermyn can't let the passage go, it troubles her. '"But, Mr Duncan," said Lady Jermyn, "newspapers do make such mistakes. It may be Lord Stratford, after all. There is no such thing as accuracy in a newspaper. Why, now, only two months ago, when we met you at Brighton, in the "Fashionable Changes,"[42] they chose to send us all to Worthing, and they spelt Jermyn with an 'a.' It is the second time they have done so. I never believe a newspaper"' (I, 124).

Newspapers and their puzzling ways come up again the following morning. 'The whole party were re-assembled at the breakfast-table', writes Lister. 'The welcome post arrived as usual, and letters and papers were soon seen picturesquely interspersed among cups, plates, egg-stands, and toast-racks', when Lady Harriet abruptly interrupts the peace of the table to take her husband's attention away from his newspaper:

'There—you political person!' said Lady Harriet, holding up a letter to her husband, who sat perusing the newspaper on the other side of the table ... 'Oh, how I hate all politics!' said she, directing her observation to the rest of the company. 'Begging the gentlemen's pardons, I don't think it improves them at all. It makes them business-like and *wiggy*. As for us women, it really ruins us completely. Don't you think so, my dear?' appealing to Miss Clifton.

'I agree with you entirely,' said the latter, 'and I know several instances of its bad effects.' (III, 193)

'The only thing I complain of', insists Lady Harriet, 'is their putting in debates at all. I mean indiscriminately into every paper. There is really not one that a lady can take up.' As Miss Clifton observes, any immediate change by the editors in the content of the papers is highly unlikely: 'We are too well satisfied with the present order of things. I am sure I myself know several ladies who never read anything but newspapers. There is old Mrs Printley reads the Morning Post through every day—quite through—every advertisement—stamp-mark and all. It exactly occupies her from the breakfast hour till three o'clock.' 'Well,' confesses another lady, 'I think I can safely say, that the united reading of the whole female part of the house of Daventry does not comprise more than Deaths and Marriages, and the Fashionable Changes. We never look at anything else—we abstain upon principle' (III, 197–8).

Growing weary of this idle newspaper chatter, the heroine, Lady Caroline, takes up the day's edition of the *Morning Post*:

She dropped the paper, clasped her hands, and raised them with a shudder to her face; and, 'Oh! he will die!' burst tremulously from her lips.
[Mr. Duncan reads the article aloud ...] 'We regret to state, that Lord Malton lies dangerously ill at the Clarendon Hotel. His Lordship's illness is supposed to have originated in the distressing event to which we alluded a few days back, and of the truth of which there is no longer the smallest doubt.' (III, 201)

All is revealed. Lady Caroline's love for Henry Granby, formerly a secret consigned to her breast alone (her parents disapprove of Granby's prospects), is suddenly startled into public knowledge by a newspaper report sold to the paper by 'creepers', independent reporters who have shadowed Granby since he has been made Lord Malton, rich, titled and a celebrity. Caroline's parents, Sir Thomas and Lady Jermyn, are delighted to learn, whatever the source of their knowledge, of their daughter's attachment to Granby now that he is rich and a lord. The novel finishes in a flourish

of celebrity triumph: 'Lady Jermyn had perused already with her mind's
eye the words, '"Viscountess Malton on her marriage, by Lady Jermyn,"
in the list of presentations at the ensuing drawing-room; and had almost
composed a description of her dress' (III, 326–7).

Towards 1828, however, novels of fashionable life begin to display a considerable suspicion of celebrity in a world that was fast coming unglued
from its traditional social mores. Sir Reginald Glanville, the hero's best
friend in Bulwer's *Pelham* (1828), warns Pelham of the dangers of print
notoriety: 'Never, my dear Pelham, be tempted by any inducement into
the pleasing errors of print; from that moment you are public property;
and the last monster at Exeter 'Change has more liberty than you' (II, 87).
In the event, it is Glanville himself who loses his liberty to invasions of
the press. Innocent of a murder of which he is accused, Glanville stands
guilty in the columns of the daily papers. The difference between the
individual, or as Benedict Anderson characterizes it, the gap between the
'representative' and the 'personal' in newspaper celebrity, leaps into sharp
focus.[43] The newspapers are delighted to find an aristocrat with real blood
on his hands. Lady Glanville interrupts a conversation between Pelham
and her daughter to ask about a story in the newspaper that, unknown
to her, describes the situation of her own son: 'Have you seen the papers
to-day, Mr Pelham?' she asks him, and, 'she pointed to an article in the
Morning Herald, which she said had occupied their conjectures all the
morning—it ran thus:—"The evening before last, a person of rank and
celebrity, was privately carried before the Magistrate at—. Since then,
he has undergone an examination, the nature of which, as well as the
name of the individual, is as yet kept a profound secret".' This newspaper
report, a matter of 'representative' character, precipitates a violent reaction in Pelham that he must hide: 'I did not therefore betray a single one
of the emotions this paragraph excited within me, but appeared, on the
contrary, as much at a loss as Lady Glanville' (III, 272). He hastens from
the Glanville home to fling himself headlong into the criminal world of
east London in search of evidence to clear his friend. Pelham discovers
the real malefactor, but for the benefit of newspaper reporters who lie in
wait to witness his appearance in court, he turns his sordid and frighten-
ing experience in the East End into a tale of knightly romance, giving
them 'copy', as it were, for the newspaper notice the next day: '"I have
come," said I, "to redeem my pledge, and acquit the innocent"' (III, 345).
Pelham's mother, a social butterfly of the first order, makes use of the
'representative' powers of the press with enthusiasm. Her son's marriage
to Ellen Glanville, Reginald's sister and the Glanville heiress, brings him

a magnificent £40,000 in dowry, but as his mother cannily suggests, 'I think it will be better to give out that Miss Glanville has eighty thousand pounds'—the story will look better in the papers (III, 349).

Bulwer's fellow authors, Lady Bury and Lady Scott, are equally ambiguous about the intrusive energy of the press, not for any inconvenience it might bring to an individual subject, but for the destabilizing consequences that aristocratic scandal might bring to the social fabric of the nation. For Bury and Scott newspapers perform the service of a brutal rat-catcher – obsessively fixed on scandal, careless of means and effects, ignorant of its own poisons, though useful indeed for hauling out aristocratic corruption.

Lady Scott's novel, *A Marriage in High Life* (1828), edited by Lady Bury, features a rich middle-class heroine, Emmeline Benson, who marries the 'handsome and manly' Ernest, Lord Fitzhenry, only son of the Earl of Arlingford. The marriage is a financial deal on both sides. For the aristocratic father of the groom, his son's marriage into the middle classes is payment for a debt he owes the bride's father. On the middle-class side, it is a triumph for the bride's City father to have the newspapers report his daughter's lofty marriage as '*at home*, by special license'. The groom, however, behaves oddly at the wedding (people notice) and more oddly indeed on his honeymoon when he refuses to go to bed with his new wife, and when at the breakfast table the next morning he can't be drawn from his newspaper (I, 74). It happens that the wicked Lady Florence Mostyn, Ernest's mistress, has extracted a promise from him that he will never make love to Emmeline, a vow he keeps. His closest physical contact with Emmeline comes during a waltz forced upon him at a public ball – 'Emmeline felt her husband's arm round her waist; her hand was clasped in his, and his breath played on her forehead. Her feelings almost overcame her! Her heart beat so violently that she could hardly breathe … complaining of faintness, she begged him, in a scarcely audible voice, to stop' (I, 192).

At the Italian Opera, Emmeline spies her husband, 'the oval head, the brown, curly hair, the attitude of the arm', in an opera box across the way leaning towards Lady Florence Mostyn. She flees the opera house for the street, but her carriage is caught, as these things happen, in a carriage accident with her husband and Lady Florence who are also in flight. 'Amid the din of voices, whips, trampling of hoofs on the pavement, and shivering of breaking lamps', Emmeline leaps into her carriage, but, in an attempt to protect her, a friend, a faithful Mr Pelham[44] who is secretly in love with her, leaps in after her. Their carriage drives towards her house;

her husband's carriage drives towards Lady Florence's. Emmeline says never a word to her parents about what has happened. They get the news in their morning paper:

A singular fracas took place at the Opera on Saturday night; not being yet informed of the particulars, we forbear making any reflections. As it is a double intrigue, and therefore neither party can complain, it is impossible to say how the affair may end. The *chère amie* of the noble lord is well known in the fashionable world both *abroad* and *at home*; and it is not perhaps surprising that the neglected wife should have *pris son parti*, and found a champion to espouse her cause. He is said to be in the *diplomatic* line, and *of course* a particular friend of the husband. One rumour states the injured wife to have eloped—another that a duel has taken place. Certain it is that two carriages with the F—Z—Y arms were seen to drive furiously out of Grosvenor-street at different hours and in different directions on Sunday afternoon. (II, 97)

It takes another newspaper report – nothing else will do – to clear Emmy, as her father now calls her, the daughter whom he had been pleased to call in his days of vanity and pride 'Lady Fitzhenry':

It is with sincere pleasure that we can confidently contradict a report in our last, respecting a certain noble pair in Grosvenor Street, in so far at least as the fair fame of *one* of the ladies is concerned. Lady F____y, we understand, merely left town in order to pay a visit to her father at Ch—l—n, where she now is. A legal separation may however be anticipated, as it is certain that the noble Lord has also most abruptly left home, and, it is whispered, not *alone*. Rumour also states that the diplomatic friend has followed the fugitives, in order, if possible, to prevent the scandal of a public *éclat*. (II, 124–5)

'Fool! idiot! that I was', says old Mr Benson, 'striking his forehead, "to be so proud of this marriage … I had rather have seen you the wife of the lowest clerk in my banking-house, than that of this Lord Fitzhenry, or any other lord in Christendom with his vile paramour"' (II, 137 ff.). When Fitzhenry's father, the old Earl, calls to make amends, middle-class Mr Benson asserts his moral authority over a corrupt aristocracy by turning him away. The faltering husband Ernest, Lord Fitzhenry, now abandoned by Lady Florence and desperately ill in Paris, returns to England only to find Emmeline willing – nay, anxious – to help him mend his morals. He learns to pray – he has never done it before – and sleeps with her prayer book under his pillow. In his last breath he thanks Emmeline for reading him 'that beautiful Essay of Miss Bowdler's on the Advantages of Sickness', an aristocratic testimonial admirably suitable for the bold-type 'classifieds' of the daily papers (II, 282–3).

Lady Bury's novel *Flirtation* (1827) also brings ominous word of aristocratic moral decay as reported in the newspapers. Lady Frances, unhappily married to Lord Bellamont, runs off with Mr Carlton, whereupon Lord Bellamont seduces Lady Dashwood. 'The Morning Post, and other prints, teemed with the *fracas* for some days', she reports, 'and then it was as much forgotten as though it had never happened. Forgotten!—where? and by whom?' cries Lady Bury with portentous solemnity, 'It is an awful question—too awful to be answered in these pages' (III, 302).

Charles White's Tory novel *Almack's Revisited* (1828) caricatures the great Whig hostess Lady Holland as 'Lady Alderney' drawing on the ambiguous status of newspaper celebrity to expose even the greatest of the exclusives. Lady Alderney yearns for fame and immortality in the grander print world, claims White, something beyond the celebrity of the daily press:

Lady Alderney's highest ambition was to outlive the ephemeral columns of the Morning Post ... She sighed in her soul to be handed down to posterity in the 'historic quarto,' edited by one of the learned of her own sex, not only as the leader of a party, but as the nucleus around which the wit, talents, and erudition of her day, clustered like bees around the honey-dripping eglantine. She would have renounced not only the pleasures of life, but even existence itself without a tear, if she could have been assured of again reviving, in the shape of a large paper copy of octavo Memoirs, edited by some amphibious Blue, under the auspices of an erudite and speculative publisher. (III, 3–4)

Newspaper celebrity reached the end of its shelf life for the exclusives around 1830. *The Young Duke*, Disraeli's second novel, written in the summer and autumn of 1829 and published in March 1831, marks its spectacular end. The protagonist of the novel, the richest young man of his day, is tied to existence solely by the thread of celebrity that follows him, an extreme representation of the excesses of his class. As might be expected from the author of *Vivian Grey*, Disraeli's *The Young Duke* is a calculated newspaper confection, 'a series of scenes', as he privately boasted, 'every one of which would make the fortune of a fashionable novel'.[45] When Disraeli's father first heard the title of his son's second novel, his response was natural enough – '*Young Duke!* What does Ben know of Dukes?'[46]

Disraeli knew well enough to attach the Duke's existence to the calculated glamour of newspaper celebrity. The history of George Augustus Frederick, the Duke of St James, begins with his fortune: 'The Duke of St. James possessed estates in the North and in the West of England, besides a whole province in Ireland. In London, there was a very handsome square and four streets all made of bricks, which brought him in yearly more cash than all the palaces of Vicenza are worth in fee-simple.' In addition, continues Disraeli, 'His rent-roll exhibited a sum total, very neatly written, of two hundred thousand pounds; but this

was independent of half a million in the funds, which I had nearly forgotten, and which remained from the accumulations occasioned by the
unhappy death of his father' (I, I). The Duke of St James, writes Disraeli,
'was now, in the most comprehensive sense of the phrase, a Public
Character ... A Sunday journal was immediately established. Of this
epic, our Duke was the hero.' 'One week, the Duke saved a poor man
from the Serpentine', the narrator reports from the journal, 'another,
a poor woman from starvation; now an orphan was grateful; and now
Miss Zouch, impelled by her necessity, and his reputation addressed
him a column and a half, quite heart-rending' (II, 48–9). The young
Duke performs every task that the Sunday papers could ask: he takes
a mistress, 'The Bird of Paradise', and with great diligence wastes his
fortune in gambling, building castles in the country, a mansion in town
and a luxurious retreat in Regent's Park. His former guardian steps in
only at the last moment to save him from bankruptcy. But Disraeli's
newspaper 'confection' falls victim before the close of the novel to a
much more powerful *real* news story, the collapse in 1828–9 of the agricultural economy. As the narrator reports:

Great agricultural distress prevailed, and the rents could not be got in. Five and
twenty per cent was the least that must be taken off his income, and with no
prospect of being speedily added on. There was a projected rail-road that would
entirely knock up his canal, and even if crushed, must be expensively opposed.
Coals were falling also, and the duties in town increasing. There was also sad
confusion in the Irish estates. (III, 84)

'The Universe' and 'The New World', two Sunday journals that devote
themselves to the Duke's glamorous excesses, promptly announce that
the young Duke is 'done up' (III, 114) and that they have a fresh young
lordship to take his place, Lord Marylebone: 'The young Duke was quite
forgotten, if really young he could longer be called. Lord Marylebone was
in the mouth of every tradesman' (III, 93–4). Consumer celebrity is thus
abandoned by fashion to the lesser streets of Marylebone and its parvenu
residents.

THE SILVER FORK NOVEL AND THE PRESS, 1830 TO 1841

Mikhail Bakhtin's *chronotope* ticks away. Repeal of the Test and
Corporation Acts is up for consideration in 1828, as well as Catholic
emancipation, both measures bitterly divisive as social and political issues. A ruling coalition of liberal Tories and Whigs falls in 1828

to a conservative Tory government under the leadership of the Duke of Wellington. Electoral reform, a Whig dream that had waxed and waned for years, suffers yet another defeat in Parliament. Even a modest proposal for borough reform, a transfer of representation from the infamous rotten boroughs of Penryn and East Redford to Manchester and Birmingham, suffers a peremptory defeat at the hands of the Tory conservatives.[47] Nevertheless, issues of constitutional change begin to stir outside Westminster. When the general election of 1830 that followed the death of George IV returned a large increase in Whig reform electors, the noise of reform entered Parliament itself.

In the sense of Pierre Bourdieu's *habitus*, or the 'feel for the game (*sens pratique*)', the parliamentary push for enfranchisement in 1830 had become the only game in town.[48] The papers and the public were captured by the political and social turbulence associated with constitutional reform. Catherine Gore, a popular new author, turned her novels of fashionable life towards this world of social and political change. For Gore, the inevitable prospect, as she understood it, of power falling into non-aristocratic hands became the political centre of her novels.

The Forsyth clan, a Scottish banker family in her *Women as They Are* (1830), the first genuinely political middle-class family in a silver fork novel, give a grand dinner to impress readers of the *Morning Post* with the fact that 'the Prime-Minister of England was about to grace their board!!' (III, 106). Gore reports their expenses for the occasion with appropriate middle-class exactness. On his way to his office in the City, Mr Forsyth stops his carriage at the goldsmiths Messrs Rundell and Bridge on Ludgate Hill to commission a Forsyth shield for the occasion, 'one of the most elaborate and mendacious imaginations of the Herald's College ... [and] a pair of splendid gilt candelabra, with a dessert service to match' (III, 108). London's most celebrated chef, Louis Eustache Ude, is contracted to cater the dinner. 'And now the fatal day had dawned upon the last fiery ordeal!—the *salmi de Langues de lapin, farci aux pistaches,*—the *Sauté de foies de chapon à la Marengo,*—and *Cuisses d'alouette panés en papillôte*, were in the very hour of alembic project' (III, 124). The gilt candelabra, etc. arrive in the morning from Rundell and Bridge in special hackney coaches in 'green-baize bags of most aureal promise' (III, 124–5). And then – Lord Willersdale sends his regrets. He has a committee meeting. 'A dinner at five and twenty guineas a head', mourns Mrs Forsyth, '—it is enough to drive one wild!' (III, 126). After an evening of appalling social gaffes, 'Mr Forsyth retired to bed with the head-ache, and the satisfactory remembrance that he had worried himself, and bored fifteen innocent individuals to the amount of 2,432*l.* 16*s.* 9*d.* Rundell and Bridge included' (III, 135).

The ladies of the Forsyth household weep themselves to sleep with their only comfort, that the next morning will provide solace with 'the following paragraph, (which had been sent to the office in the course of the preceding week) in the consolatory columns of the mild Morning Post':

Mr. Forsyth, M. P. for the borough of Catspaw, gave a splendid entertainment of Saturday last to a select party of friends; among whom were Lord and Lady Willersdale, and the Hon. Miss Dudley; the Marquis and Marchioness of C ... The banquet consisted of every delicacy in or out of season. (III, 136)

Unfortunately one of the scandal-seeking Sunday papers has received different information and presents a rival version of the Forsyths' grand affair, equally faulty in its truth and accuracy:

PLACE-HUNTING EXTRAORDINARY
We beg to call the attention of the worthy and independent electors of Catspaw to a paragraph in the 'never-sufficiently-to-be-despised, and altogether-to-be-mistrusted,' Morning Post. We understand they have at present the honour of being represented by a respectable man, of the name of Forsyth; of the firm, we presume, of Forsyth and Son, slopsellers, in the Barbican; who appears to be hospitable and vain of his hospitality. Like other pompous worthies, he advertises his dinners. And who,—tell it not in Catspaw—who, think you, my worthy and independent electors, graced, or *are said* to have graced, the banquet of this illustrious individual on Saturday se'nnight? My Lord and my Lady Willersdale! (*The head and front of our present corrupt ministry!*) ... There can be little doubt that the eyes of the sycophantic slopseller are fixed on some snug sinecure. (III, 138)

There can also be 'little doubt' that Public Opinion feeds splendidly at the two conflicting newspaper reports of Mr Forsyth's extravagant dinner table, a regular donnybrook of political, cultural and commercial values to shake the political nerves of British society in 1830.

In Gore's next novel *Mothers and Daughters* (1831), where the Westlands, a more respectfully rendered middle-class family, read the newspapers, the women too, including the political essays on free trade and the abolition of colonial slavery, it is the aristocracy that becomes the object of newspaper mockery. Lord Stapylford, an aristocrat tentatively engaged to Minnie De Vesci the heiress and heroine, has turned out badly. He is a wastrel and narcissist who displays his aristocratic airs in a manner guaranteed to set middle-class readers on edge, 'lounging on the down sofa of his apartment at Mivart's', London's most fashionable hotel, 'passing a white hand through his perfumed curls, and crumpling with the other the Morning Post into a toss-ball' (I, 277). His inevitable bankruptcy, under the management of 'Messrs. Screw, Gripe, and Co., Agents of Great St. Helen's London', becomes known to Minnie only by means of a notice placed in the morning dailies by 'Messrs. Flourish, House-agents and Auctioneers', with every detail of Stapylford's aristocratic privilege and consumer excess turned against him and his noble order:

'To Noblemen and Gentlemen,' that they had been empowered by the assignees to let on lease for a term of years, 'that capital mansion known by the name of Stapylford Park; containing a suite of state chambers 434 feet in length; thirty-five best bed-rooms, and suitable offices;—together with a lake covering an extent of 1230 acres; with five thousand acres of land, strictly preserved; besides pineries, graperies, pheasantaries, ice-houses, conservatories, menageries, aviaries, picture and sculpture galleries, &c. &c. &c.;—&c. &c. &c.' (II, 278)

The last shred of aristocratic finery goes a day later, also reported by the newspapers: 'The Private collection of A NOBLEMAN going abroad; Comprising his unrivalled cabinet of 550 snuff-boxes, besides cabinet pictures, *bijouterie*, and objects of *virtù*, collected at an incalculable expense, and to be disposed of without the least reserve' (III, 278). The *Morning Post* has its say as well, writes Gore, in 'a statement as clear, and candid, and awful, and implicatory—as dashes, and asterisks, and italics could make it—of the crimes, and misdemeanours, and fooleries of the ruined spendthrift' (II, 265).

After passage of the Reform Bill in 1832, the tectonic plates of social and political power shift in silver fork novels, placing the novels in a fresh relationship with celebrity and newspapers and post-Reform culture. Power moves house. Aristocrats must head for the boroughs and towns to get out the vote. There is a distinct fall-off in London activity with fewer nights at the opera or private walks through Berkeley Square, and no more innocent excursions to Regent Street for a little shopping.

Mrs Gore's novel *The Hamiltons* (1834), a self-conscious before-Reform and after-Reform novel, was published in 1834, but set historically in the midst of political developments from 1828 to 1832, and then continued through the years 1832 to 1834. In 1828 in the country town-village of Laxington a provincial culture of pre-Reform newspaper-reading prevails:

The Vicar and the attorney—nay! even the attorney's sister, Miss Pen. Smith ... were content with Lord Tottenham's second day's Courier and the weekly intelligence of the County Chronicle. Newspapers and magazines would have been productive of political discussions;—political discussions, of squabbles among neighbours hitherto united and content. Things were better as they were. The borough could not be kept too quiet;—nor the Earl's deputed [the agent] be too watchful against innovations. (II, 3)

With the arrival of a new family, however, the Hamiltons, who are Tory people of rank, the villagers begin to read their second day *Couriers* with greater attention to the national news. Fashionable life and national life, by implication, are still working in tandem in the year 1829:

Their interest in the proceedings of parliament was no longer restricted to the 'Ayes' and 'Noes' of the honourable members by whom it was Lord Tottenham's pleasure (or interest) that they should be represented. They already loved to read, in their stale edition of the Courier, that 'THE RIGHT HON. GEORGE HAMILTON had said a few words inaudible in the gallery'— that 'THE RIGHT HON. GEORGE HAMILTON had entertained the Lord Chancellor and a distinguished party at dinner, at his mansion in Spring Gardens.' The Right Honourable George was the first denizen of their genteel neighbourhood who had ever possessed 'a mansion' in town!—(I, 13)

The love plots of the novel ride forward on a combination of national politics and fashionable 'news'. Engagements, weddings, parties, duels, new furniture, decorations, holidays, deaths and bankruptcies, are as sedulously reported by the newspapers and read by the villagers as parliamentary speeches, political scandals and changes of government.

As for the sisters in this two-heroine novel, Susan, the younger sister, married to Augustus Hamilton, the son of the Tory minister, positively dislikes newspapers. When her brother congratulates her on her celebrity, Susan responds with shock: 'Who told you I was established as a beauty?' He replies in course, 'The newspapers ... You are now "the lovely Mrs Hamilton"—'tis a settled phrase, like "the gifted Canning," or "the great Sir Walter!!"' (I, 252). Susan answers sharply, 'I never read newspapers ... Augustus is no politician; and knows that I hate the very names of Whig or Tory' (I, 260). Nevertheless, 'Not a newspaper of the day but recorded the name of the Hon. Mr. and Mrs. Hamilton, as guest at some illustrious table; or as doing the honours of Spring Gardens to the Marquis of Shetland and my Lords A. B. C. and C. D.' (I, 212–13). Susan is now, whether she likes it or not, a political asset to the Tory Party. Marcia, Susan's older sister, married to a radical politician, reads newspapers constantly, her way of participating in her husband's political career. 'Laying aside a paper from which she had been reading to her husband the reported edition of one his own fine speeches', she is interrupted by the arrival of unexpected, but like-minded guests to her political parlour (II, 154).

Back in Laxington, national news filters through to the population in its usual way, through the news of the 'Fashionable World'. The connection, however, between fashionable news and political life, at the heart of silver fork fiction, has begun to falter. Reform politics, as Mrs Gore demonstrates in this novel, has completely changed the social coordinates of political power. One of the local ladies of Laxington, interpreting a report in the papers, strays considerably from the mark, as the novel reader, who possesses the 'real' story, knows only too well:

'Lord—lord!—my dear Lady B!' cried Pen. Smith (who flew with her congratulations to Green-oak the moment the County Chronicle announced, in its largest letters—: 'At Vienna, on the 28th of February, the lady of the Hon. Augustus Hamilton of a son and heir!'—) 'How every thing *does* seem to prosper with that dear creature! After living boxed up here at Green-oak, year after year, she makes one of the first matches in England;—takes the lead in all the tip-top company, goes to court, pleases every body;—and now, you see, the very first child's a son and heir;—a fine thriving babe, I don't doubt.' (II, 115–16)

Pen. Smith's hopes for a dynastic future of aristocratic rule are based on the faulty assumptions of the fashion columns. In fact, the child is sickly, Susan is ill, Augustus is engaged in an affair with Susan's best friend, and the child is to die, with symbolic timing, on the same day as George IV. 'There was a bond of sympathy between the dying infant and the dying king. Their infirmity reduced them to an equality' (II, 283).

There comes a great flurry of newspaper reading in *The Hamiltons* after 1830. Even Susan takes them up:

Few persons suffered more, under the system of intimidation at that moment pursued by the liberal press, than the gentle Susan Hamilton. The details of the French and Belgic Revolutions were never absent from her mind. With restless anxiety, she perused the threats of the lowest order of the public journals; and already beheld, in imagination, her husband and her husband's father, fugitives like Polignac and Peyronnet before the fury of the populace; or confined for life in those pleasant apartments on the banks of the Thames, which are entered through the Traitor's Gate! (III, 16)

The town of Laxington begins to show political restlessness in its slim source of news: 'A reading room was established, in which the Examiner newspaper and Westminster Review were unblushingly read, in open day-light, by the subscribers' (III, 20). Susan's fame in 'Fashionable World' turns sour: 'no rhapsodies in the servile papers respecting the beauty and elegance of the all-accomplished Mrs Hamilton. Everything connected

with that name was in the minority ... distasteful to the eye of that feeble
tawdry, giggling jade, called Fashion' (III, 107).

In the post-Reform era, the rituals of aristocratic life no longer possess their former newspaper significance. Augustus, Susan's husband and
a courtier at Windsor, 'could not remain blind to the fact that he was
good for no other purpose than to form a lay-figure in the gaudy pageants
of aristocratic life' (III, 127). Lord Laxington, the former Tory minister,
living abroad after Reform and being cared for by his daughter-in-law
Susan, still cannot resist reading the papers: 'Poor Susan was often grieved
to observe the restless anxiety with which Lord Laxington looked for the
arrival of the English papers; and the interest he involuntarily betrayed
in all the trivial changes of official life' (III, 262). In Laxington, the new
post-Reform culture produces a library stocked with the latest publications. 'All the new publications,—the magazines,—reviews—', exclaims
one enthusiastic resident. '*Reviews*!—pah!', volunteers a more conservative voice, 'A pack of inflammatory trash!—What leisure had we to *want*
either new books or old ... unless, perhaps, it was a Debrett's Peerage,—
when a dispute arose among us which was eldest, Harry Tottenham or
William' (III, 246–7).

Novels of fashionable life are remarkably quick to respond, as one might
expect, to the subtlest changes in society, even in fashions of newspaper
reading. The connection between political news and news of fashionable
life is recognized almost immediately as a victim of reform. Caroline
Norton's *Woman's Reward* (1835) demonstrates the significance of the loss
for silver fork novelists. Mary, the novel's heroine, has moved as far afield
as Nice, her exile the direct consequence of her brother's loss of the family fortune in a failed election bid. She ekes out a meagre living by nursing British invalids who have moved to France for the climate. One of
her patients, a young boy with consumption, asks her for 'her story'. She
attempts to divert the child's attention from the painful memories of her
recent life. '"Come," said Mary, "I will read you the news from England;
and that will amuse you".'

'No, no,' said he playfully, 'indeed I wont; I know it all by inspiration. A great
many murders have been committed, and all of them are proved to have been
committed by Irishmen, or by men whose parents were of Irish extraction; a
great many long dull speeches have been made in the House of Commons, and
a great many short foolish ones in the Houses of Lords. You will find them
under the head of "Parliamentary Proceedings," and they are all much alike.
Then, let me see—oh! Mr. Pain, of Wandsworth, has got a large gooseberry
bush in his garden; from which, four gooseberries (each measuring two inches in

diameter) were picked in the coldest week of March, the bush having flowered at Christmas. Mr. Dibbs, at Kensington, has an equally preposterous turnip; and Mr. Oxley, of Yorkshire, has found, in the hollow of a tree, a she fox bringing up a fox-hound puppy, and suckling it affectionately ... and so ends "News from England".' (III, 34)

'"Hush—hush! you will tire yourself talking so much," said Mary laughing.' After the Reform Bill, the best that the newspapers can come up with, as Mrs Norton claims, are dull parliamentary speeches, Irish murders, large gooseberries and preposterous turnips.

It is certainly true, as David Cannadine observes, that the days of inherited power had not disappeared, not by any means.[49] Nevertheless, passage of the Reform Bill had altered public opinion towards fashionable aristocratic society. Contested power, the traditional fuel of silver fork fiction, continues to run the silver fork novel, but on a much reduced scale of family struggles and county politics. Catherine Gore's *Mrs. Armytage: or, Female Domination* (1836) reduces the connection of the fashionable world and contemporary politics to a rehearsal of neighbourhood squabbles.[50] As for the social columns of the *Morning Post*'s 'Fashionable World', they become in this bitter novel little more than commercial advertisements of bourgeois social encroachment.

Mrs Jack Baltimore of deeply unfashionable Baker Street, the mother of the sadly mistreated heroine of the novel, casts 'a wistful eye upon the ball-describing details of the Morning Post, or the flashy vis-à-vis that rolled along beneath her windows' (I, 42). Her sister, Mrs Dyke Robsey, married to a rich West Indian, sets her heart 'upon giving a "déjeûner à la fourchette," as the newspapers politely call a luncheon', writes Mrs Gore with withering contempt (I, 57). 'It is true', Mrs Gore writes of the changed times, 'mail-coach roads, daily newspapers, and book-clubs, have ... diffused themselves over the provinces with more celerity than may be wholly desirable' (I, 136).

Mr Leonidas Lomax, an America adventurer and interloper in the Armytage neighbourhood, becomes Gore's prime example of the new relationship between fashion and newsprint. As Mrs Gore reproachfully observes, 'It is not alone the "leaders" of "the leading journals of Europe" which may be fairly termed the "mis-leaders of the times;" scarcely a minor "we hear," or subordinate "it is said," ... but has its influence in causing the little to pass for great, and of the great diminishing their importance' (III, 211). 'Day after day', Gore complains in *Mrs. Armytage*, 'the fog-bewildered population of the murmuring *grenouillière* of Great Britain, was taught by the magniloquence of the morning papers to venerate the newly-acquired consequence of Mr Lomax Marscourt.' This is the first of the name changes that advertise the rise of Leonidas Lomax to social celebrity. Gore follows the Lomax Marscourts through each of their commodity-graced steps in the *Morning Post*'s 'Fashionable World': their wedding coach, 'a bright canary picked out with black, and lined with watered silk of a pearl grey'; their calling cards, 'left for their Majesties at the Pavilion yesterday'; their Sunday dinner, 'at their magnificent residence in Regency Square; including ... Lady Spunge, and the Hon. Mr. and Misses Spunge', with special attention to the lapse of the Marscourt name in a previous column, 'Among the company present on Wednesday last, at her Majesty's ball, we omitted to notice the names of Mr. and the Hon. Mrs. Lomax Marscourt'; their lease of a country estate, 'We understand that Mr. Lomax Marscourt (a near connexion of the Duke of Spalding) has taken a lease for seven, fourteen, or twenty-one years, of Courtierfield Lodge, in the neighbourhood of Windsor Forest'; their new house in town, 'Mr. Lomax Marscourt, it seems, is the purchaser of the fine mansion just completing at the north-east corner of Belgrave Square'; their house decorators, 'Messrs. Ottoman and Jos have just received a commission to furnish it in a style of Oriental magnificence'; their patronage of the arts, '"The sketch of the Battle of Bunker's Hill, ... has been purchased at the price of one hundred and seventy-five guineas by a wealthy amateur, Mr. L. Marscourt, of Courtierfield Lodge'; their order of new plate, 'We learn that Messrs. Rundell and Bridge have just sent in designs for the central group of the noble service of plate now in progress for Mr. L. Marscourt, of Belgrave Square and Courtierfield Lodge' (III, 212–14). And, finally, the triumphant success of Leonidas Lomax's acquisition of a title: 'We have the pleasure to observe, in last night's Gazette, the elevation of Mr. Lomax Marscourt to the Baronetage' (III, 216).

The signs of status that once defined the power struggles of pre-Reform Britain are sold off in post-Reform Britain to the meanest of customers. The constitutional issues that gave silver fork novels their political trenchancy are no longer news of any importance, a situation with dire consequences for the silver fork genre. The politically engaged silver fork novels of 1825 to 1841 simply come to a halt. The next generation of novels about fashionable life come unmoored from their original underpinnings. The heroine of *Rank and Beauty: or, The Young Baroness* (1856), George Eliot mockingly reports, 'by dint of reading the newspaper to her father, falls in love with the *prime minister* ... through the medium of leading articles and "the *résumé* of the debates"'.[51] A Reform-era reader might well have found this plot interesting, even provocative—and why not? A newspaper-reading heroine in the 1830s could plausibly represent a step towards constitutional change, an advancement of Great Britain towards every blessing of the 'New Aera' to come. *Rank and Beauty*, however, without any such connection to the 'whole community', becomes for George Eliot in 'Silly Novels by Lady Novelists' (1856) the author's risible example of the merest nonsense, a work long past its sell-by date.

CHAPTER 5

The topography of silver fork London

A highly respectable person, Mrs. Maxworth! Should do myself the
honour of waiting upon her in Cavendish Square more frequently,
only that my horse not being accustomed to stop at any door north
of Oxford Street, I am apprehensive of giving him a bad habit.

Puppy Parkyns, in *The Fair of Mayfair* (1832)[1]

Dickens' London is everyone's version of nineteenth-century London, an
imaginative construction of the city that has now so naturalized itself
to our way of thinking that an alternative never occurs to us. Dickens,
as James Donald suggests in his *Imagining the Modern City*, taught us
how to experience urban space by emphasizing its 'here and nowness', its
historical specificity, and most significantly, its decipherability through
social, economic and administrative networks. But Donald also suggests
a second way of writing about the modern city where the *way* of seeing,
rather than the portrayal itself, becomes the focus of the experience.[2] This
is the approach that is most productive, I would suggest, in examining
urban space in novels of fashionable life.

London is the true home of silver fork fiction. Characters may visit
the country, claim they prefer it, even claim they wish they were back
in Lancashire, but London is where they can be said to be 'at home'.
In Disraeli's novel *Henrietta Temple* (1837), the young hero, arriving in
London for the first time:

stared at the magnificence of the shops blazing with lights, and the multitude
of men and vehicles moving in all directions ... Each minute the streets seemed
to grow more spacious and brilliant, and the multitude more dense and excited.
Beautiful buildings, too, rose before him; palaces, and churches, and streets,
and squares of imposing architecture ... their route appeared a never-ending
triumph. (II, 71–2)

In Mrs Gore's *Women as They Are* (1830), when three ladies arrive at
Barnet where their coach stops for fresh horses, the magnificent view

of the city from the prominence becomes the first topic of conversation. Miss Dudley, one of the travelling ladies, has never been to London:

The carriage door having been opened during the change of horses, in spite of the cutting gales of a frosty evening ... Captain Mordaunt's bronzed and good humoured face intruded itself, to inquire after his sisters' bodily health, and Miss Dudley's mental composure.

'What an agitating moment for your feelings! Does not the first glance of yonder murky haze, springing from the distant spot, "Where reeking London's smoky cauldron simmers," fill you with delicious anticipations? Do you not already behold visions of Almack's, and the glories thereof?' (III, 37)

A newly married couple in Gore's *Pin Money* (1831) living in Mayfair's Bruton Street propose to visit her mother in Berkeley Square: 'The carriage?—oh, no!—do let us walk; it is a beautiful night, and we can take the key and cross the square to Charles-street.' The young wife puts on her shawl and they take their evening walk to her mother's house through 'the rustling lilac-bushes in Berkeley-square' (I, 56, 60). In Bulwer's *Pelham* (1828), the narrator pauses to ponder London's effect on the human spirit: 'Many are the curious places in London: it has its romantic sites, and its sublime sites, and its tremendous sites; it contains matter for endless research and endless reflection' (III, 157).

As opposed to Dickens' London of shadowy systems, the London of silver fork novels exists in the imagination of its inhabitants very much as it does for the characters in Virginia Woolf's *Mrs. Dalloway*, where a walk across St James' Park or down Victoria Street to the Army & Navy Stores becomes a state of mind produced by immediate visual cues. A comparison of two socially aspiring neighbourhoods, one in a Dickens novel and the other in a silver fork novel marks the difference. Raymond Williams in *The Country and the City* selects a passage from *Little Dorrit* (1855–57) as a typical Dickens urban description. In the passage, Dickens describes Harley Street as a stiflingly dull dinner table:[3]

Everybody knows how like the street, the two dinner-rows of people who take their stand by the street will be. The expressionless uniform twenty houses, all to be knocked at and rung at in the same form, all approachable by the same dull steps, all fended off by the same pattern of railing, all with the same impracticable fire-escapes, the same inconvenient fixtures in their heads, and everything without exception to be taken at a high valuation—who has not dined with these? (I, ch. xxi)

The *Little Dorrit* passage, says Williams, demonstrates how 'the most evident inhabitants of cities' in a Dickens novel 'are buildings ... where the house and the life being lived in it are undistinguishable'.[4]

In contrast, Catherine Gore's account of a visit to the nearby neighbourhood of Regent's Park in her novel *Pin Money* (1831) produces a rather different vision of bourgeois society. Her topographic spaces reflect the unstable social transience of her aspiring Marylebone residents:

They were now in the string of carriages leading to Mrs. Luttrell's *fête*, and within view of those elaborate festive preparations, with which persons of moderate means, moderate mansions, and an acquaintance of the moderate class, affect to rival the hospitalities of the Duke of Devonshire or Lady Londonderry. The front of a tolerably proportioned house overlooking the Regent's-park, was converted by the temporary aid of floor-cloth and tarpaulin, into a conservatory smelling more of Downing's manufactory than of roses and jessamine; while stars of ill-trimmed and variegated lamps, flaring and smoking, added their unlucky odours to the malaria of the spot. The hall of Mrs. Luttrell's abode was metamorphosed by a screen of withering laurel-branches into a rural retreat; in which some eight or ten footmen,—with the glaring liveries of the family, hanging voluminously upon the shoulders of half the gang, and betraying them as hirelings for the occasion,—exerted the utmost fury of their lungs to announce the entering guests. At the door of the ball-room stood the curtseying and overheated Mrs. Luttrell. (I, 94)

Gore gives us images conceived in a relational London geography, everything temporary and moving, and nothing like the dull stolidity of the Dickens scene. Mrs Luttrell's Regent's Park entertainment exposes itself to the fashionable standards of Mayfair elegance. The great open space of Regent's Park competes with a smelly, crowded conservatory and a withering bower in the hall that is populated by a 'gang' of footmen brought in from the streets. The hostess focuses the chaos by her 'curtseying' presentation of her 'over-heated' self. An unseemly penetration of urban markers from the street invades the house – the 'gang' of footmen, Downing's manufactory, the smoking lamps – to give it a seamy public space all its own.

London streets make social space visible in silver fork novels, both indoors and outdoors, even in the most rarefied, exclusive haunts of silver fork society. The ironic lens of the narrator's urbane, cosmopolitan eye is always scanning the streetscape for private information about public lives. As a character in Disraeli's *Henrietta Temple* (1837) observes, in these novels 'everything lives and moves' (III, 136–7).

John Nash's great Regent Street project unintentionally released the imagination of silver fork novelists to construct a fiction of Mayfair and Marylebone as opposing social and political forces in the map of Reform London. 'Crossing Oxford Street' becomes the source domain for a metaphor that embraces the political, economic and cultural jockeying of aristocratic politics of the late Regency.[5] It would be hard to account for the silver fork novel without Regent Street. The new street, many years in the planning, twelve years in the building, essentially complete by 1825, producing more 'rubbish' in the construction than all the Shakespearean commentators combined, as one fictional dandy remarks,[6] provided a glamorous setting for silver fork characters to move about in. Characters shop on Regent Street, sit for their portraits there, drop by for a look at the Cosmorama, attend scientific and mechanical exhibitions, hear concerts, drive cabriolets or simply stroll the street for pleasure. 'The Toledo of Naples, the Corso of Rome, the Rue de la Paix, and the Boulevards of Paris are really nothing to Regent Street', claimed Nathaniel Parker Willis, an American observer, on first seeing the new street in the spring of 1834.[7]

In his study, *Atlas of the European Novel, 1800–1900*, Franco Moretti demonstrates how Regent Street functions in the silver fork novel as a topographic dividing wall – silver forks to the west, Dickensians to the east.[8] As an east–west dividing wall alone, however, the description falls short of capturing the street's full critical topographical significance for the silver fork novel. Regent Street was a potent new political conduit, one that turned the cliché of the old *east–west* division of 'city and town' on its axis for a new and more subtle *north–south* political configuration, one distantly related to the old east–west axis, but made profoundly different through the imminent approach of political reform.[9]

Reading from south to north on the London map, we locate the contested social spaces of silver fork London: Westminster in the south with government and the clubs; Mayfair directly north of Piccadilly, an aristocratic stronghold; then, crossing Oxford Street into Marylebone, the domicile of the nabobs, the newly titled, the newly rich and the successful professional ranks, that is to say the home of power-in-waiting. Crossing Oxford Street in either direction – from established power in Mayfair to potential power in Marylebone, or the other way around – becomes the focus of the political and social geography of silver fork fiction.

From the start, plans for the new street recognized the political significance of this new reordering of metropolitan space. Nash's 'Plan' argues that, 'By the straight direction of this street Mary-le-bone Park [Regent's Park] is brought nearer the Houses of Parliament, Courts of Law, the Treasury, Admiralty, &c. than in many other parts of the town, in the highest request of fashion', that is Mayfair itself.[10] The topographic problem for Nash as a developer, however, lay in the busy commercial

nature of Oxford Street and, equally, in its thoroughly middle-class
reputation: 'Crossing Oxford Street has always been a fashionable objection to residence north of Oxford Street', he admits in his proposal for
the new street, but, he claims, there is a solution: 'To do away with that
impression, it is proposed, that where the continuation of Portland Place
with Oxford Street unites with the new street intended from Oxford
Street to Piccadilly ... a circus should be formed, Oxford Street crossing
it from east to west, and the new street from south to north.' He suggests
that, perhaps, if a statue could go in the middle of the circus and a colonnade continued around the circus, that in riding around the circus,
'the sensation of having passed Oxford Street will be entirely done away,
and the two divisions of the town insensibly united in the best manner
possible'.[11]

Even though Nash's proposal is a transparent exercise in real estate
promotion, including the delightful prospect of a stately parade of
coaches heading north and south through his handsome 'circus', it also
throws down a significant political gauntlet. In respect to distance to
Westminster – and 'distance is best measured by time', he reminds the
reader – the new development in Marylebone is 'within 170 yards as near
as the nearest part of Grosvenor Place ... ; it is within 80 yards as near
as the west side of Grosvenor Square, and 70 yards nearer than the upper
end of Upper Grosvenor Street; it is within 90 yards as near as Stanhope
Street; it is more than one-third of a mile nearer than Portman Square
or Manchester Square' (lii). Moreover, although nothing ever came of it,
both Nash's plan and an earlier plan by John White called for a national
memorial at the top of the street, the southern end of Regent's Park. For
Nash it was to be a public building 'to receive the statues and monuments of great and distinguished men' (xxxvii); for White, a church,
'appropriate for the interment [sic] of those eminent statesmen, warriors
and philosophers, who may at future times deserve monuments to their
memories', including 'a delightful garden' where the effigies of great men,
and other national monuments, would be placed by a government committee, this done in direct opposition, he says, to the 'greediness of the
fluctuating body' represented by the aristocratic Westminster Abbey.[12] In
effect, the Regent Street project from its beginnings envisioned a challenge to the traditional political geography of the privileged classes, now
and in immortality. T. H. Shepherd's well-known view of Lower Regent
Street, looking south over Carlton House, deliberately distorts the size of
Westminster Hall and the tower of St Margaret's to emphasize the close
relationship of the new street to the new topography of government.[13]

Opposing maps of London, however, with more egalitarian visions, offer powerful competition to the hierarchies of margin and periphery implied in Nash's new *north–south* axis of power. Contemporary guidebooks for 'the stranger', for example, turn the city into a convenient entertainment for tourists, 'such a round of delights, that the town resembles Vauxhall'.[14] *Leigh's New Picture of London* (1830), a widely disseminated London guidebook, presents organized lists of services, amenities, London monuments and sites, from St Paul's to the Opera House, Finsbury Circus to Grosvenor Square, as if each entry were of equal interest and of the same importance. The democratically formatted information and equal-sized, blocky engravings of buildings contain an implicit political message for its middle-class readers, that London is efficient, accessible, safe, and as the text proudly observes, home to 'a heterogeneous mass composed of strangers from every town and province of the United Kingdom ... and people of almost every nation in the world'.[15]

G. F. Cruchley's guidebook, *Picture of London, or Visitor's Assistant* (1831),[16] constructs a topographical fiction of London 'space as a container, a co-ordinate system of discrete and mutually exclusive locations'.[17] Cruchley's sites are keyed to numbers, the numbers to a grid, and the pleasures of the city to an implicit rating of one to ten. Unfold the map, decant the information and move on to the next view, the next entertainment or next improving experience. Streets are how you get there. The rationalized version of London's streets found in the *Picture of London* could persuade only the most naive 'stranger' of its practicality with its sturdy assertion that, 'By becoming well acquainted with the leading line of the streets [the stranger] will find his way with facility to any given place on the maps.' As for the new street, Regent Street, it features in the *Picture of London* as only one among others of equal practical value: 'The most beautiful cross communication is the new line of streets beginning at Pall mall; including Waterloo place, the Quadrant, Regent street, and Portland place, leading to the Regent's park' (p. 13). The implicit political axis of Nash's new Regent Street is not acknowledged in Cruchley's account.

Silver fork novelists found this kind of guidebook both boring and misleading: 'No doubt we shall soon have folding maps of the moon, Mogged and Tegged for the touring season', the hero of Catherine Gore's novel *Cecil* (1841) remarks contemptuously (II, 278–9). T. H. Lister's hero in *Arlington* (1832) also notes the limitations of such guidebooks as reporters of social space: 'And yet Italy is so traversed by English, who, because they have turned its chief cities into watering-places, think they are really well acquainted with the country, that this want I have mentioned is never thought of. "Who wants to hear more of Italy?" they would ask: "everybody has been there." So if they get good guide-books, as they would for Cheltenham, or the Lakes, they are satisfied' (III, 132).

The 'mental maps' that silver fork novelists call upon are not the bland, utilitarian tourist guides of Mogg and Tegg that Lister cites above, but maps adjusted to contemporary economic and political topographies.[18] Take for example, the New Road, now Euston Road, London's 'by-pass' road of the time. The New Road provided a direct and convenient east–west commuter link between the socially aspiring neighbourhood of Marylebone, situated on the northern side of Oxford Street on Nash's map of power, and the City, the source of real economic power. This road features significantly in Catherine Gore's *Women as They Are* (1830), when the old father of a banker's family, the Forsyths, now residing in Marylebone, retreats sadly to his office in the City after an outrageously expensive and disastrous Mayfair-style dinner given by his ambitious wife and daughters. Forsyth takes the commuter road to his office in the City to lick his wounds: 'James Forsyth Senr. in the agony of his disappointment, mounted his favourite mare, and jogged along the new road towards the Barbican—the Alpha and Omega of his consolation: leaving his wretched wife and daughters [in Marylebone] to encounter the yet unravelled misfortunes of the day' (III, 125). The anguish of the Marylebone ladies, together with the patriarch's distracted retreat to the City, is mapped onto the topography of the New Road. The east–west coordinates of the New Road, Marylebone (aspiring fashion) and the City (money) are sorely compromised by the north–south social jockeying between Marylebone and Mayfair represented by Regent Street.

The map-informed struggle for identity in Gore's novel, in political terms as well as social, is played out on a grand scale in the Regent's Park Colosseum in Marylebone. The Colosseum, one of the great attractions of the new park (Figure 4), housed an enormous panoramic view of London designed to attract a fashionable, well-to-do audience with its extravagant painted version of London, a handsome refreshments room and attractive gardens for strolling in the grounds. Inside the building, a 360-degree view taken from the top of St Paul's, drawn by Thomas Hornor and executed by the artist E. T. Parris, burst upon visitors as they issued from a mechanical lift onto the viewing platform.[19] Stephan Oettermann describes the huge painting in *The Panorama: History of a Mass Medium* as being like 'an optical inventory, a catalogue of countless objects, down to the smallest house' – concluding curtly, 'the view of

THE COLOSSEUM IN 1827. *(Front to the Regent's Park.)* THE PANORAMA OF LONDON.

Figure 4 *The Colosseum in 1827* and *The Panorama of London*

a real estate agent'.[20] The promoters provided telescopes in imitation of those on the viewing platform at St Paul's for visitors to use for examining details of the painting. Hornor's panorama by report created a striking optical illusion, even to causing height giddiness in some viewers.[21] In fact James Elmes, a contemporary architectural critic, argued that the Colosseum's panoramic depiction of London was actually *better* than the original, 'for the prospect from the iron gallery of the cathedral is so often dimmed and obscured by the smoke and vapour which hangs over the city, that it is very uncertain when to obtain a clear prospect, except at those very early hours in the morning when access cannot be had'.[22]

Rob Shields' analysis of the West Edmonton Mall in Edmonton, Canada, with its Arc de Triomphe and other icons of great world capitals, helps explain the social magic of the Colosseum's panorama: 'This is not done with the ethic of "We are giving you the reproduction so that you will want the original" but rather "We are giving you the reproduction so you will no longer feel any need for the original".'[23] The effect of Shields' 'dis-placed sense of place', both for the visitor to the West Edmonton Mall and, I would argue, for the Reform-era visitor to the Regent's Park panorama, is to remove provincial Edmonton and Regent's Park, Marylebone, from the margins of power to the centre of power. The 'virtual' view from St Paul's, now happily situated in the elegant new Colosseum in Regent's Park, cleanses the City of its money-grubbing associations and is thus 'better' than its original. The old east–west social divisions of Town and City are simply 'disappeared' by the painting.

In a visual tour de force, the viewer of Hornor's panorama was able to see at the edges of its horizon (perhaps with the help of one of those useful telescopes) the very building in which he was standing, the Colosseum itself.[24] Then, by climbing two more sets of stairs, the visitor would be ushered onto an outdoor platform at the top of the Colosseum's dome to be presented with yet another 360-degree panorama, a 'real' one this time, but with the Colosseum now sited at the empowered centre of the panoramic view, and St Paul's and the City forced to the margins. It was a paradox the visitor could experience with his eyes and his feet: first, Hornor's indoor panorama with its patent fiction to which the 'giddy' visitor accedes, and then, second, the outdoor panorama of London seen from the top of the Colosseum with another, competing knowledge in play, a fiction still of course, and just as pressing in its claims to power as that of the first. Rather than an opposition, however, the two views are actually bland, self-congratulatory affirmations of the same absolutist panoramic topography. The newly politicized northern suburbs of

Marylebone and City money exchange a satisfying conspiratorial wink with the City itself – a 'done deal' of new power, appropriately enough enacted on the spot, across Oxford Street, in Marylebone – the political reason for Nash's new map of London.[25]

This is the mapping context that silver fork novels examine by opposing two fictions of urban space – an aristocratic as-seen-from-Mayfair London set against a middle-class moneymaking London. As one dreadful old Mayfair harridan expresses it in Catherine Gore's *Pin Money* (1831), 'There ought to be a Pict's-wall built up to support us against the incursions of such hordes of barbarians … I would sooner see every descendant of my house stretched in their grave, than disgraced by a commercial alliance' (1, 301).

Raymond Williams' analysis of the political geography of Jane Austen's novels helps place the political programme of the silver fork novels in its spatial context.[26] Williams argues that Austen's novels focus on personal conduct, and, that within a complex system of estates, incomes and social position, personal conduct is seen to create a bridge linking private moral order and social order. The price to pay for this order, he maintains, is the confinement of social settings to 'country houses and their families … to a single tradition: that of the cultivated rural gentry'.[27] If in Austen's *Pride and Prejudice*, Meryton and Longbourn or Lucas Lodge and Netherfield Park possess the power to represent relationships between private and public order, other kinds of order, argues Williams, 'must be converted to these signs of order to be recognized at all'.[28]

This is the conversion in silver fork novels, though to a different, if related social order, that links the personal and public spatial order of these novels to Jane Austen's. It is as if the immediate post-Austen authors of the 1820s and 1830s gather up Austen's characters in a box, take them to London, give them an elevation in rank and drop them onto the London map of Westminster, Mayfair and Marylebone to make their way up or down Regent Street as best they can. The familiar characters of Austen's novels struggle to establish a London social identity analogous to the one they left behind in the country. These characters, now with addresses in Brook Street, Grosvenor Square, Portman Square, Harley Street and Portland Place and, with the newly acquired manners of urban exclusives, look anxiously over their shoulders for direction from that lost world described by Raymond Williams.

Streets become the way of construing the world. Streets become the way to match the body, face, dress and rank of a character to a symbolic topography. A City man is summed up by his workplace: 'The face of the man was common-place and ordinary; one sees a hundred such, every day, in Fleet-street or the "Change"' (Bulwer, *Pelham*, III, 85). A middle-class visitor to Cheltenham: 'that tall meagre youth in the blue frock coat, and the buff waistcoat ... puts me in mind of ... a dish made in Bloomsbury Square' (*Pelham*, II, 38–9). The wealthy commercial family gets placed firmly in their topography by a snobbish aristocrat: 'Sir Somebody Westland;—one of our commercial upstarts—as rich as the Bank, and as vulgar as Oxford Street' (Gore, *Mothers and Daughters*, III, 195). Streets are for distinguishing social identity and position. As Pelham tells his friend, Sir Reginald Glanville, 'I make it a rule never to drive out with a badly dressed friend; take time, and I will let you accompany me' (I, 78–9). But they are also for private conversations, for political deals, for making social contacts that would be inconceivable indoors. Remarkably little occurs in private in silver fork novels. The hero of Theodore Hook's *Jack Brag* (1837) simply rents the door, nothing more, of a great house in Grosvenor Street and meets his friends at his Club: 'My name is on the door, and my address is on the card', he boasts to his old mother (I, 7). In silver fork novels things tend to happen on the way to some place, or on entering or leaving that place. For privacy, the heroine in Gore's *Pin Money* goes to Regent's Park to weep (II, 99–100); the hero of Disraeli's *Vivian Grey* goes to Kensington Gardens for the same purpose, there being no other really private place available in his very public world (II, 217).

In silver fork novels, movement is what the reader watches for. Identity is defined from the body's space outwards, oddly like Adrienne Rich's formulation in 'Notes towards a Politics of Location', where she argues paradoxically that the relativity of location in geographical and social terms establishes social identity, and, at the same time, challenges the fixity of rules that establish those spaces.[29] This is the condition of identity for the Dandy in silver fork fiction and his primary role – to disarrange social expectations. The Dandy travels and reports, assigns names and categories like a travelling anthropologist or a writer of guidebooks, but, rather than fixing space as middle-class guidebooks do, his accounts throw these spaces into instability, causing new spaces and new social arrangements to emerge.

In the early novels of fashionable life, between 1825 and 1830, there is excitement in the air of impending political change, of power in movement and speed, of space as negotiable. During a tedious carriage ride into Suffolk, the hero of Bulwer's *Pelham* (1828) reads political dispatches of 'what is going on' (II, 236), and on the return journey he reflects on the different social spaces of country and city: 'The man who is meek, generous, benevolent, and kind in the country, enters the scene of contest, and becomes forthwith fiery or mean, selfish or stern, just as if the virtues were only for solitude, and the vices for the city' (III, 103). Disappointed in his political contrivances, all of them arranged in the privacy of long walks in the streets with numerous political movers and shakers, Pelham calls for his horse, and heads for another part of London: 'I ... felt the free wind freshening over my fevered cheek, and turned my rein toward the green lanes that border the great city on its western side' (III, 136). Personal identities are attached to movement through the city's social spaces: 'Do as you please, Sir Reginald', says the villainous blackmailer in *Pelham*, lolling impudently on the 'costly ottoman' in Sir Reginald's rooms in Pall Mall, 'It's not a long walk from hence to Bow-street, nor a long swing from Newgate to the gallows' (III, 218).

The threat for Sir Reginald, and indeed the running irony of silver fork novels, is the actual *instability* of space in Reform London. Dinosaurs like the old duchess in *Pin Money*, cited above, are adamant that nothing will or should change their Mayfair entitlements to power and status, but silver fork novelists view the world as seen from Mayfair as a limited and comic version of contemporary reality. Catherine Gore particularly is fond of satirizing aristocratic Mayfair's grandiloquent trajectories of the city's space. In Gore's story 'The Separate Maintenance', from *The Fair of Mayfair* (1832), gossip travels 'the town from Bryanston Square to Storey's Gate, gathering matter like a snow-ball by the way' – that is, not so heroically far, except in the minds of the gossiping matrons (II, 28). And in 'The Special License', from the same collection, one particularly obnoxious young woman, a parvenue, explains how she avoids her country neighbours in London: 'Fortunately they live in some place at the other extremity of the globe—Russell Square I believe,—so that we never have the misfortune of meeting them' (III, 327).

On the other hand, Gore's mockery of Mayfair pretensions contains a profound contemporary truth, that the representative middle-class spaces despised by Mayfair exclusives have more political and social significance than they can simply understand. The heroine's eccentric aunt, Olivia Tadcaster, in *Pin Money*, meets Lady Lotus, an acquaintance from north of Oxford Street (Marylebone), the 'wrong' side, during her morning calls to visit a new bride in Park Lane (Mayfair): 'I fully intended calling on you this morning', she tells Lady Lotus, 'if I could possibly manage to get so far as Portland-place. But really, it is *so* far out of one's beat that I can seldom accomplish the journey; and I keep a little by-list of

my East Indian friends,—the directors' wives,—and one or two Calcutta
people such as Lady Cabob and Mrs Budgerow whom I picked up one
autumn in Cheltenham,—so that I may contrive to strike them all off
in one morning.' Lady Olivia, pleading prior commitments in Mayfair,
'in Arlington-street, in the civilized part of town', innocently compounds
her insult. The Empire strikes back in Lady Lotus' pointed reply: '"Next
to these charming Park-lane residences," she observed ... "I must say I
prefer an airy quarter, such as the immediate vicinity of Regent's-park.
The Duke of Droneham, who frequently calls on me in his daily drive,
is always envying our situation; and old Lady Borenough declares she
should expect to live for ever, if she resided in Portland-place"' (III, 20–1).
Broadly comic as this confrontation between established privilege and
nabob aspiration may be, the scene implicitly acknowledges that the
politicized urban space envisioned by Nash's new development of London
topography deserves better representation than the condescending notice
given it by Lady Olivia.[30]

Addresses are a *serious* laughing matter, as T. H. Lister suggests in his
novel *Herbert Lacy* (1828): '"Tell me your company, and I will tell you
what you are," says an adage of no mean wisdom, but London would
seem to scorn such extensive data, and limits the inquiry to "Tell me your
street"' (III, 79). Lister's ostensible purpose in his novel is to minimize
the 'trivial distinctions' of address, but his choice of imagery belies the
intent: 'Look at the dense throng of London society, and this will furnish
the explanation. It is a scene of desperate rivalry, where crowds press on
like mariners from a wreck, filling to the utmost the frail boats that are
to bear them to the shore, and each feeling that he should be safe if his
neighbour were drowned' (III, 79).

'It would be possible', writes Lister, 'to make out a scale of the comparative gentility of the streets and squares.' Listing the most prominent squares in descending order, he produces his proof: 'St. James's and
Grosvenor-squares would look down like rival potentates from a proud
height of dignity on their humbler brethren of Berkeley, Hanover, and
Portman; and these in return may discharge their contempt on the minor
northern fry of Cavendish, Manchester, Bryanston, and Montague' (III,
77–8). When an aspiring social riser falls on bad times, the hierarchical topography of London's streets and squares are there to measure his
fall. He must move his family to 'a quarter which, in the flippancy of
his more prosperous days, he would have called the Polar regions'. The
dreaded region is defined by its street address: 'It was one of the Alpha
Cottages, separated widely from the habitable part of the west-end by

that *impassable* barrier, the New Road', now called Euston Road (III, 48).[31]

Catherine Gore provides a scene in *Mothers and Daughters* (1831), her most intensely address-conscious novel, which captures a strong whiff of the battle smoke. Lady Maria Willingham, the ultimate termagant mother, has managed to manoeuvre her establishment from 'a damp cottage at Chiswick' to a moderately respectable address in Seymour Street in order to give her two daughters a good shot at finding an aristocrat in the marriage market. The girls are as predatory and address-conscious as their mother. One of them rather sharply informs her uncle, a general and colonial governor, formerly of Portland Place (flashy), but now living in Portman Square (highly respectable), that he mistakes rank hierarchies in planning a dinner with a mixed-guest list that includes the extra-fashionable Duke of Lisborough as proper company for a banking family, the Westlands, old friends of the General's from his days of residence in Portland Place. 'Good God! You surely do not think of such a thing!' says Eleanor, 'Men who were never dreamt of on the southern side of Oxford-street!' He retorts with a list of Mr Westlands' public accomplishments: 'a distinguished officer in his Majesty's service ..., a Director of the Honourable East India Company ..., a banker of considerable eminence [and] married to the niece of the late Attorney General'. '"My dear uncle," interrupted Eleanor, who was less in awe of the General than either her mother or sister, "what are all these people to the Duke? He never heard of them, nor *will* ever hear of them in the course of his existence! Except in such places as Bedford-square, or Devonshire-place, the Westland family rank among the nonentities of the earth ... The Duke of Lisborough never finds himself among strangers, and he would consider it an affront to be invited among a tribe of Hottentots like the Westlands"' (I, 270). Lady Willingham and her daughters are, of course, profoundly mistaken in their political and social principles and find themselves at the conclusion of the novel 'wintering in Brighton'.

Lady Scott's novel, *A Marriage in High Life* (1828), suggests the intensity of class feelings captured in silver fork addresses. The novel opens with a marriage: 'by special license, at her father's house in Harley Street, Emmeline Benson to Ernest, Lord Fitzhenry, only son of the Earl of Arlingford of Grosvenor Square' (I, I). Emmeline's father, 'an opulent city merchant and banker', considers his daughter's move from Harley Street, Marylebone, to Grosvenor Street, Mayfair, a triumph. The marriage ends with the very public adultery of Lord Fitzhenry and Emmeline's return from Grosvenor Street to her father's home in Harley Street. Old

Mr Benson, outraged by such aristocratic immorality, demands that Emmeline accompany him back to Grosvenor Street for a complete explanation: 'And, after striking his cane several times with impatience on the bottom of the carriage, he suddenly, as if he thought greater speed would relieve his feelings, bade the coachman drive faster. This injunction was the means of bringing them into Grosvenor-square' (II, 110–11). North-of-Oxford-Street invades south-of-Oxford-Street with the moral upper hand and financial clout as well. 'I am not the fool he takes me for', Mr Benson tells his daughter, 'I am not to be coaxed by a few civil speeches from a lord into a mean forbearance. A fortnight more, and I shall most assuredly visit his lordship, and he shall see whom he has to deal with' (II, 164). The reversal of the social, economic and moral power field provides a striking reinscription of political priorities on the map of London. The traditional moneyed City of the old east–west City–Town power structure has asserted itself aggressively and with moral authority on the north–south Marylebone–Mayfair axis of Regent Street.

Catherine Gore, in 'The Special License' in *The Fair of Mayfair* (1832) uses the new Regent Street axis to present a freshly mapped picture of Reform London. Mr Maxworth, a businessman of Cavendish Square, a north-of-Oxford-Street address, disapproves heartily of his son's proposed match to an aristocrat: 'You may persuade Lady Emma Aston to a temporary adoption of the habits of a banker's wife; but you will find her recur at last to all the pomps and vanities of Boscawen Castle' (III, 268–9). It turns out that the aristocratic Lady Emma is the perfect daughter-in-law whose principles are exactly consonant with the old man's. The marriage takes place with his heartfelt blessings, and, 'Among all the Maxworths and Astons ... every individual of "both their houses,"—and of St James's Square or Cavendish,—was now arrayed in smiles' (III, 350). Lady Emma and young Edward Maxworth are folded into the political and social consequences of the marriage of two London squares – one north of Oxford Street, Cavendish Square and commerce, the other one south of Oxford Street, St James' and aristocratic prestige – the perfect united image of the Whig political nation.

Four years later, the points of the silver fork urban map shift again, and Catherine Gore's novels are there to frame new Whig political alliances on London's topography. In *Mrs. Armytage: or, Female Domination* (1836), Gore follows the movement of her scarcely middle-class heroine, Marian Baltimore, from a third-rate Baker Street address to the home of her superlatively parvenue aunt, Mrs Dyke Robsey in Portland Place (an ultra-Marylebone address), whose husband is a wizened, befuddled old nabob with a seat in Parliament. Arthur Armytage, the son of the fearsome Mrs Armytage of the title, falls in love with Marian, the Baker Street/Portland Place girl, marries her and takes her home to Holywell, the Armytage country estate, where she is lorded over and abused by his despotic mother who has control of the estate and the family purse strings. The rule of Mrs Armytage, who tyrannizes in local county governance and under the domestic roof, is brought to an end when her claim to the estate is discovered to be false – a hidden codicil to Arthur's grandfather's will surfaces. Arthur takes his place as the legal owner of the estate and the long-suffering Marian ascends to her rightful position as lady of Holywell. The British names of Arthur, Marian and Holywell unite as an apotheosis of the Whig electorate – a coalition of Holywell (the gentry) and Baker Street (the middle classes, colonial money and Irish connections). Gore's symbolic combination reflects an idealized version of the very political coalition supporting the Whig government in 1836 – a fragile, unpopular mix of exactly these political forces.

But Mrs Gore's relocation of her spatial discourse away from London and back to the countryside suggests that the novel of fashionable life, essentially urban, is in serious trouble. Mrs Gore had experimented briefly in two earlier stories with the potential of representative power in the London suburbs. 'The Flirt of Ten Seasons' and 'The Separate Maintenance', both in *The Fair of Mayfair* (1832), send her heroes and heroines respectively to Putney and Fulham for education and moral training. She returns her characters to town after their sterling moral qualities are formed in these suburbs, to relocate them on the silver fork map at addresses both north and south of Oxford Street. The aristocracy, the wealthy professional classes, the government and the landed gentry are thus renewed with generous applications of suburban diligence and honesty.

Gore, however, returns to London urban space sensationally in 1841, with her novel *Cecil: or, the Adventures of a Coxcomb*, of which a contemporary critic writes, 'There never was a novel written at such a slapping pace.'[32] The narrator-protagonist, Cecil Danby, tells his story from the vantage of memory, beginning with his brilliant entrance into London society in 1810 (when Carlton House favoured the Whigs),[33] through his service in the Peninsular campaign of 1813 (which appals him), to the victory celebrations of 1814 (when Carleton House was, deplorably, Tory), to the Irish Charity Ball of 1822, and finally to the court guide, *The Red Book* of 1825, when Cecil consents to become a courtier to George IV, a conclusion he greets as a sad and wry personal defeat. In this novel, Gore chronicles the dissolution of the silver fork topography – Nash's imagined London – that had given life to the fictions of Bury, Lister, Disraeli, Bulwer and her own novels. In particular she laments its loss of power to represent the great political alliances of the day through its significant relational topography.

Cecil's family home in Hanover Square, south of Oxford Street, begins as an active political household, with Lord Ormington, Cecil's father, a Whig, spending his evenings at Parliament, and his mother enjoying a bustling aristocratic social life. The saga ends in dilapidations, Lord Ormington self-exiled in two rooms of the Hanover Square house, Lady Ormington tucked away in her private room with her patent medicines and her stuffed dog, and the Ormington children scattered over the political spaces of London. Julia, the red-headed sister, lives in Westminster with her husband, a civil servant, hardly ever appearing in Mayfair society. John, the elder brother, has a house in Connaught Place, only yards from Mayfair across the Edgware Road, but at 'the extremity of the world!' cries his mother. Cecil is a courtier, 'a state treasure … like the Houghton Pictures', and, at the time of the writing of his autobiography, 1840–1, he spends his evenings with his brother John, now widowed and a recluse.

The early promise of cultural renewal in an enlarged franchise headed by aristocratic leadership, the vision of politically liberal silver fork novels during the heady days of Reform, fails utterly. 'I saw clearly that the Kingdom of Dandyism was in its Lower Empire', writes Cecil. 'As coming events cast their shadows before them, one felt already, even in the early part of the reign of George IV, a weary chill of mind and body, foreshadowing the age of utilitarianism' (III, 168). The political and social topography of silver fork fiction, always unstable and ever moving, retreats before that chilly vision. The future that Cecil laments is, as Gore implies, a cultural and political retreat into the lifeless space of guidebooks and real estate maps. Instead of pursuing the dandy's mission of challenging, changing and altering the map of London, Cecil settles into living death as a courtier in the train of George IV – but not without an exhortation to future historians of the novel.

The great political order embodied in Nash's Regent Street retreats to another age, a nostalgic programme much more closely allied to Jane Austen's world than to Dickens'. Nash and the silver fork novelists, however, have the last word. In a delightful vision of the tenacious symbolic power of Nash's Regent Street, Cecil imagines the triumphal return of Brummel's body from France: 'It would never surprise me to find the ashes of the great ex-dandy fetched home from Caen, as those of Napoleon have been from St. Helena, to be interred at the foot of the Duke of York's column; on the identical spot where he initiated the Prince into the mysteries of Roman punch' (1, 224–5). With the Duke of York's column at the southern culmination of Regent Street, Catherine Gore resurrects the ghostly presence of Carlton House with its quintessentially urbane memories inscribed on the streetscape itself – constructing, in the classic silver fork manner, the public landscape of a private disaster. In effect, Gore's last novel of the Reform era, *Cecil*, concludes with the ever-transient geopolitical vision of the novel of fashionable life situated precisely where it all began, in Regent Street itself.

CHAPTER 6

Reform and the silver fork heroine

> She had an extensive duty to perform; she would rest her ambition
> on performing it with skill,—her immortal hopes on performing it
> without offence.
>
> Sybella Woodford, Lady Farnley, in *The Sketch Book* (1833)[1]

Authors of silver fork novels were confronted with a poignant confusion
of roles for their aristocratic heroines. The political combination of aristocratic and middle-class power that emerged during the Reform years
caused a major reassessment of the role of the titled heroine, her self-
presentation, her language, her social identity, indeed her function in a
novel. The heroine's glittering raiment of privilege would have to be shed
for more modest weeds of respectability, for the sober colours of her new
middle-class allies. The transition from the silver fork novel's pre-Reform
aristocratic woman, 'her existence was all Watteau', to the post-Reform
heroine, 'a plain, rational, common-sensical ... agreeable girl', was not
to be an easy or untroubled process.[2] Cultural pressures and the political
exigencies of reform sent novelists of fashionable life back to the study for
new designs to strengthen foundations that were fast crumbling away.

At the Glorious Revolution of 1688, when power moved from the Court
to Parliament, the language and manners of the Court came along too.
'Politeness discourse' formerly associated with courtly manners was now
considered the idiom most suitable to the new authority, the aristocratic
powers in charge of the country.[3] This discourse also descended to the
middle classes as the 'politeness' rhetoric of public opinion. The *Tatler*,
the *Guardian* and the *Spectator*, for example, assumed the social, political
and philosophical legacy of 'politeness discourse' as belonging to all 'the
Politer part of Great Britain', 'the elegant and knowing part of Mankind',
'the Quality', 'the better sort', and of course the middle-class readers of
these journals.[4]

'Politeness discourse' carried a wide range of meanings, but in early
eighteenth-century England it was identified primarily with rhetorical

performance, 'a dextrous management of our Words and Actions, whereby we make other people have better Opinions of us and themselves', a skill traditionally most potent at the highest levels of politics and diplomacy.[5] As an act of refined sociability, conversation was its highest art, the 'art of pleasing in company', for which such qualities as 'courtesy', 'civility' and 'politeness' were the leading ideals. Peter France in his 'Introduction' to *Politeness and Its Discontents* considers 'politeness' a culturally rich heritage indeed: 'I use the word', he writes, 'in its broad eighteenth-century sense to mean not only polite manners but something like what we call civilization ... an interrelated set of values which together define a certain ideal of modern European society and culture.'[6] Lawrence Klein in *Shaftesbury and the Culture of Politeness* argues that 'politeness' was to become the 'master metaphor' for all the great public issues that were absorbed into its wide social register. 'It enabled a moralized and politicized view of culture', writes Klein, that made it possible for 'those without formal political power' to exert their influence on the power centres of their culture.[7]

In other words, the 'semantic limpness' we now experience in the term 'politeness' must be re-evaluated.[8] Politeness discourse is not *mere* performance, a fine curtsey or a tip of the hat, but a rhetorical idiom employed where civility is itself the language of power. Threadbare remnants of it continue today with 'My Honourable Friend from Across the Aisle' or 'The Distinguished Representative from the State of Alaska'.

As the eighteenth century wore on, however, the discourse of politeness, or 'the art of pleasing', began to sit uncomfortably, as Michèle Cohen argues, with British 'manliness'.[9] A proper discourse of 'manliness', as Cohen paraphrases its defenders, should display the 'native plain, rough manners' and 'unpolished integrity' of the 'Ancient Briton'.[10] For British males, 'politeness discourse' would be consigned to the rubbish bin as 'Frenchified effeminacy', a sign of dissipation, insincerity and dissimulation, the idiom of fops, dandies, aristocrats and exclusive society – the *ton*.

By the late part of the eighteenth and the early nineteenth century any sign of 'politeness discourse' employed by men held an ambiguous status in conversation, perhaps not quite 'manly'. A proper example of its antithesis, *masculine* discourse, occurs in Jane Austen's *Emma* (1815) when the two Knightley brothers meet after a long separation: '"How d'ye do, George?" and "John, how are you?" succeeded in the true English style, burying under a calmness that seemed all but indifference, the real attachment which would have led either of them, if requisite, to do every thing for the good of the other' (I, ch. 12). In the same novel, naive Miss Bates is a great admirer of Frank Churchill's 'extreme politeness', as she calls it.[11] Mr Knightley tries to warn Emma against it. "'No, Emma"', he says, "'your amiable young man can be amiable only in French, not in English. He may be very 'aimable,' have very good manners, and be very agreeable; but he can have no English delicacy towards the feelings of other people: nothing really amiable about him"' (I, ch. 18).

The great problem for silver fork novelists and for their heroines, as Cohen suggests, arises from a divergence in discourses appropriate to men and appropriate to women – the 'discourse of civic humanism', rational and plain and public, goes to the men, and the 'discourse of politeness', the art of pleasing, is left to their women where it hangs on tenaciously as the 'desire to please', self-effacement, softness and 'the graces'.[12] Silver fork novelists had to assume or hope that history would grant their heroines one last performance of public power residing in this discourse. Their accomplishments would need a shift in priorities, with 'conversation' reinstated as the first and most important.

Jane Austen wrestles with politeness discourse for women in *Pride and Prejudice* (1813) when she has Mr Darcy rephrase Mr Bingley's teasing mockery of women's accomplishments – 'They all paint tables, cover screens, and net purses.' "'Your list of the common extent of accomplishments," said Darcy, "has too much truth. The word is applied to many a woman who deserves it no otherwise than by netting a purse, or covering a screen."' Caroline Bingley, always vigilant for Darcy's attention, leaps in with an enlarged curriculum: "'A woman must have a thorough knowledge of music, singing, drawing, dancing, and the modern languages, to deserve the word"', she announces, adding a few extra 'accomplishments' that a modern reader might be tempted to dismiss, unwisely, as snobbery pure and simple – "'she must possess a certain something in her air and manner of walking, the tone of her voice, her address and expressions, or the word will be but half deserved"' (I, ch. 8). Darcy does not hesitate to confirm the entire list, including Miss Bingley's self-interested addition. "'All this she must possess"', he says.

Miss Bingley has a point. Her list is solidly traditional as a programme designed to fit aristocratic women for taking an active part in polite society or 'power' society. Darcy's addition to her list, 'the improvement of her mind by extensive reading', is even more so. Elizabeth's firm middle-class rejection of Darcy's 'politeness' programme, 'I am no longer surprised at your knowing *only* six accomplished women' (I, ch. 8), will become a more difficult position for her to maintain than she understands. Even Miss

Bingley's smug recommendation of 'air of manner and walking', 'tone of voice' and 'address and expressions', as Cohen observes of politeness discourse, requires a rigorous 'self-control and discipline of both body and tongue',[13] sterling values that Elizabeth must ruefully acknowledge when she 'reflected how materially' her own 'credit' must be hurt by the repeated 'impropriety of conduct' of her nearest relatives (II, ch. 13).

From 1825 to 1830, the aristocratic heroines of silver fork novels written by male novelists – Ward, Normanby, Lister, Disraeli and Bulwer – are known to the reader more by their reputation and their social status than by their active presence in the novels. The hero admires the heroine for her elegance, her beauty, her charm and her sweetness and sometimes for her wisdom, but readers know her only at second hand. By 1832, most of the men writing these novels leave the silver fork genre behind. Whatever they formerly had to say about politics in their novels could now be said more plainly in Parliament and government, which is exactly where Bulwer, Disraeli, Lister and Lord Normanby were to take their careers. After 1830 the women authors more or less had the genre to themselves, even more so after the 1832 passage of the Reform Bill. Any serious departures from traditional feminine 'politeness' in their novels had to be treated with great caution. In real life too, a diversion from the expected 'politeness' rituals could start an outcry of surprising intensity.[14]

A. E. Chalon's double sketch of Maria Malibran (Figure 5) the blazing star of Italian opera in the late 1820s and 1830s, records a scandalous event that took place in the London opera season of 1829. Malibran appears in the upper left-hand corner of the sketch posed as a glamorous member of the opera audience, her opera glass in hand and her gaze fixed on the performance. On the opposite side, Malibran appears again, but this time in her opera costume as a lame, bedraggled and ancient crone. 'After playing Fidelma [*sic*] in Cimarosa's opera Il Matrimonio Segreto,' Chalon explains in a note on the sketch, 'Malibran went into a Pit box to see the Ballet, or rather to afford the Public a better opportunity of appreciating her powers of transformation.' The opera star's double appearance as a performer *and* as a member of polite society created a major stir: 'To see a lady of twenty-two or so … disfigure her spirited, intellectual countenance … to witness such a transformation', wrote a horrified critic in the *New Monthly Magazine* (1829), 'was a feature in the cast of characters which few of the audience were prepared for … This preposterous travesty can only be regarded as a wayward freak of caprice.'[15]

Malibran's caprice might well have disturbed a conservative, politeness-distinguished society anxious about its own prospects for the

Figure 5 *Spettatrice – Attrice* (1830), by A. E. Chalon

future – Catholics already in Parliament, Dissenters too, Jews knocking at the door, Whigs stirring up the middle classes, Radicals doing it with the working classes. As Fred Inglis notes so aptly in his recent study *A Short History of Celebrity*, it was the Reform Act that first propelled into future years of the nineteenth century the *theatre* of revolution, 'the march, the demonstration, the staged rehearsal of slogans, the flag, the masses', as a way of embodying 'the public narrative of politics'.[16] A twenty-two-year-old woman acting as if she were in control of her own destiny was bound to turn heads. 'From the first hour when Maria Garcia [Malibran] appeared on the stage', writes Henry Chorley, a contemporary witness, 'it was evident that a new artist, as original as extraordinary, was come—one by Nature endowed, not merely with physical powers, but also with that inventive, energetic, rapid genius before which obstacles become as nothing, and by aid of which the sharpest contradictions can be reconciled.'[17] Constitutional change was a desperate thing to contemplate, but a young woman altering her social role at will was a 'preposterous travesty'. Clearly women were being watched and their public performances interpreted as metaphors of social order. Malibran's double-performance struck contemporaries immediately as an aggressive social misstep.

For aristocratic heroines in novels of fashionable life in the 1830s, the celebrity power granted them by wealth and titles was an opportunity for silver fork authors to give them a political presence through public and semi-public performances of aristocratic 'politeness discourse'. Three especially significant aspects of performance were available – first, the heroine's skilled accomplishments, not necessarily private, her singing, playing an instrument, drawing and most significant, her accomplishments in conversation; second, the heroine's display-performance at the Opera, gloriously framed and held aloft in the opera box, a secular monstrance of aristocratic power; third, in home theatricals depicted in the novels, a real-life feature of aristocratic households regularly reported in the *Morning Post*'s accounts of the plays, charades and home-produced mini-operas of society's most exclusive denizens.

ACCOMPLISHMENTS

Ironically, by Jane Austen's time, 'accomplishments' had become novelistic shorthand for the disparagement not only of women's education, but often of their intellect as well. In *Pride and Prejudice*, Mr Bennet's request to his daughter Mary at a Netherfield gathering that she set aside her tedious pianoforte performance announces the depth to which 'politeness discourse' and the 'art of pleasing' had sunk: 'That will do extremely well, child', says Mr Bennet, 'You have delighted us long enough. Let the other young ladies have time to exhibit' (i, ch. 18).

Elizabeth must nevertheless display her 'accomplishments' on a visit to Rosings. Darcy moves towards the pianoforte to gain an opportunity for conversation. 'I certainly have not the talent which some people possess, of conversing easily with those I have never seen before', he confesses to Elizabeth almost at once, 'I cannot catch their tone of conversation, or appear interested in their concerns, as I often see done.' Elizabeth responds with an illustrated lesson in the art of 'politeness discourse', which classically belongs to women in polite society, as Michèle Cohen explains, as their duty to assist in the construction of men's refinement.[18] As Elizabeth does so, her rhetorical rhythms echo Darcy's:

'My fingers,' said Elizabeth, 'do not move over this instrument in the masterly manner which I see so many women's do. They have not the same force or rapidity, and do not produce the same expression. But then I have always supposed it to be my own fault—because I would not take the trouble of practicing. It is not that I do not believe *my* fingers as capable as any other woman's of superior execution.'

Darcy provides a heart-stopping moment of 'politeness discourse' in return. 'You are perfectly right', he says to Elizabeth and smiles: 'We neither of us *perform* to strangers' (emphasis added, II, ch. 8). Darcy's spontaneous offer of *his* performance as the complement to *her* performance may be the only genuinely erotic exchange he and Elizabeth have in the entire novel – if Elizabeth could only hear it.[19] It is also a demonstration of how the 'art of pleasing', the old 'politeness discourse', could become a potential fund of power for silver fork heroines.

Accomplishments, who has them and who has not, would prove a useful gauge for silver fork novelists in marking the changing fortunes of reform politics. A gentleman in Lister's *Granby* (1826), for example, teases the heroine with mock instructions in fashionable politeness, 'I hope you do not sing or play, or draw, or do anything that every body else does.' She confesses, 'I do a little—very little—in each.' He replies, 'I'm afraid you are accomplished.' That she denies, and asks him, 'What accomplishments do you allow to be tolerable?' '"Let me see," said he, with a look of consideration ... "You may *not* sing a note of Rossini; nor sketch gateposts and donkeys after nature. You may sit to a harp; but you need not play it. You must not paint miniatures nor copy Swiss costumes. But you may manufacture any thing—from a cap down to a pair of shoes—always remembering that the less useful your work the better"' (I, 95–8). The Miss Cliftons in *Granby* possess exactly these accomplishments: 'like those of most other girls: they sang, played, drew, rode, read occasionally, spoiled much muslin, manufactured purses, handscreens, and reticules for a repository, and transcribed a considerable quantity of music, out of large fair print into diminutive manuscript' (I, 103–4). In Catherine Gore's *Mothers and Daughters* (1830) a woman's needle-work is deemed as necessary for the ultra-exclusives as for the middle classes, but the French-educated daughters of the novel's title cheat on this one, setting out 'unfinished specimens of *broderie*' for admiration, '*chef d'oeuvres* of the needle ... purchased of an indigent *brodeuse* of the *Rue Vivienne*' (I, 131), according to the reports of their dearest friends.

As public debate on political reform gains ground in 1829–30, readers of silver fork novels begin to see politeness discourse take on a respectable, middle-class spirit. Mr Leslie Winyard, a notorious seducer in Lady Bury's *The Exclusives* (1830), whispers to Lady Glenmore, praising her delightful accomplishment in singing duets. 'For instance', he says in soft tones, 'how very much more enchanting it is to be singing a duet with you, than sitting at an opera, hearing the artificial execution of those who sing by profession! For surely the true intention of music is that it should express our own feelings.' Lady Glenmore answers with great care. 'There was a secret sense of genuine purity in her heart, which made her dislike the license of his gaze', and 'fixing her eyes on him with all the composure of perfect innocence', she rejects him firmly in the coded language of 'politeness discourse': 'It is very delightful to me to go to the Opera', she says to her insinuating companion, 'and the perfect finish of the singing of professional people teaches me to improve my own' (I, 61–2).

A Reform heroine's choice of the music she sings or plays acquires a pointed political significance. In *The Exclusives* Lady Glenmore, a Whig, must perform before an audience made up of a large group of hostile Tory women. She chooses a piece from Handel, highly respectable, English-by-adoption, 'not like your French frippery'.[20] 'And though she began unwillingly', the proper modest posture, 'all the men were in unfeigned raptures'. She is exceedingly careful not to *exhibit*: 'Once or twice Lady Glenmore paused when there was a change in the movement, and half rose, saying, "This is too long, you will be tired;"—but she was permitted a *douce* violence, and, reseating herself, finished the whole *scena*' (III, 70). That is well done indeed. One of the Tory women, Lady Tenderden, 'sat biting her lips in despite for having pressed her to the trial of her skill'. And the Comtesse Leinsengen, leader of the Tory clique, 'observed to Lord Baskerville, as he placed himself by her, "I am quite glad to put de taste of dat horrid dull *Teseo* out of my mouth. How people can be so *baroque* as to choose such long old-fashioned things, good for nothing but your German professors!"' (I, 71).

Foreign music must be tucked away in a dark cupboard by all Reform-minded heroines, whereas unreformed aristocrats and middle-class imitators carry on as usual. The aristocratic amateurs in Mrs Gore's *The Opera* (1832) thus practise Bellini in their afternoons (II, 184). When the two *à la mode* sisters in *Mothers and Daughters* (1830) visit exclusive friends in Arlington Street, Mayfair, they find the group 'already attempting the score of a new opera of Spontini's, which had just arrived from Berlin among some equally important diplomatic despatches' (II, 26).[21] In Bury's *The Devoted* (1836), 'The Miss Elvins', earnest middle-class girls, 'were called "*musical*" ... screeching through Rossini's impossibilities with perfect self-satisfaction' (I, 54). Socially aspiring Lady Beckford in Gore's *The Cabinet Minister* (1839) foolishly admits into her home 'French or Italian singers, of whose morals she knew worse than nothing ... [to] assist in the more difficult concerted pieces of Mozart or Cherubini' (I, 79).

When the modest middle-class attorney's daughter, Margaret Barnsley, in Gore's *Stokeshill Place* (1837), must display her accomplishments, they are admirably home-grown. She goes 'trembling to the instrument' where she delights her aristocratic listeners 'at the excellence of her performance, and the purity of style acquired from the able organist of Westerton'. These aristocrats cannot contain their surprise 'at the diffidence which, during her stay at the Abbey, she had disclaimed all pretension to musical accomplishments' (i, 193). Sir Henry Woodgate, the hero, stays home from the Italian opera to hear the middle-class heroine sing English songs: '[He] found himself listening to Margaret's performance of some canzonets of Withers, at the express desire of Lord Withamstead, who loved young voices married to old music. Her singing, like her talking was devoid of pretension; and the old man was grateful to her for not flourishing over simple English ballads, like the false taste of the Drewes', a local aristocratic family of fashionable girls (ii, 252).[22]

Drawing and painting follow a similar redirection of taste, from foreign to domestic. Honoria, the heroine of Lady Bury's *The Disinherited* (1834), loves landscape paintings, she says, of the *English* school. When she goes on an excursion to Hadleigh Castle, 'Her drawing materials were never forgotten, and she soon found a spot where the darkness of the building was finely relieved by a long line of light glittering on the estuary immediately behind it, while a range of white clouds settled themselves most advantageously as a boundary to the distance, and formed a frame to the picture, which would have been otherwise flat and tame' (i, 244). The national appreciation of John Constable's *Hadleigh Castle* (1829) was never put to better use by a heroine. In contrast, in *Women as They Are*, Mrs Gore's novel of 1830, a socially aspiring middle-class mother boasts of the foreign accomplishments acquired by her diligent daughter at a boarding school in Bath: 'I think I can show you some specimens of Poonah which will amaze you', Mrs Daly says to her aristocratic visitor, Lady Willersdale. 'Specimens of Poonah?' asks Lady Willersdale, '—is it a mineral?'[23] 'Of Poonah work, and oriental tinting', says Mrs Daly, 'which I find have quite superseded sketching and drawing in modern education' (ii, 65).

In *Belmont's Daughter: A Fashionable Novel* by E. H. Macleod, a novel designed to flatter the middle classes and published in the same politically tumultuous year of 1830, a Miss Belmont, middle class and possessed of many worthy talents, weds an aristocrat only to find that her hard-earned accomplishments are wasted and unwanted in exclusive company:

'The hours she had imagined would (when they obtained an establishment of their own) have been devoted to those pursuits which had been her delight from infancy—in reading—in small musical parties—in the discussion of different literary productions—where were they?—Spent at the opera—the ball—or splendid parties' (II, 23–4). The trope had been used five years earlier by Lord Normanby, a Whig politician, in his novel *Matilda: a Tale of the Day* (1825) where the heroine finds that in her marriage to a 'frigid' aristocratic, 'her talents were wasted—her accomplishments unnoticed' (I, 44). She gazes into her magnificent jewel box in despair: '"I cannot talk to *you*," she ejaculated; "I cannot confide to you my feelings,—yet it is to you, to such as you, to such cold and senseless splendour, that I am wedded"' (I, 45).

Gore's collection of tales the year after the passage of the Reform Bill, *The Sketch Book of Fashion* (1833) features a story, 'The Old and the Young Bachelor', with a middle-class woman, Sybella Woodford, who marries an aristocrat, Lord Farnley, only to discover that it is *her* accomplishments that must uphold the duties of her husband's rank, with no help whatsoever from him or his chilly aristocratic kin. Worse, hints Mrs Gore, all is not right in the bedroom. 'There was something in the artificial dignity of his address incapable of giving way, even in the intimate communion of wedded life', she explains. 'He often seemed to examine her with a curious eye; to be trying to assure himself that he had not made too great a sacrifice in yielding up his liberty in favour of so obscure a person' (III, 45).[24] Sybella soldiers on triumphantly with her accomplishments, her hard-earned politeness discourse, a shot in the arm for her husband's foolish, enfeebled, torpid aristocratic family. If she cannot find happiness as a wife, she must seek it in performing her aristocratic duties. Her husband resents her triumphs. In redesigning the sculpture gallery, for example, 'It was not that Sybella had the bad taste to interfere in his projects or rectify his designs', says Gore, 'But she made no secret of her own; the superiority of which was so evident, that Lord Farnley was wise enough to see the ridicule to which he should expose himself in so unequal a contest.' The fame of Sybella's polite accomplishments spreads throughout the neighbourhood: 'Sybella composed a *proverbe*; Sybella devised a charade, which the amateur performers of the neighbourhood lauded as superior to the cleverest productions of Scribe.' Her aristocratic husband may seethe, but, 'To have protested against the merit of these performances, would have been to render himself ridiculous' (III, 50).

AT THE OPERA

The King's Theatre, London's Italian opera house, is a favoured spot for silver fork novelists to examine the political health of the aristocracy, or lack of it. Located in the Haymarket almost exactly midway between power centres, close to the Houses of Parliament, the clubs and the salons of Mayfair, the King's Theatre presented a twice-weekly opportunity, on Wednesdays and Saturdays, for the higher orders to display their aristocratic gauds of power.[25] Partington's *National History and Views of London* (1834) fixes its engraved illustration of the King's Theatre at centre-page, with lesser London sites, the University Club, the Egyptian Hall, the Burlington Arcade and Crockford's, grouped around it as humble auxiliaries.[26] Rudolph Ackermann's 'Twelve Views of London Sites Seen through Arches' (1820) grants the King's Theatre equal visual status with Westminster Abbey, the Palace of Westminster, Whitehall and the Horse Guards.[27]

For the major women novelists, Catherine Gore, Charlotte Bury and Lady Blessington, a heroine's attendance at the opera can never be a simple or private amusement. The aristocratic heroine's presence in her box, her opera glass at her side, is a politeness performance designed for public consumption:

There she sat;—her ivory arm, in all its perfection of graceful symmetry, carelessly reclining on the crimson cushion. Her eyes, without even an affectation of interest in the business on the stage, glancing through her glossy curls ..., her small and delicately rounded waist displayed as she lifted her glass, or turned her beautiful head towards the persons standing in the background. (Gore, *The Opera*, III, 192)

The contemporary practice of the opera house management of identifying the boxes with 'the names of their female proprietors' shocks the foreign-born hero of Gore's *The Opera* (1832). In a letter to a friend in Paris, Adrian marvels that the women's names, 'according to English custom, are affixed above each several door' (I, 123). A contemporary publication, a *List of the Subscribers* (1839), provides a map of the house with the owner's name linked to each numbered box. Theodore Hook's middle-class Mrs Thompson in *Love and Pride* (1833) attends exhibitions at the Royal Academy solely to match portraits of '"Lord Whiskin in the uniform of the North Somerset Militia," and "Lady Mary Fopsey, and child," in order that she might find them out when she next saw them at the Opera' (I, 45).

An opera box at the King's Theatre thus occupies a social space somewhere between a woman's private drawing room and the public stage. 'Is there any more delightful place for a *tête à tête* than an opera box?' (II, 174) a matron exclaims as she welcomes a friend to her box in Lady Bury's novel *The Devoted* (1836). Lord Normanby, the author of *Matilda: A Tale of the Day* (1825), is more tempered in his appreciation. Normanby confesses, 'An opera box, is perhaps, of all places in the world, the best fitted for the necessary operation of undergoing an awkward or embarrassing interview. The doubtful light—the divided attention—the confused noise—are all highly favourable ... to the concealment of real feelings' (I, 178). In Gore's *The Opera*, one dandy suggests to another, 'What say you to addressing the lady yourself, and on neutral ground?—Let us return to-night to the Opera, and if you have courage to enter her box, she cannot refuse to answer your questions' (I, 130).

By virtue of its general visibility, however, the opera box is also a stage where the heroine must be acutely aware of her performance. Henry Chorley in his *Thirty Years of Musical Recollections* (1862) remembered Lady Blessington as a major scene-stealer at the King's Theatre: 'Opposite the Royal box was to be seen another celebrity—much observed ... Her queenly and sweet beauty (animated, withal, whenever she spoke, and set off by her peculiar dress) was of itself sufficient to attract remark ... Her wit, too, which her books in no respect represent ... It enchanted the men.'[28]

Lady Blessington's short guide to the season's fashionable amusements, *The Magic Lantern* (1822), falls into the characteristic double-bind that silver fork novelists faced, of giving an account of fashionable society that could also be used as an etiquette manual for readers with social aspirations. She provides two contrasting opera-box performances in the guide, a well-bred aristocratic one (Right) and an uneasy middle-class one (Wrong):

A frequenter of the Opera will soon distinguish the casual occupiers of a box from the owners. The dress, the air of self-possession and ease, with which the latter enter, and present themselves in the front of their boxes; a little premeditated bustle in opening and shutting the door, drawing and undrawing the curtain and moving the chairs, attract the attention of the audience to their boxes, and they support the staring and levelling of glasses pointed at them, with a well bred *nonchalance* that shows them well accustomed to it. (65)

The offenders, Lady Blessington's middle-class aspirers, receive a sharp knuckle-rap for their misjudged performance:

while those who hire a box for the night, enter it with an appearance of *mauvaise honte* that keeps them back for the first five minutes after their entering, and when they do come forward, their flushed faces mark the dread which they feel at encountering the eyes of so great a crowd of spectators, and their over dressed heads shew how much trouble they have taken to adorn themselves for the unusual exhibition. (65)

Theodore Hook exploits the political significance of such middle-class intrusions into aristocratic territory by pillorying the Misses Podgers, comic characters in his *Sayings and Doings* (1824), for their ungainly intrusion into a box at the King's Theatre: 'companions in finery, noise, and vulgarity; they were attendant nymphs on their father, a retired Plymouth slop-seller' (1, 56).

Novelists more liberal than Hook, such as Mrs Gore and Lady Bury, take their political cue from Lord John Russell, the radical Whig politician, who makes a clear distinction between 'good' aristocrats and 'corrupt' aristocrats: 'If by aristocracy those persons meant are [those] … who seek honours without merit, places without duty, and pensions without service—for such an aristocracy I have no sympathy; and I think the sooner its influence is carried away with the corruption on which it has thriven, the better for the country, in which it has repressed so long every wholesome and invigorating influence.'[29] Gore and Bury turn their opera boxes into a witness box, a space for unmasking unworthy aristocrats who refuse to show a proper correlation between moral authenticity and their privileged social class.[30]

In Lady Bury's novel *Flirtation* (1827), the right-thinking aristocratic heroine, Lady Emily Lorimer, attends a performance of Rossini's *Tancredi*, where her presence provokes a comparison with 'corrupt' aristocrats nearby:

Her animated countenance expressed, without reserve, the delight she experienced, unlike the *nonchalant* manners of the greater part of the audience, (of those in the boxes, at least) which might lead a beholder, unversed in the secret, to suppose they came there to perform some necessary but dull duty. (11, 276)

These inattentive, 'nonchalant' aristocratic box holders are indeed at the opera to perform 'power', the political 'duty' of their rank. Ironically, they hold an outdated script for the wrong 'performance'. The blasé response they display to the onstage performance is exactly the condition that enables the sexual vice of 'flirtation' at the opera, the moral flaw that gives rise to the title of the novel. Lady Emily's rapt attention to the onstage performance links her to the connoisseurs, largely from the upper middle classes seated in the pit.[31] Lady Emily, the author insists, is *not* performing in her opera box. She is '*natural*', not '*nonchalant*'. 'She hears nothing but Calidori's "Quanto dolce nell alma"' (ii, 281).[32] Yet, as a consequence, she becomes the person 'stared at' and criticized by Old Corruption as inadequate. 'Really!' says a dandy in the next box:

Lady Emily's beautiful features are quite disfigured sometimes by all those violent commotions ... It is only permissible for a lady to suffer the corner of her mouth just to turn, when the irresistible Mr. Liston is on the stage, and she may hold the corner of her pocket-handkerchief to the eye when Madame Pasta acts Medea. But really those sobbings and showerings—and then the laugh, which may be heard in the next box! (iii, 3–4)

Lady Emily in fact 'performs' her part to perfection in Lady Bury's opera-box drama of 'Aristocratic Reform' and explicitly in the idiom of 'feeling' appropriated to that cause in the year 1827. Lord Mowbray, a liberal-minded, Whig aristocrat, attracted by her honesty and sincerity, cannot resist visiting Lady Emily's opera box: 'as I have for some time observed you from the pit engaged entirely with what was passing on the stage, I conceived that I might venture to steal in, determined not to interrupt your amusement, by my conversation, at least, but merely to make my bow and retire again' (ii, 283–4).

Topics of conversation, the proper ones to introduce into an opera box, become the silver fork novelist's regular trope for smoking out unworthy aristocrats. Countess Leinsengen, a scheming Tory activist, baits Lord Albert d'Esterre, the hero of Lady Bury's novel *The Exclusives* (1830), with the 'tedium' of a 'dull English Sunday', a topic designed to sound him out as a political ally. She gets her answer: 'Lord Albert d'Esterre looked still more cold and grave, as he drew himself up and leant against the back of the box, saying, that "it was an unfitting time and place for such discussions, and that he begged to be excused from entering on them".' A fashionable guest in the same box confirms Tory corruption by complaining of the early closing hour on Saturday nights: '"But dear me the Opera is ended," looking at his watch, and turning to Lady Tilney. "Oh those tiresome bishops—really I wish people would not meddle with what (hem!) they have nothing to do,—we are deprived of half our ballet on the Saturdays (hem!)"' (i, 156).

Following the successful passage of the Reform Bill in 1832, the opera house suffered a steep decline in importance in silver fork novels. Mrs Gore's novel of 1834, *The Hamiltons*, set in the years 1828 to 1834, suggests that aristocratic displays of glamour and wealth, particularly at the opera, had been a significant political miscalculation for the Tory government that may have contributed to their electoral losses of 1830–1:

The season and the session, meanwhile, had opened together; and opened with auspicious promise to the quietists of the court party. All was sunshine … Ireland grumbled a little, the manufacturers groaned,—and the continent occasionally growled in the distance;—but *who* could give ear to such inharmonious sounds, when Donzelli and Malibran were singing;—or who deign to notice the menacing gestures of a mob of wretches who cried aloud that their bread was taxed, and their children starving, when Taglioni, the handmaid of the graces, was making her debut at the Opera!—The Bayadare was in possession of every heart and every eye;—where was there an ear or a voice disengaged for the gaucheries of the most High Court of Parliament? (II, 280)

Marcia Berkely, married to a radical politician in *The Hamiltons*, explains to an inquisitive young caller why she no longer attends the opera: 'I have married into a situation of life which forbids much participation in public amusements', she says to the girl. '"But you love music?" persisted Blanche, glancing at a harp and piano, and a profusion of music books which appeared to be in much use.' 'Very much', says Marcia, 'it serves to lighten many a solitary hour. But professional music I seldom hear. In every position of society one is obliged to sacrifice something' (II, 267–8). Marcia's younger sister Susan marries the son of a Tory cabinet minister and discovers that her duties inevitably involve attendance at the opera. 'But must I be presented, and go to the opera immediately?— Can we not be quiet, for a short time', she begs her husband, 'till I get accustomed to London?' (I, 171). She cannot. Her father-in-law, Lord Laxington, insists upon her taking an opera box at once: 'he could not more advantageously mollify the hearts of his countrymen than by appearing in public accompanied by a beautiful daughter-in-law' (I, 177). Even after her husband destroys their marriage by his scandalous infidelity with her best friend, Susan must still appear with her father-in-law in her box at the opera. Susan's wayward husband, bitterly regretting his loss, can view her only from afar: 'He stood sometimes watching his wife from the pit at the Opera, as she leaned back in her box (in compliance with Lord Laxington's desire for her constant appearance in public), pale, marble-like and beautiful, but without a smile—without a hope,—like a spring-tide whose flowers have been withered by untimely frosts' (III, 131). Politeness discourse takes a cruel toll on the aristocratic heroine of this silver fork novel.

Sutherland Edwards in his *History of the Opera* (1862) laments the sharp decline of aristocratic opera attendance in real life: 'On the whole, the Opera has become less aristocratic, less respectable, and far more expensive than of old', he writes. He quotes the earlier work of Mount Edgcumbe on this regretted state of affairs, 'tickets bearing the names of ladies of the highest class have been presented by those of the lowest, such as used to be admitted only to the hindmost rows of the gallery'.[33] Mrs Gore takes note of this real-life change in opera attendance in her novel *Mrs. Armytage* (1836) to suggest a political origin. Her villain Sir Leon Marscourt (formerly Leonidas Lomax), a South Carolina slave owner and Tory sympathizer, celebrates his elevation to the baronetage by splurging magnificently on an opera box for his wife, Lady Marscourt, at the King's Theatre. 'Tarnation grand!' observes Mrs Gore in wry acknowledgement of Reform's democratizing consequence (III, 355).

HOME THEATRICALS

If opera attendance dries up for the aristocratic heroine, home theatricals continue to offer her opportunities for displaying her accomplishments and politeness skills. Home theatre had been pressed into service in the previous generation by Maria Edgeworth in *Patronage* (1814), by Frances Burney in *The Wanderer* (1814) and, most notably, by Jane Austen in *Mansfield Park* (1814). In each of these novels it is used as a trope for examining the heroine's performance when her 'accomplishments' are required to perform a dramatic role foreign to her social identity.[34] The dangers faced by Edgeworth's and Burney's heroines, mainly the fear of being shunned by the hero or put out of doors by a patron, are of no interest to the later silver fork novelists. Jane Austen's version of the theatricals in *Mansfield Park*, published in the same year as Edgeworth's and Burney's, becomes a more useful working model. The extension of the moral issues raised by *Lovers' Vows* into the main action of Austen's novel, particularly in the sexual tensions and jealousies of her amateur performers, provides silver fork novelists with a pattern for extending the charades, plays and mini-operas of their silver fork plots into tropes for illuminating the politics of class. T. H. Lister's *Arlington* (1832) does just this, mounting a home theatrical at Lady Crawford's house, an echo of Austen's Mary Crawford, where the woman engaged to marry the hero disguises her flirtation and her eventual affair with a fellow actor in otherwise unnecessary rehearsal sessions.

Letitia Landon's *Romance and Reality*, published in 1831, commences with a heroine reminiscent of Austen's Emma, 'young, pretty, and spoilt' (I, 2), also from the genteel middle classes, who must face a full-blown confrontation with aristocratic values during a visit to fashionable friends in London. Emily's first assignment is to play a Greek slave in a charade: 'The subject of the picture was Roxelana receiving a present of the Sultan from a young Greek girl.' The countess, her hostess, 'personified the brilliant coquette to perfection', says Landon, and as for Emily, clearly overwhelmed by her new aristocratic company, 'It was impossible to give a more perfect representation of a young Greek girl parted from her home and her affections ... the subdued and drooping attitude, nothing could more accurately depict the "delicate Ionian pining" for her own free and mountain village' (II, 175–6).

A second entertainment called for by the countess, a game of 'Proverbs', demands a dramatic scene that will display the meaning of a common saying. The one selected for illustration is '"*chemins divers—-même but*"—"divers roads, and the same end"'.[35] In the performance, writes Landon, 'the countess and Emily were two sisters, each of whom affect an attachment to the cavalier they care not for, to pique the one they prefer'. The countess takes the part of the 'sentimental' sister, leaving to Emily the part of the 'lively' sister, which is very bad luck indeed for Emily. The two gentlemen of the party who are to take the male parts in the 'proverb' are the very persons whose roles match the positions they occupy in Emily's life. As the designated 'lively' sister in the 'proverb', Emily must reject the man she secretly *does* love, Edward Lorraine (a handsome ultra-Tory), who does *not* love *her*, to act a 'love' for a man who actually does love her, Cecil Spencer (a plain and indolent Tory), whom she does *not* love. Her immediate and urgent task is to disguise with her politeness skills the misery she feels in this painful reverse, a doubling of her real, but secret situation.[36] Her dissembling, enabled by her skills in politeness, succeeds so well that the countess calls the piece to a halt. She had expected Emily 'to make a good side scene', says Landon, 'and was more surprised than pleased by a display that cast herself quite into the background' (II, 176). Crossed in love and deeply unhappy with her life of politeness discourse, which she experiences as a series of constant social dissembling, Emily enters a convent in France, then escapes to England where she dies of grief. Landon's novel is a tale of love frustrated by the constraints of politeness discourse, a language that gives the heroine no speech of her own to articulate what she desires, even to herself, thus leaving her with no choice but retreat to a nunnery. A memorial stone in the village church marks the end of the *chemin* for Emily: 'Emily Arundel / The Last Survivor of her Family / Aged 21' (II, 248).

Perhaps the most sensational example of home theatricals in a silver fork novel is produced in 1832, the year of the Reform Bill itself, by Mrs Gore's novel *The Opera*. The piece chosen by its amateur actors for the entertainment of the Duke of Cardigan and his invited guests is a 'tiny pastoral opera' by Charles Simon Favart (1710–92) entitled *Annette and Lubin*.[37] Its relevance to this intensely political year would be obvious to any opera buff, but is made clear in the narrative for general readers. The lead characters are two 'peasant' lovers, Annette and Lubin, who successfully resist all the scheming efforts of the villainous feudal and civic powers who attempt to block their union.[38]

Unsuspected by the Duke of Cardigan and his noble friends, however, their most celebrated guest for the amateur performance, the international opera star 'La Silvestra', was born a peasant, 'Stephanine Haslinger', and was the youthful lover of Adrian Maldyn, son of Lord Abbotscourt. La Silvestra arrives in London to exact revenge on Lord Abbotscourt for parting her from Adrian, and on Adrian for willingly abandoning her. She sets out with cunning deliberation to challenge the system of aristocratic privilege that had brutally disregarded her feelings as a young woman.

The diva uses her professionally honed politeness skills to direct a fifth column assault on the British aristocracy into whose socially exclusive company she is welcomed with enthusiasm, her admission vouched for by her 'celebrity', her 'feeling voice' and her 'faultless manners'. The transformation of the peasant Stephanine Haslinger into the celebrated 'La Silvestra', glamorous opera star and 'perfectly genteel' Mlle Sandoni, daughter of the respectable old Colonel Sandoni (as it is given out), rightly prompts forebodings in her former lover, Adrian, who remains silent about La Silvestra's real identity in order to protect his own position in London society. 'There is something to me almost awful in the perfection of dissimulation practised by this woman', Adrian writes of La Silvestra, 'it seems abetted by the inspiration of an evil spirit!' (II, 206).

The transformation of a peasant girl into a fit associate for aristocrats in 1832 would naturally touch public anxieties about a political reform frequently described by its opponents as reckless 'experiment' that if enacted would collapse the walls separating the social classes. The arrival of the opera star at the coincident opening of Parliament and the Opera season of 1831 marks the intersection in the novel of these intertwined events: 'Next week', Adrian writes a friend, 'parliament will meet and ... next week the Opera will open;—and thenceforward something will be going on in London. The great sea-monster will lash its tail, and we shall all share its reanimation' (I, 319).[39]

La Silvestra presents her self-constructed history as 'Mlle Sandoni' in all the rhetorical pieties of *respectability*, a middle-class credential essential to La Silvestra's acceptance into liberal aristocratic society in this year.[40] 'The devotion of a young and timid girl, descending from the dignified respectability of a private gentlewoman to all the humiliations of a theatrical life for the sake of an infirm father', old Colonel Sandoni, writes Mrs Gore, 'was sufficient to bespeak the good will of Gertrude and Mrs Perceval' (II, 269), two of the genteel company. La Silvestra's manipulative ease with the rhetorical language of middle-class respectability, along with her 'perfect' display of aristocratic politeness skills, gives her a decided advantage over her foes. 'Even Constance Fitzgerald', notes the author, 'on other occasions so vigilant and discriminating, found reason to admire and praise the tokens of gentle blood visible in her elegant demeanour, the expression of feminine gentleness adorning her countenance' (II, 134). 'She is a charming creature; so frank,—so *naïve*,—so unlike what I expected in a public performer', says another charmed aristocrat, 'How I hate the word profession when applied to so ladylike and delicate a person!' (II, 165). Adrian Maldyn can only wonder at the completeness of the peasant diva's social transformation:

Were those mellifluous accents which had recently so melted my soul, the same whose coarse Lower-Austrian dialect had breathed, that night, a tender farewell to her '*Schatzerl*'?—Was that fairy foot in its sandal of silvery satin, the same which had plodded away in its buckled hob-nailed shoe, on the announcement of Brother Remigious' approaching snuffle. (II, 113)

Conservative elements of aristocratic society, however, harbour no sentimental illusions about admitting a mere 'player' to their ranks: 'We are none of us safe!' says an elderly matron, 'If such people as this Mademoiselle Sandoni are to be introduced into our private circles, merely because they have a sweet voice and an ingratiating manner, all the barriers of society may as well be turned over at once. We shall find figurantes on the bench of peeresses, and ... ' (II, 277).

A twist in the novel's plot gives a particularly painful meaning to the *Annette and Lubin* theatrical entertainment. La Silvestra, the ex-peasant, now an honoured guest, takes her private revenge in witnessing the aristocratic Adrian Maldyn, her former lover, play the part of 'Lubin' in the opera, where his 'peasant' lovemaking to 'Annette', his aristocratic girl friend, mirrors with earthy double entendres the rustic love affair of their own shared past. 'At the risk of disappointing the whole party', Adrian-the-polite complains to a friend, 'I found myself obliged to walk through his part!—Nothing could be more provoking than to appear in this disadvantageous position, in the presence of one so like to triumph in my awkwardness as the prima donna of the Italian Opera' (II, 237). La Silvestra's grim pleasure in the Favart rehearsals may be disturbing in itself, but the political meaning of this scandalous power reversal, a peasant girl witnessing the discomforts of an aristocrat playing a peasant, would not be lost on any reader in the year of the novel's publication. This is 'politeness discourse' turned upside-down.

Mrs Gore's deepest sympathies are invested in her plain-spoken, revolutionary diva. The aristocracy in Gore's *The Opera* is a class divided, weak, clannish and in rapid decline, both morally and spiritually. In one grand final scene, La Silvestra's disdain for an effete, vicious and frozen British aristocracy tears back the politeness veil that covers the social and political chasms of contemporary society. The great diva turns around for a final gesture of victory. Having taken revenge on all her enemies – Lord Abbotsford drops dead when he recognizes her, the aristocratic heroine dies of grief in a madhouse and Adrian dies of a broken heart – La Silvestra is the only figure left standing at the final curtain. She turns her back on England with sovereign contempt, prepared for yet another triumphal tour of the Continent.

Lady Bury, keenly aware that the rituals of 'politeness' were running out of time, felt it necessary to instruct her middle-class readers in *The Devoted*, of 1836, in the now arcane rituals of aristocratic entertainments: 'Be it known to the curious of posterity, that charades are acted enigmas—words of which the syllables comprehend various meanings, and afford scenes to develop the story of the little drama' (II, 125). Her cast of characters, close variations on figures in *Mansfield Park*, include Ethel (Fanny), companion to her cousin Lady Elizabeth Altamont (Mary Crawford) and St Aubyn (Edmund), a clergyman, who is in love with Lady Elizabeth, and not Ethel (Fanny), who of course is secretly in love with him. Lady Elizabeth must choose between St Aubyn, the man she loves, and his older brother the heir to the title and estate, a man she does not love. Ethel, like Austen's Fanny, must wait on Lady Elizabeth's pleasure.

The home theatrical, entitled 'Bondage', mirrors in its gothic plot the triangle of the politically driven love-plot which points ominously to Lady Elizabeth's wavering but ultimately immovable attachment to status, rank and wealth. 'Bondage', the title of the home theatrical, casts a long shadow over the novel. When St Aubyn, like Edmund Bertram, is asked to participate in the play, he uses his clergyman's position to refuse: 'Dear Lady Elizabeth, these scenes I ought not to mingle in', he tells her, 'I have perhaps been already too much in them' (II, 138). Following the performance, Lady Elizabeth seeks him out. 'One only thing was wanting to the gratification of Lady Elizabeth: it was the expressed homage of Mr. St. Aubyn. She had seen him, it is true, with his eyes riveted on her during the performance; but when all approached to give her the meed of applause, he from whom it would have been most grateful was silent. At length she contrived to draw near the place where he had stood during the whole performance.' St Aubyn's disapproval includes the home theatre as an institution, but even more, Lady Elizabeth's pointed display of her superlative politeness skills. His objection recalls Edmund Bertram's, but projects a subtly different focus:

'Mr. St. Aubyn,' she said ... 'Tell me, do you not think we acted *tolerably?*'
'A great deal *too* well, Lady Elizabeth.'
'Too well! How ridiculous! What do you mean?'
'My meaning cannot be briefly told; and I had far rather not be pressed to its disclosure.'
'Nay, now you frighten me,' she replied: 'I dare not attend to you, or I shall be quite unfit for the duties of the evening.'
'Duties!' exclaimed Mr. St. Aubyn with marked emphasis and a scornful smile. (II, 154–5)

St Aubyn's contemptuous response, 'Duties!', carries its own message about the now obvious failure of aristocratic reform. Lady Elizabeth's valuation of 'duties' is subjected to a more exacting measure than she intends.[41]

In the event, it is Lady Elizabeth's 'bondage' to outdated aristocratic values that guides her to choose St Aubyn's elder brother, the heir, in preference to St Aubyn the clergyman. Her father, Lord Altamont, who is responsible for having taught Lady Elizabeth the 'duties' of her station, conducts his own barren life in the 'bondage' of aristocratic social precedence. The 'politics of the day were hateful to his tenets', she writes, political philosophy was 'unbecoming persons of high rank', and the French Revolution was the result of 'the introduction of what were called men of letters into society' (I, 20–1).

The traditional affinity of the silver fork novel for depicting struggles for power itself, a relatively simple matter, is no longer adequate, as noted, to describe the post-Reform politics of civic projects, poor laws and factory legislation. Nevertheless, Lady Bury uses *The Devoted* to register her alarm at the incompetence of the post-1832 Whig 'reform' governments, which remain in her opinion too aristocratic and too much like pre-Reform governments. In 'The Closing Chapter' of *The Devoted*, she loses patience. Aristocratic government, including Lord Melbourne's Whig cabinet, top-heavy with aristocrats, falls under the heavy weight of her condemnation. 'As it is, Lord Altamont', a clear-sighted, if scolding character says to the rank-proud father of Lady Elizabeth, whose life has been ruined by her father's aristocratic principles of excessive 'politeness': 'This is now your heritage: dress it up as you may, with coronets and ribbons and orders, and all the insignificance of the regalia of life, it will be but the skeleton of your departed consequence' (III, 321).

Moreover, Lady Bury provides a distinctly mixed conclusion for the 'bondage' of love that makes Ethel's life a misery in pining for the unavailable St Aubyn. In her dying breath, Lady Elizabeth begs St Aubyn, to whom she confesses an *eternal* love, to marry the middle-class Ethel, her cousin-companion. St Aubyn, now known as Lord Fitzarlington (ironically, he inherits), of course discovers that 'Ethel was as perfect as a human being can be'. Moreover, 'He became by degrees very fond of her … ; he knew that it was in the power of him to make her happiness; he would fulfil his loved-one's dying request, he *would* marry Ethel Delamere.' And so he does. 'With the smiles of their children and the blessing of their dependants', concludes Bury, 'life is to them a pleasant waiting place for death' (III, 327), a shocking conclusion for a reader looking for the happiness of a marriage plot. Whatever political promise a union between the aristocracy (Lord Fitzarlington) and the middle classes (Ethel) might have held four years earlier at the height of excitement for reform in 1832, the actuality has provided a sense of decided disillusionment in this novel.

In Catherine Gore's post-Reform novels, she frequently finds it useful to introduce middle-class characters who can be brought forward to teach her young aristocrats, puzzled and thoroughly clueless, about political and social changes in post-Reform Britain. *Fraser's* reviewer recognizes the ploy and singles it out for praise: 'Amid all the whirl of society, Mrs. Gore never loses sight of the pure and the simple', he writes. 'In illustration of this we would refer to the character of the governess in *Stokeshill Place*, and to Dr. Grant in *Mrs. Armytage*', two adamantly middle-class figures Mrs Gore designates to introduce their privileged pupils to the middle-class way of the world. In *Stokeshill Place* the heroine goes to her governess to seek advice about a coming election in which her father is a candidate, asking if the governess doesn't think that her father's tenants will follow the traditional pattern of 'loyal servants' by casting their votes for him – the polite assumption, one might say, of an empowered class. The governess, who knows better, exclaims, 'No! my dear—never!—No! such influences will never more be established in England. There is too great an extension of trade. There are too many power-looms and cotton factories at work.' The heroine continues haplessly, 'You think the age has assumed too federal a character to admit of a re-concentration of the feudal principle?' Her governess, who can hardly believe the extent of her pupil's aristocratic fantasies, is flabbergasted. "*My dear!*"—demanded Miss Winston, fancying that her pupil's head was again excited by delirious fever. "What can you possibly mean?"' (II, 12).[42] The second of Gore's middle-class characters praised by *Fraser's*, the vicar Dr Grant in *Mrs. Armytage* (1836), must explain to his former pupil, Arthur Armytage, who wavers in removing his mother from control of his estate, that he has no legal choice but to follow the instructions of the newly discovered codicil to his grandfather's will that deprives the tyrannical, abusive Mrs Armytage of her power. 'Every question is more or less a question of equity', says Dr Grant, spelling it out in the simplest possible terms to his former student. 'Even to the tenants on the estate, you owe it that they should be subjected to the control of their lawful landlord. The very leases signed by Mrs. Armytage are null and void', and, he adds, 'you, as being cognizant of the fact, make yourself a party to the fraud' (III, 262). Politeness rules do not apply in this new age, as Mrs Gore well knows.

Politeness discourse as it fades from the heroines' lives, does remain potent as a weapon to be used, politely, against the female authors themselves. The male reviewer for the Tory periodical *Fraser's*, January 1838, for example, smokes out Mrs Gore's liberal Whig bias in her recently published *Stokeshill Place* (1837) only to let the lady author off with condescending politeness. 'The moral, as intended by Mrs. Gore in her tale', he writes, 'is obvious … the prejudices of the aristocracy are too strong to be carried by any assailant, even though he be armed with every intellectual and mental quality ever bestowed upon man.' 'But why', he adds disingenuously, 'has Mrs. Gore made all her exclusives Tories?' This gentle, patronising attack running beneath the criticism may have satisfied *Fraser's* Tory readers, but it is hard to believe that it was altogether welcome to a woman whose novel *Stokeshill Place* had pointedly questioned the role of aristocratic politeness discourse in her heroine's life. The *Fraser's* reviewer concludes his remarks on *Stokeshill Place* by announcing that it can be 'safely' recommended 'to the world at large', his praise resting solely on Gore's *politeness*, that is, his own certain knowledge that Mrs Gore has first-hand experience of exclusive society and thus knows 'the art of pleasing' first hand: 'Throughout every scene of this novel', he writes, 'Mrs. Gore has manifested consummate taste, acute powers of description, and infinite skill and judgment.' Praise indeed.

Epilogue

Life is to them a pleasant waiting place for death.
                                    Lady Bury, *The Devoted*[1]

An epilogue demands a brief look at the beginning, but particularly at the end of a phenomenon such as the silver fork novel. The market for novels of fashionable life, as contemporaries recognized, was a remarkable development in the history of prose fiction. 'It is inconceivable', an American observer wrote, 'what a vast literary taste there is in England; that is to say, a taste for literary scandal, tittle-tattle, reviewing and magazining.'[2] Contemporary critics hostile to novels of fashionable life focused mainly on their commercial success. 'Every year and every month sends forth new ones', complained Maginn.[3] 'We believe that since novel-writing has become a trade, never was it lower than at present.'[4] A reviewer from *The Athenæum* accused Colburn's novels of putting 'literature on a footing with Liquid Blacking'.[5] *Blackwood's* asserted that 'the mere suspicion of having written a book, [will] be sufficient ground for expulsion from the society of gentlemen'.[6]

Undoubtedly the hostility of contemporary nineteenth-century critics to 'trade' literature contributed to the disappearance of silver fork fiction from the canon. But just as problematical for their reputation was the attitude of the authors themselves, all of them susceptible to internalization of their contemporary social and literary culture. Within the pages of their novels could be found the seeds of destruction that would assist in their dismissal from public memory. As a self-advertising strategy, silver fork authors sought strenuously to dissociate their own works from the 'popular' *inauthentic* novels of rival novelists. As Bulwer has a disgruntled dowager in his *Pelham* (1828) complain, 'Of all the novels on society with which we are annually inundated, there is scarcely one which gives even a tolerable description of it.' '*Not* strange', says her obliging listener, 'Most of the writers upon our little, great world, have seen nothing of it' (III, 48). A young woman (not an exclusive) in Lister's *Arlington* (1832) asks a gentleman, who really is one, 'What is an exclusive?' confessing that all she knows on the subject comes from 'a Novel called "Exclusiveness Unveiled"', but, as she admits, 'I don't know much more now than I did before I read it, though I heard it was to open many mysteries.' Lister's gentleman, disingenuously disclaiming any knowledge of such things, 'Not being one myself', produces a string of clichés from silver fork novels as his 'knowledge' of society. A friend reproves him, 'Too bad, upon my word ... to confirm that girl in all her errors, and fill her brain with fresh chimeras' (1, 128). Such self-derogation could only confirm the next generation in its contempt for silver fork fiction.

Also, the political collapse of Whig-fuelled designs and aspirations for the Reform settlement simply brought the significance of the silver fork novel's engagement with it to a close. Novels of fashionable life were no longer part of the march of Progress, but clearly the retrograde and reactionary fossils of an unenlightened era with different political goals. Thackeray pillories them on these grounds in 'The Book of Snobs' (1846–47): 'What Peerage-worship there is all through this free country! ... "Your merits are so great," says the nation, "that your children shall be allowed to reign over us, in a manner. It does not in the least matter that your eldest son be a fool: we think your services so remarkable, that he shall have the reversion of your honours when death vacates your noble shoes."' Adding, 'If anybody wants to know how intimately authors are connected with the fashionable world, they have but to read the genteel novels.'[7]

Claudia Johnson's brave attempt to sort out the canonical history of the Romantic novel in a recent essay provides a tentative map for uncovering the fate of the silver fork novel, its lost colony.[8] Johnson draws attention to two early nineteenth-century canons of the novel, one which 'didn't take', Anna Laetitia Barbauld's collection of novels, *The British Novelists* (1810–20), and another that *did*, Walter Scott's collection, *Ballantyne's Novelist's Library* (1821–4). Scott's aim in his collection, writes Johnson, was to foreground novel-writing as a masculine profession, a goal that chimed exactly with that of male novelists and literary critics of the 1820s and 1830s in their desire to catch the wind of professionalism that was blowing the middle classes to power in the Reform and post-Reform years.[9] In contrast, Barbauld puts the novel into a 'heterosocial discursive space', Johnson writes, making a place for women in the conversation of novel writing. Barbauld's collection, as Johnson notes, includes twenty-two novelists, 'fourteen are men and eight are women', whereas in Scott's *Ballantyne's Novelist's Library* 'twelve are men, [only] two are women'.[10] For Barbauld, novels are politically active, they 'take a tincture from the learning and politics of the times, and are made use of successfully to attack or recommend the prevailing systems of the day'.[11] They are intended, as Johnson explains, to 'intervene in and alter specific political "systems"'.[12]

Barbauld's commitment to the political significance of novels locates silver fork fiction in a vigorous, still-alive contemporary canon, albeit not the ultimately normative canon of Walter Scott. Barbauld's canon gives equality to the woman's tradition, claiming that 'surely it will not be said that either taste or morals have been losers ... The names of D'Arblay, Edgeworth, Inchbald, Radcliffe, and a number more will vindicate this assertion.'[13] Moreover in singling out Burney, Edgeworth and Radcliffe, the novelists that Jane Austen also puts up against the male tradition in *Northanger Abbey* (I, ch. 5), Barbauld provides a contemporary link to the political fictions of silver fork novels.

Twentieth-century criticism has been hamstrung by Scott's famous dictum that novels present the 'probable'. As Claudia Johnson writes, 'the leading principle of twentieth-century histories of the novel is that novels are narratives of private life, that they turn inward, forming subjectivities that occlude or mystify the political'.[14] In contrast, Mrs Barbauld has no apologies for the fictiveness of plot. As Barbauld considers Henry Fielding's *Tom Jones*, she observes that the reader rests secure in the knowledge that Tom's 'history will come to an agreeable term ... And why does he foresee all this? Not from the real tendencies of things, but from what he has discovered from the author's intentions.'[15] Barbauld 'imagines novel readers not to be idle, young, too impressionable, or wishful', writes Johnson, 'but to be alert proto-narratologists altogether conscious that a novelist is executing fiction according to discernible designs and in relation to understood conventions'.[16]

Any notion, for example, that Jane Austen might be mixed up in such an unseemly crowd could only be an aggravation to New Criticism. For F. R. Leavis and Ian Watt, writes Johnson, 'Austen is where "the great tradition" of the English novel begins.'[17] Faced with Mrs Gore's confession that she was indebted to 'Miss Austin [*sic*]', Matthew Whiting Rosa in his New Critical study, *The Silver-Fork School: Novels of Fashion Preceding Vanity Fair* (1936), hurries forward with defensive protests. There is 'perhaps' a female kinship when 'a little vindictiveness drives their pens', he writes, 'Yet one feels a difference in their work not to be atoned for by any amount of similarity in aim or subject. The delicate clarity of an Austen novel is as remote as can be from the prolix cumbrousness of a Gore novel.'

Or, to set the difference again, he continues, 'When Disraeli described Mrs Gore as a "sumptuous personage—looking like a full-blown rose," we feel that he should have met Jane Austen in order to give us a simile for her derived from some more retiring plant.'[18]

Silver fork aspirations for a Whig version of reform, always an immiscible mix of a 'reformed' aristocracy and the 'respectable' and 'genteel' middle classes, were to evaporate by 1841, the final nail driven in the coffin by the dismal history of the stumbling aristocratic government of Lord Melbourne. Mrs Gore takes stock of aristocratic politics in her novel *Cecil* (1841) when she has Cecil, now an ageing dandy, review the failures of Whig reform. Complaining that the British are never able to unite their talents, Cecil constructs a list of those who could have 'saved the nation', naming himself first of course, then two other fictional dandies, Henry Pelham and Vivian Grey, along with three real-life political figures – Brougham, Lyndhurst and Macaulay – then three novelists, Mrs Gore, Lady Morgan and Mrs Norton and, additionally, the waxworks entrepreneur Madame Tussaud. He finishes with a raft of well-known contemporary male writers and, finally, two politicians, Daniel O'Connell and Lord Cardigan, yoking an unpopular Irish politician and a disgraced English lord.[19] 'The truth is', he confides, 'that, like a straw thrown up to determine the course of the wind, the triflers of any epoch are an invaluable evidence of the bent of the public mind. *They* are always floating on the surface,—always ostensible!—*They* are a mark for general observation. *They* are the only *really* public men. Posterity will see, in Brummel and Castlereagh, the leading characters of the Regency' (I, 122–3). Brummel the dandy and Castlereagh the war leader, 'the only *really* public men', says Cecil, 'belong together as master designers of silver fork spaces in Regency England: the private and the public, Almack's and All Europe'.

Winifred Hughes, perhaps the most acute of writers on silver fork novels, finds the failure of the silver fork novel to lie in irreconcilable conditions inherent in the conflicting demands of middle-class fiction and the social circumstances of the aristocracy.[20] Mrs Gore's anti-heroical 'dandy' Cecil, says Hughes, is keenly aware of the representative part he plays as an aristocrat. Like the aristocracy itself, she writes, Cecil Danby has no reason to exert himself, very like the criticism levelled by contemporaries at Lord Melbourne's laid-back performance as prime minister. 'The dynamics of social mobility are simply irrelevant to Gore's born aristocrats.' Unlike 'the middle-class protagonist' who can be rewarded with stability and consumer comforts, Cecil is 'historically displaced' in middle-class society.[21] His whimsical fantasy of saving the nation, like Gore's

Whig hopes for aristocratic political reform, dissolve with the silver fork novel itself into solipsistic dreamings of what could have been.

With the principles of Barbauld's canon in operation, however, novels of fashionable life might well be considered a late political blossoming of the woman's tradition of the novel. The Editor of the 'Preface' of the Bentley edition of *Sense and Sensibility* boldly announces in 1833, 'Miss Austen is the founder of a school of novelists; and her followers are not confined to her own sex, but comprise in their number some male writers of considerable merit.' 'In Barbauld's formulation', writes Johnson, 'novelistic canons supplement, critique, or contest political systems rather than displace or stand as alternatives to them', which is, I offer, an unexpectedly keen description of the role silver fork novels play with such enthusiasm in the age of Reform.[22]

Appendix

The following list comprises the names and works of silver fork authors referred to in this study, plus a few additional authors of special interest, the authors listed in alphabetical order followed by a brief biographical note, with the works of each author listed in the order of their date of publication followed by a **Plot Summary** and informal **Comments** on the individual work.

ANONYMOUS

Anonymous, *Hyde Nugent, a Tale of Fashionable Life*, 3 vols. (London: Henry Colburn, 1827)

Plot Summary: The St Quentin and the Nugent families with adjoining properties are the closest of friends though of opposite political opinions, Mr St Quentin, a Whig (and just turned out of office by a Tory at the commencement of the novel) and the Nugent family, a traditional Tory family. They exist peacefully together as friends, noted as an unusual example, by not talking politics and by keeping their conversations to hunting, rents, tithes, poor-rates and parish business. The man who has taken Mr St Quentin's parliamentary place considers himself to be 'both whig and tory as occasion required, but who was held to be neither by those who scrutinised his character'. The lack of party identification is regarded as admirable. Young Hyde Nugent loses Georgina, his beloved, when he misbehaves with a ballerina at the Opera. Georgina falls into a fever when she discovers the dalliance and dies. Nugent is taken to the Continent to recover. It is hinted that he eventually finds happiness with a woman named Augusta. The villains of the piece get their comeuppances through unwise marriages and consequent financial catastrophes.

Comments: The novel addresses the delinquency of the governing classes, particularly their attendance at the Opera House on Saturday nights, 'the night before the Sabbath', where the 'glittering pageant of the opera dancers' whose libidinous display of limbs – 'they ought to recollect that there *are* modest and virtuous women in the house' – will affect the 'warm imaginations' of the young 'even while in the house of prayer'(I, 177). The novel's frank promotions of political independence, domestic values and religious piety appear aimed at a middle-class readership receptive to these principles.

BLESSINGTON, MARGUERITE, COUNTESS OF (1789–1852)

Marguerite Gardiner Farmer, a countess by marriage, was ostracized from London's most exclusive society for social missteps past and present. Born into an Irish land-owning family impoverished by her father's financial extravagance, she was forced by her father into marriage at age fourteen with a local gentleman, Captain Maurice St Leger Farmer, who was insane, as her father well knew. Marguerite was locked up, beaten and generally abused by her husband. She fled, found 'protection' with Captain Thomas Jenkins as his so-called 'wife' and, in 1813, left him for her future husband Charles, Viscount Montjoy and Earl of Blessington. Lord Blessington paid off Jenkins with a thousand pounds. The Blessingtons were able to marry in 1818 following the accidental death of Farmer, her deranged husband. Lady Blessington's past was questionable, but not necessarily fatal to a London social life. The scandal that kept the women of society away was more recent: her relationship with Count d'Orsay, her step-daughter's handsome young husband. This threesome, after the death of Lord Blessington, were rumoured to be living in Paris in a scandalous *ménage à trois*. When Lady Blessington returned to London in 1830, d'Orsay came with her.[1] As a widow on an inheritance far smaller than her style of life demanded, Lady Blessington took up writing to support her fairly grand establishment. She edited literary annuals (*The Book of Beauty* and *The Keepsake*) and wrote novels of fashionable life, among these *The Repealers* (1833), *The Victims of Society* (1837) *The Confessions of an Elderly Gentleman* (1837) and *The Governess* (1839). More famous in her time as a celebrity than as a writer, Lady Blessington is now remembered for her *Conversations of Lord Byron* (1834) and for the luscious portrait of her by Thomas Lawrence (1822) that hangs in London's Wallace Collection.

Blessington, Lady, *The Magic Lantern; or, Sketches of Scenes in the Metropolis* (London: Longman, Hurst, Rees, Orme and Brown, 1822)

Plot Summary: This short journal-style piece (72 pages) offers a tour of four of London's most fashionable sites of leisure: the Auction, the Park, the Opera and the Egyptian Hall. An account of London's fashionable exclusives and their behaviour at these sites, it also satirizes the awkward efforts of middle-class imitators to match them in style and elegance.

Comments: The narrator offers keen observations of the contemporary social scene, directing her narrative to an imagined audience of genteel readers. The characters are stereotypical representatives of society: the laconic dandy, the silly young girl, the aristocratic beauty, the City merchant with his wife and daughters. The particularized and detailed liveliness of the London scene together with the narrator's personal engagement show Lady Blessington to be a talented observer of fashionable life. Her sharp-eyed description, a news reporter's account of action and response, explores the urban effervescence that later characterizes silver fork fiction at its best.

Blessington, Lady, *The Repealers, a novel*, 3 vols. (London: R. Bentley, 1833)

Plot Summary: The plot of this novel is almost indecipherable. It is constructed around social pains and embarrassments that bear traces of Lady Blessington's personal experience of exclusion from aristocratic society that, by rights, she ought to have belonged to through her marriage to Lord Blessington. Her most persistent tormentor, the real-life Lady Charleville, is represented in the novel as the fictional Lady Abberville. When Lord and Lady Oriel (a version of the Blessingtons) go into Irish exile because Lady Oriel's reputation has been harmed by falsely reported scandal, they are embraced by the Irish people. The Repealers burn the houses of other Anglo-Irish landlords, but pass by Lord and Lady Oriel's on the night they burn the Abbervilles' house, only rescuing these hated English landowners at the last minute with taunts of derision.

Comments: The characters in the novel discuss recent silver fork literature, giving praise to selected authors: Letitia Landon's *Romance and Reality* (1831), "'I have read her novel,' said Lady Oriel, 'and think it exceedingly clever; the dialogue epigrammatic and sparkling, displaying all the freshness and gaiety of youth, with the observation of maturity'" (II, 227); praise of Mrs Gore: 'the authoress of, what shall I say, half the popular novels of the day, among which there is not a single failure; her books give you all the sparkle of fashionable life, without any of its inanity, and her fecundity of imagination is as extraordinary as her facility of language; she appears never to tire herself, and certainly never tires her readers, for she is always brilliant and often profound' (II, 228–9). 'Some of the upper-class characters' in Blessington's novel according to recent biographers, 'are indeed portraits: the Prime Minister Lord Rey is Lord Grey; Lady Guernsey is Lady Jersey; and Mrs Grantley, who looks "the very personification of a muse," is Caroline Norton (whom Blessington did not like).'[2]

Blessington, Lady, *Two Friends, a novel*, 3 vols. (London: Saunders and Otley, 1835)

Plot Summary: The story starts well with a programme of political divisions: the sober, liberal MP, Mr Desbrow, and the flighty aristocrat, Lord Arlington, who are good friends from Cambridge days. The present political situation, immediately post-Reform, is outlined with spirit. This appears to be a political compromise novel – good and bad attributed to both sides. The plot unfortunately descends into love dalliances and confusions that hijack the promised political plot. We are told that the liberal MP's uncle/guardian is a liberal only because, as a Tory, he was prevented from marrying the love of his life by a proud, conservative aristocratic family. Thus the basis for our MP's education in liberal principles is deeply undercut. The aristocratic friend, Lord Arlington, is truly a scattered moral force, with a good heart, but tempted by the excesses of aristocratic leisure life, a habit of gambling and an infatuation with Lady Walmer, the wife and sister of two of his friends. Lady Walmer is no innocent herself. She seduces Arlington into elopement, a scandal that provides enough confusion to last the novel, with his true love 'Lady Emily' wanting nothing to do with him when she discovers his history with Lady Walmer.

Comments: The novel is a combination of aristocratic gossip, mistaken identities and gross newspaper falsifications that drive its plot for its three volumes of sentimental confusions.

Blessington, Lady, *The Confessions of an Elderly Gentleman* [title page, 1836] (London: Longman, 1837)

Plot Summary: The episodic narrative is determined by six portraits of imaginary women supplied by the illustrator Thomas Parris. Lady Blessington concocts a tale to go with each portrait, each one featuring the Elderly Gentleman's reminiscences about his brief, failed relationships with each of the women.

Comments: The portraits are in the mode of the popular annuals, with the reader's attention drawn to each picture for clues to support the character, disposition and rank of each woman as she is represented in the text. The format suggests *Consumer's Report*, each picture an illustration of the product, followed by a discussion of its merits and demerits.

Blessington, Lady, *The Victims of Society*, 3 vols. (London: Saunders and Otley, 1837)[3]

Plot Summary: An epistolary novel. Lady Blessington's modern editors, Ann R. Hawkins and Jeraldine R. Kraver, summarize the plot of *Victims* as the story of Lady Augusta Vernon, 'open and trusting … confident that society will not believe ill of a woman if she has not behaved ill'. Lady Augusta finds otherwise. She is 'influenced throughout the novel by two older women: the well-bred Lady Mary Howard Delaward and the French-reared—and thus "unprincipled and heartless"—Caroline Montressor'.[4] The novel follows this rigorously determined pattern, but with a special emphasis on the treachery of fashionable London society and the consequent loss of an innocent woman's reputation, no doubt drawing on Lady Blessington's own painful experience in aristocratic society, but also with possible immediate reference to the 'criminal conversation trial of Caroline Norton' then in process.[5] Lady Augusta dies from her relentless mistreatment: 'She passed away from this life without a struggle or sigh … Never was there any thing more touching than the appearance of Augusta in the sleep of death.' Her friends immediately send away 'express for two of the best artists from London, to make a picture, and a cast, from which a bust is to be executed of her', a kind of special silver fork immortality.[6] Caroline Montressor, driven by her own demons, commits suicide in criminal disgrace.

Comments: *Hunt's London Journal* singled out *The Victims* and *The Repealers* among Blessington's novels as 'particularly popular with circulating-library readers'.[7] The novel was written in the midst of financial struggle. Lady Blessington was at work on *The Victims of Society* in January 1837, having finished *The Confessions of an Elderly Gentleman* by December 1836. When she published *Victims* in mid April 1837, she was simultaneously at work editing *The Book of Beauty* and had begun the next issue of *Gems of Beauty*, a collection of her poetry. The author's claim in the 'Preface' to write social satire, 'paint[ing] the manners of the day', rather than giving individualized portraits of contemporaries, a standard protection clause of silver fork novelists, includes an interesting assessment of the power of media celebrity for novel readers, who 'are apt to take up a novel as we go to an exhibition, less to criticise the creations of fancy, than to search for the portraits of our friends'.

Blessington, Lady, *The Confessions of an Elderly Lady*
(London: Longman, 1838)

Plot Summary: Another series of women's portraits, but this time the extended narrative of Lady Arabella, who tells a bitter, paranoid tale of the treacheries of other women, the offenders' engraved pictures provided as a prompt for each tale. The collection concludes with Lady Arabella permanently embittered, resigned to life as a single person.

Comments: *Confessions of an Elderly Lady* is a disturbing psychological study of the protagonist's self-delusion, paranoia and frustrated ambition, but also of a society that perverts the natural instincts of women through restrictive limitations that drive them into devious paths of action.

Blessington, Lady, *The Governess*, 2 vols. (London: Longman, 1839)

Plot Summary: 'Clara Mordaunt was the only child and orphan of a merchant, whose unsuccessful speculations had led to bankruptcy and—suicide' (1, 3). Clara must seek work. She answers an advertisement in the papers for a governess, is accused of an affair with her employer's husband and must seek employment elsewhere. The novel is much indebted to Burney's *The Wanderer* (1814) for its employment trials and to Burney's *Evelina* (1778) for an embarrassing night at the opera for the heroine with one of her employers, a Madame Duval figure. Clara is rescued from her difficulties by middle-class Quaker relatives living in Clapham Common. Ultimately a fortune, 'immense wealth', is left to her by her late aunt's brother, General Bertie of the East India Company, enabling Clara to re-enter polite society.

Comments: There is a moral lesson in this tale for abusive employers: 'Mrs. Williamson, and the Manwarrings, in future ever treated the governess who undertook the instruction of their children with more humanity; giving as a reason, that there was no knowing whether they might not, at some future period, become heiresses, or countesses, and so turn out useful acquaintances' (II, 330–1).

BULWER, EDWARD (1803–73)

Edward George Earle Lytton Bulwer Lytton [*formerly* Edward George Earle Lytton Bulwer], first Baron Lytton, was born into a family with self-conscious claims to station.[8] His name(s) gave his contemporaries great amusement. He was Edward Bulwer, however, during his career as a silver fork author. Bulwer began to write for a living when his mother withdrew funds to mark her disapproval of his choice of a bride. His 'dandy' novel *Pelham* (1828), a witty, ironic view of fashionable life, drove Thomas Carlyle, outraged by it (or by reports of it in *Fraser's*), to write *Sartor Resartus* (1833–4). Bulwer went on to publish two more novels in the silver fork mode, *The Disowned* (1829) and *Godolphin* (1833). He set aside writing novels of fashionable life to pursue a political career, but with only moderate success, returning to follow a literary career with great success.

Bulwer, Edward, *Pelham; or, The Adventures of a Gentleman*, 3 vols. (London: Henry Colburn, 1828)

Plot Summary: Pelham, the son of a 'moderate whig' father and a fashionable mother (armed with irresistible Chesterfieldian advice for her son) gives the reader a peripatetic tour of his own career as a dandy. Pelham's narrative position is that of wry instructor in the arcane customs and opinions of his dandy race. He takes the reader first to Paris where the right and wrong restaurants are touched on, what is fashionable to order for a meal, what is not, which hotel is the best appointed for discerning travellers, where to be seen, where not to be seen. He returns to England for a tour of the comically middle-class pleasures of Cheltenham and, finally, to London where his life is expressed through urban signs: the street he lives on, the shops in which he allows himself to be seen, the parts of town in which he travels and the cut of his clothes. Included in the tour of his life is the melodramatic tale of his friend, Sir Reginald Glanville, wrongly accused of murder, framed by villains and eventually rescued from prison by Pelham who undertakes a dangerous expedition into London's *terra incognita*, the East End, where he uncovers proof of the plot aimed at destroying his friend. Pelham marries Reginald's sister who is otherwise a mere cipher.

Comments: Bulwer's *Pelham* is the quintessential late-1820s dandy novel. The hero wins a parliamentary seat as a Whig, but the seat is challenged and presented to a candidate who supports the government (Tory). Later offered a seat by the government in return for his support, he is sorely tempted, but refuses in order to await the time he can return as an independent gentleman, ambitious not for 'fame', as he had been in his dandy guise, but for 'greatness'. The audience for Pelham's tour of dandy life is manifestly dual: those social exclusives who will appreciate the keen irony of his self-revelations and those middle-class aspirants to fashion eager to gather his cunningly distributed crumbs of information about exclusive society. Pelham's skills in managing aristocrats, bankers, shopkeepers, even the criminal classes, support his claims as a liberal aspirant to power in a period of unsettling social and political change.

Bulwer, Edward, *The Disowned*, 3 vols., 3rd edn [1st edn in December 1828] (London: Henry Colburn, 1829)

Plot Summary: The novel is set vaguely in the 1780s and 1790s, but the politics and social issues belong to the world of the late 1820s. The plot is divided between two sets of protagonists, the sad history of Algernon Mordaunt and his beloved Isabel St Leger, an impoverished orphan, and the adventures of Clarence Linden, an aristocratic hero fallen on slender times who must seek out a life in middle-class London. Mordaunt and Isabel are married, though at the wedding Mordaunt has misgivings: 'an icy and thrilling foreboding curdled to his heart!' Rightly so, since the legal case for his inheritance is lost: 'It is past, Isabel: henceforth we have no wealth but in each other. The cause has been decided—and—and—we are beggars!' (I, 323) He dies and is buried on a hill, separate from his family, leaving a child whose story the author promises in another novel. The second protagonist, Clarence Linden, is more fortunate. Although he undergoes serial humiliations in his associations with the middle classes, he is rescued by a wealthy mentor and conquers both society and politics by dint of elegant manners and his appointment as private secretary to Lord Aspenden. In the final pages, the hero, now Lord Ulswater, marries his beloved, a wealthy heiress, Lady Flora Westborough.

Comments: Putting to one side the echoes of Bulwer's marital problems in this novel, the issues of social change in the late 1820s are met with less confidence here than in *Pelham*. The frustrations of genteel employment are examined in authorial asides, the shame of selling artistic talents of any sort, the drudgery of writing 'fashionable novels' in particular. But the major delights of *The Disowned* are the middle-class characters that the aristocratic Clarence Linden meets in London, especially his landlady, the redoubtable Mrs Copperas: 'We possess accommodations of a most elegant description—accustomed to the genteelest circles' (I, 108–9), she assures Clarence. Dinners, intellectual evenings and amateur musicales follow upon his taking rooms with Mrs Copperas, so painful to his spirits that Clarence doubts with reason that he will be able to manage the 'base, pretending, noisy, scarlet vulgarity of the middle ranks' (I, 136). His mentor informs Clarence, preparing him for the inevitable inclusion of the middle classes in his life, that a 'man will never be a perfect gentleman who lives only with gentlemen. To be a man of the world, we must view the world in every grade, and in every perspective' (I, 142–3).

Bulwer, Edward, *Godolphin, a novel*, 3 vols. (London: Richard Bentley, 1833)[9]

Plot Summary: Constance Vernon's father, a failed politician, on his deathbed extracts from his daughter the promise that she will take revenge on the aristocracy for its refusal to allow him, as a man of talents from 'middle life', to be admitted to the innermost councils of power in the government. Constance must never marry for love, but only for power. Constance, who is ambitious, beautiful, well-educated and eager to engage in a political life, marries Lord Erpingham, a wealthy dull-witted aristocrat, even though she loves Percy Godolphin, a talented, comparatively poor, reduced member of the aristocracy. With her radical political sentiments she strives to sabotage the aristocracy from within. Godolphin, meanwhile, falls under the spell of Augustus Saville, a dark version of the dandy, a man of fashion, clever, cunning and handsome, admitted to the most exclusive aristocratic circles, but also a gambler, a speculator (wealthy through lending and investing his dubiously obtained winnings in the stock market) and a man of luxurious habits. With a small fortune left to him by a cousin, Godolphin follows Saville to Europe to take up the life of a disengaged, luxurious aristocrat under Saville's tutelage, living only for his own pleasure and ease. Lord Erpingham dies, Constance and Godolphin are married, but do not immediately find happiness together. Their lives and ambitions have diverged too much. With the advice of a mutual friend they retire from the world and engage in domestic affections where they do find happiness. Both join in rejoicing at the advent of the Reform Bill of 1832 and its eventual effect, they predict, of removing the 'obstacles to genius ... which have been fatal, not to myself alone', says Constance, 'but to all I have admired and loved; which render the great heartless, and the lowly servile; which make genius either an enemy to mankind or the victim to itself ... shall, if never utterly removed, at least be smoothed away into more genial and unobstructed elements of society' (III, 306).

Comments: *Godolphin* moves away from the novel of fashion towards the social problem novel. Bulwer engages the condition of aristocratic women, disenfranchised from political power, but placed paradoxically in the London world of political life where their 'duties' are ambiguous at best. Constance Vernon can also be seen as a symbolic stand-in for Men of Talent from 'middle life', like Bulwer, who are denied power by aristocratic exclusivity. The criminal law and poor laws need attention, it is claimed, but the great aristocrats care only for issues that concern property, the source of their own wealth. The fashionable culture of social gossip, repartee, newspapers, the *Morning Post*'s 'Fashionable World', advertisements of domestic services, estate auctions and property sales,

the usual feast of silver fork fiction, are eschewed for the more essayistic concerns of political journals and magazines.

BULWER, ROSINA (1802–82)

Rosina Anne Doyle Bulwer Lytton, born into a family of moderate social standing in Ireland, came with her mother to England in 1812, where she entered the
society of French aristocrats who had escaped the Revolution. She and Edward
Bulwer were married in 1827. They were separated in 1836. After the separation
she turned to writing to support herself, finding her £400-per-year settlement
inadequate to her style of life. After *Cheveley* she published twelve more novels,
literary essays and a number of autobiographical works.

Bulwer, Rosina, *Cheveley; or, The Man of Honour*, 3 vols. (London: Bull,
1839)[10]

Plot Summary: 'The first two volumes of *Cheveley* depict the unhappy marriage
of the Cliffords, the boorish and unfaithful Lord De Clifford and his blameless
wife, who falls passionately in love with the Marquis of Cheveley. In the third
volume, the plot is resolved when Lord De Clifford falls from his horse and dies.
The novel was widely regarded as being a *roman à clef*, the revenge taken by
Rosina Bulwer on her husband, Edward Bulwer, for his unfaithfulness and violence, both portrayed in De Clifford.'[11]

Comments: Rosina Bulwer's *Cheveley* (1839) was merely her first salvo in a half-
century campaign of hatred for her husband Edward Bulwer, a feeling that
characterized the relationship on both sides. Rosina's superb ear for spoken conversation, however, catches the brutal and stupid malice of her mother-in-law,
Mrs Bulwer, with satisfying and unerring skill.

BURDETT, MRS (C. D.) (*FL.* LATE 1820–30S)

Biography: not found.

Burdett, Mrs (C. D.), *At Home. A Novel*, 3 vols. (London: Henry
Colburn, 1828)

Plot Summary: Mr Fielding a country parson, a younger son and brother to
Lord Alton, is also father to the lovely and virtuous Julia, who after her mother's
early death spends much of her childhood with Lord and Lady Ellesmere, parents to Lord Calvert, the hero of the novel with whom she secretly falls in love.
Lord Calvert upon his majority goes to France, falls in with a crowd of dandies, picks up their habits and eventually leads them as a style-setter, though
he is wise enough to see through the triviality of the dandy pose. In Paris he

meets Lord Fitzosborne, a seasoned dandy who has been sent by his father, Lord Tralee, a parvenu office holder dependent on the Tory Party, to seduce Calvert away from the firm Whig principles of his father Lord Ellesmere and get Calvert's support for the Tory government. Lord Tralee and his son Fitzosborne are deeply involved in an extortion scheme involving the excise tax in Ireland, a scandal that will be exposed unless certain measures of the Whig opposition are defeated. Fitzosborne, charming and good-looking, is the villain of the piece, a dangerous dandy, and a speculator in politics, love and finance – scheming, calculating and successful almost to the end. He persuades Julia to consent to marriage with him, misleading her about Lord Calvert's true feelings for her – this in order to secure her fortune and thus cover the financial hole left by his father's pilfering. Just in time, it is revealed that Fitzosborne is already married and has a child. He takes his own life. Julia suffers the fever that accompanies such revelations, but recovers after Lord and Lady Ellesmere 'alternately folded her to their hearts'. In a very short time she marries Lord Calvert at which, 'the long lines of tenantry, that had for miles escorted the bridal equipages ... danced till the rising sun superseded all other illumination' (III, 358).

Comments: This tale of social and political scheming marks the beginnings in post-Reform politics of the transition from the political parties into which one is born, to modern political parties organized around party platforms and parliamentary voting blocs. Lord Ellesmere, old style, opposes such a change: "'No party, Calvert, no party," hastily interrupted the Earl. "Never consider politics as a profession. Be independent in your principles as you are in your circumstances; but never condescend to be a party-man'" (I, 192). Lord Fitzosborne and his father Lord Tralee are of course party men in the modern sense, that is political hacks looking out for their own interests. The hallowed Whig heritage of the Glorious Revolution, of 'Hampden and Lord Albemarle', is not theirs. The novel concludes as Whig loyalties in silver fork novels tend to do, cementing principle and party by a series of aristocratic marriages within family groups.

BURY, LADY CHARLOTTE [SUSAN CAMPBELL] (1775–1861)

Lady Charlotte Bury, the youngest daughter of the Duke of Argyll, served as lady-in-waiting to Queen Caroline from 1810 to 1815, a position that obliged her to become a witness for Caroline's defence in the 'Delicate Investigation', not good for Lady Charlotte's social reputation, but an event that established her as a strong, public Whig proponent for the rest of her life. Her first marriage to Colonel John Campbell, a near-penniless cousin, ended with his death in 1809, leaving Lady Charlotte hard-pressed for money, hence her court appointment. Her second marriage in 1818 to the Reverend John Bury, the tutor to her daughters, shocked society. Twice-widowed (the Reverend Bury died in 1832) and having both times married men as poor as herself, Lady Charlotte drudged at writing for her living. In 1833, she wrote requesting the payment of a debt owed her, claiming that she could not eat until it was repaid.[12] Her silver fork novels, *Flirtation* (1827), *The Separation* (1830),[13] *The Exclusives* (1830), *The Disinherited; and The Ensnared* (1834), *The Devoted* (1836) and *Love* (1836) are earnest works, burdened with melodramatic plots and tragic endings, but they carried considerable cachet with contemporaries as reliable *romans à clef.* *The Exclusives,* for example, was immediately followed by a 'Key', *The Separation* was advertised by Bury's publisher as revealing the secrets of a real-life event, and *Flirtation* achieved a certain amount of popularity suggested by its three editions in a single year. Her lasting literary fame, however, rests on her *Diary Illustrative of the Times of George the Fourth* published anonymously in 1838, but attributed by contemporaries to Lady Charlotte for knowledge of the Court that only she possessed.

Bury, Lady Charlotte, *Flirtation*, 3 vols. (London: Henry Colburn, 1827)

Plot Summary: *Flirtation* focuses on two sisters, Lady Emily and Lady Frances, one a flirt (Lady Frances) and one not (Lady Emily). Lady Frances marries for money, flirts in her opera box, loses the affection of her husband, runs up a mountain of debts, falls into the hands of a seducer and dies in misery. The lower ranks in this novel suffer from 'flirtation' as well. Miss Macalpine, who naively credited the false advances and protestations of the first Lord Mowbray, remains single for life, though still devoted to the Mowbray family. There are a significantly large number of characters who suffer from 'flirtation'. Rosalinda, an Italian heiress in the *Grandison* tradition, misinterprets the common politeness of the present Lord Mowbray when he visits Italy, follows him back to England, but to no avail. She forfeits her inheritance in leaving Italy, is driven to employment as an opera singer and dies in Pimlico of a broken heart. Rose Devlin, a country girl seduced by a local squire, Mr Carlton, is discovered by Lady Emily in London working as a prostitute. Rose's father follows her to London only to die after finding her. Her mother goes mad in the parish workhouse. Lady Emily, the non-flirting sister, all that is good, humble, obedient and of service, enjoys nature, home decoration and pious reading. She becomes the willing companion of her elderly uncle when he falls on hard times and must leave London for more humble quarters in Clifton. Lord Mowbray rescues Lady Emily from a wicked attempt by Mr Carlton 'and his ruffians' to abduct her, another echo of *Grandison*, seeks her hand in marriage and builds a small temple of love in his garden to commemorate the first day he conversed with her.

Comments: *Flirtation*, though published by Colburn and capitalizing on the vogue for silver fork novels, belongs to an earlier generation of women's fiction in terms of its story and frame of reference. Miss Macalpine resembles a Susan Ferrier Scotswoman, comic, naive, blunt and speaking home truths to sophisticated aristocrats. Rosalinda's experimentation with employment is reminiscent of Frances Burney's heroine in *The Wanderer*, with the same sorry results. The *Grandisonian* echoes are obvious in the tale of the Italian girl who follows an English lord to England. It is difficult to see this story as having any direct reference to the two heroines of *Sense and Sensibility*, though Willoughby is a 'flirt'. There is a Lady Dashwood in the final pages of Lady Bury's novel whose adultery with a noble lord gives rise to the same sort of newspaper scandal as Mr Crawford's and Maria Rushworth's elopement in *Mansfield Park*: 'The *Morning Post* and other public prints teemed with the *fracas* for some days, and then it was as much forgotten as though it had never happened. Forgotten!—where? and by whom? It is an awful question—too awful to be answered in these pages.' (III, 356).

Bury, Lady Charlotte, *The Exclusives*, 3 vols. (London: Henry Colburn and Richard Bentley, 1830)

Plot Summary: There are at least three mini-plots in this novel, all of them dependent on the promises of a *roman à clef* for sustaining interest. First, there is the mockery of women who enforce the laws of exclusivity, Lady Tilney and her group. Second, there is moral criticism directed at the loose morality of the exclusive class. Third (and fourth), there are two romantic stories, both of them dependent on mistakes of communication that come in such a structured, ritual-based aristocratic society. Real feelings are lost in the characters' busy struggle to stay afloat in high society. The first story is that of Lord Albert d'Esterre and Lady Adeline Seymour, who love each other but are hindered through the wicked designs of exclusive society: George Foley aims to marry Adeline's fortune; Lady Hamlet Vernon is out to seduce and possibly marry Albert. All is explained, finally, in the last pages of the last volume. The second love plot is that of Lord Glenmore and Lady Glenmore. Lady Glenmore is targeted for seduction by the wicked and very persuasive Mr Leslie Winyard. Lord Glenmore is convinced of Lady Glenmore's infidelity by incriminating circumstances. He confronts her, she confesses to her inexperience and her errors in social judgement, but claims innocence, which is true enough. He forgives her. But the author, like Mrs Gore in *Women as They Are* (1830), makes sure that Lord Glenmore takes his share of the blame for leaving his wife to navigate exclusive society without his guidance while he devotes himself to government. For reasons of political honour he resigns his post, and he and Lady Glenmore drop their exclusive acquaintances in order to return to the country.

Comments: The lack of a central, controlling plot is the bane of this novel, as it is for many silver fork novels, but this one is especially twittering. The delights of a *roman à clef* have little lasting or sustaining power. The love plots are so predictable that they go for nothing. The excitement is on an ad hoc basis, largely created around the constrained codes that make for misinformation, repression and suppression of feelings. When public spaces must make do for private communication – the opera, in two important scenes; a visit to a Molière play (the theatre box), dinner parties, Almack's – these things happen. With the best of good intentions, characters who act with candour and innocence are at a disadvantage. Lady Bury is much concerned with the different value systems represented in public and private life, with, of course, private life given the author's stamp of approval. Burney's novels are the likely source of the insistent tropes illustrating social inhibitions that block communication in polite society.

Bury, Lady Charlotte, *The Separation*, 3 vols. (London: Henry Colburn and Richard Bentley, 1830)

Plot Summary: The story of Lord Fitzharris, a protagonist in the 'dandy' mode of Disraeli's *Vivian Grey* and Bulwer's *Pelham*, takes a surprising turn when Lord Fitzharris leaves London for France where he falls in love with a penniless French woman, Lenora, whom he marries in a Catholic ceremony. Lord Fitzharris loves Lenora, but cannot reconcile himself to admitting the marriage in England since his family's finances depend on his marrying well. He abandons his foreign wife (and son) in England, having first tried selling her as mistress to a friend. He then bigamously marries the heiress of a rich merchant family, 'the Lawrences of Russell Square' (by this time living in Grosvenor Square). The new Lady Fitzharris is an example of all that is good, moral and right about English middle-class womanhood. Far better, more 'noble' than her aristocratic husband and in-laws, she attends Lenora on her deathbed and adopts Lenora's son by Lord Fitzharris, her own child by Lord Fitzharris having died soon after birth. Lenora, after a harrowing mad scene, dies 'in the rites of her own religion and in the faith of all Christians'. Lord Fitzharris, 'lived on, but it is feared that his repentance had no foundation to rest upon, and he died as he had lived— unblessed, unhonoured'.

Comments: Bury's *The Separation* addresses the fabric of fashionable life only in separate bits and pieces. The characters visit the opera, drive on Regent Street and witness an after-theatre street fracas in Covent Garden. But literally 'the charm of the opera' as 'the great theatre of London society' supplies the overheated rhetoric and melodramatic structure of the novel, providing a scene, for example, in which the dying Lenora, Lady Fitzharris and the bigamous husband are gathered for a grand confrontation. There are also infant deaths, death by poisoning and plentiful lunatics. Lady Bury's operatic sensibility provides an opportunity for her reflections on the gender-strapped predicament of women, but the here and now of fashionable society is mercilessly invoked for its inability to 'feel' or even comprehend the tragedies of her heroines. In the minds of London exclusives the history of Lenora and Lady Fitzharris is merely a newspaper story, a passing scandal of the moment, an entertainment for the breakfast table.

Bury, Lady Charlotte, *Journal of the Heart,* Preface by Lady Bury, 1st edn 1830 (London: James Cochrane and Co., 1835)

Summary of Preface: This volume is a collection of short pieces by 'the Hon. Anne Seymour Damer', and comes with 'some account of her Life and Character' written by Lady Bury, her 'cousin', as she is called in a letter included in the prefatory material. The 'Preface' that comes with this volume is reprinted from 'Preface to the Second Edition of *Belmore*' (a novel by Anne Seymour Damer) and was written by Lady Bury in 1827 (p.3). Lady Bury's 'Preface' is short and included in other preliminary matter. She notes Mrs Damer's career as a sculptor, her present claim to fame, almost in passing: 'Of her works as a sculptor, if they do not claim the highest meed of praise, they yet merited and obtained great admiration. Lord Byron once mistook one of her heads (I believe that of Mr Lamb) for a bust of Grecian art' (p. 10). Lady Bury's strongest interest is displayed in relating the consequences of Mrs Damer's unhappy marriage: 'But though Mrs. Damer was uninfluenced by any motive of necessity to enter the lists of fame, the happiest ties of woman's life were denied to her. During the short time that she was a wife she behaved excellently well to a singularly depraved husband; and at his death she despoiled herself of every thing to pay his debts, as far as her means allowed, even to the very diamond buckles of her shoes' (p. 6).

Comments: Anne Seymour Damer's collection of stories hangs on the thread of a 'journal' kept by the heroine to record the 'feelings' she experiences on a tour of the Continent, 'A Journal of the Heart' being the title of her first entry: 'I went to the Opera—beautiful music! The Griselda music grows upon one like all real pleasures ... yet sometimes music is *too* painful, and a time may come when I may not be able to bear it' (pp. 17–18).

Bury, Lady Charlotte, *The Disinherited; and The Ensnared,* 3 vols. (London: Richard Bentley, 1834)

Plot Summary: These are two short novels published together. *The Disinherited* begins with a comic sketch of the vulgar commercial family of Sir Robert Leslie, sparing one daughter, Honoria, who has spent her childhood as a companion to Alfred Montagu the son of Lord Montagu, a business associate (in some mysterious way) of her father. She falls in love, as per usual, with young Alfred, but his father disinherits him for taking up the profession of artist. The novel provides excellent details of young Alfred's failed attempts to sell his art, concluding with a refusal of his work by a publisher of 'ladies albums'. Sir Robert's son Augustus returns from the Middle East to flaunt himself as a dandy. His other daughter, Letitia, spends her time shopping and looking for a husband. Honoria, the good daughter, is shipped off for a visit to Lord Montagu's country house with her father's hope that Lord Montagu will marry her and save him from bankruptcy. Honoria discovers a letter hidden in a book on the top shelf of the library revealing that Lord Montagu has not only mistreated his wife, Alfred's mother, but has abandoned his French mistress, now deceased, and left his illegitimate daughter to earn her bread as a seamstress. When Lord Montagu proposes to Honoria, just as her father had hoped, she refuses him outright. Her family's fortune is lost, her father dies of a heart attack, Lord Montagu commits suicide, and she and her mother must move to humble lodgings in Sydenham. Alfred Montagu the artist, now Lord Montagu, having inherited the title and estate because his estranged father had neglected to name an alternate heir, encounters Honoria by accident at the hackney-coach stand at Elephant and Castle on the way to Lincoln's Inn to see her lawyer. They rediscover their love and are married. The wicked characters, Honoria's siblings Augustus and Letitia in particular, are punished by loss of the father's fortune; the good people, Honoria and Alfred with all their friends find money and happiness.

Plot Summary: In the second tale, *The Ensnared*, Lord de Courcy's love affair with a married woman, Lady Constance Percy, is revealed when her husband unexpectedly discovers a portrait of his wife painted for Lord de Courcy displayed in the painting room of the artist Sir Frederick Marchmont. 'This tale was written', claims the Preface, 'with the express endeavour to show the ultimate misery and wide-extended mischief which are the inevitable consequences of all attachments that are not founded on principle and sanctioned by virtue.'

Comments: The main plots of both stories do little more than insist that aristocrats are wicked and rich merchants are vulgar, two serious issues in the social imagination. In contrast, the minor plots enfolded in the main plots of both of Bury's short novels break new ground. Bury shows a generous appreciation for the uncertain economic prospects of men and women who must live by their own hands, women especially, but men, too, as Alfred Montagu's 'disinherited' condition bears witness. Moreover, it is servants, family retainers, shopkeepers, coachmen and ordinary citizens of no social standing who come to the rescue of the young protagonists when no one else steps forward to challenge the corruption that darkens the higher orders.

Bury, Lady Charlotte, *The Devoted*, 3 vols. (London: Richard Bentley, 1836)

Plot Summary: Two cousins are contrasted: Lady Elizabeth Altamont, who is devoted to reason alone; and Ethel Delamere, her impoverished cousin, who values feeling (virtuous feeling) above reason. Lady Elizabeth loves Mr St Aubyn, a country vicar, the younger brother of Lord Deloraine. Ethel loves St Aubyn as well, but secretly. The choice before Lady Elizabeth is whether to marry Mr St Aubyn for love, or to marry Lord Deloraine, his elder brother, for wealth and title. In a related plot, Delamere, Ethel's brother (lame and passionate) also loves Lady Elizabeth, but with the awkward complexity that he has cause of revenge against her father, Lord Altamont. Lord Altamont is responsible for encouraging the love of Delamere's mother, but shifts her off onto his younger brother in marriage, who, when he discovers her prior relationship with Lord Altamont, disowns his crippled son and his wife. At a house-party theatrical, Delamere directs a game of charades with the word 'bondage' as the key, intentionally setting out the life choices for each of the players. Lady Elizabeth, in the event, rejects marriage with Delamere, relinquishes St Aubyn and marries Lord Deloraine for his estate and title – with dire consequences. Her child dies, her husband dies, the Deloraine title descends to St Aubyn, the man she loved in the first place. She dies. St Aubyn marries Ethel, Miss Delamere, who has loved him from the first and has led a life of silent torment at the hands of Lady Elizabeth who taunts Ethel by exhibiting her own power over St Aubyn.

Comments: The contrast between feeling and reason represented in the two female cousins operates more or less according to structure. But Delamere, Lady Bury's Byronic poet and reluctant politician, brings a perspective on the relationship between aristocratic entertainments – gambling, the arts, painting, theatre and opera – and the principles of the Whig aristocracy that makes *The Devoted* the most challenging of Bury's works. The home theatre episode in *The Devoted* owes much to the theatricals in Austen's *Mansfield Park* with its participants, as in the Austen novel, morally implicated in the choice of the parts they play. The similarities between Ethel Delamere and Fanny Price in their love interests are also drawn from *Mansfield Park*. The theatrical charades, particularly in regard to the key word, 'bondage', may have found a second life in Charlotte Brontë's *Jane Eyre* (1847).

DISRAELI, BENJAMIN (1804–81)

Benjamin Disraeli, middle-class, born into a scholar's family in Bloomsbury, published his best-known novel of fashionable life *Vivian Grey* (1826) anonymously, although his publisher, Henry Colburn, put it about that the novel was written by an exclusive, a man of the first rank. *Vivian Grey* was a sensation. Disraeli followed it with *The Young Duke* (1831), a potboiler of consumer excess, after which he began successfully to make his way in London's fashionable circles. *Henrietta Temple* (1837), his last silver fork novel, was published in the year he entered Parliament, his primary career goal. In the 1840s, after the vogue for fashionable fiction had passed, Disraeli published his famous 'Young England' novels: *Coningsby* (1844), *Sybil*, (1845) and *Tancred* (1847).

Disraeli, Benjamin, *Vivian Grey*, 3 vols. (London: Henry Colburn, 1826)

Plot Summary: Vivian's story is the education and progress of an ambitious young dandy's attempt to enter political life. Part comedy, part melodramatic tragedy, it is, finally, a highly unstable characterization. The reader is encouraged to like Vivian, but Vivian is also ambitious and coldly efficient in manipulating others, utterly selfish without either moral or political principles. His father has only a life interest in a £2,000-a-year income, so Vivian must earn his own way in life. He cultivates the manners and mannerisms of the exclusives, using his access to them in order to manipulate their power to his own advantage. He constructs an Opposition party out of the second-rate power holders that he is able to bring under his control, or so he believes. When he falls from favour, he leaves the country for Germany to experience a failed affair with a girl named Violet Fane.

Comments: Ellen Moers' comparison of Disraeli's *Vivian Grey* with Bulwer's *Pelham* (1828) puts Disraeli's novel in the perspective of other dandy writing: 'Pelham is a dandy who conceals a serious moral purpose behind his affectations; Vivian is a dandy whose lust for power defies concealment, and whose dandyism is a pose to gild immoral means used for an immoral end ... Pelham's motto reads: "Manage *yourself*, and you may manage all the world." Vivian Grey's credo runs: "A SMILE FOR A FRIEND, AND A SNEER FOR THE WORLD, is the way to govern mankind" ... Pelham's wit is fresh, spontaneous, impudent; Vivian's is always calculated and often sinister.'[14]

Disraeli, Benjamin, *The Young Duke*, 'A Moral Tale, though Gay', 3 vols. (London: Henry Colburn and Richard Bentley, 1831)

Plot Summary: The claustrophobic tale of an enormously rich child, then youth, then man. He is left under the care of a good guardian (only moderately wealthy, and a Catholic, too), but one who is hampered from acting for his ward because of his chronically ill wife. The young Duke is thus given over to his rich, high-fashion relatives who intend him to marry their daughter, and in bringing up the young Duke, spoil him thoroughly. He comes of age, wastes his fortune in architectural projects, expensive furnishings, a mistress and finally, disastrously, in gambling. He appeals to his good guardian, the Catholic Mr Dacres, who helps the young Duke salvage what he can – a small amount of property relative to what he had, but still an immense fortune. The young Duke marries his guardian's daughter, May, with whom he has fallen passionately in love. He also makes an impressive speech in the House of Lords, taking the side of Catholic emancipation, his only genuine accomplishment in life until his marriage with May.

Comments: In some ways, Disraeli's hero, the young Duke, is the story of *Mansfield Park*'s Henry Crawford rewritten with Henry as the hero. That is very much the interpretation Margaret Fuller (1810–50), the nineteenth-century American writer and feminist, takes: 'The English novelist, Disraeli, in his novel of the "Young Duke", made a man of the most depraved stock be redeemed by a woman who despises him when he has only the brilliant mask of fortune and beauty to cover the poverty of his heart and brain, but knows how to encourage him when he enters on a better course.'[15] *The Young Duke*, it must be admitted, is a very long tale for present-day readers to get through. Each one of the young Duke's excesses must be described in lengthy detail, accounts of material luxuries, expenses and entertainments, fantasies of fortune that a middle-class author might entertain with the help of the *Morning Post*'s most exuberant accounts of exclusive life in its 'Fashionable World' columns.

Disraeli, Benjamin, *Henrietta Temple, a Love Story*, 3 vols. (London: Henry Colburn, 1837)

Plot Summary: The story laments the condition of pre-Reform Catholics of noble blood who are prevented from acting in the political life of the nation. Their energies are thrown upon 'the Empire of fashion'. The hero, Ferdinand Armine, has a commission in the Guards obtained for him by a family friend and spiritual advisor. Thinking that he will be his father's heir, he begins to spend money borrowed on that promise in a reckless way. He finds unexpectedly that he will not be the heir, so he returns to England to marry his cousin Katherine, who is the heiress of the fortune. Katherine falls in love with him and they make plans to marry. However, on a country walk, Armine meets Henrietta Temple by accident in the woods near home. It is instant love on both sides, which presents a knotty problem for reader and author in regards to the previous engagement. Miss Temple is also a Catholic. Henrietta finds out about Katherine and leaves for Italy where she is courted by a nice, kind, gentlemanly sort of fellow. Ferdinand follows her. Disraeli's improbable solution is to have Ferdinand marry Henrietta (who still loves him), and Katherine, whose feelings were not all that strong for Ferdinand anyway, marry the kind gentleman who was courting Henrietta. Meanwhile, Henrietta inherits an immense fortune so all live happily ever after.

Comments: Ferdinand, as the love plots show, can easily be taken as a debt-ridden, impulsive, irrational, self-indulgent weakling. He is frustrated only by his own selfish, foolish judgement and his careless treatment of two worthy women. But there is much description of interior decorating interest to amuse the reader – 'The room, without being inconveniently crowded, was amply stored with furniture, every article of which bespoke a refined and luxurious taste: easy chairs of all descriptions, most inviting couches, cabinets of choice inlay, and grotesque tables covered with articles of virtú' (1, 193). There is a fictionalized version of William Crockford (1776–1844), low-born owner of London's most fashionable gambling house, and a recognizable version of Lady Blessington's son-in-law and likely lover, Count d'Orsay, as Count Alcibiades Mirabel, a man of constant good cheer and generosity, who eventually bails Ferdinand from debtors' prison by winning a large sum at gambling. The reader is also taken to seedy loan offices in the City as Ferdinand falls into financial ruin. Ferdinand reforms, we are told, and, 'after the passing of the memorable act of 1828', he becomes a Catholic MP, 'adhering to the Whig politics' of his family, but always standing ready, says Disraeli, who had turned Tory before 1837 when this novel was published, to 'ultimately support that British and national administration which Providence has doubtless in store for these outraged and distracted realms' (III, 329).

EDEN, EMILY (1797–1869)

Emily Eden, born into a large aristocratic Whig family who were active in national politics, was educated at home, read widely and was encouraged by her family in her interest in politics. She became an important Whig hostess. Eden published a novel in 1859, *The Semi-Detached House*, which, after its success, she followed with a novel written much earlier in 1829, *The Semi-Attached Couple*, published by Bentley in 1860.

Eden, Emily, *The Semi-Attached Couple* [written in 1829] (London: Bentley, 1860)

Plot Summary: Eden's novel is a genuinely amusing, wry and sentimental novel of family rivalries and young love. There are two young women, two pairs of lovers, each with relationship troubles. The first pair, Helen and Lord Teviot, from respective gentry and aristocratic backgrounds, can't understand one another. 'Lord Teviot's haughty sense of superiority is made pointed in the novel by allusions to Austen's *Pride and Prejudice*.'[16] The second couple, Eliza and Colonel Beaufort, have an opposite problem: 'Poor girl! little did she think that while she sat quietly in the carriage, pondering over Colonel Beaufort's tritest remarks, hoarding up as the most important recollections that he liked reading the newspaper, and did not care about poetry; that ... the ungrateful creature had dismissed from his mind all the conversations that had ever passed between them ... and that she was merely to him a good-humoured little Miss Something, whom he had met at St Mary's' (II, 73).

Comments: Winding through the love interests, there are political points for Eden to score against an internally divided Tory Party. A fictionalized version of Lord Liverpool's death in 1827 sums up the state of the Tory Party in 1828–9:

he took to his bed and died. His cabinet was broken up. It had been, after the usage of all cabinets, divided into two factions, opposed on all important points to each other, but forming what is by courtesy called an united cabinet, under the gentle sway of the worn-out nonentity at their head. He was gone. Six or seven newspapers, with broad black borders, announced the death of one of the greatest men of the age ... An equal number of papers, after professing, with becoming candour and humanity, that they warred not with the dead, raked up all the old scandal they could collect against the deceased ... they prophesied the utter annihilation of the ministerial party, and announced that in twenty-four hours they should be able to give a correct list of the new cabinet about to be formed by the powerful leader of the opposition. All the idle men in London rushed to their clubs, and such high betting had not been known since the last Epsom races. (II, 102–4)

GORE, CATHERINE (1799–1861)

Catherine Gore, the daughter of a well-to-do wine merchant, with connections in the aristocracy on her mother's side, married into the fringes of the aristocracy. Her husband, Charles Gore, the youngest son of the Earl of Aram, was an officer in the 1st Regiment of the Life Guards, a position that brought his wife access to exclusive society. He was forced to leave the Life Guards on account of bad health, and as a British diplomat he moved the family to Paris for eight years. There was always an urgent need for more money. Over three decades, Mrs Gore published more than seventy titles totalling more than 200 volumes – plays, poetry, tales, novels, also the editorship of annuals, a dreary task she loathed. The quality of her novels is mixed, understandably considering the pressure on her to produce, but some of them bear up well, particularly *Women as They Are* (1830), *Mothers and Daughters* (1831), *Pin Money* (1831), *The Hamiltons* (1834), *Mrs. Armytage; or Female Domination* (1836), *Stokeshill Place; or the Man of Business* (1837) and *The Cabinet Minister* (1839), which are especially readable. In her most ambitious novel and her masterpiece, *Cecil; or, The Adventures of a Coxcomb* (1841), she brings the silver fork genre to a close with her hero's tale of aristocratic inflexibility and failure in both his public and private life.

Gore, Catherine, *Women as They Are; or, The Manners of the Day*, 3 vols. (London: Henry Colburn and Richard Bentley, 1830)

Plot Summary: Helen Mordaunt, eighteen years old, achieves 'an excellent marriage' to Lord Willersdale, an aristocrat, a politician at the highest levels, and forty-one years old. She is confused, feels none of the traditional feelings of 'love', doesn't much like how delighted her parents are to get rid of her, and can't really rejoice in their happiness at her future material prosperity. Lord Willersdale, the best of men, is solicitous for her happiness, but is reserved and keeps his distance. He wants her to love him for himself. Neither one of the two has the slightest idea about how to effect a connection. They go to London, she gets involved in fashionable London engagements. She is not corrupted by them, she just enjoys dancing and is young, healthy and physical. She also gets involved in scandal, quite by accident. She herself is not at fault, but tongue-waggers are always ready. Lord Willersdale loses his government position in a change of party; he fights a duel for her honour (quite unnecessarily); Helen is given the opportunity to show her love for him by nursing him: many tears. She insists that they go to Ireland to reclaim his health. They thrive there, but must return to London after the winter for him to become prime minister. The story then more or less repeats itself with another villain and a second scandal. The novel concludes with explanations all around. Helen gives her husband a stern wife's talk about not giving her any guidance for behaviour in exclusive society. He is all apologies.

Comments: This is Mrs Gore's first novel of fashionable life and is a serious exploration of the stresses that modern life – social status, celebrity, a consumer culture – can bring to a marital relationship. The main issue, the age gap in the marriage of a forty-one-year-old politician to an eighteen-year-old girl still finding her identity, brings all of these issues into powerful focus.

Gore, Catherine, *Pin Money; a Novel*, 3 vols. (London: Henry Colburn and Richard Bentley, 1831)

Plot Summary: There are three primary plots that meander their way through the novel.

Plot 1: Frederica's officious aunt, Lady Olivia Tadcaster, has insisted that Frederica be granted 'pin money', a small independent income, in her marriage settlement. This happens against the better judgement of her husband, Sir Brooke Rawleigh. She mismanages this income, gets into embarrassing debt, mostly by being too obliging to fashionable friends who trick and lure her into spending more than she should. She is pursued by a notoriously licentious rake, a remarkably plausible figure and powerful in fashionable and government circles, Lord Calder. He is tall, dark, handsome, lays down the law in society, and is extremely clever and personally engaging. Frederica is never tempted to stray from Sir Brooke, whom she loves, but she repeatedly falls into compromising situations engineered by Lord Calder. As Mrs Gore makes clear, Lord Calder is much more intelligent, cultured and socially skilled, and he has a more powerful mind than 'poor Sir Brooke'. Much of the plot is made up of marital misunderstandings occasioned by Frederica's participation in London fashionable life enabled by her pin money. Sir Brooke is a country squire, happy in his country consequence, a good man, handsome, lovable, loved and very likeable, just not too smart. His wife is loyal and deeply in love with him. Mrs Gore has fun with his sullen behaviour, door slamming and his trials in becoming an MP. He buys a seat, must do the duties, dislikes it all, but thinks it necessary to his position. He would much rather spend the evening with his lovely wife. And she would like to be with him, too.

Plot 2: The Waddlestone story. Leonora Waddlestone is the granddaughter of a 'soapboiler'. Her father, Mr Beverley, a promising attorney, has married into a City fortune, but taken his wife's family name with her fortune. Mr Beverley is a gentleman, highly respectable and a participant in the highest cultural circles – of artists, collectors, music – but her mother, the soapboiler heiress, is a vulgar embarrassment. It appears that Leonora is engaged to Lord Launceston, Frederica's brother, but Launceston is in reality involved in an elaborate ruse with his friend Colonel Rhyse, to act the lover so that Rhyse will be allowed to visit Leonora with him. Rhyse and Leonora are secretly engaged, but Mrs

Waddlestone insists on her marrying 'a Lord'. The ruse is only revealed at the very end.

Plot 3: Lord Launceston, Frederica's brother, is a reformed spendthrift who remains short of money, but falls in love with his mother's poor companion, Lucy Elbany. Lucy is in actual fact Lady Mary, the cousin he was promised to in his infancy by their parents. He refuses to honour his parental engagement to Lady Mary Trevelyan, so his mother introduces Lady Mary as 'Lucy', her poor companion. Since Lady Mary has been in Italy for many years with her father Lord Trevelyan, Launceston doesn't recognize her, nor do any of the London people who might be supposed to know her. This ruse is revealed in a dénouement scene at the end. Meanwhile Lady Rawleigh (our heroine Frederica) has been much disturbed by what seems to be Launceston's double dealing with women. And she dislikes Lucy intensely not only for usurping her mother's love, as it appears she does, but also for getting in the way of Launceston's 'proper' marriage to his cousin Lady Mary. Lucy's true identity as Lady Mary is revealed to Launceston, Frederica and the reader at the end in a staged scene borrowed from the conclusion of Edgeworth's *Belinda*.

Comments: *Pin Money* is a celebration of marriage, of the joys of life in London and of the delight in consumer pleasures laid out in their most tempting and sparkling form. Commercial wealth rubs up against aristocratic wealth, gentry wealth clashes with aristocratic, and cultural prejudices blunder into each other in comic confusion. There are a few yawns for the reader during occasional set pieces and in the baggy plotting, but Gore's wit and irony make up for it.

Gore, Catherine, *Mothers and Daughters; a Tale of the Year 1830*, 3 vols.
(London: Henry Colburn and Richard Bentley, 1831)

Plot Summary: The moral plot follows a straight and simple road. Lady Maria Willingham, 'neither handsome, clever, nor amiable', is widowed and left with three daughters. The two eldest daughters, Claudia and Eleanor, who are placed with her, become mercenary marriage competitors in the aristocratic marriage market. Both girls lose love and fortune through their own unsuccessful machinations. The youngest daughter, Minnie, is raised by more provincial relatives from the middle classes, her uncle General De Vesci and his wife. Lady Maria and her two older girls go off to the Continent to polish their elegance. Minnie, in contrast, all that is natural and good, is rewarded by marriage to her true love, her cousin Charles Willingham, who treats her like a sister for most of the novel, inflicting suffering on Minnie very much like Fanny Price's in Austen's *Mansfield Park*, until he can be brought around. This Fanny Price trope gets a second exposure in the novel with Minnie's cousin, Mary Willingham, the smallpox-scarred daughter of Minnie's father's brother. Mary is in love with Frederick Lorimer who is in love with Mary's cousin Eleanor (who, like Mary Crawford, loves him, but refuses him as a second son with no fortune), and then mistakenly is believed by Mary to be in love with her cousin Minnie. But Frederick, like Austen's Edmund Bertram, proposes marriage to Mary when he comes to recognize the inner beauty of her character. Most of the romantic plot is mere piffle, though Eleanor and Claudia are given moments of painful and comic humiliation.

A secondary plot in *Mothers and Daughters* bears the weight of the political and social upheavals of the late 1820s. The wealthy banking family of the Westlands enters the novel as the extended family of General De Vesci's wife. Minnie, the De Vesci's niece and intended heiress, spends time at the Westlands' home in Marylebone on a regular basis of polite visits. The Westland family, as opposed to the corrupted circle of high life aspired to by Lady Maria Willingham and her girls, consists of seriously worthy persons. But as parvenus, the Westlands amuse Mrs Gore as she explores the customs and rituals of Marylebone society with the unsparing eye of a social anthropologist. In contrast, however, to the excesses of aristocratic life, the sign of that higher class's failings, the Westlands' gorgeous display of middle-class wealth is, if undeniably vulgar, also solid proof of British glory and a golden witness to their competence to govern. 'More than one member of the Westland family, indeed, was seated in that honourable House', Mrs Gore claims, 'and Miss De Vesci … found herself obliged to swallow her patés and cutlets in daily audience of the recapitulated debates of the preceding night. In these, and throughout all similar discussions, the name of her cousin Charles found honourable mention.' Charles, Minnie's future husband, stands as Mrs Gore's ideal political figure, one of the 'independent members of the House', who in the late 1820s and early 1830s seemed a key to the possibility of parliamentary reform. Charles Willingham, says Mrs Gore, 'was a patriot in the purest sense of the word' (III, 52–3).

Comments: Mrs Gore's Westland family are the first seriously competent middle-class characters in silver fork fiction, an English family perfectly qualified to take part in the government of the nation. Their representation becomes the standard that is repeated in future novels by Gore and by other silver fork authors.

Gore, Catherine, *The Opera, a novel*, 3 vols. (London: Henry Colburn and Richard Bentley, 1832)

Plot Summary: The story of Adrian Maldyn, an Irish aristocrat, reared in exile in Bavaria by his father, and Adrian's early affair with Stephanine Haslinger, a Bavarian peasant girl, its tragic consequences played out years later in the fashionable world of Reform-period London. Adrian arrives in London to find the city politically abuzz with Reform and with the arrival of a celebrated new opera star, La Silvestra, who unknown to anyone else is the very peasant girl he had seduced and abandoned years before, Stephanine

Haslinger. La Silvestra has arrived in London with the purpose of exacting revenge on Adrian and his father by spoiling Adrian's chances of marriage and the continuance of the family line. The intricacies of the plot are played out through a series of *Mansfield Park*-like amateur rehearsals of an opera to be performed at the home of the Earl of Cardigan, where La Silvestra is welcomed into the aristocratic theatrical troupe as a social equal. Partial revenge comes with La Silvestra's attendance, as an honoured guest, to witness Adrian play the part of a rustic lover in this home-produced opera in which he re-enacts the role he played in real life in Stephanine's seduction. La Silvestra reveals her peasant identity in the concluding pages of the novel in a startling scene in which she rejects the Earl of Cardigan's proposal of marriage with a spirited and strong echo of Elizabeth Bennet's rejection of Mr Darcy in *Pride and Prejudice*.

Comments: Possibly in response to predictions of Great Britain's imminent social and political collapse with the impending Reform Bill of 1832, this novel catches the intense social anxiety that greeted its rocky passage in Parliament. Stephanine Haslinger the Bavarian peasant, as La Silvestra, is easily able to manipulate the aristocratic actors who play at being peasants. The hero, unable to expose La Silvestra's origins, witnesses her success with shocked horror: 'There is something to me almost awful in the perfection of dissimulation practised by this woman; it seems abetted by the inspiration of an evil spirit!' Mrs Gore, who dutifully claims to be appalled as well, also admires and sympathizes with the successes of the class-leaping La Silvestra, the only character energetically alive in a novel otherwise peopled by dried-up, ineffectual, self-destructive aristocrats.

Gore, Catherine, *The Fair of Mayfair*, 3 vols. (London: Henry Colburn and Richard Bentley, 1832)

General Note: A collection of six short 'novels' distributed over three volumes. These stories derive from a point of view central to the political climate of the 1820s, the earlier time, entertaining as they do general representations of the corrupt morals and political principles of a ruling class resistant to reform.

'The Flirt of Ten Seasons', I, 3–233
Plot Summary: A contrast of the diligent hard-working, virtuous family of Mrs Raymond, a widow, living in Fulham for economy's sake, with the fashionable aspirations of richer relatives, the Germaines, who live in Mayfair and have contempt for their poorer relatives. The Raymonds prosper in the world by dint of their merits – literary talent, liberal politics, kindness and generosity of spirit. The Germaines lose out in the marriage market through their ambition to curry favour with the fashionable world and are left at the conclusion 'wintering in Brighton'.

'The Separate Maintenance', I, 237–348; II, 3–220

Plot Summary: Lady Henrietta Wellwood insists on a 'separate maintenance' clause in her marriage settlements on the advice of an interfering aunt. When she and Sir Henry Wellwood fall into differences at the scheming of the same aunt and her friends, Lady Wellwood puts the separate maintenance clause into action. She regrets it even at the time and more so when her estranged husband goes to fight abroad in the Napoleonic wars. She moves to Putney where she sets up a modest but tasteful cottage appropriate to her limited income. The military husband, while returning her dog which had followed him from the neighbourhood to London (a trope borrowed from Frances Burney's *Cecilia*), discovers that Henrietta has a shrine featuring his portrait as a military officer, a hussar, in her little family altar of miniatures. The couple fall in love again and are reunited.

'Hearts and Diamonds: or Fifty Years Ago', II, 223–329; III, 3–36

Plot Summary: The story of Lady Stratherne, 'the gayest, and fairest, and frailest of the beauties of Ranelagh', told fifty years after her death by an elderly contemporary and friend. Lady Stratherne, an old school chum, meets the narrator in Hyde Park and introduces her to the fast-living exclusive society she runs with. Lady Stratherne's guilty secret is that she gambles, but only because her husband pays her no attention. She loses an extravagant sum at play and to save her honour, commits suicide with opium, dying with her distraught husband and two children at her side.

'A Divorcée', III, 39–152

Plot Summary: Amelia, the daughter of a poor family in Bath, the Kendals, in Bath marries the very rich Mr Allanby. She is taken to his hall in the country where she is miserable, lonely and unable to become used to the rigid life of the country squirearchy. He imports some female relatives, but they are part of the same stiff social world. Amelia makes friends with a sweet, disabled, Christian woman nearby, Jane Esthope, the daughter of a former incumbent of the vicarage. Amelia's husband, as a Member of Parliament, removes his wife to London where, 'Mischief, in her most smiling mask, sits like the beautiful witch in Thalaba at an everlasting spinning-wheel, weaving a mingled yarn of sin and sorrow for the daughters of Fashion' (III, 87). Mrs Allanby does every public duty that her husband, the county member, could desire of her, but the artificiality of fashionable life tarnishes both her beauty and her morality. Her husband has no time for her, she is seduced by a rake, taken to Paris and abandoned. She comes back to her first home in the country where she dies in Jane Esthope's cottage, 'a *divorcée*!'

'My Grand-daughter', III, 155–267

Plot Summary: This tale, set in the eighteenth century, features a parvenu who makes a fortune, works at getting a title, marries a peeress, truckles to all her relatives, worships rank and has a daughter. 'For many succeeding years, Sir Gilbert existed for the duty of attending levees and intruding at drawing-rooms; giving dinners to the aristocratic kinsmen of his wife and daughter and ... above all of qualifying the new Lady Ormleen [his daughter] to wear her ermine gracefully, and extend the magnificent connections of the family.' The daughter's spirit is narrowed by the conception of London society her father teaches her, 'that the society of London consists of some three thousand individuals exclusively concentrating the wit, learning, accomplishments, and merit of the Kingdom. She had no more idea of extending her interest beyond this aristocratic ecliptic of the social firmament, than of looking for roses and lilies in a plantation of Savoy cabbages' (III, 160).

'The Special License', III, 270–375

Plot Summary: Young Edward Maxworth is in love with Lady Emma Aston. Edward's banker father, Mr Maxworth, disapproves heartily, believing that, 'You may persuade Lady Emma Aston to a temporary adoption of the habits of a banker's wife; but you will find her recur at last to all the pomps and vanities of Boscawen Castle ... It would destroy all the comfort of my old age, to find a flimsy fiddle-faddle woman of fashion stuck up like a doll by my fireside, to sneer at the habits of my house, and deride a condition of life whose respectability is beyond her power of comprehension' (III, 268–9). Everything, however, works out well: Lady Emma is a sensible girl; Mr Maxworth's daughter Emily falls in love with Lady Emma's brother, Lord Aston – and that too is good. The Aston family is decent and welcoming to the banker's family, and the banker's family, in return, appreciates the Astons. The villains are the Parkyns, a family of nouveau riche, like the Maxworths, but with pretensions to status. The social confrontation takes place in the suburbs, near Box Hill, where the Parkyns and the Maxworths both have country retreats. Mrs Parkyns is the true villain, a social climber who corrupts, first, her son 'Puppy' Parkyns with her ambitions for him as a dandy and, second, her daughter Grace, who is set to catch Dick, the younger son of the Maxworth family, in marriage. But Grace's demands in her marriage settlement, presented by her foppish brother Puppy to old Maxworth, are so outrageous that the match is abruptly terminated.

Comments: The stories in this collection are connected by their common support of the middle classes, their virtues and respectability, as opposed to the vices and exclusiveness of the aristocracy. Such a programme would have gained political traction in the year 1832 when wealthy representatives of banking, manufacturing and trade were reaching for political enfranchisement.

Gore, Catherine, *The Sketch Book of Fashion*, 3 vols. (London: Richard Bentley, 1833)

General Note: A collection of six short 'novels' distributed over three volumes.

'The Pavilion', I, 3–135

Plot Summary: A satirical examination of the 'dandy' culture and the kind of women who thrive in it. The action occurs 'four years after Waterloo' and the story features the wife of the new Prussian ambassador, Countess of Rippenheim, who arrives in London with positive preconceptions of English culture, only to be steadily disabused of her opinion by the frivolity and malice she finds in exclusive London society. 'Well, well', writes Mrs Gore, 'a season in London will scarcely fail to endow her with the right use of her eyes, ears, and understanding … How is it possible for foreigners to be forewarned against the extraordinary instances of *mésalliance* which betray them, in this country, into the society of *parvenues* of every description; actresses, opera dancers, farmer's daughters—all sorts and conditions of women' (I, 8). As for the genuinely exclusive inhabitants, 'She would as soon have expected to find a scorpion hidden under the leaves of a garden rose, as that the languor of her air and the graciousness of her manners could be made a matter of ridicule among those who met her with such eager invitations and overtures of friendship' (I, 12). The tale demonstrates Mrs Gore's disenchantment with English society in 1833, not only in the manners of its exclusive classes, but in the new openness of social movement as well. As for aristocratic women, the misguided standards that aristocratic men employ in choosing their wives reflect not only on the limitations on women's social roles, but the faulty principles that guide that governing class as well. Describing a courtier's concerns in canvassing the marriage market, 'His anxiety, therefore, in the selection of a wife, was less directed to secure a pretty little doll to sit in his drawing-room, embroidering work-bags, or murdering Herz's sonatas for his amusement, after the fashionable pattern of domestic life,—than to find a woman worthy to adorn his rank in the eyes of the world, as well as in his own … qualified to walk hand in hand with him in the saloons of royalty; participate with him in an endless round of festivity and dissipation' (I, 121).

'My Place in the Country', I, 139–255

Plot Summary: Mr Martindale, a merchant, returns from the Cape of Good Hope with a £90,000 fortune and soon marries a woman of his own rank who wishes to figure in fashionable London society. She insists that he acquire a 'place in the country' as a mark of exclusivity, but soon finds that she hates everything about country life. Her husband's fortune has been much depleted by the expense of buying an estate, but the fortunate failure of the deed to their property saves the couple and they are able to leave their 'desolate' rural existence for the comforts of urban life with other mercantile families living near Hanover Square.

'The Second Marriage', I, 259–307; II, 3–183

Plot Summary: This is the story of a young woman, Julia Trevelyan, raised like Emma Woodhouse in great retirement, by a Mr Woodhouse-type father overly concerned for her health and a mother, who, like Mrs Bennet in *Pride* *and Prejudice*, talks embarrassingly to anyone and everyone about her daughter's chances of snagging a rich baronet suitor in marriage. Sir Alan Redwood, the suitor, like Darcy, represses his desire for the heroine, who in turn, must be silent about her love for him. He is recently widowed, has an infant daughter and is confused about his loyalties to his dead wife and his child. When the misunderstandings of the courtship are cleared up, the marriage takes place, but the couple starts marriage on the wrong foot. The heroine, Julia, is confused about her role in county life and in an enlarged family of former in-laws and the little daughter. She also is too young to appreciate the formal manners of her husband's grand household or his close attention to the business of the estate: 'No! he was *not* hers!—never, never could be hers.—He belonged to his dead wife,—his living child ... to any and every one but *her* ... to stewards, tenants, gamekeepers, and constables! Every human being at Farminghurst seemed to have a claim on his time, a title to his personal interest' (II, 77). Redwood is a Mr Knightley sort of person in this respect, a responsible, active landlord attentive to his tenants and the local community. There is a brief appearance of Julia's former governess, Miss Wilmot, Miss Taylor-like who, as in *Emma*, is full of good advice, but of no real help to the heroine since she is herself recently married and busy with a growing family of her own. Other allusions to Austen's works appear in the vein of *Northanger Abbey*, where Julia, like Catherine Morland, trembles in dark passages in Redwood's modernized Gothic house. She comes upon a 'funeral achievement of the late Lady Redwood, with its black bordering, and skull and cross bones' on the staircase, which paralyzes her with terror, and she mistakes Redwood for a ghost and faints. Irritations mount. Redwood wears a ring that Mary, the dead wife, gave him on her deathbed. Julia destroys, innocently, a grove 'sacred to the memory' of Mary. She thinks Redwood is a cold, unresponsive husband; he thinks she is a cold, fashionable woman. She returns to her own family in despair where she falls desperately ill with grief. Redwood arrives to save her life with renewed declarations of love and gives her a lengthy account of his history with his first wife, Mary, with whom it seems he, unhappily, also had a restrained and chilly relationship. Julia recovers and returns to Yorkshire to engage in the responsibilities of a married woman with the help and advice of the late wife's middle-aged sister, Martha, who teaches her how to visit the poor, care for the sick and carry out her new duties as substitute mother to Redwood's young daughter and as the dutiful châtelaine of a great estate.

'The Old and the Young Bachelor', II, 187–312; III, 3–56

Plot Summary: The 'old bachelor', the guardian of Sir Francis (Frank) Norton, has secretly plotted to marry his ward to charming, lovely, spontaneous Sybella Woodford, a woman of Frank's own rank in the country gentry. The alliance falls through because of the manipulations of Frank's other guardian, the 'young bachelor', Lord Farnley, an aristocrat with social ambitions for his friend Frank. Lord Farnley successfully encourages Frank's marriage with an aristocratic woman instead of the gentry-born Sybella. When Lord Farnley later meets Sybella, he falls in love with her and marries her himself. Each of these 'mixed' marriages is a disaster. Sybella cannot find happiness as the wife of a careless, cold aristocratic husband who is neither interested in nor capable of meeting the challenges of the new age. She must look to the satisfactions of the duties of her elevated station, which she performs with triumphant success. The gentry-born Frank is, in turn, saddled with a frigid aristocratic wife and must now live with her in the company of her vexatious, rank-conscious family and their associates.

'A Manoeuvrer Outwitted; or Relations from India', III, 59–148

Plot Summary: Mrs Bentham, the widow of a civil servant in the East India Company, returns to London in straitened financial circumstances and sets out to make her fortune by setting up as richer than she is, pushing her way into exclusive society. Sly and cunning, she pits her wit against a family of mean-spirited, heartless Scottish aristocrats who take her up when they think it is to their financial advantage and then abandon her as her plans fail. The closely observed satire directed at parvenu social manipulations and aristocratic financial meanness are especially revealing of the economic pressures experienced by marginal participants in fashionable society.

'The Intrigante', III, 151–330

Plot Summary: The story of a married woman whose affairs with men of rank raise herself and her husband to wealth and fashion: 'ambition which presented men and women to her view only as dupes and victims;—which made her life a plot;—her diversion a stratagem,—her husband a tool,—her lover a stepping stone,—her very children the mere perpetuators of her success. Affection, duty, virtue, were empty sounds in the ears of the cold-blooded and venal *intrigante*' (III, 266). The Sunday newspapers bring her career to a close: 'Mrs Clermont's natural nothingness,—her acquired importance,—nay, the exact means by which it had been achieved, were dexterously exhibited Sunday after Sunday, in as many different shapes as the itinerant fan-juggler can conjure out of a folded sheet of paper' (III, 269–70). Like Becky Sharp in Thackeray's *Vanity Fair*, however, Lady Anne, the 'intrigante' lands on her feet, since, as Gore writes, she cared 'nothing for the state or its service (setting aside the salary thereunto attached) than for the politics and constitution of Cochin China ... [S]he extended her smiles to both sides of the House ... and soon came to be handsomer and more agreeable among the "outs" who were soon to be the "ins,"—than among the "ins" who were soon to be "outs."—It was noticed that during the last season of Lord Farrington's administration, she shared her opera box with the lady of a leading opposition lord; and though, till the fatal crisis, she was regarded, by what was termed her *own* party, as a friend in the enemy's camp, it soon became pretty evident that she had been quite as much of an enemy in their own' (III, 277–8).

Comments: The cumulative effect of the tales in *The Sketch Book of Fashion* presents a sour-sharp commentary on a world in social and political flux, supporting Gore's claim in the 'Preface' that the tales were written pre-Reform, 'the last of a series of Novels, of a class created by the peculiar spirit of the last reign, and manifestly at variance with that of the present times' (i, iii–iv). The 'ins' and the 'outs' are equally despicable, Tories and Whigs, aristocrats and the middle classes. The middle classes manipulate the vices of the aristocracy to their own benefit, sometimes able to pull out of the trap, as in 'My Place in the Country', but more often caught in the destructive undertow of the corrupt aristocratic society they wish to join.

Gore, Catherine, *The Hamiltons*; or, *The New Æra*, 3 vols. (London: Saunders and Otley, 1834)

Plot Summary: The tale follows the general structure of *Sense and Sensibility* with two sisters, Susan, the younger sister with strong sensibilities, and Marcia, the older sister with instincts of rationality and common sense. Marcia marries a professional man, the lawyer Bernard Forbes (a radical in the pattern of Lord Brougham), to make a strongly moral and politically involved couple. Susan marries a decadent Tory aristocrat, suffers greatly from the moral corruptions of her husband and the professional aspirations of her father-in-law, a Tory minister. When her father-in-law receives a peerage (Lord Laxington), Susan must reluctantly shoulder the duties of aristocratic life. Her husband has an affair with her best friend and is killed in an honour duel by the husband he has cuckolded. After suitable grief and convalescence Susan marries a marquess and a Whig, Lord Claneustace. Their marriage is the model aristocratic partnership (a match for the professional partnership of her sister Marcia's marriage) and a glowing display of the aspirations of Whig government through the couple's exemplary management of the Claneustace estate in their gardening, farming, railways, canals, mines, etc.

Comment: This is the most party-specific of Gore's novels, set among the failures of Tory government in the years before and immediately after 1830 when Wellington's government gave way to the Whig government of Lord Grey. The partisan politics of Gore's novel is prompted, however, by the power politics of 1834, a year in which the Whigs were briefly tumbled from office for the return of a Tory government promoted by William IV. The dependence of the Hamiltons, the Tory family, on the public treasury is the focus of Gore's anti-Tory narrative in which she regularly depicts a general arrogance and a laxness of morals associated with all her Tory characters. Augustus Hamilton, Susan's wandering husband, is a genuine treat – in love with Susan, guilty, ashamed, witty, teasing and mildly sadistic, operating at full throttle in Gore's land of unhappy marriages. Thackeray went to school on this one. The dual-sister plot makes it possible to engage discussions of radical politics as well. Marcia, the elder sister, has a radical salon in Bloomsbury where contemporary issues that might seem alien to silver fork society can be aired through her husband's radical principles.

Gore, Catherine, *Mrs. Armytage; or, Female Domination*, 3 vols.
(London: Henry Colburn, 1836)

Plot Summary: Mrs Armytage, the widowed mother of two children, Sophia and Arthur, has an independent income, whereas her children are, besides a few hundred pounds of their own, dependent upon her for their support. Mrs Armytage's masculine training as a girl and her love of power – the patriarchal system that she has usurped and taken onto her own shoulders – has perverted her 'maternal' feelings. The daughter Sophia is driven to an early death (Mrs Armytage hides a proposal of marriage from Sophy's beloved); her son is bankrupted (no help arriving from his mother); and her daughter-in-law (an unwelcome addition to her family from the commercial classes) has her honour besmirched, largely at the hands of her mother-in-law. It is finally revealed after much suffering and injustice that Mrs Armytage has no genuine right to any of her assumed powers. A paper is discovered proving that the legal arrangements she has been acting under have no effect and that a codicil to the will of Arthur's grandfather has left everything to Arthur. Arthur is driven to reveal this to his mother solely to protect his wife, Marian, from dishonour. Mrs Armytage goes off to the Continent to die, but is brought back to be forgiven at Holywell Hall as she falls into a final decline. Marian and Arthur become the ideal British couple, remarked and loved in their neighbourhood for their private and public virtues, especially the wife, the *new* Mrs Armytage.

Comments: The moral is thoroughly political, having to do with the holdover of the principles of an *ancien régime* run amok with unjust powers. Mrs Armytage exhibits the old system as a perversion of order made more strikingly visible by way of gender. The political analogy involves a specific problem faced by the contemporary Whig political coalition of old- and new-style adherents to the party. Mrs Armytage represents the conservative old-style Whig squirearchy. The neighbouring family of aristocrats, modern and liberal-thinking Whigs, respect the widow for her good qualities, tolerating her eccentric and rigid opinions with compassion and understanding. All the other villains of the novel are Tories, including a neighbouring parvenu landowner who opposes her interests in a local election, and a group of 'fashionable' Tory aristocrats in the nearby town who oppose her with their own candidate. There is also a social interloper and aspirant for title and distinction, a Yankee, Mr. Leonidas Lomax, a South Carolina slave owner who allies himself with the Tory villians of the piece. Mrs Armytage's son Arthur, liberal and generous in spirit and expansive in his sense of class – he has married a woman from the commercial class – is a modern Whig. He wins the local borough seat (against his mother's candidate) in an election run by the rules of the new system of Reform. Arthur's eventual triumph over the narrow principles of his old-style Whig mother as a modern Whig married to a middle-class woman with Irish connections is an example to the nation. It also mirrors the electoral situation of the Whig Party in 1836.

Gore, Catherine, *Stokeshill Place; or The Man of Business*, 3 vols.
(London: Henry Colburn, 1837)

Plot Summary: Two intersecting plots run through *Stokeshill Place*: the story of Mr Barnsley, the 'Man of Business', a canny attorney who works himself up from clerk to son-in-law of the chief attorney and thereafter the recipient of £135,000 as his wife's inheritance from her father. With this stake he purchases Stokeshill Place, a country estate, and sets about to establish himself as a landed gentleman among the local townsmen, gentry and aristocracy. The second plot concerns his daughter, Margaret, an heiress, accomplished and beautiful, but who as the daughter of 'the Man of Business' is socially compromised by her father's background in trade. The first two volumes tell of Margaret's troubles in local society and in fashionable London society. The last volume concerns itself overwhelmingly with her father's financial destruction – his bankruptcy through another's fraud, the exposure of his forgery of a legal document (to protect Margaret's fortune) and his suicide. Margaret's resurrection in the final pages as the newly created heiress of a rich uncle returned from India and her consequent marriage to the widowed new owner of Stokeshill Place arrives, it feels, as an author's afterthought.

Comments: The novel, set in pre-Reform Bill England, presents issues that belong to the political and social upheavals of post-Reform 1837. As a 'new' man, Barnsley manages the business affairs of his aristocratic neighbours and fellow townsmen with great efficiency and probity, including his management of the local workhouse for which he is heartily hated by the locals (Gore's nod to the 1834 Poor Laws). As a potential MP his skills in business would make him the sort of man who is necessary, Gore argues, to the running of a modern parliamentary government. But Barnsley's ambition to rise socially is proffered as his tragic flaw, and his political defeat is considered the symbolic expression of an immoveable social prejudice, from villagers to aristocrats, against the power of his money (or talent) to secure him a place in the traditional governing classes. Margaret's on-going problems in the fashionable world run parallel to her father's in the political. Her fortune attracts the worst of aristocratic predators: 'Lord Shoreham was ignoble in all his ideas and ambitions.—Brereton a solemn coxcomb.—George Holloway a lump of clay,—and Edward Sullivan a lump of sugar' (II, 37–8). Her marriage in the last pages to the widowed Sir Henry Woodgate, the representative of the ancient family of Stokeshill Place, reinstalled there by his late wife's fortune, attempts a compromise, of sorts, between old and new. Stokeshill Place, the novel's troubled site of historic intransigence, is demolished and the new Sir Henry and Lady Woodgate (Margaret) move to Hanover Square, London, for Sir Henry to be near his parliamentary duties and for Margaret to attend her 'Oriental' uncle whose hypochondria, like Jane Austen's Mr Woodhouse's, demands the constant attention of his loving niece.

Gore, Catherine, *The Cabinet Minister*, 3 vols. (London: Richard Bentley, 1839)

Plot Summary: An expansion of the Fanny, William, Edmund configuration of Jane Austen's *Mansfield Park*. Two impoverished young relations of old Sir Gideon Woodbridge, Bessy and Frank Grenfell, are taken into Hursley Park by his reluctant widow as subordinate members of the family: Bessy as servant-companion to her Tory aunt, Lady Mary (a vicious combination of Lady Bertram and Mrs Norris), and Frank as companion to Sir Henry, her son, who is Frank's age. With Sir Henry's financial support, Frank attends Eton and Christ Church, where both young men are converted to the Whig cause much to the chagrin of Sir Henry's violently Tory mother. Frank, who makes a mark in London society is briefly turned from his political course by a Tory woman of fashion, but returns to the Whig Party to become the cabinet member of the title, knighted by King William IV for his valuable services. Bessy, the Fanny Price figure, an ardent supporter of Whig politics in her own right, refuses a grandly advantageous offer of marriage from Lord Warkworth, a pompous, arrogant Tory college acquaintance of her brother and her cousin, though it incurs the wrath of her abusive aunt. But, as Bessy has been nursing a secret love for Sir Henry for most of the novel, her fidelity is rewarded, like Fanny Price's, by marriage to her cousin in a blissful union of Whig sympathies. Frank, the statesman, marries a Whig renegade from a Tory family, Julia Loveden, who appears in the novel as a lively social observer in the style of Austen's Mary Crawford.

Comment: The story commences in the Regency Crisis of 1810, and ends with condensed accounts of ensuing events in Whig history, from the mid-to-late 1820s to the post-Reform years of William IV. The narrative present of 1839, however, is firmly positioned in the contemporary political consciousness of the novel: two years after the accession of Victoria, with the Whig Party in the midst of a grave political crisis through its own internal weakness, division, and a vigorous challenge from Peel's revived Tory Party. The reader is repeatedly directed to draw parallels and lessons from 'now' and 'then'. Frank Grenfell's generous, open nature and his ease in high society, for example, could be drawn from a generic Whig posture, but more likely echoes contemporary opinion of the Whig prime minister Lord Melbourne's character: he was 'a gentleman, liberal and straightforward, with no meanness, and incapable of selfish trickery and intrigue'.[17] Lord Warkworth, Bessy's rejected suitor and the Tory *bête noire* of Sir Henry and Frank at Christ Church, is 'dictatorial, pompous, and serious about honours', 'a mere knowledge-pump!', 'a solemn fop'. This may suggest the Tory leader Peel (he took a double first at Christ Church and was known for his arrogance and coldness), but more probably it is aimed at Gladstone who also achieved a double first at Christ Church. He was denounced famously by Macaulay in the *Edinburgh Review* (April 1839) the same year as Gore's novel, as 'the rising hope of those stern and unbending Tories'.[18] Frank's opinion of Warkworth is only a variation of Macaulay's: 'I own it fires my blood to find the opposition of this narrow-minded blockhead to every measure calculated to forward the interests of humanity ... hailed by the country as patriotism, and by the court as loyalty!'(III, 284).

Gore, Catherine, *The Dowager; or, The New School for Scandal*, 3 vols. (London: Richard Bentley, 1840)

Plot Summary: The novel's action originates in the house of the Countess Dowager of Delmaine, an ancient harridan who lives to plague her children, her grandchildren and her neighbours with her malicious gossip that causes one of her neighbours to mutter, 'There's a whole novelist's library in the brain of that hateful old Dowager!' (I, 23). From her lair on Upper Grosvenor Street, she manufactures the sort of gossip that breaks up friendships, causes duels, endangers marriages and generally creates domestic mayhem in her circle. A significant secondary plot concerns the husband of one of her neighbours who is targeted for seduction by a cabal of Tory ladies who want to bring him into the Tory Party. In the final pages all is explained, all forgiven and the Dowager dies unloved and alone: 'How charming—how delightful!' cries Lady Gransden from across the street. 'Next spring what a happy circle will be collected on the spot to which we have all looked with terror, as the den of the Dowager!' (III, 318).

Comments: The Dowager is an unwelcome survivor of the old pre-Reform politically narrow Mayfair, her divisive presence becoming a danger to the broad coalition of new alliances in the unstable Whig Party of 1840. The young families of the story, all of them Whigs, liberals and radicals, are set at dangerous sixes and sevens by the Dowager's interfering tale-bearing, making them vulnerable to Tory predators such as, for example, the cabal of women who pursue the wavering Whig lord from across the street. Moreover, the feuds she promotes among their Whig and Whig-leaning relatives make them unable to unite effectively against their common enemy, the Tory opposition. The energy of Gore's social-political representations in earlier novels, however, is seriously diluted in this novel as defeat looms for Lord Melbourne's Whig government with crushing inevitability in 1841: 'And all the time, the newspapers went on gravely announcing, day after day, *whose* dinners were eaten by *whom*, what balls were iced by Gunter and fiddled to by Tolbecque' (II, 120), she writes, falling more or less into the same pattern herself in the waning of silver fork political energy in this novel.

Gore, Catherine, *Cecil; or, The Adventures of a Coxcomb*, 3 vols. (London: Richard Bentley, 1841)[19]

Plot Summary: The autobiographical account of Cecil Danby, younger son of Lord and Lady Ormington, and his career as a dandy, self-consciously addressing his life as participant in the span of social history running from the late eighteenth-century to the much-altered world of 1841: his entry into Regency society, his service in the Peninsular campaign, his hero's return, his guilt in the accidental death of his elder brother's son, his consequent volunteer service at Waterloo, his wanderings on the Continent and finally his return to a post-war London of economic expansion and social upheaval. Cecil's involvement with a string of women, each treated as a social type, his own arch self-awareness – a disturbing mix of candid and defensive – his family relations and the ever-present secret, his illegitimacy and the tragic relationship with his 'father' Lord Ormington, fill the outline of his personal narrative.

Comments: *Cecil* is Mrs Gore's most serious and ambitious novel, one that attempts the same social and historical reach as Thackeray's *Vanity Fair*. Politically touched by her sense of the failure of Whig aspirations, the impending fall of the Melbourne government and her strong sense of the close of an era, the novel is both a nostalgic and bitter critique of aristocratic attitudes and political weakness in the late Regency and the first decade following Reform. It is also a self-conscious valediction to the silver fork novel, a short-lived genre set in motion by Reform. As Cecil remarks,

At the moment in question, there were half a dozen of us who might have revolutionized the coteries. At this present writing, there are a score who might revolutionize the country,—Cis Danby, Henry Pelham, Vivian Grey,—Brougham, Lyndhurst, Macaulay;—Rogers, Moore, Lutrell, Ginger Stubbs;—Morgan, Gore, Norton, Tussaud;—Lockhart, Fonblanque, Dickens,—Carlyle, Sydney Smith, Dicky Milnes, Dan O'Connell, and Lord Cardigan, who might form a tremendous battalion if they could only manage to shave in the same shop—. Luckily, we abominate each other.—I defy even the five thousand horse power of genius to force us into conspiracy. (III, 291–2)

HOOK, THEODORE (1788–1841)

Theodore Hook, the political satirist, deserves mention parenthetically as a novelist of fashionable life, mainly as the target of William Hazlitt's 'silver fork' attack on his novels – 'provided a few select persons eat fish with silver forks, he considers it a circumstance of no consequence if a whole country starves'[20] – but also for *Sayings and Doings* (1824–8), an amusing collection of novellas about fashionable life, as well as *Maxwell* (1830), *Gilbert Gurney* (1836) and *Jack Brag* (1837), satires and comic anecdotes situated on the margins of fashionable fiction. Hook's career was heavily involved in politics, just as were the other men writing fashionable fiction, though Hook spent his life primarily as a journalist and as the editor of Tory political journals. Hook is also an exceptional figure in novels of fashionable life for his ultra-Tory political opinions. Most of the silver fork novelists were radicals, liberals or out-and-out Whigs. The Tory exceptions are Hook, Letitia Landon and Charles White.

Hook, Theodore, *Sayings and Doings: a Series of Sketches from Life*, 3
  vols. (London: Henry Colburn, 1824) [A second series was published
  in 1825, and a third in 1828]

Plot Summary: Each of the three series contains a collection of tales. They are
reviewed by contemporaries with detailed plot summaries. See Theodore Hook's
Sayings and Doings (1824, 1825, 1828), in P. D. Garside, J. E. Belanger and S. A.
Ragaz, *British Fiction, 1800–1829*.[21]

Comments: The reviews of Hook's *Sayings and Doings* by contemporaries are
glowingly favourable for the first two series. The third series, 1828, is treated with
more reserve for a perceived harshness in the stories and apparent misogyny. *La
Belle Assemblée* in 1824 writes: 'These volumes display an extraordinary knowledge of life and nature, and a most happy talent for the delineation of character
and manners. The satire is and, altogether, the style is so racy and piquant—
there is so much truth and felicity in the sketches—that it is impossible not to be
delighted with the work' (*La Belle Assemblée*, n.s. 29 (Apr 1824), pp. 167–9).[22] The
best known of the stories in *Sayings and Doings* are 'Martha the Gypsy', 'Passion
and Principle', 'Cousin William' and 'Gervase Skinner'.

Hook, Theodore, *Maxwell*, 1st edn 1830 (London: Richard Bentley, 1840)

Plot Summary: The major characters are Mr Maxwell, his son Edward (Ned) and
his daughter Katherine (Kate, Kitty, Kittums), her beloved Charles (Charley Boy)
Somerford, whose mother is thought to be a 'natural child', parentage unknown,
though in the final pages Charles is discovered to be the heir to the title and
estate of the Earl of Lessington (i.e. 'less *ton*'). Although Kate is in love with
Charles, Mr Maxwell, ambitious for his daughter and ashamed of Charles' low
origins, has him sent off to India, making him break with Kate, and refuses to
allow a marriage. Kate is seemingly unaware of her father's sleight of hand in the
matter. Mr Maxwell manoeuvres her into marrying his stockbroker Mr Apperton
because Charles does not write to her and is reported to be ill, dying, not prosperous, etc. Mr Apperton, in a painful irony, is illegitimate too, as it unexpectedly
turns out, with a mother who is the landlady of the Cat and Cauliflower in the
Ratcliffe Highway. Apperton, Kate's stockbroker husband, is tight-fisted, penny-
pinching and an unfeeling slave to market values. Kate is pretty much a piece
of furniture to him, though a useful key to Mr Maxwell's fortune. Apperton is
also a crook who invests his father-in-law's entire fortune in a dicey bank that
goes bust. Edward (Ned) is in love with a woman he glimpses crossing Long
Acre, a passion that he maintains with no encouragement from her or from her
family for all three volumes, with, in fact, positive discouragement from his family because of an untold 'secret' about the girl. The plot only reveals the secrets
of her origin and fortune in the very last chapter. Walk-on characters – comic
middle-class folk (one or two with very serious criticisms of upper-class values)
and a string of silly aristocrats (except for the sentimental, aristocrat grandfather,

Lord Lessington) – bring timely political significance to an involved and lengthy exposition of the two love stories (Kate's and her brother Ned's). Finances, the risky economy (stocks falling), a crooked stockbroker husband for Kate, and threat of debtors' prison for the entire family, keep the plot on the boil.

Comments: This is Hook's most carefully constructed novel. He follows a Tory political programme that elevates the sentimental middle classes (the heroine, her family and their friends, including a rich wine merchant's family), denigrates the commercial middle classes (the rich stockbroker husband and his more humble Cat and Cauliflower family) and mocks the aristocracy as a class of incompetent, bumbling, pompous, corrupt, self-interested fools. The newspapers are the calendar keepers of the novel with advertisements, naval reports, the stock market, City rumours in the dailies, fashionable gossip in the *Morning Post* and bankruptcies in the *Gazette*, marking the progression of plot events.

Hook, Theodore, *Gilbert Gurney* (London: Whitaker, 1836) and *Gilbert Gurney Married* (London: Colburn, 1838)

Plot Summary: 'Thinly disguised portraits and a string of anecdotes from real life.'[23]

Hook, Theodore, *Jack Brag* (London: Richard Bentley, 1837)

Plot Summary: A satire on freeloading and middle-class aspirations to social station. Anecdotes and short tales.

Comments: Edward Bulwer in an essay 'The Works of Theodore Hook' in the *Westminster Review*, 6 (1838), pp. 169–98, writes, 'the novels of Mr Hook would make the felicity of a life, a silver fork. The sum of human knowledge with him is to know a lord: the understanding is a faculty given to men to decide on dishes: the life of a man a period of time allotted for wearing starched neckcloths. The mission which Mr Hook has come into the world to tell, is contained in one precept;—act not *Bloomsburily*. The danger of which he has warned mankind is plebeian dinners' (p. 184). Hook's bumptious humour carries the day in many of his stories.

HUDSON, MARIANNE SPENCER (*fl.* 1825–6)

Marianne Spencer Stanhope Hudson, the author of *Almack's* (1826), is remembered for this single novel. Prince Pückler-Muskau notes it for its social accuracy in his journal of London life: 'You may partly conceive the burlesque effect such a fashionable novel produces on people in the middling society of London, who are continually groping in the dark after "le bel air", are consequently in perpetual terror and agony, lest they should betray their inacquaintance [*sic*] with the great world, and thus make themselves exquisitely ludicrous.'[24] Maria Edgeworth found pleasure in Hudson's novel as well: 'I particularly like the dialogue in the third volume, where Lady Anne Norbury debits and credits her hopes of happiness with her two admirers: no waiting-maid could have written that.' She continues, 'In the second volume, also, I think there is a scene between Lord and Lady Norbury in their dressing-room, about getting rid of their guests and making room for others, which is nicely touched: the Lord and Lady are politely unfeeling; it is all kept within bounds.'[25] *Almack's*, clearly entering celebrity territory, was immediately followed by a 'Key' to society figures which the publisher prefaced with a puff that serves as a good description of most fashionable fiction during the pre-Reform years of the 1820s: 'these volumes ... are extremely satirical, extremely personal, very clever ... perhaps, the best picture of the gayest fashionable life that has ever issued from the press'.[26] The 'Key' to Hudson's *Almack's* marks out the novel's middle-class audience with condescending irony, but also makes a clear statement about the readership Hudson expected to find: 'Of course, we write not to inform duchesses and countesses; but citizens and country cousins must thank us for enabling them to talk of the supreme *bon ton* and Almack's, and shew their acquaintance with who's who in the grand topic of the day.' Hudson's *Almack's* achieved such popularity that Charles White exploited her title in his silver fork novel *Almack's Revisited* (1828).

Hudson, Marianne, *Almack's, a Novel*, 2nd edn, 3 vols. (London: Saunders and Otley, 1826)

Plot Summary: Lionel Montague, younger son of the Montague family, now much reduced in fortune through the dissolute life of his elder brother in economic exile on the continent, visits the new tenants of his ancestral home, Sir Benjamin Birmingham, his wife Lady Birmingham and their daughter Barbara. The Birminghams' wealth is a mix of mercantile and West Indian, its foundation derived from an earlier marriage of Lady Birmingham. The daughter Barbara is the year's prize in the marriage market with a fortune of £20,000 p. a. Barbara, educated by a clergyman's family of genteel status while her parents lived in the West Indies, is a model of decorum and 'truly feminine' feelings, with none of the vulgarity of her family's background. Lionel Montague, too, is a model: a hero returned from the Spanish campaigns, an economist who lives without debt on his limited income, and an esteemed independent MP. He falls in love with Barbara, but is unhappily aware that her mother, Lady Birmingham, has higher aims for her in marriage. Lady Birmingham is an inflated version of Jane Austen's Mrs Elton, inheriting her barouche landau, donkey cart and staff of supernumerary servants along with her deafness to social gaucheries. Far more pressing than the Lionel and Barbara romance is Lady Birmingham's successful assault on exclusive society and her achievement of the *sine qua non* of the fashionable world, a ticket of admission for herself and her daughter to Almack's. The romance plot concludes summarily with Lionel's wastrel brother killed in a duel (in a footnote) and Lionel's succession to the estate with 'its fine landed property' and his future title as Sir Lionel Montague, thus enabling him to marry the heroine with Lady Birmingham's blessing.

Comments: The influence of the *roman à clef* is still strong in Hudson's silver fork novel. The 'Key to *"Almack's"*' (1827), published 'by demand', presents a list of initialled names, supposedly identifiable in exclusive society. The novel does not move into full political engagement, although Hudson includes an episode with a Tory family and a Whig family tossed together for a stiff country visit. The plot and characters of *Almack's* are firmly anchored in the conventions of women's fiction of the previous generation and in plot devices, characters and even phrases drawn from Jane Austen's novels, and also from Frances Burney's and Maria Edgeworth's. Other self-conscious styles are drawn from fashion columns, advertisements and legal notices in the newspapers, all much studied by the novel's characters. There is also a section set aside for parodies of fashionable letter-writing, including a series of sample letters by 'gentlemen' and 'ladies' very much indebted to Mary Crawford's mocking version of her brother's letters and Lady Bertram's expansive page-fillers in *Mansfield Park*. In this sense *Almack's* is typical of the silver fork genre, presenting contemporary upper-class mores drawn from middle-class sources (women's fiction, newspapers, reviews) and intended partly as a satire of the fashionable world's response to the intrusion of middle-class interlopers, but also as instruction to attentive middle-class readers as to how such entry might be successfully accomplished.

JAMESON, ANNA (1794–1860)

The daughter of an Irish miniature-painter and his English wife, Anna Jameson was educated at home. The family settled in London in 1798, and at age sixteen Jameson became a governess. She married a lawyer, Robert Jameson, in 1825, but separated from him in 1829. Her writing career supported her parents and sisters, much of it occupied with female grievances, the plight of governesses and the need for wider employment opportunities for women.[27]

Jameson, Anna, *Diary of an Ennuyée*, 1 vol. (London: Henry Colburn, 1826)

Plot Summary: Influenced by Germaine de Staël's *Corrine*, this work is offered as the diary of a broken-hearted young governess travelling in France and Italy. The 'author' compares fashion in Paris and in London, the streets of Paris to the streets of London, the lake at Geneva to the Panorama of Lake Geneva currently on display in London, La Scala in Milan to the King's Theatre in the Haymarket. She notes the paintings and sculpture she sees in Venice, the ones she likes and the ones that are not 'favourites'. She notes that Samuel Rogers is to be seen daily in the Tribune from eleven to twelve o'clock, and recounts his continued love of good food. She dies, suddenly, for lack of mail from England: 'I may confess, that till now, a faint—a very faint hope did cling to my heart.

I thought it might have been just possible; but it is over now—*all* is over!' Her
next lines, says the editor, are 'not legible', and 'Four days after the date of the
last paragraph, the writer died at Autun in her 26th year, and was buried in the
garden of the Capuchin Monastery, near that city' (p. 354).

Comments: This 'diary', travel literature for social aspirants, makes a safety gesture in the beginning pages to Thomas Moore's *The Fudge Family in Paris* (1818)
as a prophylactic fence around its own more elegant responses to the Continent.
The text is designed to signal the 'right' responses to foreign travel, churches,
paintings and sculpture, as well as the proper sort of names to drop, 'Byron'
and 'Samuel Rogers'. Ten years later Catherine Gore drew on the public's familiarity with this work by entitling one of her own works *Diary of a Désennuyée*
(London: Henry Colburn, 1836).

LANDON, LETITIA (1802–38)

Letitia Landon, born into a middle-class professional family, was the eldest of
three children. At the death of her father when she was seventeen, she became
the breadwinner for the family, writing to support her mother and to put her
brother through Oxford.[28] She considered herself a professional author without
apology. She first made her way in literary society through the merits of her
poetry as 'L. E. L.' and followed by becoming a voluminous writer for periodicals and for the annuals, two of which she edited, *Heath's Book of Beauty* and
the *Scrap Book*. She also wrote three novels. Her first novel, *Romance and Reality*
(1831), includes important passages on political philosophy, contemporary literary figures and the most pressing political issues of the day. Her second novel,
Ethel Churchill (1837), though set in the early eighteenth century, includes a vivid
section on the miseries of writing for a living in the nineteenth century, a fate
Landon knew well. *Ethel Churchill* also features gripping pictures of Poor Law
failures of the late 1830s. *Lady Anne Granard; Keeping Up Appearances* (1842), a
novel published posthumously and finished by an unknown hand, begins with
a bright imitation of Austen's *Pride and Prejudice*, a close version of the Bennets
and their overabundant number of daughters, but descends into melodrama.

Landon, Letitia, *Romance and Reality*, 3 vols. (London: Henry Colburn
and Richard Bentley, 1831)[29]

Plot Summary: Emily Arundel is in love with Edward Lorraine, who is indifferent to her. Cecil Spencer is in love with Emily Arundel, who is indifferent to
him. Cecil marries his childlike cousin Helen after Emily's death.

Comments: The romance plot obviously counts for little in *Romance and Reality*.
It is the loose structure on which Landon hangs the observations of a self-con-
scious writer who is keenly aware of the professional world in which she functions.
She takes up the tradition of women's fiction, with assessments of Austen, Burney

and Edgeworth. She makes the perceptive observation that Scott's example has had its influence on novels like her own, the fashionable novel. She addresses specifically works by Bulwer, Disraeli and Lord Normanby. She notes the power of daily newspapers to influence culture and politics with their advertisements of services and consumer goods, the political editorials, parliamentary speeches, and their news of the fashionable world and governing classes. The Tory bias of this novel appears most sharply in her character 'Mr. Delawarr', a thinly disguised version of the Catholic-emancipation Peel, roundly confronted with the charge, 'False to your party—still falser to yourself' (II, 301).

Landon, Letitia, *Ethel Churchill: or, The Two Brides*, 3 vols. (London: Henry Colburn, 1837)

Plot Summary: The novel is set in the early eighteenth century. Henrietta the flawed heroine marries the emotionally frigid Lord Marchmont for wealth and rank. She is filled with feelings, wants to communicate them to him, but he is like facing a 'north wind'. Her uncle, who lives in retirement with his books and laboratory, sees the misery ahead for her and says so. The newly married Lady Marchmont (Henrietta) goes to visit Ethel Churchill in her humble cottage across the churchyard to spend time till her husband Algernon, Lord Marchmont, returns home. She joins a group of young people – Ethel Churchill, Walter Maynard, for whom she clearly has strong feelings, Norbourne Courtenaye and Lavinia Fenton. Walter Maynard is a poet. Norbourne is a model aristocrat. Lavinia Fenton is the historical figure, the Polly Peachem in Gay's *The Beggar's Opera* who marries her lover the Duke of Bolton. At the story's beginning, Henrietta loves Maynard, Lavinia loves Maynard, Maynard loves Ethel, Ethel loves Norbourne Courtenaye. The young people play a 'truth' game, each telling what he or she wishes in life. Henrietta wishes 'for universal admiration'; Maynard wishes 'for fame—glorious and enduring fame'; Lavinia wishes 'to be a lady—have an embroidered damask gown, and ride in a coach and six'; Norbourne confesses, 'I would wish to love' (I, 46). The novel explores each wish. Maynard becomes a hack, dies 'with a gurgle', surrounded by his friends. Lavinia, as in real life, marries the Duke of Bolton and gets her coach and six. Ethel marries Norbourne. Henrietta uses the poisons she has learned to make in her uncle's laboratory to murder the men who have betrayed her – her husband the society monster (he has 'a genius for furniture') and her seducer Sir George Kingston. She falls into 'Incurable Insanity!' Ethel and Norbourne vow, 'She will be our sister.'

Comments: The novel may be set in the early eighteenth century, but it includes superb examples of contemporary urban life in nineteenth-century London. Walter Maynard's depression as a hack writer shows Landon's own first-hand experience: 'My works sell; but look at the amount of labour, and calculate how poor is the recompense! Half that toil, half that talent, given to any other pursuit, would have ensured wealth' (III, 129).

Landon, Letitia, *Lady Anne Granard; Keeping Up Appearances*, 3 vols.
(London: Henry Colburn, 1842)

Plot Summary: The plot begins as a 'domestic story of the present day', a revised version of Austen's *Pride and Prejudice*, including the requisite five daughters, a spendthrift mother desperate to get her daughters 'off her hands' and a weak, broken-spirited husband-father. The estate is to be left away from the family through the lack of a male heir. Among the characters there is a motherly 'Mrs Palmer', a variation on 'Mrs Jennings' in *Sense and Sensibility*, who also has the writing talents of 'Lady Bertram' in *Mansfield Park*, 'of making the smallest possible quantity of matter cover the largest possible quantity of space ... [A]ny body ... can give some sort of account if any thing remarkable has occurred; but the great art is to write a long letter when you have nothing to say' (I, 60). The girls all make excellent marriages in spite of their interfering mother.

Comments: The novel was published posthumously, the second half written by another hand. The first half is bright and satiric, the second half much less so, but focused on Tory and Whig struggles in local politics.

LISTER, THOMAS HENRY (1800–42)

Thomas Henry Lister was born into the wealthy squirearchy and married a woman of the aristocracy. He knew fashionable life at first hand. He published his 'dandy' novel *Granby* (1826) to acclaim and went on to write *Herbert Lacy* (1828) and *Arlington* (1832) in the fashionable mode. After 1832, Lister left his novel-writing to take significant administrative posts under successive Whig governments through the 1830s.

Lister, Henry, *Granby. A Novel*, 3 vols. (London: Henry Colburn, 1826)[30]

Plot Summary: The hero, Henry Granby, has been raised by his uncle, the General. Granby is very fond of his uncle, genuine mutual affection here, but is troubled by the fact that he has been raised to no profession and that the General does not want him to take up one. Granby's mother has been something of a spendthrift – raised luxuriously and unable to change after marriage. His father loses what is left of the fortune in a bank speculation. Granby falls in love with Caroline Jermyn, whose pompous, rather dim father is the Tory placeman from Rottentown: 'He thought religion was a good thing, and ought to be kept up, and that, like cheap soup, it was excellent for the poor.' The Jermyns do not approve of Granby (he is poor) and forbid Caroline to encourage him. Vincent Trebeck, a dangerous modern dandy, ambitious to join exclusive society in London and much interested in Caroline's fortune, is not a mere clothes horse, but a cunning and successful political and social manipulator. Granby's cousin Tyrrel, another of Granby's enemies and the supposed son and heir of Lord Malton, is actually illegitimate, though passed off as the heir by his father. All this comes out upon the death of the General, at which time Granby becomes Lord Malton. Tyrrel, the false claimant, commits suicide and Trebeck, the dandy, disappears from the narrative. Lady Jermyn happily commences to dream of the *Morning Post* and its report of her daughter's marriage: '"Viscountess Malton on her marriage, by Lady Jermyn" in the list of presentations at the ensuing drawing-room; and had almost composed a description of her dress' (III, 327).

Comments: A typically high-spirited and intensely London novel of the mid-1820s. The novel draws pointedly on women's fiction, in particular Austen's *Northanger Abbey* and *Pride and Prejudice*, and Burney's *Evelina*. Politically, Catholic emancipation is offered as the talisman of the admirable characters; Tory political principle is represented by Sir Thomas Jermyn (of [mid-1820s] Rottentown) with his complacent support for any and all Tory measures. Granby is the independent, liberal-minded hero; Trebeck the unscrupulous social manipulator, and Tyrrel the drug-haunted, gambling and criminally minded heir (supposed) to the Malton title and estate. The closing union of the liberal-independent Granby and the sensible Caroline Jermyn is intended to mark the way forward for the nation's political future.

Lister, Henry, *Herbert Lacy*, 3 vols. (London: Henry Colburn, 1828)

Plot Summary: Herbert Lacy, from an aristocratic family, falls in love with Agnes Morton, from a rising family, her grandfather having made his fortune in manufacture (iron) and become owner of the Dodswell estate in order 'to sink the manufacturer in the country gentleman'. His son, Agnes' father, spends extravagantly in an effort to make his way in local aristocratic society. Agnes, independently heiress to £80,000, is prohibited from receiving more than £400 a year until she is married on condition of her financial guardian's permission, or until she reaches twenty-five years of age. The guardian is Mr Sackville, a villain of the Trebeck variety (see *Granby*), only much worse – smooth talking, handsome, unprincipled politically and totally plausible socially. Sackville encourages Mr Morton, Agnes' father, who is deeply in debt, to sign over to him his Dodswell estate and also, into the bargain, to insist that his daughter Agnes marry him. Sackville has his eye on Agnes' £80,000 inheritance independent of her father. Agnes consents with protest and tears, begging for one year's respite. The family moves to London where they can live economically on Agnes' £400 per annum, avoid their unsympathetic country neighbours and present Lister with a prime opportunity to describe the declensions of London social life. Lacy meanwhile enters Parliament as a liberal-minded gentleman with no party affiliation, though he supports Catholic emancipation, limitations on the game laws and even ponders, possibly, some changes in the corn laws. Mr Sackville meanwhile is exposed to the rigours of the law by a nervous confederate for forging letters that have fomented problems between the Morton and Lacy families. Agnes the manufacturer's granddaughter and Lacy the aristocrat's son are united in marriage in the concluding pages. Lacy's stiff old father apologizes to his son for not having recognized the value of men of Mr Morton's sort: 'I have learned to shake off some portion of my former exclusiveness, and to applaud the liberal spirit of these times, which presents no insurmountable barrier to any species of ambition' (III, 283–4).

Comments: *Herbert Lacy* falls short of the high spirits of *Granby*, but maintains a lively appreciation of London's urban spectacle. The wicked doings of Mr Sackville give a welcome touch of villainy to enliven the bland plot. There are also the Bagshawes, low-born relatives of the Mortons very like the Branghtons in Burney's *Evelina*, who expose the affectations of their social betters with mortifying accuracy. The central protagonists, the Mortons and the Lacys, on the other hand, serve largely as symbolic figures who offer Lister the occasion to address changes in the economics of power.

Lister, Henry, *Arlington. A Novel*, 3 vols. (London: Henry Colburn and Richard Bentley, 1832)

Plot Summary: Lord Arlington, the father of the hero-protagonist, has been killed in mysterious circumstances while out shooting. The narrative commences in 1800, with the story of his young son, now Lord Arlington, an account of his education (scanty), his life in London (fashionable), his failed engagement to a woman of fashion, the loss of his inheritance to an American 'heir' (later proved to be a fraudulent claim) and his consequent self-exile to a remote estate in the 'North of England' where he studies the politics and economics of Bentham, Mill and Adam Smith, and turns his estate into a model community. The tale concludes in the late 1820s with the now mature Lord Arlington's return to London to assume his duties in the Upper House and to recover his inheritance through the exposure of the fraud related to his late father's death and to marry his first love, the daughter of an admirable gentry family, who has been pining for him during his six-year absence.

Comments: The plot of the fashionable world, successful in *Granby* and in *Herbert Lacy*, now fails to support the aims of Lister's political concerns. The first volume takes the hero to fashionable London; the second volume rehearses Austen's trope of amateur theatrics in *Mansfield Park*, even to including a character named 'Lady Crawford', too much rehearsing on the part of the two secret lovers and with the same scandalous dénouement. Volume three abandons the fashionable plot altogether to replace it with a series of essays offered as conversations on politics and economics between Lord Arlington and his advisor Mr Hargrave. This is not without interest. One character, a merchant, Mr Baxter, argues vigorously for the abolition of the aristocracy, forcing the hero to articulate his own reasons, provisional and fairly tepid, for continuing with the present system. Arlington's guiding principle of 'men, not measures' lights his path through the passion and confusion of the political debates of its year of publication, 1832, thus making constitutional change almost palatable to his aristocratic sensibilities: 'He learned to weigh circumstances more accurately in the balance of reason ... to observe ... in action that "golden mean" of tempered hope and rational pursuit, by which we are rendered least accessible to calamity and best prepared for its reception' (III, 322).

MACLEOD, E. H. (*FL.* 1820–30)

Biography: not found.

Macleod, E. H., *Geraldine Murray,* 4 vols. (London: A. K. Newman, 1826)

Plot Summary: Captain Lexington falls in love with proud Lady Geraldine. Lady Geraldine marries Lord Hungerford; Captain Lexington marries someone else. Lexington falsely persuades Lady Hungerford that her husband has been unfaithful to her. She elopes with him, but discovers that she has been tricked. Geraldine's 'impetuosity and haughtiness of temper' (III, 230–1) leads her to this sorry fate, says the author, 'by which means she suffered the excitements of a foundless [*sic*] jealousy to destroy all her happiness, and render her a prey to Lexington's passion'. She dies in poverty in 'an obscure village in _____shire' (III, 249).

Comments: *Geraldine Murray* is a pious, middle-class version of the *Morning Post*'s 'Fashionable World' hearkening to an earlier literary tradition critical of aristocratic excess. Lady Geraldine is severely punished with poverty, repentance and a Clarissa-like death, refusing, like Richardson's heroine, to see her seducer on her deathbed. Lexington, like Lovelace, flees the country, 'not with a view of regaining his peace of mind; he felt and KNEW that was for ever broken' (III, 263).

Macleod, E. H., *Belmont's Daughter: a Fashionable Novel,* 4 vols. (London: A. K. Newman, 1830)

Plot Summary: Annabel, the daughter of a parson, elopes with an aristocrat, Lord Belgrade, who takes her to London to lead a life of excess (plays, the opera, balls, Sunday travel) and soon runs off with another woman. The heroine removes to the country to spend her days in charity and good works for the poor in a country village. Upon her husband's death (she forgives him on his deathbed), the author hints that Mr Morgrave, the man who had first loved her, will eventually inspire love in her heart and she will marry him for a future life of virtuous happiness.

Comments: *Belmont's Daughter* displays a thoroughly middle-class understanding of aristocratic failings. The pious heroine finds that she and her husband have very different ideas of life. Lord Belgrade, for example, insists that she play the pianoforte before a group of a company of at least thirty people. The orchestra begins, she tries, but, 'nature had not endued her with sufficient strength—and after the first verse, which was a complete failure, she fainted'. It is revealed that Annabel's mother was seduced by Lord Belgrade's father. Annabel was never told why her father forbade her any connection with Belgrade. If she had known, her elopement would never have happened, the implication being that if the father is bad, the son is too, and thus goes the aristocracy.

NORMANBY, LORD (1797–1863)

Constantine Henry Phipps, Lord Normanby, son of the first Earl of Mulgrave, was created the first Marquess of Normanby in 1838. He published three fashionable novels of note, *Matilda* (1825), *Yes and No* (1828) and *The Contrast* (1832). A significant figure in the Whig Party from the early 1820s, Lord Normanby's career as an author of fashionable novels came to a halt after Reform, when he assumed a series of administrative posts under successive Whig governments.

Normanby, Lord, *Matilda; A Tale of the Day*, 2 vols. (London: Henry Colburn, 1825)

Plot Summary: Starting off in the pattern of Austen's *Persuasion*, Matilda Delaval and Augustus Arlingford fall in love and form a tacit engagement, but are prevented from pursuing it by her guardian who forbids her to see Arlingford because he is the second son and will not inherit. Arlingford leaves for Europe to sort out the business matters of his spendthrift older brother and is reported by the scandalous paper, the *John Bull*, to have taken up with an Italian lady. With this ammunition, plus the persuasions of an older friend, Matilda's guardian tricks her into marrying Sir James Dornton, a nouveau riche gentleman from Manchester, the possessor of a recently purchased baronetage and, as comic relief, some embarrassing Manchester relatives. Arlingford, now Lord Ormsby upon the death of his older brother the wastrel, returns to England to find his fiancée married to another man. When all the characters remove to the Continent, the two former lovers are thrown together repeatedly by her husband, Sir James, who covets the association with aristocratic status and Lord Ormsby's signature, as well, permitting a railway to run through the Ormsby estate. The earlier love of Matilda and Augustus, never quenched, smoulders on. Sir James believes falsely that an illicit connection has been formed. He treats Matilda cruelly and is hastening back to England with her when Ormsby, pursuing the carriage, observes Dornton strike Matilda. He removes her from Dornton's abusive treatment. 'Thus in an unguarded moment, by this one act, had one of the most virtuous of her sex fallen from the topmost heights of rank and reputation down to the level of the most wretched outcasts from society' (II, 267). After her divorce from Dornton, Matilda and Ormsby marry. Matilda dies in childbirth, as does the child of their union. Lord Ormsby 'sought some relief to his feelings in active service in the cause of the Greeks' (II, 379).

Comments: The plot of the novel reflects Lord Normanby's close engagement with Whig politics. The villains are all Tories: Matilda's guardian, Lord Wakefield, is a borough monger; the *John Bull* that publishes falsehoods is an infamous Tory scandal sheet; Sir James Dornton, Matilda's husband, is a Tory speculator running railways through ancient British estates; Mrs Hobson, Dornton's sister, takes home-town Manchester pride in Peterloo: 'What was that great gentleman, who so civilly wrote to thank our people for killing the Radicals?' Lord Ormsby's mother, on the other hand, always had 'a partiality for a *liberal*' which is reflected in the novel's arguments for Catholic enfranchisement, Italian independence, disapproval of harsh game laws and concern for the corruption of parliamentary elections. The union of Tory politicians and financial powers in the City demonstrates itself in the marriage 'settlement' Lord Wakefield strikes with Sir James Dornton: Sir James will forgive Lord Wakefield's debts if Lord Wakefield will persuade Matilda with her heiress' fortune to marry him. The conclusion of the novel, the chaotic and doomed marriage of the liberal/radical Lord Ormsby and the much abused Matilda mirrors not only the political frustration of Normanby's own life in 1825, but the general confusion of alliances between liberal Tories and out-of-power Whigs in that year, and for the next three.

Normanby, Lord, *Yes and No: A Tale of the Day*, 2 vols. (London: Henry Colburn, 1828)

Plot Summary: The story traces the fates of three young men: Mr Oakley, politically radical, but abrasive and unyielding; Mr Germain, his cousin, with unsettled political opinions leaning towards the liberal, but also drawn to the distractions of exclusive society; and Mr Fitzalbert, a rake and dandy with a sinister and calculating political intelligence. There is a contested borough election among Oakley (a Whig), Germain (a liberal Tory) and a Mr Stedman (an ultra-Tory). Fitzalbert maliciously pulls strings behind the scenes. Germain wins his seat, but only by forming a coalition with Mr Stedman and the ultras. Oakley gets elected through another route. After Oakley succeeds to the title and estate of his misanthropic uncle, Lord Rockington, he falls in love with Lord Rockington's illegitimate daughter, Helen Mordaunt, ideally domestic and intelligent, who has loved him from afar. Oakley, however, is killed in a duel with Fitzalbert after he has accused Fitzalbert of cheating Germain out of his estate at cards, correct but an impulsive insult. At the conclusion, Germain marries a strong-minded, politically liberal woman, Lady Jane, who can help him manage his political career and tell him how to vote. Fitzalbert is left to continue his career in fashionable society unstopped. Oakley leaves two substantial estates in his will, one to Helen Mordaunt and the other to Germain.

Comments: The political implications replicate the contentious political conditions of 1828. They focus on Oakley's Whiggish pride and 'obstinacy' in refusing concessions to others possessing any opinion different from his own. Oakley is thus a political failure, even though he is well informed, has high principles and is devoted to his duties as a Member of Parliament. Germain, though he is easily lured away from his MP duties as a classically irresponsible aristocrat and a devotee of fashionable society, is a better MP than Oakley because he is capable of the social and political tact that must be used with middle-class electors, a group given abundant space in this novel. Moreover, Germain is not corrupt, like the dandy Fitzalbert. Under the good management of his solid wife, Lady Jane, Germain will become an acceptable political figure. Stedman, the ultra-Tory, is discounted with contempt, but nevertheless remains in government at the conclusion of the novel.

Normanby, Lord, *The Contrast*, 3 vols. (London: Henry Colburn and Richard Bentley, 1832)

Plot Summary: The hero, Lord Castleton, falls in love with a country girl from Lancashire, Lucy Darnell, on a house party visit to the north of England. He had in the past been in love with Gertrude, Lady Gayland, but they have been separated through the machinations of a fortune hunter attracted by Lady Gayland's inheritance. Castleton marries Lucy, but the return of the couple to London brings trouble to the marriage. Lucy's country speech is an embarrassment, and her inability to appreciate opera or tolerate the nakedness of the dancers causes much disquiet. Lady Gayland befriends Lucy and shelters her from criticism. But Lady Gayland and Castleton find that they are still in love and she, sensing danger, withdraws to the Continent to effect a complete separation from Castleton. Lucy is drowned in a storm on a visit to her country relatives. 'She, "to whom in life pomp had been her only bane", is buried in the Castleton family vault with all aristocratic pageantry and honours.' The author maintains it is too soon, 'to anticipate the date when that elasticity of spirit, which is the never-failing attribute of the human mind … shall, with the assistance of time, have triumphed over mortal sorrow', and, presumably, will make way for Lady Gayland's return from the Continent and her marriage to Lord Castleton.

Comments: The novel offers a typical response of the fashionable novel to the agitated reform rhetoric of 1832. Normanby brings the 'purity' of a picturesque moral vision into contact with the sophistication of urban life, a symbolic 'contrast' embodied in the two women, Lucy and Lady Gayland, marking the unnerving possibilities that confound the promise of a 'reform' future. As in two other fashionable novels of 1832, Gore's *The Opera* and Lister's *Arlington*, the certainty of change and the rigidity of fashionable life fail to sit comfortably with one another, even for characters and authors with the most well-meaning liberal sentiments.

NORTON, CAROLINE SHERIDAN (1808–77)

Caroline Norton was born into a family famous for its acting background (her grandfather was Richard Brinsley Sheridan) and well-connected socially, but not wealthy. She made an unfortunate marriage to George Norton, primarily to relieve her mother's financial situation. Norton was a wife-beater. After a final separation, she was largely responsible for her own support. George Norton, in need of money, commenced public divorce proceedings naming Lord Melbourne as corespondent, which, though the case was thrown out, caused a scandal that followed Caroline for the rest of her life. In her literary career she wrote poetry, novels, edited *La Belle Assemblée* (1832), *The English Annual* (1834–8), *The Keepsake* (1836) and contributed widely to the annuals. Norton was also politically active, an ardent Whig, publishing in the summer of 1837, 'for private circulation, a pamphlet entitled *Observations on the Natural Claim of the Mother to the Custody of her Infant Children, as affected by the Common Law Right of the Father*', and following it with pamphlets on the subject which contributed to passage in 1839 of the 'Infant Custody Bill'.[31]

Norton, Caroline, *The Wife, and Woman's Reward*, 3 vols. (London: Saunders and Otley, 1835)

Plot Summary: There are two tales. *The Wife* concerns a woman who marries without love after she is jilted by the man she loves. Her husband is unfaithful, but she brings him back with her virtue and persuasiveness.[32] The second story, *Woman's Reward*, is a brother–sister story in which the sister is abused and mistreated by a violent brother. Mary, the heroine, promises her dying father she will look after Lionel, the younger brother. Mary does not marry, has a very small income and lives at Hastings. Lionel spends his fortune on an election, loses it, has many debts and is nearing bankruptcy. The new politics of partisanship and financial favours is satirized. Lionel marries a flighty woman, continues to exhibit a violent temper by abusing his wife who elopes from the house with Algernon Percy, a notorious seducer, taking her child with her. Lionel's debts land him in prison where he is visited by his sister Mary who finds 'him standing half dressed in the midst of the apartment, glaring wildly around him, an open razor in his hand, and his throat bared for the purpose of self-destruction'. Mary saves her brother from suicide, but he dies only moments later from shame and guilt: 'A faint sigh escaped his lips, and he feebly pressed her hand; presently he opened his wide dark eyes, and muttered hurriedly—"My father calls me;"—and in another moment, that restless heart had ceased to beat—that fine vigorous frame lay cold and nerveless on the couch of death ... Lionel, was but a painful memory to a few grieving hearts; and to the rest of the world—nothing' (III, 23). Mary goes to France where she lives cheaply and nurses British invalids dying of consumption. She gets a letter from an old flame asking her to marry him. She does, but remains forever embittered by her experiences with a violent man, her own brother.

Comments: Mrs Norton's experiences of life are revealed not so much in the plot, but in the generally depressed, dreary tone that afflicts both tales. 'Sales were disappointing, but this publication led to an offer from the same publishers for a travel book.'[33]

OWENSON, SYDNEY, LADY MORGAN (1776–1859)

Sydney Owenson, daughter of an Irish actor and a tradesman's daughter, married Charles Morgan, a physician, only after he had been granted a knighthood. She could then enter married life as Lady Morgan, a title highly useful to her in her publishing career. She is remembered mainly as a writer of Irish national tales, travels and, during the 1830s, as a literary journalist. Though she herself wrote about the ruling classes, the gentry and aristocracy in Ireland, she joined the critical attacks on fashionable novels in her writing for *The Athenæum* during the 1830s.[34] In the late 1830s she wrote an important series of essays in this periodical where she relegated silver fork novels to the lowest ranks of literature.

SCOTT, CAROLINE LUCY DOUGLAS, LADY SCOTT (1784–1857)

Caroline Douglas Scott was born into a titled Anglo-Scottish family. She published her first novel *A Marriage in High Life* with the help and supervision of her cousin, the author Lady Charlotte Bury. She published another fashionable novel, *Trevelyan*, in 1831. In 1856, her novel *The Old Grey Church* was published, an evangelical novel of fashionable life, famously excoriated by George Eliot in her essay 'Silly Novels by Lady Novelists' (1856).[35]

Scott, Caroline, *A Marriage in High Life*, ed. Lady Charlotte Bury, 2 vols. (London: Henry Colburn, 1828)

Plot Summary: Emmeline Benson, the daughter of one of the most opulent merchants in London, is married to Ernest, Lord Fitzhenry, the only son of Lord Arlingford. Lord Fitzhenry has a mistress, Lady Florence Mostyn, who is wicked, bewitching and tenacious. She extracts a promise from Lord Fitzhenry on his wedding day that his marriage to Emmeline will be in name only. He keeps to his word. The novel is thus about Emmeline's unhappy predicament as 'a wife and not a wife' – her suffering from the contempt of fashionable London, her pain at having to see her husband in the company of another woman at the opera and, implicitly, her sexual frustration in living in the house with Lord Fitzhenry with the door to his bedroom closed to her. In the last quarter of the novel, Ernest goes abroad, becomes sick, develops consumption and bitterly regrets the way he has treated his wife. Lady Florence Mostyn abandons him. Emmeline hastens to Paris to nurse her errant husband and read to him from 'that beautiful Essay of Miss Bowdler's on the Advantages of Sickness'. He dies repentant in her arms. A kindly gentleman, Mr Pelham, who has defended Emmeline throughout the novel, remains to marry her when and if she can forget her love for her husband.

Comments: The plot of Lady Scott's novel fits squarely into the social and political agitation of its year of publication, 1828, presenting the public with a fashionable novel that solidly supports the claims of the middle classes to be more 'respectable' and morally superior to the ruling, aristocratic class. Mr Benson's outrage when he finally discovers his daughter's situation focuses the political point of the novel succinctly: 'I had rather have seen you the wife of the lowest clerk in my banking-house, than that of this Lord Fitzhenry, or any other lord in Christendom with his vile paramour' (II, 137).

WARD, ROBERT PLUMER (1765–1846)

Robert Plumer Ward initially practised law, but in 1795 he published a history of the law, which he followed with other law treatises that brought him political notice, a seat in Parliament, further publications in favour of Pitt and his allies, and a continuing career in various government administrative posts. With retirement, and the death of his wife in 1821, Ward turned to fiction and published *Tremaine, or the Man of Refinement* in 1825. A second novel, *De Vere, or the Man of Independence*, followed in 1827, which 'may have prompted Canning's quip that Ward's law books were as interesting as novels and his novels as dull as law books'.[36]

Ward, Robert, *Tremaine, or the Man of Refinement*, 2nd edn (London: Henry Colburn, 1825)

Plot Summary: Tremaine, a dandy and aristocrat, goes to the country after an active life in town (government and fashion) to withdraw and enjoy the intellectual life of retirement. Also, and more to the point, his political party the Whigs have been excluded from power by the Prince Regent. He finds the country a bore and bad for his health, but refuses to admit this. His childhood tutor and friend, a local clergyman/landowner, takes him under his wing and introduces him to a useful life in the country. Mr Evelyn, the friend, also has a daughter Georgina who makes unfashionable, but delightful conversation, rides horses well and, in spite of her lack of fashionable accomplishments, charms Tremaine. The first volume ends with his attraction to Miss Evelyn growing and his estimation of a life in the country increasing. The second volume looks as if it is going to take him to London, but it does not. It introduces people from London to the country, 'exclusives' who demonstrate all their vices and aristocratic faults. The third volume consists largely of didactic essays pitting Mr Evelyn's orthodox piety and arguments for religion against Tremaine's penchant for a more loosely understood Deism. Tremaine must be converted to orthodoxy before Georgina will consider marrying him, though she loves him deeply. She won't trust her immortal soul with an irreligious husband. They separate, she pines away, nearly dies and must be taken to the south of France where she and Tremaine meet again. He is converted by Evelyn, the entire volume being turned over to his religious conversion and the marriage project.

Comments: It's worth noting that this novel, in spite of a reputation for dullness, has parts that are genuinely a treat to read. There is the influence of Sterne, and repeatedly the sweetness and wry perception of Goldsmith's *Vicar of Wakefield*, with Mr Evelyn's fatherly laughter at his daughter as an example. When Georgina protests that she will not marry a suitor who is 'so very old', forty years of age, her father notes that Tremaine is nearly forty. She replies that he is not, he is only thirty-eight years old. 'That makes the difference', he tells her and kisses her goodnight. Also, Evelyn is occasionally the gentle butt of humour for his clergyman's prudery – his position on the immorality of opera, for example. As it is in Goldsmith, however, such gentle mockery of the vicar is absent when it comes to his clergyman's duties as a teacher of morality. Some of the social comedy in the novel has a Branghton-like boisterousness. But much of the bumpkin humour serves to teach Tremaine how to lower his aristocratic pride and deal plainly and fairly with his country neighbours – an early example of the Reform dynamic, especially in its ideas as to the political future of aristocratic Whig pride.

WHITE, CHARLES (1793–1861)

Charles White published *The Adventures of a King's Page* (1829), *The Belgic Revolution of 1830* (1835), *The Married Unmarried* (1837) and *Three Years in Constantinople; or, Domestic Manners of the Turks* (1845). White's only novel of fashionable life, *Almack's Revisited*, was first published as *Herbert Milton* by Saunders and Otley in 1828, then reissued as *Almack's Revisited* in the same year, possibly to capitalize on the popularity of Marianne Spencer Hudson's recent *Almack's* (1826), also published by Saunders and Otley. The *Literary Gazette* advertised White's novel as if it were in competition with Hudson's novel, presumably a publisher's puff: 'We consider ALMACK'S REVISITED to be superior to the first *Almack's* which has made so great a noise, and become so universally popular.'[37] *Almack's Revisited* was to become White's key title and the associated name by which his future productions were advertised.

White, Charles, *Almack's Revisited*, 1st printing known as *Herbert Milton*, 3 vols. (London: Saunders and Otley, 1828)

Plot Summary: There are two Herbert Miltons in the novel: first, Sir Herbert whose advancement from an unprovided younger son to a respected official in the East India Company begins the novel; second, his Eton-educated son Herbert whose romance with a Miss Manby provides the narrative thread (slender) for the action of the novel. The history of Mr Manby, the heroine's supposed father, is also narrated in the first volume as it intersects fatally with Sir Herbert's. When young Herbert reveals to his father that he has married Miss Manby against his father's wishes, Sir Herbert dies of a haemorrhagic fit as he confesses to young Herbert that he has 'married his own sister'. Young Herbert departs England in an act of wilful self-destruction, joining Wellington for the last days of the Spanish campaign. He dies in battle. A villainous cousin, the spendthrift and gambler Alfred Milton, presumptive heir to the Milton estate, takes immediate measures to despoil the estate for its cash value, to sell its woods, household goods and portraits to the highest bidder. Just in time a gentleman appears (too late to prevent Herbert's death) to prove that 'Miss Manby' is not Sir Herbert's daughter at all, but is 'Emily Mowbray' who was exchanged during a shipwreck with a lookalike child (Sir Herbert's) who died in the sinking of the ship. Herbert's best friend and the trustee in charge of his will, Captain Sidney, sorts out the inheritance rights and confronts Alfred, the villain who has engineered the whole catastrophe. The wicked Alfred in an effort to horsewhip Sidney misses aim, loses his balance, plunges into a chasm and expires 'in the falls of Dead Man's Dance'. The widowed Lady Herbert, now the proud mother of young Mowbray Milton, Herbert's son and heir, assumes the custodial management of the Milton estate. 'She has not quitted Milton Park since the period of her first removal to its walls, her whole time being employed in watching over her son, and in dispersing in acts of charity the noble fortune of which she is in possession' (III, 361).

Comments: The novel has a strong Tory bias. Wellington is introduced worshipfully as 'the great chieftain' when young Herbert is introduced to him: 'As the hero extended his hand to bid adieu to the young soldier, the thrill which it imparted to the whole frame of the latter seemed to animate his soul with a portion of that immortal fire which flowed in the veins of the conqueror himself' (I, 145).

Notes

CHAPTER I   CULTURAL CONTEXTS

1 William Hazlitt, 'On Patronage and Puffing', *Ainsworth's Magazine*, 2 (1842), pp. 42–3, cited by Nicholas Mason, '"The Quack has Become God": Puffery, Print, and the "Death" of Literature in Romantic-Era Britain', *Nineteenth-Century Literature*, 60, no. 1 (June 2005), pp. 1–31. Citation p. 13.

2 Clifford Siskin, 'Epilogue', in Deidre Lynch and William B. Warner (eds.), *Cultural Institutions of the Novel* (Chapel Hill: Duke University Press, 1996), pp. 423–40. Citation p. 426.

3 Walter Benjamin, *The Arcades Project*, trans. Howard Eiland and Kevin McLaughlin (Cambridge, MA: Harvard University Press, 1999), Q2, 6, p. 531.

4 Alexander Zevin, 'Panoramic Literature in 19th Century Paris: Robert Macaire as a Type of Everyday', http://dl.lib.brown.edu/paris/Zevin.html, pp. 12, 9.

5 *Westminster Review*, 1829, 'Newspaper Press', p. 216. Cited by Jonathan Mulrooney, 'Reading the Romantic-Period Daily News', *Nineteenth-Century Contexts*, 24, no. 4 (Dec. 2002), pp. 351–77. Citation p. 359.

6 Clifford Siskin, 'VR Machine: Romanticism and the Physical', *European Romantic Review*, 12, no. 2 (Spring 2001), pp. 158–64. Citation p. 160. From David Deutsch, *The Fabric of Reality* (London: Penguin, 1977), pp. 95–6.

7 Clifford Siskin, 'Novels and Systems', *NOVEL: A Forum on Fiction*, 34, no. 2 (Spring 2001), p. 209.

8 As John Stuart Mill writes in 'The Spirit of the Age', *The Examiner*, 9 Jan., 1831, 'The Grand achievement of the present age is the *diffusion* of *superficial* knowledge; and that surely is no trifle, to have been accomplished by a single generation.'

9 Stephan Oettermann in *The Panorama: History of a Mass Medium*, trans. Deborah Lucas Schneider (New York: Zone Books, 1997) argues that the term 'panorama' came about first with the technical term coined in the late eighteenth century to describe 'a "circular vista, overview (from an elevated point)" of a real landscape or cityscape', and was followed soon after by 'a metaphorical use to mean a "survey" or "overview" of a particular field of knowledge … Throughout the nineteenth century these three meanings of the word existed side by side' (p. 7).

10 'There are two panoramic exhibitions in the British metropolis belonging to Messrs. Burford at Leicester Square, and No. 168, Strand, at each of which there are generally views of two celebrated places. Admission to each view, 1s.; and description, containing an outline sketch of the panorama, 6d.' *Leigh's New Picture of London* (London: Samuel Leigh, 1830), p. 315.

11 The panorama in the Colosseum, Regent's Park, 'far surpasses in extent and accuracy every thing of the kind hitherto attempted ... The various objects are depicted as seen from the top of St. Paul's where Mr. Horner made the original sketches in 1821 ... The Gardens surrounding the Colosseum are laid out so as to appear much more extensive than they really are. They comprise conservatories, waterfalls, fountains, a Swiss cottage, &c. Admission Panorama alone, 1s.; Panorama, ball, and saloon for works of art, 3s.; Conservatories, fountains, and Swiss cottage, 2s.; the whole, 5s.' *Leigh's New Picture of London*, p. 316. See Oettermann for a full description with excellent illustrations, of the Colosseum in Regent's Park (pp. 132–40).

12 'The Cosmorama is intended to present correct delineations of the celebrated remains of antiquity, and of the most remarkable cities and edifices in every part of the globe. The exhibition-room is fitted up in an elegant style, and is divided into galleries, each comprising seven accurate and well-painted views, which, being seen through glasses, have the appearance of reality. The subjects are changed every two or three months. Open from 11 till dusk. Admission, 1s., descriptive catalogue, 6d.' *Leigh's New Picture of London*, p. 317.

13 'The Diorama in Regent's Park is decidedly superior both to the panorama and the cosmorama in the fidelity with which the objects are depicted, and in the completeness of the illusion ... [T]he optical deception is complete, and it is difficult for the spectator to persuade himself that he is only contemplating a work of art. Admission, boxes, 3s., amphitheatre, 2s., description, gratis' *Leigh's New Picture of London*, p. 315. See Oettermann for the history of this offshoot of the panorama (pp. 69–83): 'The dioramas seemed to offer a quick and easy substitute for travel, almost as if they were not pictures of distant places but the distant places themselves, now right next door' (p. 78).

14 See Judith Flanders, *Consuming Passions: Leisure and Pleasure in Victorian Britain* (London: Harper Perennial, 2007), pp. 266–7.

15 Gordon Mackenzie cites this contemporary review in *Marylebone, Great City North of Oxford Street* (London and Basingstoke: Macmillan, 1972), p. 135.

16 William Greenslade's phrase for Chad Newsome's Paris in 'The Power of Advertising: Chad Newsome and the Meaning of Paris in *The Ambassadors*', *ELH*, 49, no. 1 (Spring 1982), pp. 99–122. Citation p. 102.

17 Flanders, *Consuming Passions*, p. 267.

18 Dror Wahrman, *Imagining the Middle Class: The Political Representation of Class in Britain, c. 1780–1840* (Cambridge University Press, 1995), pp. 14–15.

19 Marguerite Blessington, *The Magic Lantern: or, Sketches of Scenes in the Metropolis* (London: Longman, Hurst, Rees, Orme, and Brown, 1822).

20 Lady Blessington's genuinely lively writing skills were lost for more profitable jobs in editing annuals and producing occasional potboilers. However, her poem, *The Belle of a Season* (London: Longman, Orme, Brown, Green and Longmans, *c.* 1839), richly illustrated by A. E. Chalon, shows her considerable talent for comic verse and her sharp eye for the rhythms and foibles of fashionable chatter.

21 Pierce Egan, *Life in London: or the Day and Night Scenes of Jerry Hawthorn, Esq. And His Elegant Friend Corinthian Tom, Accompanied by Bob Logic, the Oxonian, in the Rambles and Sprees through the Metropolis*, 'Dedicated to His Most Gracious Majesty, King George the Fourth', 'Embellished with thirty-six scenes from Real Life, designed and etched by I. R. and G. Cruikshank; and enriched also with numerous designs on wood, by the same artists' (London: Sherwood, Neely, and Jones, 1821).

22 Anon. [Egan, Pierce 'improbable'], *Real Life in London: or, The Further Rambles and Adventures of Bob Tallyho, Esq. and his Cousin the Hon. Tom Dashall, &c. through the Metropolis* (London: Jones & Co., 1821; II published 1822).

23 Nathaniel Parker Willis, a contemporary American observer of London's fashionable world, writes of Bulwer's behaviour in society: 'The author of *Pelham* is a younger son, and depends on his writing for his livelihood; and truly, measuring works of fancy by what they will bring, a glance round his luxurious rooms is worth reams of puffs in the Quarterlies. He lives in the heart of fashionable London, entertains a great deal, and is expensive in all his habits, and for this pay Messrs. Clifford, Pelham, and Aram—most excellent bankers.' Cited by George Paston in *Little Memoirs of the Nineteenth Century* (London: Grant Richards, 1902), p. 178.

24 Robert Blake, *Disraeli* (New York: St. Martin's Press, 1967), pp. 56, 73–4.

25 See J. Fitzgerald Molloy, *The Most Gorgeous Lady Blessington*, 2 vols. (London: Downey & Co., 1896), especially II, pp. 160–92, and Michael Sadleir, *The Strange Life of Lady Blessington* (New York: Farrar, Straus, and Company, 1947), pp. 186–238.

26 G. C. Boase, 'Bury, Lady Charlotte Susan Maria (1775–1861)', rev. Pam Perkins, *Oxford Dictionary of National Biography* (Oxford University Press, 2004). www.oxforddnb.com.ezproxy.libraries.claremont.edu/view/article/4147.

27 Winifred Hughes, 'Gore, Catherine Grace Frances (1799/1800–1861)', *Oxford Dictionary of National Biography* (Oxford University Press, 2004). www.oxforddnb.com.ezproxy.libraries.claremont.edu/view/article/11091. The Disraeli citation comes from Matthew Rosa, *The Silver-Fork School: Novels of Fashion Preceding* Vanity Fair (New York: Columbia University Press, 1936), p. 134.

28 'Catherine Gore: Life', screen within Susan Brown, Patricia Clements, and Isobel Grundy (eds.), *Orlando: Women's Writing in the British Isles from the Beginnings to the Present.* Cambridge University Press Online, 2006. http://orlando.cambridge.org.

29 Mason, p. 22, n. 68, for an account of recent scholarly debate on changes in the poetry market during the late 1820s and early 1830s.

30 Citation from *Lord Beaconsfield's Letters*, ed. R. Disraeli, 1887, p. 71, in Glennis Byron, 'Landon, Letitia Elizabeth (1802–1838)', *Oxford Dictionary of National Biography* (Oxford University Press, 2004). www.oxforddnb.com. ezproxy.libraries.claremont.edu/view/article/15978.

31 'Identifying itself as a commodified form, her poetry forecloses that final (romantic illusion) of art: that it lives in a world elsewhere', writes Jerome McGann in 'The Failures of Romanticism', in Tilottama Rajan and Julia M. Wright (eds.), *Romanticism, History, and the Possibilities of Genre: Re-forming Literature 1789–1837* (Cambridge University Press, 1998), pp. 270–87. Citation p. 283.

32 Paston, *Little Memoirs of the Nineteenth Century*, p. 182. Rosa gathers gossip about Colburn's payment to authors in *The Silver-Fork School*: 'For Hook's *Sayings and Doings*, first series … he paid £600; for the second series he paid one thousand guineas, a sum later increased by £200 and £150. To Lady Morgan for her *Florence MacCarthy* he paid £2,000. Ainsworth, in writing to his friend Crossley that at any time he could get £500 for a fashionable novel, was in no way exaggerating … We have seen what he paid Disraeli for *Vivian Grey*, £200 for the first part, and £600 for the second. Five hundred pounds was the first payment for *Tremaine*, and much more was added when the book proved profitable', p. 188.

33 'Sydney Owenson, Lady Morgan: Life,' in Brown, Clements and Grundy, *Orlando*.

34 *Westminster Review*, 9, no. 20 (April 1829), 'Weekly Review', p. 476. Cited by Mulrooney, pp. 351–77. Citation p. 357.

35 Mason, pp. 8–9.

36 In order to ensure good reviews of his novels, Colburn made himself proprietor of 'the *New Monthly Magazine*, the *Literary Gazette*, and *The Athenæum*', later taking shares in the *Sunday Times* and the *Court Journal* as well. See Mason, pp. 14–15.

37 John Sutherland, 'Henry Colburn Publisher', *Publishing History*, 19 (1986), pp. 59–84. Citation p. 61.

38 *Ibid.*, p. 63.

39 *Ibid.*, p. 62.

40 J. Sutherland cites Michael Sadleir's claim that Colburn died 'leaving £35,000', an enormous fortune, p. 60.

41 Rosa, Matthew Whiting, *The Silver-Fork School: Novels of Fashion Preceding 'Vanity Fair'* (New York: Columbia University Press, 1936).

42 Edward Bulwer, *England and the English*, 1st edn London 1833 (Paris: Baudry's European Library, 1834), p. 252.

43 'In 1833 duties on advertising were … reduced by two shillings to 1s. 6d … Between 1833 and 1834, the number of advertisements in newspapers increased by some 35 per cent.' James Raven, *The Business of Books: Booksellers and the English Book Trade 1450–1850* (New Haven: Yale University Press, 2007), pp. 346–7.

44 Mulrooney, p. 354.

45 Jennifer A. Wicke, *Advertising Fictions: Literature, Advertisement, and Social Reading* (New York: Columbia University Press, 1988), p. 2.

46 Zevin, pp. 12, 9.

47 Michel Foucault, 'Body/Power', in C. Gordon (ed.), *Power/Knowledge: Selected Interviews and Other Writings 1972–1977* (Brighton: Harvester, 1980), p. 55. Cited by Sean Hides, 'The Geology of Material Culture and Cultural Identity', in Susan M. Pearce (ed.), *Experiencing Material Culture in the Western World* (London and Washington, DC: Leicester University Press, 1997), p. 25.

48 Wicke, pp. 1–3, 16.

49 Robert Montgomery, 'Introductory Epistle to an Eminent Puffer', *The Puffiad* (London, S. Maunder: 1828), p. 15. Cited in Mason, pp. 26–7.

50 Anonymous review of 'Pin Money', *Westminster Review*, no. 15 (Oct. 1831), pp. 433, 434. Generously cited by Alison Adburgham, *Silver Fork Society: Fashionable Life and Literature from 1814 to 1840* (London: Constable, 1983), pp. 213–14.

51 William Hazlitt, 'The Dandy School', from *The Examiner* (18 Nov. 1827), in P. P. Howe (ed.), *The Complete Works of William Hazlitt*, 21 vols. (London and Toronto: J. M. Dent and Sons, 1934), xvi, pp. 143–9. Citation p. 146.

52 Richard Salmon, 'The Secret of the Spectacle: Epistemology and Commodity Display in *The Ambassadors*', *The Henry James Review*, 14, no. 1 (Winter 1993), pp. 43–54. Citation p. 44.

53 Simon During, 'Regency London', in James Chandler (ed.), *The Cambridge History of English Romantic Literature* (Cambridge University Press, 2009), pp. 335–54. Citation p. 335.

54 *Ibid.*, p. 337.

55 Margaret Linley, 'A Centre that Would Not Hold: Annuals and Cultural Democracy', in Laurel Brake, Bill Bell and David Finkelstein (eds.), *Nineteenth-Century Media and the Construction of Identities* (Basingstoke: Palgrave, 2000), pp. 54–76. Citation, p. 54.

56 *Ibid.*, p. 55.

57 Wolfgang Iser, *The Implied Reader: Patterns of Communication in Prose Fiction from Bunyan to Beckett* (Baltimore and London: Johns Hopkins University Press, 1974), pp. 275, 279.

58 Richard Bjornson, 'Cognitive Mapping and the Understanding of Literature', *SubStance*, no. 30 (1981), pp. 51–62. Citations pp. 52–3, 55.

59 Greenslade, p. 106.

60 Mulrooney, p. 360, from Daniel Stuart, 'Anecdotes of Public Newspapers', *Gentleman's Magazine* (July 1838), pp. 23–7.

61 *The Times*, Tuesday, 25 Sept. 1821, 'ONE HUNDRED BEAVER HATS.— ROBERT LLOYD, of 92 Newgate-street, original maker and inventor ... Silk hats, with double edges, 18s. each. N. B. Just published, Lloyd's 4th edition of a Treatise on Hats, 1s.'

62 John Vernon, *Money and Fiction: Literary Realism in the Nineteenth and Early Twentieth Centuries* (Ithaca and London: Cornell University Press, 1984), p. 8.

63 *Ibid.*, p. 20, citing J. Hillis Miller, 'Afterword' to Signet edition of Dickens' *Our Mutual Friend* (New York, 1964), p. 904.

64 With the introduction of paper money in 1793, the number of banks in England increased from 280 in 1793 to 626 in 1815. See Vernon, p. 33: figures cited from Robin Martin Reeve, *The Industrial Revolution, 1750 to 1850* (University of London Press, 1971), p. 167.

65 William St Clair, *The Reading Nation in the Romantic Period* (Cambridge University Press, 2004), Appendix 8, p. 576.

66 *Grant's London Journal*, pt 1, no. 3 (Jan. 1840), cited by James Hamilton in *London Lights: The Minds that Moved the City that Shook the World, 1805–1851* (London: John Murray, 2007), p. 198.

67 During, p. 339.

68 Vernon, p. 53.

69 Jane Austen, *Sanditon*, in Janet Todd and Linda Bree (eds.), *Later Manuscripts*, p. 156, in *The Cambridge Edition of Jane Austen*, gen. ed. Janet Todd, 9 vols. (Cambridge University Press, 2008).

70 Jane Austen, *Persuasion* (iii, ch. 9), Janet Todd and Antje Blank (eds.), p. 71, in *The Cambridge Edition of Jane Austen*, gen. ed. Janet Todd, 9 vols. (Cambridge University Press, 2006).

71 Mulrooney's 'Reading the Romantic-Period Daily News' suggests that even for the working classes the habit of reading a daily newspaper was, by 1829, as common as patronage of a coffee house (pp. 357–8).

72 Nikki Hessell's 'News and Newspapers: Readers of the Daily Press in Jane Austen's Novels', *Persuasions*, no. 31 (2009), pp. 248–54, records Jane Austen's early awareness of 'the implications of such a dramatic change in the nation's reading habits'.

73 Mulrooney, p. 359.

74 Wicke, in *Advertising Fictions*, writes, 'The litany of literature Leavis cites is notable because it is speech-based ... What advertising really kills for Leavis is literature as transfigured speech, the art he places at the root of creative language use', p. 9.

75 Charles Lamb, *The Letters of Charles Lamb*, ed. E. V. Lucas, iii (New York: AMS, 1968; London: Methuen, 1935), pp. 242–3.

76 Stephen Colclough's *Consuming Texts: Readers and Reading Communities, 1695–1870* (Basingstoke: Palgrave, 2007) cites Leah Price's observation of Victorian readers in regard to their 'unrecorded reading': 'the "sheer bulk of many Victorian genres", she argues, required "their consumers to skip and to skim, to tune in and zone out"', p. 168. Leah Price, 'Reader's Block: Response', *Victorian Studies*, 46, no. 2 (Winter 2004), pp. 231–42.

77 Barbara M. Benedict, 'Sensibility by the Numbers: Austen's Work as Regency Popular Fiction', in Deidre Lynch (ed.), *Janeites: Austen's Disciples and Devotees* (Princeton University Press, 2000), pp. 63–86.

78 *Ibid.*, pp. 69–82.

79 David Allan, *A Nation of Readers: The Lending Library in Georgian England* (London: The British Library, 2008), p. 124.

80 *Ibid.*, p. 149. The same price structure, writes Allan, recurs at John Brown's Wigan circulating library in 1821.
81 *Ibid.*, p. 151. Stephen Colclough's account of working men's personal libraries in *Consuming Texts*, however, emphasizes their lack of money as making access to books among working men limited and difficult. Moreover, interest in novels appears slight, he writes, among groups of working men bent on self-improvement (pp. 146–62).
82 Allan, p. 154.
83 Ellen Miller Casey, 'Silver-Forks and the Commodity Text: Lady Morgan and *The Athenæum*', *Women's Writing*, 16, no. 2 (Aug. 2009), pp. 253–62. Casey's essay cites Morgan's book reviews from *The Athenæum*, 1839 to 1840, in which Morgan attacks novels of fashionable life for their close relation to commercial culture.
84 Lady Morgan [Sydney Owenson], review of *Jack Sheppard: A Romance* [by William Harrison Ainsworth], *The Athenæum*, 626 (26 Oct. 1839), p. 803. Cited in Casey, p. 257.
85 Lady Morgan [Sydney Owenson], review of *The Dowager*, *The Athenæum* 678 (14 Nov. 1840), p. 899. Cited in Casey, p. 258.
86 Lady Morgan [Sydney Owenson], *Jack Sheppard*, p. 804. Cited in Casey, p. 257.
87 Cited in Casey, p. 258, from Lady Morgan's review of Mrs Gore's *The Dowager* in *The Athenæum* 678 (14 Nov. 1840), p. 899.
88 Colin Campbell, 'The Romantic Ethic and the Spirit of Modern Consumerism: *Reflections on the Reception of a Thesis Concerning the Origin of the Continuing Desire for Goods*', in Pearce, pp. 36–48.
89 *Ibid.*, pp. 37–8.
90 Richard Salmon, *Henry James and the Culture of Publicity* (Cambridge University Press, 1997) pp. 6–7. See Jürgen Habermas, *The Structural Transformation of the Public Sphere: An Inquiry into a Category of Bourgeois Society*, trans. Thomas Burger with the assistance of Frederick Lawrence (Cambridge, MA: MIT Press, 1991), p. 7.
91 Wicke, p. 6.
92 *Ibid.*, p. 17.
93 Hazlitt, 'Dandy School', p. 146.
94 The politics of literary criticism was a troubling fact of life for authors in the Reform period, as John Strachan explains in *Advertising and Satirical Culture in the Romantic Period* (Cambridge University Press, 2007), p. 259. Strachan cites Robert Montgomery's complaint in *The Age Reviewed* (1828): 'You can scarcely mention a magazine or a paper, that has not a certain publisher and critic, who play a literary shuttlecock most admirably. Besides all this perfidious venalism, there are party rancour, envy, malice, pique, and all the concomitants of little minds, constantly affecting the critics', p. 131.
95 Salmon, 'The Secret of the Spectacle', p. 48. Salmon cites Wolfgang Fritz Haug, *Commodity Aesthetics, Ideology and Culture* (New York: International General, 1987), p. 122. See also Allan, p. 155, for the plate 'The Reader remade', which depicts a woman's body reconstructed from books she has read from the circulating libraries.

96 I am indebted to Salmon, *Henry James and the Culture of Publicity*, pp. 132–3, for his lucid explanation of this argument.

97 Winifred Hughes, 'Silver Fork Writers and Readers: Social Contexts', *NOVEL: A Forum on Fiction*, 25, no. 3 (Spring 1992), pp. 328–47. Citation p. 336.

98 Deidre Shauna Lynch, *The Economy of Character: Novels, Market Culture, and the Business of Inner Meaning* (Chicago and London: University of Chicago Press, 1998), p. 157.

99 'blazon, n.' *OED* Online. March 2011. Oxford University Press. www.oed.com/view/Entry/20024.

100 Salmon, 'The Secret of the Spectacle', p. 48.

101 Norman Gash, *Aristocracy and People: Britain 1815–1865* (Bungay, Suffolk: Edward Arnold, 1979), p. 168.

102 For an account of *Fraser's* ultra-Tory politics, see Robert Lapp, 'Romanticism Repackaged: The New Faces of "Old Man" Coleridge in *Fraser's Magazine, 1830–35*', *European Romantic Review*, 11, no. 2 (Spring 2000), pp. 235–47.

103 Linley, p. 59. Carlyle might be counted among contemporary readers as another who missed the point of Bulwer's irony in *Pelham*.

104 Gore employs diamonds again in *Mothers and Daughters* (1831) for a value comparison: 'Lady Stapylford's diamonds at Carlton House ... were as regular matters for newspaper discussion as the Slave Trade, or the annual debate on Emancipation' (II, p. 67).

105 Jean Baudrillard, *For a Critique of the Political Economy of the Sign*, trans. Charles Levin (New York: Telos Press, 1981), p. 67. Baudrillard compares a wedding ring (symbol) with an ordinary ring (fashion) that anyone can substitute for another, an object of consumption, pp. 66–7.

106 Mrs Gore's *Mothers and Daughters* (1831), which appears between *Women as They Are* (1830) and *Pin Money* (1831), is also concerned with the relationship of money and status, but presents it as a Bourdieu-like habitus in action, 'a feel for the game' as played through the aggressive social manipulations of the mother-villain of the piece, Lady Maria Willingham. Commodity objects arrive in this novel strictly 'as advertised', mostly surface, and with prices attached.

107 Pierre Bourdieu, 'The Market of Symbolic Goods', in Randal Johnson (ed.), *The Field of Cultural Production* (New York: Columbia University Press, 1993), pp. 112–41. Citation p. 114.

108 A magnificent fortune of £30,000 a year. Invested at an interest rate of 5%, there will be £5,000 per year from the £100,000 on marriage and £25,000 annually in interest from the £500,000 she will eventually inherit.

109 Lynch, *Economy of Character*, p. 126.

110 Claudia Johnson, '"Let Me Make the Novels of a Country": Barbauld's "The British Novelists" (1810/1820)', *NOVEL: A Forum on Fiction*, 34, no. 2 (Spring 2001), pp. 163–79. Citation p. 172.

111 Lynch, *Economy of Character*, p. 256.

112 Frederic Jameson, *The Political Unconscious: Narrative as a Socially Symbolic Act* (London and New York: Routledge, 1989), pp. 206–8.

113 Lynch, *Economy of Character*, p. 127.
114 *Ibid.*, p. 150.
115 *Ibid.*, for citation.

CHAPTER 2   THE WOMAN'S TRADITION: EDGEWORTH,
BURNEY AND AUSTEN

1 Henry Lister, *Granby. A Novel* (London: Henry Colburn, 1826), (1, p. 148).
2 Winifred Hughes, 'Elegies for the Regency: Catherine Gore's Dandy Novels', *Nineteenth-Century Fiction*, 50, no. 2 (Sept. 1995), pp. 189–209. Citation p. 205.
3 [Henry Taylor], 'Novels of Fashionable Life', *Quarterly Review*, 48 (1832), pp. 177, 165. Cited in Hughes, 'Elegies for the Regency', p. 205. Hughes argues that the weakness of structure in novels of fashionable life lies in 'the shape-lessness of aristocratic experience', where social advancement, the primary plot of middle-class fiction, is irrelevant, an observation that would account for the sense of political despair that haunts Gore's *Cecil* novels.
4 Salmon, 'The Secret of the Spectacle, p. 44.
5 Campbell, pp. 36–48. Salmon, 'The Secret of the Spectacle', p. 50.
6 Catherine Gore, in a letter, 14 July 1832, to the editor of the *New Monthly Magazine*, cited by Michael Sadleir, *Bulwer and His Wife: A Panorama, 1803–1836* (London: Constable & Co, 1933), pp. 301–2.
7 Pearce, in 'Foreword: Words and Things', in *Experiencing Material Culture in the Western World*, continues the distinction: 'while serious fiction … concerned itself with social relationships … popular fiction, by contrast, shaped itself by drawing on the materially centred elements in the same inherit-ance' (p. 9). 'Popular fiction parallels life in that it offers its readers what they would wish to have or to be … Serious fiction … tells us more about living and about ourselves, while popular literature leaves us knowing more, which is not the same thing' (p. 7).
8 The beginnings of a woman's canon seem to be in Landon's mind. The Minerva Press novels are at the bottom, with considerably more respectable novelists, Robinson, Radcliffe and Smith placed next up the ladder, then the primary candidates for canonical status – Edgeworth, Burney and Austen.
9 It should be noted that Landon's depreciation of Austen's *Pride and Prejudice* did not prevent her from borrowing the plot and characters of this novel for the beginning of her novel *Lady Anne Granard* (published posthumously, 1842).
10 Edward Copeland, *Women Writing about Money: Women's Fiction in England, 1790 to 1820* (Cambridge University Press, 1995), pp. 15–34.
11 Henry Lister, *Edinburgh Review*, 51 (July 1830), pp. 444–62. Citation p. 447.
12 The portrait that Lady Delacour reveals from behind the 'green curtain' in Edgeworth's *Belinda* (ch. xxi, 'The Denouement') clears the way for Virginia to marry Captain Sunderland instead of Clarence Hervey, a case of mistaken identity. In *Pin Money*, the identity of 'Lucy' the companion is revealed as one and the same with Lady Mary Trevelyan, another case of mistaken identity.

13 April Kendra, 'Silver-Forks and Double Standards', *Women's Fiction*, 16, no. 2 (August 2009), pp. 191–217, notes the entire dependence of Edgeworth's Lady Delacour and Gore's Lady Danvers on the world of London society for their identity and self-worth (p. 213, n.26). T. H. Lister dismisses the significance of Lady Danvers' political ambition in the *Edinburgh Review*, 51 (July 1830): 'Neither can we admire the lady's overweening agonies on the occasion of a thinly-attended party;—and why thinly attended? Because her brother is just gone out of office. We think this reason will excite a smile among those who know how slight is the influence of office in what is called the fashionable society of London,—how little politics are allowed to mingle with its festivities,—how little the idlers, who throng for amusement to the house of a fête-giving lady, care whether her nearest relatives are Whig or Tory, *in* or *out*', p. 453.

14 See Frances Burney, *Evelina, or a Young Lady's Entrance into the World*, 3 vols. (London: T. Lowndes, 1778), I, letter xxi, for similar Branghton misadventures at the opera.

15 Charlotte Grandison in Samuel Richardson's *Grandison* (1753) is the early progenitor of this figure. There is, in fact, a Mr Grandison in *Almack's*, the Whig MP for the county (II, p. 3).

16 Kathryn Sutherland, *Jane Austen's Textual Lives: From Aeschylus to Bollywood* (Oxford University Press, 2005), p. 1.

17 Deidre Lynch (ed.), 'Introduction', *Janeites: Austen's Disciples and Devotees* (Princeton University Press, 2000), p. 11.

18 Janine Barchas, 'Mrs. Gaskell's *North and South*: Austen's Early Legacy', *Persuasions*, 30 (2009), pp. 53–66. Kathryn Sutherland sets the relationship in historical context in '*Jane Eyre*'s Literary History: The Case for *Mansfield Park*', *ELH*, 59, no. 2 (Summer 1992), pp. 409–40. Jocelyn Harris notes Austen influence in her essay, 'Jane Austen, Jane Fairfax, and Jane Eyre', *Persuasions*, 29 (2008), pp. 99–109. Early adaptations of other Austen novels are noted by June Sturrock in '*Emma* in the 1860s: Austen, Yonge, Oliphant, Eliot', *Women's Writing*, 17, no. 2 (August 2010), pp. 324–42. Elsie B. Michie in 'Frances Trollope's *One Fault* and the Evolution of the Novel', *Women's Writing*, 18, no. 2 (May 2011), pp. 167–81, finds the relationship of Darcy and Elizabeth in *Pride and Prejudice* an inspiration for exploring altered understandings of marriage in 1840.

19 Charles Beecher Hogan, 'Jane Austen and Her Early Public', *Review of English Studies*, n.s., 1 (1950), pp. 39–54. Annika Bautz in *The Reception of Jane Austen and Walter Scott* (London and New York: Continuum, 2007), p. 81, also cites early praise of Austen, including John Lockhart's public *Letter to the Right Hon. Lord Byron* (1821), anonymous praise in the *Retrospective Review* (1823), Miss Mitford's *Our Village* (1824), Walter Scott's review of Lister's *Granby* (1826), T. H. Lister's review of Gore's *Women as They Are* (1830) in the *Edinburgh Review* (July 1830), Sir Egerton Brydges' *Autobiography* (1834) and Coleridge's *Table Talk* (1835).

20 B. C. Southam, *Jane Austen: The Critical Heritage* (London: Routledge & Kegan Paul, 1968).

21 Bautz, p. 81. Bentley purchased copyrights from Henry and Cassandra Austen in 1832 and from Egerton in 1833.

22 Bautz also argues that publication of Austen's nephew's *Memoirs* in 1870 'reflects rather than initiates [popular] interest in the novels', p. 81.

23 Edward Bulwer Lytton [Bulwer had inherited, hence the name change], *My Novel: or Varieties in English Life* (Edinburgh and London: W. Blackwood and Sons, 1853), 'Book the First: Initial Chapter'. A writer for Richard Horne's collection, *The New Spirit of the Age*, 6 vols. (London: Smith, Elder and Co., 1844), claimed that in one respect Gore outmatches Austen: 'If she [Gore] rarely reaches the quiet humour of Madame D'Arblay, and never realizes the Dutch fidelity of Miss Austen', he argues, 'she preserves, upon the whole, a more sustained flight than either', p. 237.

24 Lister's character 'Lady Harriet' echoes criticism in an unsigned review in the *British Critic* (March 1818): 'In imagination, of all kinds, she [Austen] seems to have been extremely deficient ... her characters, her incidents, her sentiments, are obviously all drawn exclusively from experience.' Southam, *Critical Heritage*, p. 80.

25 *Edinburgh Review* (July 1830), p. 449.

26 Sir Walter Scott, *Journal, 1825–26* (Edinburgh: Oliver and Boyd, 1939), p. 135. Cited in Hogan, p. 50.

27 The editor's claim (p. xiii) appears following Henry Austen's 'Memoir of Miss Austen' (see Kathyrn Sutherland (ed.) *J. E. Austen-Leigh: A Memoir of Jane Austen* (Oxford University Press, 2002), p. 154), an unacknowledged appropriation from Richard Whately's review of *Northanger Abbey* and *Persuasion* in the *Quarterly Review* 24, no. 48 (January 1821), pp. 352–76.

28 Clara Tuite, *Romantic Austen: Sexual Politics and the Literary Canon* (Cambridge University Press, 2002), pp. 75–7. Margaret Linley addresses the critical establishment's objection to male participation in the feminine-identified Christmas annuals in her essay 'A Centre that Would Not Hold', pp. 54–76. For male authors it meant a welcome addition to their income, but the term 'prostitution' crops up repeatedly to discourage male participation in annuals, pp. 60–2.

29 'To Cassandra Austen', 11 February 1801, *Jane Austen's Letters*, ed. Deirdre Le Faye, 3rd edn (Oxford University Press, 1995), no. 34, pp. 79–81.

30 Le Faye, *Letters*, no. 31, no. 144. Mrs Welby was a niece of Mrs Leigh Perrot, Austen's aunt; 4 Sept. 1816. These events are cited in the *Morning Post*, 12 Jan. 1801 and the *Morning Post*, 4 Sept. 1816. Hessell, 'News and Newspapers', pp. 248–54, notes Austen's practice of including newspapers in her novels.

31 Jane Austen's Edmund Bertram in *Mansfield Park* looks 'over the various advertisements of "a most desirable estate in South Wales"—"To Parents and Guardians"—and a "Capital season'd Hunter"', iii, ch. 3.

32 William Galperin, in Lynch, *Janeites*, pp. 86–114, especially pp. 90–1. See also Lynch, 'Introduction', *Janeites*, p. 11.

33 'Opinions of *Mansfield Park*: Collected and Transcribed by Jane Austen', in Southam, *Critical Heritage*, pp. 48–51.

34 Southam, *Critical Heritage*, p. 80.

35 Andrea Hibbard, '*Vivian Grey* and the Silver-Fork Etiquette of Authorship', *Genre*, 32 (Winter 1999), pp. 252–7.

36 Lister, *Edinburgh Review* (July 1830), in Southam, *Critical Heritage*, p. 114.

37 David Gilson, 'Jane Austen, the Aristocracy, and T. H. Lister', *The Jane Austen Society: Report for 2002* (Chawton: The Jane Austen Society, 2002), pp. 56–65, sees Austen parallels in Lister's *Granby* in a Mr Edwards, who rambles like Miss Bates, and in Lady Jermyn, a controlling woman like Fanny Dashwood, who turns a general invitation of hospitality into a specific invitation for her own advantage. Vincent Trebeck's conversation with Caroline Jermyn (I, pp. 95–8) on the subject of female accomplishments, has overtones of Mr Darcy and Miss Bingley on the same subject in *Pride and Prejudice*. Gilson also cites Harold Child, in 'Lesser Novelists', in A.W. Ward and A.R. Waller (eds.), *The Cambridge History of English and American Literature*, XII, ch. 11 (New York: G. P. Putnam's Sons; Cambridge University Press, 1916), pp. 272–9, citation p. 274, saying of Mr Trebeck, the villain in *Granby*, that 'it is difficult not to regard [him] as a perverted Darcy'. A passage in a conversation between Granby and Trebeck (II, ch. 7) about girls being 'out', is reminiscent of a similar passage in *Mansfield Park* between Mary Crawford and her brother Henry. Gilson also notes in Lister's *Herbert Lacy* that there are characters named the Bingleys (ch. 4), that the heroine's mother is 'a weak, dawdling woman' like Lady Bertram, and that Lacy converses with Agnes, the heroine, under the cover of music while Miss Bagshawe 'trilled away at an air out of "Semiramide"', a parallel to Elinor Dashwood's private chat with Lucy Steele in *Sense and Sensibility* as Marianne plays the piano. In Lister's *Arlington*, Gilson observes that Lister 'uses an amateur theatrical in a country house to expose the characters of some of his principal personages in a manner that recalls *Mansfield Park*' and that one of them is named Lady Crawford, who, like Mary Crawford, looks past the genuinely iniquitous flirtations of Julia Savile at the rehearsals.

38 Hibbard, p. 257.

39 Gash, *Aristocracy and People*, p. 147.

40 Donald Southgate, *The Passing of the Whigs, 1832–1886* (London: Macmillan, 1965), pp. 7–8.

41 M. L. Bush, *The English Aristocracy, a Comparative Synthesis* (Manchester University Press, 1984), p. 77.

42 Hazlitt, 'The Dandy School', p. 146.

43 Gash, *Aristocracy and People*, p. 6.

44 *The Cabinet Minister*, published in 1839, is set in the Regency crisis of 1810–11, particularly the clash of loyalties in its aftermath. The political issue at stake in this novel belongs, by analogy, to 1839. Will the hero remain loyal to the Whig Party or betray it for a chance of advancement with the Tories? There had been a steady drain of Whig electors to the Tories since 1832. In 1839, this had reached crisis proportions. See Eric J. Evans, *The Forging of the Modern State: Early Industrial Britain, 1783–1870*, 2nd edn (London: Longman, 1996), pp. 258–61.

45 Katie Trumpener, 'The Virago Jane Austen', in Lynch, *Janeites*, pp. 140–65.
46 Beth Fowkes Tobin in *Superintending the Poor: Charitable Ladies and Paternal Landlords in British Fiction, 1770–1860* (New Haven and London: Yale University Press, 1993), for example, discovers a 'radical Tory condemnation of the gentry' in Austen's *Persuasion*, 'for failing to perform their duty and to fulfil their obligations to society', a political sentiment that runs throughout Whiggish critiques of aristocratic politics in silver fork novels, pp. 96–7.
47 *Monthly Review*, 2nd series 107 (August 1825), pp. 434–5, in P. D. Garside, J. E. Belanger and S. A. Ragaz (eds.), *British Fiction, 1800–1829: A Database of Production, Circulation and Reception*, designer A. A. Mandal. www.british-fiction.cf.ac.uk: DBF record number, 1825A066.
48 See Evans, *Forging of the Modern State*, pp. 257–8: 'The incident marks a constitutional watershed. Never again would a British monarch dismiss a ministry.'
49 Hibbard, p. 257.
50 Edward Neill's *The Politics of Jane Austen* (Basingstoke: Macmillan Press, 1999), pp. 48–50, offers a comparison of 'Blake' and 'Jane Austen' to illuminate Austen's resistance to 'ruling-class ideology' and to 'counter current over-emphasis on "a Jane Austen" locked into a strident defence of Toryism'. Here we find the deepest level of kinship between Austen's novels and Mrs Gore's equally complex considerations of power.

CHAPTER 3   REFORM AND THE SILVER FORK NOVEL

1 Mrs C. D. Burdett, *At Home, a Novel*, 3 vols. (London: Henry Colburn, 1828), I, p. 64.
2 Charles Jameson Grant (*fl.* 1830–52), caricaturist: 'While his prints of this period often displayed considerable inventiveness and an often bizarre or grotesque comic imagination, they were very much a product of a market in which the artist's individual ideology was subservient to that of his publishers and their audience, being pro moderate electoral reform and anti radicalism and revolution. Despite this, he developed a menagerie of favourite *bêtes noires* ... including Henry Brougham, Ernest, duke of Cumberland, and the duke of Wellington and Lord Grey—principal players in the drama surrounding the Reform Act of June 1832.' R. J. Pound, 'Grant, Charles Jameson', *Oxford Dictionary of National Biography* (Oxford University Press, 2004). www.oxforddnb.com.ezproxy.libraries.claremont.edu/view/article/66121.
3 Celina Fox, in *Graphic Journalism in England during the 1830s and 1840s* (London and New York: Garland Publishing, 1988), notes that the single caricature print 'has been described as an instantaneous reaction to a political event and forms, as such, a temperature chart of popular opinion', p. 73.
4 Peter Jupp, *British Politics on the Eve of Reform: The Duke of Wellington's Administration 1828–30* (New York: St. Martin's Press, 1998), p. 241.

5 Lord Holland declared the 'death of "party government"' in 1826. Cited in Jupp, p. 242.

6 Evans, *The Forging of the Modern State*, p. 201.

7 'Whig party discipline slackened from 1823. The Whigs after 1822 were rarely able to raise more than 100 supporters in any parliamentary division.' Eric J. Evans, *Britain before the Reform Act: Politics and Society, 1815–1832* (London: Longman, 1989), p. 41.

8 Frank O'Gorman, *The Long Eighteenth Century: British Political and Social History, 1688–1832* (London: Arnold, 1997), p. 279.

9 Evans, 'A Note on Approximate Strengths of Parties and Groups in the Commons, 1784–1832', in *Forging of the Modern State*, pp. 402–4.

10 *Ibid.*, p. 402.

11 Jupp, p. 241. Jupp explains, 'In the early nineteenth century all parties were coalitions of active leaders, regular followers and occasional supporters, but only the first and a proportion of the second groups were connected by party allegiance', pp. 291–2.

12 Hook's biographer, Byron Brightfield, presciently observes that Hook held 'an almost American cynicism towards both politics and politicians', in *Theodore Hook and His Novels* (Cambridge, MA: Harvard University Press, 1928), p. 273. 'The first series of Theodore Hook's "Sayings and Doings: A Series of Sketches from Life"' writes Brightfield, 'was published by Colburn and Bentley, and appeared on February 21, 1824 ... It was reprinted three times before the spring of 1825, and Hook received two thousand pounds as his share of the profits ... Accordingly, three more volumes, the 2nd series of "Sayings and Doings", appeared on January 26, 1825', p. 224.

13 In Lister's *Herbert Lacy*, the Whiggish hero, young Herbert, is praised for exactly the opposite principle: 'He adhered to no particular party, and felt no magic, in the words, "Whig," or "Tory," "Ministry," or "Opposition." Measures, not men, were his object. He saw, in the present organization of the state, the result of a long course of slow and unremitting changes, and he knew no reason why the hand of innovation, which had been hitherto beneficial, should now be arrested' (III, pp. 64–5).

14 Dror Wahrman, in his influential study *Imagining the Middle Class*, finds the precursor of this association in the 1790s, an image which resonated 'as country ideology or as a ... derivative of classical republicanism. Central to this rhetoric was the ancient agrarian idea of the small independent landed proprietor as the bearer of civic virtue ... Now it is indubitable that elements of this familiar and influential oppositional idiom reappeared, somewhat haphazardly, in the "middle-class" language of the 1790s', pp. 61–2.

15 Evans, *Forging of the Modern State*, pp. 260–1.

16 *Fraser's Magazine*, 5, May 1832, p. 455. Cited by Leslie Mitchell, *The Whig World, 1760–1837* (London: Hambledon Continuum, 2005), p. 6.

17 Gash, *Aristocracy and People*, p. 147.

18 Arthur Aspinall, *Lord Brougham and the Whig Party* (Manchester University Press, 1939), p. 134.

19 Ellen Moers, *The Dandy: from Brummell to Beerbohm*, first published 1960 (Lincoln and London: University of Nebraska Press, 1978), p. 91.

20 Gary Kelly, *English Fiction of the Romantic Period, 1789–1830* (London and New York: Longman, 1989), p. 223.

21 David Cannadine, *Aspects of Aristocracy: Grandeur and Decline in Modern Britain* (London and New York: Penguin Books, 1995), p. 19.

22 David Cannadine, *The Decline and Fall of the British Aristocracy* (New York: Random House, 1999), pp. 20, 18.

23 O'Gorman, p. 281.

24 Linda Colley, *Britons: Forging the Nation, 1707–1837* (New Haven: Yale University Press, 1992), p. 328.

25 Aspinall, *Lord Brougham and the Whig Party*, p. 135.

26 Southgate, *The Passing of the Whigs*, p. xv. Leslie Mitchell's study, *The Whig World* 1760–1837 (London: Hambledon Continuum, 2005) explores the complications, as does his essay, 'The Whigs, the People, and Reform', in T. W. C. Blanning and Peter Wende (eds.), *Reform in Great Britain and Germany, 1750–1850* (Oxford University Press, 1999), pp. 25–41.

27 Aspinall, *Lord Brougham and the Whig Party*, p. 232.

28 Wahrman, p. 252.

29 Eric J. Evans, *Parliamentary Reform, c. 1770–1918* (London: Longman, 2000), p. 19.

30 Southgate, p. 4.

31 Jupp, pp. 7, 273.

32 Ironically, it was the Tory politician Robert Peel who was able to see the handwriting on the wall in the early 1820s. Le Marchant, 19 August 1831, reports that Charles Lloyd, the Bishop of Oxford, had told him years earlier of a conversation with Robert Peel on reform. Lloyd had said of Peel, 'Peel considers a revolution at no great distance—not a bloody one and perhaps not one leading to a republic, but one utterly subversive of the aristocracy … This was about seven years ago', Le Marchant remembers (i.e. in 1824). 'I thought it so extraordinary, parliamentary reform being then almost hopeless', in Arthur Aspinall (ed.), *Three Early Nineteenth Century Diaries* (London: Williams and Norgate, 1952), p. 118.

33 Jupp, p. 273.

34 Cited by Michael Brock, *The Great Reform Act* (London: Hutchinson University Library, 1973), p. 100.

35 Derek Beales, 'The Idea of Reform in British Politics, 1829–1850', in T. W. C. Blanning and Peter Wende (eds.), *Reform in Great Britain and Germany, 1750–1850* (Oxford University Press, for The British Academy, 1999), p. 165.

36 House of Lords, 7 Oct., 1831. Cited in Southgate, p. 6.

37 J. W. Croker to H. Brougham, 14 March 1839, in *The Correspondence and Diaries of the Late Rt Hon. John Wilson Croker*, ed. Louis J. Jennings (London: Murray, 1884), ii, p. 353. Cited in Mitchell, *The Whig World*, p. 6.

38 Lord Minto to Lord Lansdowne, 6 January 1830, in Kenneth Bourne, *Palmerston: The Early Years* (London: Allen Lane, 1982), p. 305; cited in Mitchell, *The Whig World*, p. 6.

39 Mitchell, *The Whig World*, p. 112.

40 Wellington to Gleig, 11 April 1831. Cited by Arthur Aspinall in his 'Introduction' to *Three Nineteenth Century Diaries*, p. xxxv.

41 Mitchell, *The Whig World*, p. 102.

42 Beales, p. 167.

43 Colley, p. 344.

44 Mitchell, 'The Whigs, the People, and Reform', pp. 32–3.

45 Edward Royle in *Revolutionary Britannia? Reflections on the Threat of Revolution in Britain, 1789–1848* (Manchester University Press, 2000) writes, 'The election campaigns of 1830, 1831 and 1832 took politics to almost every market town, if not every parish, in the country … In Dorchester, a hand bill was stuck around the town at the end of October 1831, denouncing those who had voted against the Reform Bill in the Lords and listing government pensioners', pp. 85–6.

46 Gash, *Aristocracy and People*, p. 147. Asa Briggs, in 'Middle-Class Consciousness in English Politics, 1780–1846', *Past and Present*, 9, no.1 (1956), p. 70, suggests that there was fear in parliamentary circles that the mercantile and manufacturing classes would unite with the working classes against the landed classes to push for reform, even revolution. This fear is reflected by a contemporary John Sinclair, *Thoughts on Parliamentary Reform* (Edinburgh, 1831), p. 20: 'The elective franchise ought only to be intrusted to those who would exercise it with most wisdom and independence, and as wisdom and independence certainly prevail more in the middling ranks than in the whole mass of the people, the elective franchise should accordingly be principally enjoyed by them.' See Evans, *Parliamentary Reform*, p. 23; also Wahrman, p. 298.

47 Evans, *Forging of the Modern State*, p. 178.

48 David Cannadine, *The Rise and Fall of Class in Britain* (New York: Columbia University Press, 1999), p. 23.

49 Marguerite Blessington, *The Magic Lantern*, p. 22.

50 Brock, p. 24. Eight manufacturers were also returned in the same election, writes Brock.

51 Wahrman, pp. 14–15.

52 Evans, *Forging of the Modern State*, p. 178.

53 Southey in Cannadine, *Rise and Fall of Class in Britain*, p. 74; Melbourne, in Ian Newbould, *Whiggery and Reform, 1830–41* (Stanford University Press, 1990), p. 58.

54 Cannadine, *Rise and Fall of Class in Britain*, pp. 74–5.

55 Newbould, p. 58.

56 Hughes, 'Silver Fork Writers and Readers', p. 342.

57 Bush, p. 77.

58 I am indebted, with gratitude, to Hughes, 'Silver Fork Writers and Readers', p. 345, for the rhyming 'collision' and 'collusion' of classes.

59 Bush, p. 77. The goal of Whig reform, to exclude the labouring classes, was no secret to contemporaries: 'As the radical journalist Henry Hetherington put it … "The Bill was, in effect an invitation to the shopocracy of the enfranchised towns to join the Whigocrats of the country, and make common cause with them in keeping down the people, and thereby quelling the rising spirit of democracy in England."' Cited by Hugh Cunningham in *The Challenge of Democracy, Britain 1832–1918* (London: Longman, 2001), pp. 32–3. Michael J. Turner, in *British Politics in an Age of Reform* (Manchester University Press, 1999), notes that Edward Thompson's *The Making of the English Working Class* (London: V. Gollancz, 1963) has as its central thesis that 'By 1832 the most significant factor in politics was the presence of the working class', p. 5. Edward Royle and James Walvin's study *English Radicals and Reformers, 1760–1848* (Brighton: Harvester Press, 1982), discusses the grave disappointment of the labouring classes after the Reform of 1832, in chapter 9, 'The Great Betrayal, 1830–1837', pp. 142–59.

60 Wahrman, p. 10.

61 Fine words, but it must be noted that Sir William's acceptance of Mr Morton, now restored to considerable property, is a small step indeed for an aristocratic society that still hovers in and out of the reactionary 'upper' and 'lower' model described by Cannadine, *Rise and Fall of Class in Britain*, pp. 20, 30–5.

62 Bulwer, A review of Letitia Landon's *Romance and Reality*, *New Monthly Magazine, 32* (Dec. 1831), pp. 49–50.

63 Wahrman, p. 10.

64 Lister misses or ignores the context of Gore's rhetorical irony in his defence of this 'excellent wife' in his review of *Women as They Are* in *Edinburgh Review*, 51 (July 1830), p. 453.

65 Claire Nicolay in 'Delightful Coxcombs to Industrious Men: Fashionable Politics and Performance in *Cecil* and *Pendennis*', *Victorian Literature and Culture*, 30, no. 1 (2002), pp. 289–304, emphasizes Catherine Gore's politics, her overtly partisan Whig sympathies and her strong dislike of the Tory Party, p. 292.

66 Voltaire, *Mérope*, III, ii (1743). 'Qui sert bien son pays n'a pas besoin d'aïeux', 'Who serves his country well has no need of ancestors.'

67 'The Reviewer', in *Bell's Weekly Messenger*, extract from the *Commercialist and Weekly Advertiser*, Sunday, 1 Jan. 1832.

68 The operas that Gore cites in this novel, most of them in recent performance at the King's Theatre, include among the better known, Rossini's *Otello*, *Il Turco in Italia*, *Semiramide* and *L'Inganno Felice*, Piccinni's *La Buona Figliuola*, Paisiello's *La Pazza per Amore*, Bellini's *Il Pirata*, Vaccài's *Giulietta e Romeo*, and Mozart's *La Clemenza di Tito* and *Idomeneo*.

69 Henrietta Maria Bowdler, author of the expurgated *Family Shakespeare* (1807), shared the heroine's distaste. As Gilbert Elliot, earl of Minto, reports, the young Henrietta Bowdler 'said she never looked at [the dancers in operas] but always

kept her eyes shut the whole time, and when I asked her why, she said it was so *indelicate* she could not bear to look'. N. Perrin, *Dr Bowdler's Legacy: A History of Expurgated Books in England and America* (New York: Atheneum, 1969), p. 69, in M. Clare Loughlin-Chow, 'Bowdler, Henrietta Maria (1750–1830)', *Oxford Dictionary of National Biography* (Oxford University Press, 2004). www.oxforddnb.com.ezproxy.libraries.claremont.edu/view/article/3028.

70 Royle, Edward, *Revolutionary Brittania? Reflections on the Threat of Revolution in Britain, 1789–1848* (Manchester University Press, 2000), pp. 67–91 presents an appraisal of radical threats and government responses to the potential for violent revolution in these three years. Royle reports that the radical Francis Place considered that 'The Days of May', 1832, two weeks in which the Reform Bill hung in the balance, had brought the nation near to armed revolution: 'We were within a moment of general rebellion', he recorded on 20 May. E. P. Thompson agrees in *The Making of the English Working Class*, writing memorably, 'In the autumn of 1831 and in the "days of May" Britain was within an ace of revolution', pp. 75–6.

71 'By "revolution" [Lord] Grey simply meant democracy', writes Hugh Cunningham in *Challenge of Democracy*: 'There was no one, said Grey, "more dedicated against annual parliaments, universal suffrage, and the ballot, than I am." Far from introducing democracy, the Act was designed to prevent it ... The diarist Greville noted that the government "are conscientiously persuaded that this Bill is the least democratical Bill it is possible to get the country to accept"', p. 32.

72 Evans, *Forging of the Modern State*, p. 228.

73 Lord Holland to Grey, cited *ibid.*, 'It was an almost unchallenged assumption among members of the unreformed Parliament that the middle classes possessed a power which, if properly harnessed, must carry all before it', pp. 260–1.

74 *Ibid.*, p. 221.

75 'The Whigs, abetted by the Tories, were anxious to conciliate the middle classes. Neither of the parliamentary parties had an interest in creating a resentful and hostile middle-class radical party. After 1832 both Whig and Tory governments were forced to show themselves sensitive to public opinion in order to earn middle-class electoral support.' O'Gorman, p. 374.

76 Edward Bulwer, *England and the English*, p. 252.

77 *Ibid.*, p. 252.

78 *Ibid.*, pp. 96–7.

79 *Ibid.*, pp. 85, 99. Lyn Pykett's essay 'A Woman's Business: Women and Writing, 1830–80', in Marion Shaw (ed.), *An Introduction to Women's Writing: From the Middle Ages to the Present Day* (London: Prentice, 1998), pp.149–76, argues that women's fiction after the 1832 Reform Bill engaged in a fusion of women's genres, including the silver fork novel as the 'social problem novel'.

80 Evans, *Forging of the Modern State*, p. 260.

81 *Ibid.*, p. 259.

82 Edward Bulwer, *England and the English*, p. 133.

83 Disraeli, *Vindication of the English Constitution* (London: Saunders and Otley, 1835), p. 181. Cited in Mitchell, *The Whig World*, p. 164.

84 Mitchell, *The Whig World*, p. 169.

85 Gash, *Aristocracy and People*, p. 183.

CHAPTER 4 NEWSPAPERS AND THE SILVER FORK NOVEL

1 Catherine Gore, *Cecil: or, The Adventures of a Coxcomb*, 3 vols. (London: Richard Bentley, 1841), II, p. 277.

2 Haydon's painting was completed between October and November 1831. Robert Woof, 'Haydon, Benjamin Robert (1786–1846)', *Oxford Dictionary of National Biography* (Oxford University Press, 2004). www.oxforddnb.com. ezproxy.libraries.claremont.edu/view/article/12750.

3 David Solkin offers an excellent reproduction and discussion of Wilkie's *Chelsea Pensioners* in his study *Painting Out of the Ordinary: Modernity and the Art of Everyday Life in Early Nineteenth-Century Britain* (New Haven and London: Yale University Press, 2008), pp. 200–4. There is an enlarged close-up of the man reading the newspaper to the crowd, the central action of the painting, p. 202.

4 Brian Winkenweder, 'The Newspaper as Nationalist Icon, or How to Paint "Imagined Communities"', *Limina: A Journal of Historical and Cultural Studies*, 14 (2008), p. 89.

5 Jane Austen, *Northanger Abbey* (I, ch. 14), Barbara M. Benedict and Deirdre Le Faye (eds.), pp. 110–11, in *The Cambridge Edition of Jane Austen*, gen. ed. Janet Todd, 9 vols. (Cambridge University Press, 2006).

6 Benedict Anderson, *Imagined Communities: Reflections on the Origin and Spread of Nationalism*, first published 1983, rev. edn (London, New York: Verso, 1991), p. 26.

7 *London Gazette Extraordinary*, supplement to *The Times*, 22 June 1815, p. 3. See Winkenweder, p. 96, for the relationship of *The Times* and the *Gazette*.

8 Anderson, p. 26.

9 'Newspapers', *Westminster Review*, 1.3 (July 1824), pp. 210–11.

10 'June 19, 1835', in Charles Greville, *The Greville Diary*, ed. Philip Whitwell Wilson, 2 vols. (London: William Heinemann, 1927), I, p. 494.

11 Mikhail Bakhtin, from 'Forms of Time and of the Chronotope in the Novel: Notes Towards a Historical Poetics', in Michael Holquist (ed.), trans. Caryl Emerson and Michael Holquist, *The Dialogic Imagination: Four Essays* (Austin: University of Texas Press, 1981), p. 250.

12 Anderson, p. 24.

13 Anderson, pp. 26–7, 30, 35.

14 Paston, *Little Memoirs of the Nineteenth Century*, p. 194.

15 Aled Jones, *Powers of the Press: Newspapers, Power and the Public in Nineteenth-Century England* (London: Scolar Press, 1996), pp. 29, 39–40.

16 The *Courier* was a conservative paper, the *Morning Chronicle* a liberal-to-radical paper, and the *Morning Post* a conservative paper that carried social

columns devoted to fashionable aristocratic events. The *Herald* was best known for its reports on crime.

17 Anderson, p. 33, n. 54.

18 Cited in Sadleir, *Bulwer and His Wife*, p. 302, from a letter to Bulwer, dated by Sadleir, 4 July 1832.

19 Timing was significant enough to Smith's customers for him to supplement his protestations in the advertisement, 'to convince his friends that no exertion is wanting on his part he will, from the 1st of December, keep a list of the time that each Morning Paper is delivered to him, and the coach they are sent by. This list will be printed Monthly, the 1st number on the 1st of January, 1832, and may be had gratis by every customer of each Agent on that day; to ensure its faithfulness a copy will be sent to the Editor of each Morning Paper', p. 1.

20 Jane Austen did as well, according to a recent essay by Hessell, 'News and Newspapers', pp. 248–54.

21 A recent lament in *The Times Literary Supplement* (5 June 2009), makes this point about the social loss in cessation of the *Detroit Free Press*, a daily. Michael Greenberg, the author, cites 'Matt' in his column 'Freelance': 'The *Free Press* was practically the only thing my old man and I could talk about without fighting … It was this open letter that got passed around every morning, this great chunk of disaster stories and gossip. You didn't need electricity, you didn't need a living room or a computer or even a home. You just needed to exist and it would find you, because it was everywhere', p. 16.

22 Mulrooney, pp. 351–77. Citation p. 354.

23 Deutsch, *The Fabric of Reality*, pp. 120–1; cited in Siskin, 'VR Machine', p. 161.

24 Mulrooney, p. 358.

25 Anderson, p. 35.

26 [Archibald Alison], 'The Influence of the Press', *Blackwood's Edinburgh Magazine*, 36 (Sept. 1834), pp. 373–91 [373–4, 376–7, 379–81], in Andrew King and John Plunkett (eds.), *Victorian Print Media: A Reader* (Oxford University Press, 2005), pp. 25–31.

27 Cited by Christopher Hibbert, *Disraeli: A Personal History* (London: Harper, 2004), p. 24, from W. F. Monypenny and G. E. Buckle, *The Life of Benjamin Disraeli, Earl of Beaconsfield*, 2 vols. (rev. edn; London: John Murray, 1929), i, p. 77.

28 Moers, *The Dandy*, p. 89.

29 *Ibid.*, p. 84.

30 St Clair, p. 577.

31 T. S. Surr, in *The Magic of Wealth*, 3 vols. (1815), a novel suggested by Brian Southam, *Jane Austen: A Student's Guide to the Later Manuscript Works* (London: Concord Books, 2007), pp. 117–18, as a possible inspiration for Jane Austen's 'Sanditon', presents a breakfast table with a different newspaper for each diner: the *Morning Post* for the hostess perusing 'a tale of a mystery in high life', the *Morning Chronicle* for the humble companion looking for the title of a new

novel, the *Morning Herald* for the chaplain seeking scandal, and *The Times* for a guest who wishes to consider 'the impending destinies of the world' (I, p. 129).

32 Jones, p. 141.

33 *Literary Gazette*, 22 Apr. 1826, cited in Hibbert, p. 24.

34 On 24 May 1825, before the financial crash, J. Bennet wrote to Robert Finch, 'there appears to be an immense quantity of capital everywhere ... and people are speculating mad. Shares are to be had in any thing you may fancy from Gas to Oysters. What think you to a Steam Company for washing linen and brushing coats.' Cited in Hamilton, *London Lights*, p. 259, from Finch Papers, II, ff. 110–11, Bodleian.

35 Baudrillard, p. 119.

36 Bourdieu, *Outline of a Theory of Practice*, p. 183. Cited by Randal Johnson (ed.), *The Field of Cultural Production* (New York: Columbia University Press, 1993), 'Editor's Introduction', p. 8.

37 Baudrillard, pp. 38–9.

38 *Ibid.*, p. 32.

39 Barbara's costume with 'no taste for finery or parade' echoes Emma Woodhouse's dress at her wedding to Mr Knightley: 'Very little white satin, very few lace veils; a most pitiful business!' Jane Austen, *Emma* (III, ch. 19), Richard Cronin and Dorothy McMillan (eds.), p. 528, in *The Cambridge Edition of Jane Austen*, gen. ed. Janet Todd, 9 vols. (Cambridge University Press, 2005).

40 Mulrooney, p. 358.

41 'Newspaper Press' in the *Westminster Review*, 10, no. 19 (Jan. 1829), pp. 216–37. Citation p. 216.

42 The 'Fashionable Changes' column mentioned by Lady Jermyn is a subheading of the *Morning Post*'s 'Fashionable World' section.

43 Anderson, pp. 32–3.

44 The same names go the rounds in silver fork novels: Pelham, Fitzwilliam, Fitzallen, Augustus, Arlingford, Berkley and Berkeley, Mordaunt and many more.

45 From Disraeli, 'To William Meredith'. Cited in Hibbert, p. 39.

46 *Ibid.*, p. 39.

47 The 'demonstrably corrupt boroughs of Penryn and East Redford' had been brought to the attention of Parliament in 1826. In 1828, Huskissonites wanted to 'transfer their seats to Manchester and Birmingham'. The Huskissonites' defeat resulted in their withdrawal from Wellington's government; Evans, *The Forging of the Modern State*, p. 215.

48 See Johnson, *The Field of Cultural Production*, p. 2.

49 For the British aristocracy's ability to renew itself after Reform, see Cannadine, *Aspects of Aristocracy*, p. 36.

50 *Mrs. Armytage* was the novel that brought Mrs Gore 'nearest to being a novelist of the first rank', according to Harold Child, 'Lesser Novelists', A. W. Ward and A. R. Waller (eds.) *The Cambridge History of English and American*

Literature, 15 vols. (New York: G. P. Putnam's Sons; Cambridge University Press, 1916), XII, i, pp. 272–9. Citation p. 274.

51 George Eliot, *Silly Novels by Lady Novelists* (London: Penguin, 2010), p. 9, first published in *Westminster Review*, 66 (Old Series), 10 (New Series) (Oct. 1856), pp. 442–61.

CHAPTER 5   THE TOPOGRAPHY OF SILVER FORK LONDON

1 Catherine Gore, 'The Special License', *The Fair of Mayfair*, 3 vols. (London: Henry Colburn and Richard Bentley, 1832), III, p. 366.

2 James Donald, *Imagining the Modern City* (London: The Athlone Press, 1999), pp. 1–4.

3 Raymond Williams, *The Country and the City*, first published 1973 (London: The Hogarth Press, 1985), p. 156.

4 *Ibid.*, pp. 156–7.

5 Gordon Mackenzie in *Marylebone, Great City North of Oxford Street* (London and Basingstoke: Macmillan, 1972) discusses the social significance of the street in his aptly titled chapter 4, 'Oxford Street Frontier', pp. 72–98.

6 Gore, *Cecil*, I, p. 89.

7 Paston, p. 169.

8 Franco Moretti, *Atlas of the European Novel, 1800–1900* (London and New York: Verso, 1998), pp. 70–84.

9 Mackenzie claims Harley Street as already enabling a reorientation of London's communication axis with its first residents in 1752: 'Harley Street became the main axis of that grid of streets occupying the area between Baker Street, on the west, and Portland Place on the east; and between the "New Road" [Euston], on the north, and Oxford Street on the south', p. 99.

10 John Nash, 'Report of Mr. John Nash, Architect in the Department of Works; with Plans for the Improvement of Mary-le-bone Park', in John White (ed.), *Some Account of the Proposed Improvements of the Western Part of London, by the Formation of the Regent's Park, the New Street, the New Sewer, &c., &c.* (London: W. & P. Reynolds, 1814), p. l. John Nash's proposal in White's *Account*, cited here, is included as an appendix, pp. xxi–lxii.

11 *Ibid.*, pp. l–li.

12 White, pp. 92–3.

13 J. F. C. Phillips, *Shepherd's London* (London: Cassell, 1976), p. 44.

14 The guidebook structure is followed in the anonymous middle-class work *Real Life in London*, I, pp. 271–2.

15 *Leigh's New Picture of London* is advertised as 'presenting a Luminous Guide to the Stranger, on all subjects connected with General Information, Business, or Amusement', p. 353. The earliest *Leigh's* guide in The British Library is dated 1818.

16 G. F. Cruchley, *Cruchley's Picture of London, or Visitor's Assistant* ... 'to which is Affixed a New Map of London' (London: G. F. Cruchley, 1831).

17 Neil Smith and Cindi Katz provide a useful discussion of urban spaces in their essay, 'Grounding Metaphor: Towards a Spatialized Politics', in Michael Keith and Steve Pile (eds.), *Place and the Politics of Identity* (London and New York: Routledge, 1993), pp. 67–83. Citation p. 75.

18 The *Literary Gazette* (16 August 1823), shows advertisements for Mogg and Tegg's edition of *Paterson's Roads of England and Wales and the Southern Parts of Scotland*, with other titles representing the popularity of the genre in adjacent classifieds: a *Guide to the Lakes, with Cumberland, Westmorland, and Lancashire* and a *Guide to All the Watering and Sea Bathing Places*, p. 528.

19 The effect of surprise may have been enhanced by an elegant little lift that magically rose from the ground floor to the viewing level: 'There is a curious contrivance in this building', reported a foreign visitor: 'We entered the building. "Step into this room", said he. A door opened, and we entered a beautiful little bijou of a place. Upon a table in the centre were several books and magazines. I took up one. A bell rang. I was getting amused with the magazine. Again a bell rang. The door opened. "You can step out here if you please," said a man … We stepped out, and my astonishment was great at finding that I had ascended to the top of the building, room and all. The room is purposely contrived to ascend and descend, to save visitors the fatigue of travelling up the all-but-interminable staircase.' Cited in Mackenzie, p. 134.

20 Oettermann, p. 137.

21 Jefferys Taylor, *A Month in London: Or Some of Its Modern Wonders Described* (London: Harvey and Darton, 1832), p. 80.

22 James Elmes, *Metropolitan Improvements: or London in the Nineteenth Century* (London: Jones and Co., 1828), p. 78.

23 Rob Shields, *Places on the Margin: Alternative Geographies of Modernity* (London and New York: Routledge, 1991), p. 55.

24 Ralph Hyde, in *Gilded Scenes and Shining Prospects: Panoramic Views of British Towns, 1575–1900* (New Haven: Yale Center for British Art, 1985), reproduces this detail from Horner's map, 'The Colosseum in the Distance', figure 67, p. 143.

25 I am indebted to Neil Smith and Cindi Katz's discussion of travel metaphors in their essay 'Grounding Metaphor' for my reading of the two panoramas, pp. 78–9.

26 Williams, *Country and the City*, pp. 112–19.

27 *Ibid.*, p. 113.

28 *Ibid.*, p. 115.

29 Adrienne Rich, 'Notes towards a Politics of Location', in *Blood, Bread, and Poetry: Selected Prose* (New York: W. W. Norton, 1986). I am indebted to Smith and Katz, 'Grounding Metaphors', pp. 76–7, for their analysis of Rich's text.

30 Edward Soja's *Postmodern Geographies: The Reassertion of Space in Critical Social Theory* (London and New York: Verso, 1989) introduced me to the spatial concepts that guide this essay. I am especially indebted to Soja's chapter 5, 'Reassertions: Towards a Spatialized Ontology', pp. 118–37.

31 'Alpha Road ran between Park Road and Lisson Grove, to the west of Regent's Park. Houses on either side of it, designated Alpha Cottages, began to be built *c.* 1808.' *The Tate Gallery 1984–86: Illustrated Catalogue of Acquisitions* (London: Tate Gallery, 1988), pp. 74–5.

32 Horne, *A New Spirit of the Age*, I, p. 235.

33 'CARLTON HOUSE (at the period of which I treat) had not yet put on its judge's condemning cap. It was the Carlton House of the Prince, not of the Regent;—was the Carlton House of the Whigs, not of the Tories;—the bivouac of the Opposition, not the tabernacle of Church and State', *Cecil* (I, p. 229).

CHAPTER 6   REFORM AND THE SILVER FORK HEROINE

1 Catherine Gore, 'The Old and the Young Bachelor', in *The Sketch Book of Fashion*, 3 vols. (London: Richard Bentley, 1833), III, p. 47.

2 Gore, *Cecil*, I, p. 101; III, p. 195.

3 Lawrence E. Klein, *Shaftesbury and the Culture of Politeness: Moral Discourse and Cultural Politics in Early Eighteenth-Century England* (Cambridge University Press, 1994), p. 2.

4 *Ibid.*, p. 3.

5 Abel Boyer, *The English Theophrastus* (1702), pp. 106, 108. Cited in Klein, pp. 3–4.

6 Peter France, *Politeness and Its Discontents: Problems in French Classical Culture* (Cambridge University Press, 1992), p. 2.

7 Klein, pp. 8–14.

8 An arresting term used by Klein in this context, p. 13.

9 Michèle Cohen, *Fashioning Masculinity: National Identity and Language in the Eighteenth Century* (London and New York: Routledge, 1996), pp. 61–2. See also her study, '"Manners" Make the Man: Politeness, Chivalry, and the Construction of Masculinity, 1750–1830', *Journal of British Studies* 44 (Apr. 2005), pp. 312–29.

10 Cohen in 'Manners', pp. 322–3, paraphrases Richard Hurd's *Dialogues on the Uses of Foreign Travel* (London: A. Millar, 1764).

11 As Miss Bates observes, 'Mr. Frank Churchill was so extremely ... I shall never forget his extreme politeness', *Emma* (III, ch. 2), Cronin and McMillan (eds.), p. 349.

12 Cohen, *Fashioning Masculinity*, pp. 9, 74.

13 Cohen, 'Manners', p. 313. Emma Major, in her 'The Politics of Sociability: Public Dimensions of the Bluestocking Millennium', *Huntington Library Quarterly*, 65, no. 1/2 (2002), pp. 175–92, argues that late eighteenth-century 'politeness discourse' in Elizabeth's conversational circle shifts 'toward public identification with the national' conceived in terms of Benedict Anderson's 'community of nation' [*Imagined Communities*], and that 'from the late 1760s, the political becomes central ... to their polite society', pp. 182–5.

14 Jon Mee, '"Severe contentions of friendship": Barbauld, Conversation, and Dispute', in Heather Glen and Paul Hamilton (eds.), *Repossessing the Romantic Past* (Cambridge University Press, 2006), pp. 21–39. Mee describes disagreements among 'bluestocking' women on the proper woman's voice in public discourse, including the significance of 'Politeness' and its implications. Elizabeth Montagu maintains that 'the genuine effect of polite letters is to inspire candour, a social spirit, and gentle manners' (p. 27). Anna Barbauld was not so sure: 'There is a great difference between a paper written *by* a Lady, and *as* a lady. To write professedly as a female junto seems in some measure to suggest a certain cast of sentiment, and you would write in trammels' (p. 35).

15 Henriette Sontag, Malibran's contemporary rival in London, with her reputed gentility and her unlimited access to high society through her engagement to a nobleman, had a much easier time with London's fashionable society than Malibran. Howard Bushnell in *Maria Malibran: A Biography of the Singer* (University Park and London: Pennsylvania State University Press, 1979) recounts the different receptions given to Malibran and Sontag in exclusive society as rival stars, pp. 98–9, 108.

16 Fred Inglis, *A Short History of Celebrity* (Princeton University Press, 2010), p. 77.

17 Henry F. Chorley, *Thirty Years of Musical Recollections*, 2 vols. (London: Hurst and Blackett, 1862), 1, p. 12.

18 Cohen, *Fashioning Masculinity*, p. 2.

19 The erotics of politeness discourse are considered by Cohen, *ibid.*, pp. 36, 47.

20 In Marianne Spencer Hudson's *Almack's* (1826), a gentleman asks for Handel's 'Alexander's Feast': '"I call Handel's, music for the Gods … not like your French frippery"' (1, p. 132).

21 Vincenzo Bellini (1801–35), opera composer, the contemporary of Donizetti and Rossini. Gaspare Spontini (1774–1851), opera composer to Empress Josephine in 1805. Conductor of the Berlin Court Opera, 1820–41.

22 Marianne Spencer Hudson steals a march on Gore and Bury in her *Almack's*, where her middle-class heroine, Barbara Birmingham, modestly announces as she begins, '"I never could catch the Italian style," said she, "much to mamma's mortification. Mine is mere ballad-singing; but if it will give you any pleasure, I will try"' (1, p. 130). She sings 'Auld Robin Gray' much to the delight of the company – 'Her voice was not powerful, but it was so sweet, and so pathetic.' The maiden aunt requests that they conclude with 'God save the King', but is overruled by her brother, '"No, no!" said Mr. Mildmay, "'Rule Britannia' must be the grand finale"' (1, p. 132).

23 Poonah painting is a 'process, fashionable in early 19th-cent. England, employing or imitating an oriental style in which pictures are produced on thin paper (or occasionally silk) using thick body colour, little or no shading, and no background' (*OED*). It never gained much respect. The *OED* cites Thackeray, Letter (5 July 1836), 'She … does nothing but poonah-painting and piano forté.'

24 Letitia Landon's novel *Ethel Churchill* (1837) also includes a 'feeling', intelligent young woman who suffers a like deprivation in her marriage to an emotionally cold aristocrat, 'a disciplinarian in small matters' who 'has a genius for furniture' and 'piques himself on armchairs' (I, p. 63). Gilbert Osmond, a similarly deficient husband in James' *The Portrait of a Lady* (1881), prides himself, like Landon's character, on 'a genius for upholstery' (ch. 38).

25 Studies that discuss the political significance of the opera house are Jane Rendell's, 'London's Italian Opera House: Exchanging Looks', *Visual Culture in Britain*, I, no. 2 (2000), pp. 1–23; Edward Copeland, 'Crossing Oxford Street: Silver Fork Geopolitics', *Eighteenth-Century Life*, 25 (Spring 2001), pp. 116–34; Edward Copeland, 'Opera and the Great Reform Act: Silver Fork Fiction, 1822–1842', *Romanticism on the Net*, no. 34–5 (2004).

26 Charles Frederick Partington, *National History and Views of London and Its Environs*, 2 vols. (London: Simpkin and Marshall, 1834), I, p. 154.

27 Artist, anonymous, published by Rudolph Ackermann, 1820, The Guildhall Library, London. London Metropolitan Archives, catalogue number p7497564.

28 Chorley, I, p. 81.

29 *Parliamentary Debates*, ser. 3, ii. cc. 1086–7, 1 Mar. 1831.

30 Hibbard, p. 251.

31 Gore makes the distinction between boxes and pit (stalls) in her novel *Pin Money* (1831), when Mr Lexley, a lawyer and broker of parliamentary seats confesses, '"I never venture among the stalls. If you hazard a word in a tone louder than the pianissimo of Nicholson's flute, every member—that is every dilettante—turns fiercely round, as if you were out of order"' (I, p. 90).

32 Bury probably misremembered 'Calidori' for Maria Caradori-Allan (1800–65), whom Chorley praises as 'one of the first class singers of the second rank'.

33 Sutherland Edwards, *History of the Opera*, 2 vols. (London: Allen, 1862), II, p. 135.

34 I am indebted to Jocelyn Harris for reminding me of this.

35 Given Landon's Tory sympathies, the 'proverb' may allude to the pressing need for Ultras and the moderates in the Tory government to seek the same road, to vote together in order to keep in office in 1830–1.

36 Fanny Price's East Room ordeal of reading Edmund Bertram's part in *Lovers' Vows* with Mary Crawford as 'Amelia' may provide the model for such a repression of private misery.

37 Alfred Iacuzzi, *The European Vogue of Favart: The Diffusion of the Opéra-Comique* (New York: Publications of the Institute of French Studies, 1932), gives a thorough account of Favart's comic operas and 'vaudevilles', with special attention to *Annette and Lubin*, the 'tiny pastoral' performed in Gore's novel. Gore may have at least two variations of Favart's vaudeville in mind, *L'Amour Naif* (1762) or a version known as *Annette and Lubin* (also 1762), or possibly even Charles Dibden's English translation (1778) of the piece. Another variation, *Le Caprice amoureux, ou Ninette à la cour*, is recorded by

Iacuzzi, p. 134. Its more courtly elegance would perhaps mirror the aristocratic society of Gore's novel, but the earthy double entendres of *Annette and Lubin* fit the complex class distinctions of La Silvestra and Adrian's relationship more closely.

38 'Favart's works were enormously popular abroad in translations and resettings as well as in their original versions.' Bruce Alan Brown and Paulette Letailleur, 'Favart (i)', Grove Music. Oxford Music Online: www.oxford-musiconline.com.ezproxy.libraries.claremont.edu/subscriber/article/grove/music/42563pg1.

39 The operas that Gore cites in this novel, most of them in recent performance at the King's Theatre according to Chorley, contain plots and characters that reflect the political and social anxieties contained in the novel: Rossini's *Otello*, *Il Turco in Italia*, *Semiramide* and *L'Inganno Felice*, Piccinni's *La Buona Figliuola*, Paisiello's *La Pazza per Amore*, Bellini's *Il Pirata*, Vaccài's *Giulietta e Romeo*, Mozart's *La Clemenza di Tito* and *Idomeneo*. They may also refer to La Silvestra's position in society: *La Buona Figliuola*, 'The Good Daughter', by Piccinni, taken from Samuel Richardson's novel *Pamela*, is the story of a servant girl who resists her master's attentions, eventually marrying him. 'Ah perdona' from Mozart's *La Clemenza di Tito*, referred to by Adrian in passing, would alert readers that Adrian and La Silvestra's love, like the affair in Mozart's opera, hangs on a power disparity, but one with little chance of ending so benignly as Mozart's.

40 For the political purposes of the aristocratic Whigs, writes Wahrman, 'Expressions of "middle-class idiom" ... became an almost ritualistic commonplace', p. 305.

41 In Gore's *Women as They Are*, Lord Forreston expresses his disapproval of the heroine's participation in home theatricals much like Edmund Bertram in *Mansfield Park*: 'I will frankly own to you', he says, 'that I am sorry to find Lady Willersdale and yourself among the theatrical group. I should regret to see you act too well; and I *shall* regret to find you act indifferently, which I am persuaded will be the case. All English women act ill—they are encumbered by their natural decency' (iii, p. 190). The heroine acts anyway, but satisfies the hero with ladylike ineptitude: 'There was a delightful *gaucherie* in her movements;—a blushing reluctance in every word she uttered, which revealed the unextinguished modesty of the English gentlewoman' (iii, p. 196).

42 Although *Stokeshill Place* (1837) is set historically in pre-Reform days, the political thrust of Mrs Gore's novel is post-Reform. The changes in voting patterns after the introduction of the Municipal Corporations Act in 1835, reported by Cunningham, was to be 'in many ways as important as the reform of national government in 1832 ... The Act dissolved over 200 old corporations, mostly Tory-controlled, and set up in their place 179 municipal boroughs to be governed by elected councils, with all ratepayers having the vote ... [I]t introduced a much more representative system of government into older towns', p. 42.

EPILOGUE

1 Lady Charlotte Bury, *The Devoted, 3 vols.* (London: Richard Bentley, 1836), III, p. 327.

2 James Kirke Paulding, *A Sketch of Old England, by a New England Man* (New York: Charles Wiley, 1822), p. 127.

3 William Maginn, 'Mr. Edward Lytton Bulwer's Novels; And Remarks on Novel-Writing', *Fraser's Magazine* (May 1830), p. 510. Cited by Rebecca Edwards Newman in '"Prosecuting the *Onus Criminus*": Early Criticism of the Novel in *Fraser's Magazine*', *Victorian Periodicals Review*, 35, no. 4 (Winter 2002), pp. 401–19. Citation p. 411.

4 William Maginn, 'The Novels of the Season', *Fraser's Magazine* (Feb. 1831), pp. 95–113. Cited in Newman, p. 405.

5 [Anon.] 'The Divan', *The Athenæum*, (23 Sept. 1829), p. 599. Cited in Mason, p. 25. Wicke, pp. 19–26, analyzes the literary and social significance of 'Warren's Blacking' (an early employer of Charles Dickens).

6 *Blackwood's* (July 1828), from '*Noctes Ambrosianae*', p. 98. Cited in Mason, p. 25.

7 William Makepeace Thackeray, '*The Book of Snobs, by One of Themselves*' (1846–47), in Gertrude Himmelfarb (ed.), *The Spirit of the Age: Victorian Essays* (New Haven and London: Yale University Press, 2007), pp. 95–6, 100.

8 Johnson, 'Let Me Make the Novels of a Country', pp. 163–79.

9 According to Johnson, 'Scott's edition makes a history of the novel that proleptically creates and vindicates Scott himself', p. 174.

10 *Ibid.*, p. 170.

11 Barbauld, *The British Novelists*, 1, pp. 58–9. Cited in Johnson, 'Let Me Make the Novels of a Country', pp. 169–70.

12 Johnson, 'Let Me Make the Novels of a Country', p. 172.

13 Barbauld, 1, p. 2. Cited in Johnson, 'Let Me Make the Novels of a Country', p. 172.

14 Johnson, 'Let Me Make the Novels of a Country', p. 172.

15 *Ibid.*, p. 171.

16 *Ibid.*, p. 171.

17 *Ibid.*, p. 165.

18 Rosa, p. 128.

19 The yoking of O'Connell, the cunning Irish politician and sometime Whig ally, and the Earl of Cardigan, James Thomas Brudenell (1797–1868), moves past whimsy. Brudenell, known for 'adultery and bravado', opposed the Catholic Relief Bill, and was 'attacked in the press, hissed and booed at in theatres ... further reviled for the "atrocity" of ordering a flogging after divine service on Easter Sunday 1841'. John Sweetman, 'Brudenell, James Thomas, Seventh Earl of Cardigan (1797–1868)', *Oxford Dictionary of National Biography* (Oxford University Press, 2004). www.oxforddnb.com. ezproxy.libraries.claremont.edu/view/article/3765.

20 Hughes, 'Elegies for the Regency', pp. 189–209.

21 *Ibid.*, pp. 206–8.

22 Johnson, 'Let Me Make the Novels of a Country', p. 177.

APPENDIX

1 'Marguerite Gardiner, Countess of Blessington: Life', in Brown, Clements and Grundy, *Orlando*.

2 *Ibid.*

3 *The Victims of Society* is available in a modern scholarly edition in *Silver Fork Novels, 1826–1841*, 6 vols., gen ed. Harriet Devine Jump, eds. Ann R. Hawkins and Jeraldine R. Kraver, VI (London: Pickering & Chatto, 2005).

4 *Ibid.*, p. xxiii.

5 *Ibid.*, p. xxv.

6 *Ibid.*, p. 243.

7 'Marguerite Gardiner, Countess of Blessington: Life', in Brown, Clements and Grundy, *Orlando*.

8 Andrew Brown, 'Lytton, Edward George Earle Lytton Bulwer, 1st Baron Lytton (1803–1873)', *Oxford Dictionary of National Biography* (Oxford University Press, 2004). www.oxforddnb.com.ezproxy.libraries.claremont. edu/view/article/17314.

9 *Godolphin* is available in a modern scholarly edition in *Silver Fork Novels, 1826–1841*, 6 vols., gen. ed. Harriet Devine Jump, ed. Jump, III (London: Pickering & Chatto, 2005).

10 *Cheveley* is available in a modern scholarly edition in *Silver Fork Novels, 1826–1841*, 6 vols., gen. ed. Harriet Devine Jump, ed. Marie Mulvey-Roberts, V (London: Pickering & Chatto, 2005).

11 'Rosina Bulwer Lytton, Baroness Lytton: Life', in Brown, Clements and Grundy, *Orlando*.

12 'Lady Charlotte Bury: Life', in Brown, Clements and Grundy, *Orlando*.

13 Contemporaries noted that *The Separation* (1830) seemed to be a novel drawn from models thirty years out of date. It was, in fact, a rewrite of a novel Bury had written thirty years before under the influence of her friend Susan Ferrier's work. Her later novels also show Ferrier's influence. See 'Lady Charlotte Bury: Life', in Brown, Clements and Grundy, *Orlando*.

14 Moers, *The Dandy*, p. 94.

15 Margaret Fuller, in Joslyn T. Pine (ed.), *Women in the Nineteenth Century* (New York: Dover, 1999), p. 85. I am indebted to Sandra Alagona of Claremont Graduate University for this citation.

16 'Emily Eden: Life', in Brown, Clements and Grundy, *Orlando*.

17 Charles Greville, *The Greville Memoirs*, ed. Henry Reeve, 3 vols. (London: Longmans, Green, 1874), III, p. 118.

18 H. C. G. Matthew, 'Gladstone, William Ewart (1809–1898)', *Oxford Dictionary of National Biography* (Oxford University Press, 2004). www. oxforddnb.com.ezproxy.libraries.claremont.edu/view/article/10787.

19 *Cecil* is available in a modern scholarly edition in *Silver Fork Novels, 1826–1841*, 6 vols., gen. ed. Harriet Devine Jump, eds. Andrea Hibbard and Edward Copeland, VI (London: Pickering & Chatto, 2005).

20 Hazlitt, 'The Dandy School'. Citation p. 146.

21 Cited by Garside, Belanger and Ragaz, *British Fiction, 1800–1829*, 1824A052, 1825A042, 1828A051.

22 See the record for Theodore Hook, *Sayings and Doings* (1824), in Garside, Belanger and Ragaz, 1824A052.

23 Graeme Harper, 'Hook, Theodore Edward (1788–1841)', *Oxford Dictionary of National Biography* (Oxford University Press, 2004). www.oxforddnb.com. ezproxy.libraries.claremont.edu/view/article/13686.

24 E. M. Butler (ed.), *A Regency Visitor: The English Tour of Prince Pückler-Muskau, Described in His Letters, 1826–1828*, from the original translation by Sarah Austin (London: Collins, 1957), pp. 163–4. Cited in Garside, Belanger and Ragaz.

25 Augustus J. C. Hare (ed.), *The Life and Letters of Maria Edgeworth*, 2 vols (London: Edward Arnold, 1894), II, pp. 150–1. Cited in Garside, Belanger and Ragaz.

26 'Key to *"Almack's"*', reprinted from *The Literary Gazette* of 9 December, 1826 (London: W. A. Scripps, 1827).

27 'Anna Jameson', in Virginia Blain, Patricia Clements and Isobel Grundy (eds.), *The Feminist Companion to Literature in English* (London: B. T. Batsford, 1990), pp. 569–70.

28 'L. E. L.: Life', in Brown, Clements and Grundy, *Orlando*. Also, Mike Landon, 'The Death of L. E. L. – A Retrospective Inquest', *Women's Writing*, 16, no. 3 (Dec. 2009), pp. 445–51.

29 *Romance and Reality* is available in a modern scholarly edition in *Silver Fork Novels, 1826–1841*, 6 vols., gen. ed. Harriet Devine Jump, ed. Cynthia Lawford, II (London: Pickering & Chatto, 2005).

30 *Granby* is available in a modern scholarly edition in *Silver Fork Novels, 1826–1841*, 6 vols., gen. ed. Harriet Devine Jump, ed. Clare Bainbridge, I (London: Pickering & Chatto, 2005).

31 'Caroline Norton: Life', Brown, Clements and Grundy, *Orlando*.

32 *Ibid.*

33 *Ibid.*

34 Casey, pp. 253–62.

35 'Caroline Scott: Life', in Brown, Clements and Grundy, *Orlando*.

36 Clive Towse, 'Ward, Robert Plumer (1765–1846)', *Oxford Dictionary of National Biography* (Oxford University Press, 2004). www.oxforddnb.com. ezproxy.libraries.claremont.edu/view/article/28703.

37 See the record for 'Charles White' in Garside, Belanger and Ragaz.

Bibliography

NOVELS

Anon., *Hyde Nugent, a Tale of Fashionable Life*, 3 vols. (London: Henry Colburn, 1827).

Austen, Jane, *The Cambridge Edition of Jane Austen, gen.* ed. Janet Todd, 9 vols. (Cambridge University Press, 2008).

Blessington, Lady, *The Confessions of an Elderly Gentleman* (London: Longman, 1837).

The Confessions of an Elderly Lady (London: Longman, 1838).

The Governess, 2 vols. (London: Longman, 1839).

The Lottery of Life and Other Tales (London: Henry Colburn, 1842).

The Repealers, a novel, 3 vols. (London: R. Bentley, 1833).

Two Friends, a novel, 3 vols. (London: Saunders and Otley, 1835).

The Victims of Society, 3 vols. (London: Saunders and Otley, 1837). Also, *Silver Fork Novels, 1826–1841*, 6 vols., gen. ed. Harriet Devine Jump, *The Victims of Society*, eds. Ann R. Hawkins and Jeraldine R. Kraver, IV (London: Pickering & Chatto, 2005).

Bulwer, Edward, *Devereux; a Tale*, 3 vols. (London: Henry Colburn, 1829).

The Disowned, 3 vols. (London: Henry Colburn, 1828).

Godolphin, a novel, 3 vols. (London: Richard Bentley, 1833). Also, *Silver Fork Novels, 1826–1841*, 6 vols., gen. ed. Harriet Devine Jump, *Godolphin, a Novel*, ed. Harriet Devine Jump, III (London: Pickering & Chatto, 2005).

Paul Clifford (London: Henry Colburn and Richard Bentley, 1830).

Pelham; or, The Adventures of a Gentleman, 3 vols. (London: Henry Colburn, 1828).

Bulwer, Rosina, *Cheveley; or, The Man of Honour*, 3 vols. (London: Edward Bull, 1839). Also, *Silver Fork Novels, 1826–1841*, gen. ed. Harriet Devine Jump, 6 vols., *Cheveley*, ed. Marie Mulvey-Roberts, V (London: Pickering & Chatto, 2005).

Burdett, Mrs C. D., *At Home. A Novel*, 3 vols. (London: Henry Colburn, 1828).

English Fashionables Abroad, a novel, 3 vols., 1st edn 1827 (London: Henry Colburn, 1837).

Burney, Frances, *Cecilia* (London: T. Payne & Son; T. Cadell, 1782).

Evelina, or a Young Lady's Entrance into the World, 3 vols. (London: T. Lowndes, 1778).

The Wanderer, 5 vols. (London: Longman, Hurst, Rees, Orme and Brown, 1814).

Bury, Lady Charlotte, *The Devoted*, 3 vols. (London: Richard Bentley, 1836).

The Disinherited; and The Ensnared, 3 vols. (London: Richard Bentley, 1834).

The Exclusives, 3 vols. (London: Henry Colburn and Richard Bentley, 1830).

Flirtation, 3 vols. (London: Henry Colburn, 1827).

Journal of the Heart, 1st edn 1830 (London: James Cochrane and Co., 1835).

The Separation, 3 vols. (London: Henry Colburn and Richard Bentley, 1830).

Disraeli, Benjamin, *Henrietta Temple, a Love Story*, 3 vols. (London: Henry Colburn, 1837).

Vivian Grey, 3 vols. (London: Henry Colburn, 1826).

The Young Duke, 'A Moral Tale, though Gay', 3 vols. (London: Henry Colburn and Richard Bentley, 1831).

Eden, Emily, *The Semi-Attached Couple* (London: Bentley, 1860) and *The Semi-Detached House* (London: Bentley, 1859), gen. ed. Martin Seymour-Smith, introduced by Anthony Eden (London: Victor Gollancz, 1969).

Edgeworth, Maria, *Belinda*, ed. Kathryn J. Kirkpatrick, 1st edn 1801 (Oxford University Press, 1994).

Patronage, 4 vols. (London: J. Johnson & Co., 1814).

Egan, Pierce, *Life in London: or the Day and Night Scenes of Jerry Hawthorn, Esq. and His Elegant Friend Corinthian Tom, Accompanied by Bob Logic, the Oxonian, in the Rambles and Sprees through the Metropolis* (London: Sherwood, Neely, and Jones, 1821).

[Egan, Pierce 'improbable'] *Real Life in London: or, The Further Rambles and Adventures of Bob Tallyho, Esq. and his Cousin the Hon. Tom Dashall, &c. through the Metropolis: Exhibiting a Living Picture of Fashionable Characters, Manners, and Amusements in High and Low Life*, 2 vols. (London: Jones & Co., 1821, [II, 1822]).

Ferrier, Susan, *Marriage*, ed. Rosemary Ashton *[1818]*, (London: Virago Press, 1986).

Gore, Catherine, *The Banker's Wife; or, Court and City*, 3 vols. (London: Henry Colburn, 1843).

The Cabinet Minister, 3 vols. (London: Richard Bentley, 1839).

Cecil; or, The Adventures of a Coxcomb, 3 vols. (London: Richard Bentley, 1841). Also, *Silver Fork Novels, 1826–1841*, 6 vols., gen. ed. Harriet Devine Jump, *Cecil*, eds. Andrea Hibbard and Edward Copeland, VI (London: Pickering & Chatto, 2005).

Diary of a Désennuyée (London: Henry Colburn, 1836).

The Dowager; or, The New School for Scandal, 3 vols. (London: Richard Bentley, 1840).

The Fair of Mayfair, 3 vols. (London: Henry Colburn and Richard Bentley, 1832).

The Hamiltons; or, The New Æra, 3 vols. (London: Saunders and Otley, 1834).

The Heir of Selwood, 3 vols. (London: Henry Colburn, 1838).

Mothers and Daughters; a Tale of the Year 1830, 3 vols. (London: Henry Colburn and Richard Bentley, 1831).

Mrs. Armytage; or, Female Domination, 3 vols. (London: Henry Colburn, 1836).

The Opera, a novel, 3 vols. (London: Henry Colburn and Richard Bentley, 1832).

Pin Money; a novel, 3 vols. (London: Henry Colburn and Richard Bentley, 1831).

The Sketch Book of Fashion, 3 vols. (London: Richard Bentley, 1833).

Stokeshill Place; or The Man of Business, 3 vols. (London: Henry Colburn, 1837).

Women as They Are; or, The Manners of the Day, 3 vols. (London: Henry Colburn and Richard Bentley, 1830).

Gore, Catherine [Albany Poyntz] 'The Body-Coachman', *Bentley's Miscellany* (London: Richard Bentley, 1841), 10, pp. 87–96.

[Albany Poyntz], 'Diary of a Dining-out Man', *Bentley's Miscellany* (London: Richard Bentley, 1841), 9, pp. 280–92.

[Albany Poyntz], 'The Lady's Maid', *Bentley's Miscellany* (London: Richard Bentley, 1841), 10, pp. 157–63.

[Albany Poyntz], 'The Link Man', *Bentley's Miscellany* (London: Richard Bentley, 1841), 9, pp. 635–44.

[Albany Poyntz] 'Secrets of the Blue Chamber', *Bentley's Miscellany* (London: Richard Bentley, 1841), 9, pp. 399–412.

Hook, Theodore, *Gilbert Gurney* (London: Whitaker, 1836).

Gilbert Gurney Married (London: Colburn, 1838).

Jack Brag (London: Richard Bentley, 1837).

Love and Pride, 3 vols. (London: Whitaker & Co., 1833).

Maxwell, 1st edn 1830 (London: Richard Bentley, 1840).

The Ramsbottom Papers (London: John Camden Hotten, n.d.).

Sayings and Doings, a Series of Sketches from Life, 3 vols. (London: Henry Colburn, 1824).

Sayings and Doings, 3rd series, 3 vols. (London: Henry Colburn, 1828).

Sayings and Doings Considered, with On Dits, Family Memoirs, &c. &c. &c. (London: T. and J. Allman, 1825).

Hudson, Marianne Spencer, *Almack's, a Novel*, 3 vols., 2nd edn (London: Saunders and Otley, 1826).

Jameson, Anna, *Diary of an Ennuyée* (London: Henry Colburn, 1826).

Landon, Letitia, *Duty and Inclination*, 3 vols. (London: Henry Colburn, 1838).

Ethel Churchill: or, The Two Brides, 3 vols. (London: Henry Colburn, 1837).

Lady Anne Granard; Keeping Up Appearances, 3 vols. (London: Henry Colburn, 1842).

Romance and Reality, 3 vols. (London: Henry Colburn and Richard Bentley, 1831). Also, *Silver Fork Novels, 1826–1841*, 6 vols., gen. ed. Harriet Devine Jump, *Romance and Reality*, ed. Cynthia Lawford, 11 (London: Pickering & Chatto, 2005).

Lister, T. H., *Arlington. A Novel*, 3 vols. (London: Henry Colburn and Richard Bentley, 1832).

    Granby. A Novel (London: Henry Colburn, 1826). Also, *Silver Fork Novels, 1826–1841*, 6 vols., gen. ed. Harriet Devine Jump, *Granby. A Novel*, ed. Clare Bainbridge, 1 (London: Pickering & Chatto, 2005).

    Herbert Lacy, 3 vols. (London: Henry Colburn, 1828).

Macleod, E. H., *Belmont's Daughter: a Fashionable Novel*, 4 vols. (London: A. K. Newman, 1830).

    Geraldine Murray, 4 vols. (London: A. K. Newman, 1826).

    Tales of Ton, 1st series, 4 vols. (London: A. K. Newman, 1821).

Normanby, Lord, *The Contrast*, 3 vols. (London: Henry Colburn and Richard Bentley, 1832).

    Matilda; A Tale of the Day, 2 vols. (London: Henry Colburn, 1825).

    Yes and No: A Tale of the Day, 2 vols. (London: Henry Colburn, 1828).

Norton, Caroline Sheridan, *The Wife, and Woman's Reward*, 3 vols. (London: Saunders and Otley, 1835).

Scott, Caroline Lucy [Lady Scott], *A Marriage in High Life*, ed. Lady Charlotte Bury, 2 vols. (London: Henry Colburn, 1828).

    Trevelyan, 3 vols. (London: Richard Bentley, 1831).

Surr, T. S., *The Magic of Wealth*, 3 vols. (London: Cadell and Davies, 1815).

Ward, Robert Plumer, *De Clifford; or, the Constant Man* (London: Henry Colburn, 1841).

    De Vere; or, the Man of Independence (London: Henry Colburn, 1827).

    Tremaine; or the Man of Refinement, 2nd edition (London: Henry Colburn, 1825).

White, Charles, *Almack's Revisited*, 3 vols., first printing known as *Herbert Milton* (London: Saunders and Otley, 1828).

    The Married Unmarried (London: Henry Colburn, 1837).

CONTEMPORARY SOURCES

Anon., 'Advertisements', *Quarterly Review* 97 (June and Sept. 1855), pp. 183–225.

    'The Advertising System', *Edinburgh Review* 155 (Feb. 1843), pp. 2–43.

    'Fashionable Life' and 'Fashionable Changes', regular columns in *The Morning Post*.

    'Key to "*Almack's*"', pamphlet reprinted from *The Literary Gazette* of 9 December, 1826 (London: W. A. Scripps, 1827).

    Mogg and Tegg's *Guides*, advertisement in *The Literary Gazette*, 16 August 1823, p. 528.

    'Newspapers' in *The Westminster Review*, 1.3, July 1824, pp. 194–212.

    'One Hundred Beaver Hats', advertisement in *The Times*, Tuesday 25 Sept. 1821, p. 1.

    Review of 'Pin Money', *Westminster Review*, no. 15 (Oct. 1831), pp. 433–4.

    'The Reviewer', in *Bell's Weekly Messenger*, extract from the *Commercialist and Weekly Advertiser*, Sunday, 1 Jan. 1832.

Ackermann, Rudolph, 'Twelve Views of London Sites Seen through Arches' (1820), The Guildhall Library, London. London Metropolitan Archives, catalogue number p7497564.

Alison, Archibald, 'The Influence of the Press', *Blackwood's Edinburgh Magazine*, 36 (Sept. 1834), pp. 373–91, in Andrew King and John Plunkett (eds.), *Victorian Print Media: A Reader* (Oxford University Press, 2005), pp. 25–31.

Austen, Henry, 'Memoir of Miss Austen', 5 Oct. 1832, in Kathryn Sutherland (ed.), *J. E. Austen-Leigh: A Memoir of Jane Austen* (Oxford University Press, 2002).

Austen, Jane, *Jane Austen's Letters*, ed. Deirdre Le Faye, 3rd edn (Oxford University Press, 1995).

'Opinions of *Mansfield Park*: Collected and Transcribed by Jane Austen', in B. C. Southam (ed.), *Jane Austen: The Critical Heritage* (London: Routledge & Kegan Paul, 1968), pp. 48–51.

Barbauld, Anna Laetitia, '30 August, 1804' in Anna Letitia Le Breton, *Memoir of Mrs. Barbauld* (London: 1874), p. 39.

The British Novelists; with an Essay and Prefaces, Biographical and Critical, 50 vols. (London: Rivington, 1820).

Bentley, Richard (ed.), *Novels by Miss Jane Austen*, 5 vols. (London: Richard Bentley, 1833).

Blessington, Lady, *The Belle of a Season: A Poem* (London: Longman, Orme, Brown, Green and Longmans, *c.* 1839).

The Book of Beauty, 1834 (London: Longman, 1834).

Conversations of Lord Byron (London: Henry Colburn and Richard Bentley, 1834).

Desultory Thoughts and Reflections (London: Longman, 1839).

Flowers of Loveliness (London: Ackermann & Company, 1836).

The Idler in France (London: Henry Colburn, 1841).

The Idler in Italy (London: Henry Colburn, 1839).

The Literary Life and Correspondence of the Countess of Blessington, Robert Madden (London: T. C. Newby, 1855).

The Magic Lantern; or, Sketches of Scenes in the Metropolis (London: Longman, Hurst, Rees, Orme and Brown, 1822).

Brownlow, Emma Sophia, Countess, *The Eve of Victorianism: Reminiscences of the Years 1802 to 1834* (London: John Murray, 1940).

Bulwer, Edward, *England and the English*, 1st edition London 1833 (Paris: Baudry's European Library, 1834).

My Novel: or Varieties of English Life (Edinburgh and London: W. Blackwood and Sons, 1853).

Review of Letitia Landon's *Romance and Reality* in *New Monthly Magazine*, 32 (Dec. 1831), pp. 549–50.

'The Works of Theodore Hook', *Westminster Review*, 6 (1838), pp. 169–98.

Busby, T. L., *Costume of the Lower Orders of London, Painted and Engraved from Nature* (London: Baldwin and Company, 1820).

Carlyle, Thomas, *Sartor Resartus*, published serially in *Fraser's* (London, 1833–34).

'Signs of the Times' (1829), in Gertrude Himmelfarb (ed.), *The Spirit of the Age: Victorian Essays* (New Haven and London: Yale University Press, 2007), pp. 31–49.

Chorley, Henry F., *Thirty Years of Musical Recollections*, 2 vols. (London: Hurst and Blackett, 1862).

Collas, Achille, *The Authors of England: A Series of Medallion Portraits of Modern Literary Characters, Engraved from the Works of British Artists* (London: Charles Tilt, 1838).

Croker, J. W., *The Correspondence and Diaries of the Late Rt Hon. John Wilson Croker*, ed. Louis J. Jennings (London: Murray, 1884).

Cruchley, G. F., *Cruchley's Picture of London, or Visitor's Assistant ... 'to which is Affixed a New Map of London'* (London: G. F. Cruchley, 1831).

Dickens, Charles, *Little Dorritt* (London: Bradbury and Evans, 1857).

Dighton, Richard, *Characters at the West End of Town* (London: Thomas MacLean, 1825).

City Characters (London: Thomas MacLean, 1824).

Disraeli, Benjamin, *Disraeli's Reminiscences*, eds. Helen M. Swartz and Marvin Swartz (London: Hamish Hamilton, 1975).

Vindication of the English Constitution (London: Saunders and Otley, 1835).

Edgeworth, Maria, *The Life and Letters of Maria Edgeworth*, 2 vols., ed. Augustus J. C. Hare (London: Edward Arnold, 1894).

Edwards, Sutherland, *History of the Opera*, 2 vols. (London: Allen, 1862).

Eliot, George, *Silly Novels by Lady Novelists* (London: Penguin, 2010), first published in *Westminster Review*, 66 (Old Series), 10 (New Series) (Oct. 1856), pp. 442–61.

Elmes, James, *Metropolitan Improvements: or London in the Nineteenth Century* (London: Jones and Co., 1828).

Fuller, Margaret, *Women in the Nineteenth Century*, ed. Joslyn T. Pine, 1st edn 1845 (New York: Dover, 1999).

Granville, Harriet, *The Letters of Harriet Countess Granville, 1810–1845*, ed. F. Leveson, 2 vols. (London: Gower, 1894).

Greville, Charles, *The Greville Diary*, ed. Philip Whitwell Wilson, 2 vols. (London: William Heinemann, 1927).

The Greville Memoirs, ed. Henry Reeve, 3 vols. (London: Longmans, Green, 1874).

Hazlitt, William, 'The Dandy School', from *The Examiner* (18 Nov. 1827), in P. P. Howe (ed.), *The Complete Works of William Hazlitt*, 21 vols. (London and Toronto: J. M. Dent and Sons, 1934), XVI, pp. 143–9.

'The Periodical Press', from *Edinburgh Review* 38 (May 1823), in P. P. Howe (ed.), *The Complete Works of William Hazlitt*, 21 vols. (London and Toronto: J. M. Dent and Sons, 1934), XVI, pp. 211–39.

Heath, Charles, *Heath's New Gallery of British Engravings* (London: David Bogue, 1845).

Heath's Portfolio of Engravings, 'After the First British Masters; Comprising Portraits of the Children of the Nobility, Illustrations of Venetian and Other Tales, and Female Costumes of Various Nations' (London: A. Fullarton and Co., n.d.).

Picturesque Views of London (London: Hurst, Robinson, and Co., 1825).

Horne, R. H. (ed.), *A New Spirit of the Age*, 6 vols. (London: Smith, Elder and Co., 1844).

Howard, George, Viscount Morpeth, later 7th Earl of Carlisle, 'The Lady and the Novel', F. M. Reynolds (ed.) *The Keepsake for 1835* (London, 1835), pp. 27–8.

Hunt, Leigh, 'Prospectus', *The Examiner* (3 Jan. 1808), pp. 6–8.

Hurd, Richard, *Dialogues on the Uses of Foreign Travel* (London: A. Millar, 1764).

Jerdan, William, *National Portrait Gallery of Illustrious and Eminent Personages of the Nineteenth Century*, 4 vols. (London: Fisher, Son, and Jackson, 1830–34).

Kidd, W., *Kidd's How to Enjoy London: or, London in All Its Glory: For the Use of Strangers and Visitors*, 9th edn (London: W. Kidd, *c.* 1830).

Knight, Charles, *Passages from the Life of Charles Knight* (New York: G. P. Putnam, 1874).

Lamb, Charles, *The Letters of Charles Lamb*, ed. E. V. Lucas, III (New York: AMS, 1968; London: Methuen, 1935).

Laporte, P. F., *Her Majesty's Theatre: A List of the Subscribers for the Season 1839* (London: Andrews, Ebers, Hookham, and Mitchell; W. Seguin and Sams, 1839).

Leigh, Samuel, *Leigh's New Picture of London* (London: Samuel Leigh, 1830).

Lister, T. H., rev. of '*Women as They Are* by Mrs. Catherine Gore', *Edinburgh Review*, 53 (July 1830), pp. 444–62.

Lockie, John, *Topography of London, Facsimile of John Lockie's Gazetteer 1813* (London Topographical Society, 1994).

Maginn, William, 'Fashionable Novels', *Fraser's Magazine* (Apr. 1830), p. 321.

'Mr. Edward Lytton Bulwer's Novels: And Remarks on Novel-Writing', *Fraser's Magazine* (May 1830), p. 510.

'The Novels of the Season', *Fraser's Magazine* (Feb. 1831), pp. 95–113.

Masson, David, *British Novelists and Their Styles* (Cambridge: Macmillan, 1859).

Merle, Gibbons, 'Newspaper Press', *Westminster Review*, 10 (1829), pp. 216–37, in Andrew King and John Plunkett (eds.), *Victorian Print Media: A Reader* (Oxford University Press, 2005), pp. 342–5.

Mill, John Stuart, 'The Spirit of the Age', *The Examiner*, 9 Jan. 1831, in Gertrude Himmelfarb (ed.), *The Spirit of the Age* (New Haven and London: Yale University Press, 2007), pp. 50–90.

Montagu, Elizabeth, *The Letters of Mrs. Elizabeth Montagu*, 4 vols., reprint of 1809, Cadell and Davies, ed. (New York: AMS Press, 1974).

Montgomery, Robert, *The Age Reviewed* (London: W. C. Wright, 1828).

'Introductory Epistle to an Eminent Puffer', *The Puffiad* (London: S. Maunder, 1828).

Moore, Thomas, *The Fudge Family in Paris* (London: Longman & Co., 1818).

Morgan, Sydney Owenson, review of *The Dowager*, in *The Athenæum*, 678 (14 Nov. 1840), p. 899.

review of *Jack Sheppard: A Romance* [by William Harrison Ainsworth], in *The Athenæum*, 626 (26 Oct. 1839), pp. 803–4.

Nash, John, 'Report of Mr. John Nash, Architect in the Department of Works; with Plans for the Improvement of Mary-le-bone Park', in John White (ed.), *Some Account of the Proposed Improvements of the Western Part of London, by the Formation of the Regent's Park, the New Street, the New Sewer, &c., &c.* (London: W. & P. Reynolds, 1814).

Oliphant, M., *Annals of a Publishing House*, 2 vols. (Edinburgh: William Blackwood, 1897).

Parliamentary Debates, ser. 3, ii. Cc. 1086–7, 1 March, 1831.

Partington, C. F., 'Of the London Institution', in *National History and Views of London and Its Environs*, 2 vols. (London: Simpkin and Marshall, 1834).

Paston, George, *Little Memoirs of the Nineteenth Century* (London: Grant Richards, 1902).

Paulding, James Kirke, *A Sketch of Old England, by a New England Man* (New York: Charles Wiley, 1822).

Peacock, T. L., 'Essay on Fashionable Literature', in H. F. B. Brett-Smith and C. E. Jones (eds.), *Halliford Edition of the Works of Peacock* (London: Constable & Co., 1924–34), VIII, p. 274.

Pigot and Co.'s National, London, & Provincial Directory for 1832–3–4, 5th edn (London: Pigot, 1834).

Pückler-Muskau, *A Regency Visitor: The English Tour of Prince Pückler-Muskau, Described in His Letters, 1826–1828*, ed. E. M. Butler, trans. Sarah Austin (London: Collins, 1957), pp. 163–4.

Reiman, Donald H. (ed.), *The Romantics Reviewed: Contemporary Reviews of British Romantic Writers*, 5 vols. (New York: Garland, 1972).

Richardson, Samuel, *The History of Sir Charles Grandison*, 6 vols. (London: Richardson, 1753).

Ritchie, Leitch, *Beauty's Costume: A Series of Female Figures in the Dresses of All Times and Nations* (London: Longman, 1838).

Sala, George Augustus, *Twice Round the Clock: Or the Hours of the Day and Night in London* (1858), reprinted (New York: Leicester University Press, 1971).

Scott, Sir Walter, *Journal, 1825–26* (Edinburgh: Oliver and Boyd, 1939).

Sinclair, John, *Thoughts on Parliamentary Reform* (Edinburgh, 1831).

Sneyd, Walter, *Portraits of the Spruggins Family, arranged by Richard Sucklethumkin Spruggins, Esq.* [pseud.], arranged for publication by Frances, Countess of Morley (London, 1829).

Stevenson, William. 'On the Reciprocal Influence of Periodical Publication', *Blackwood's* (Nov. 1824), p. 519.

Stuart, Daniel. 'Anecdotes of Public Newspapers', *Gentleman's Magazine* (July 1838), pp. 23–7.

[Taylor, Henry], 'Novels of Fashionable Life', *Quarterly Review*, 48 (1832).

Taylor, Jefferys, *A Month in London: Or Some of Its Modern Wonders Described* (London: Harvey and Darton, 1832).

Thackeray, William Makepeace, 'The Book of Snobs, by One of Themselves' (1846–47), in Gertrude Himmelfarb (ed.), *The Spirit of the Age: Victorian Essays* (New Haven and London: Yale University Press, 2007), pp. 91–106.

'Novels by Eminent Hands' in *Miscellanies: Prose and Verse*, in *Works*, 8 vols. (London: Bradbury & Evans, 1856), ii, pp. 383–445.

Westmacott, C. M., '*C. M. Westmacott, to E. L. Bulwer*' (London: James Ridgway, Piccadilly, 1833) [pamphlet].

Whateley, Richard, unsigned review of *Northanger Abbey* and *Persuasion* in *Quarterly Review* (January 1821), xxiv, 352–76, from B. C. Southam (ed.), *Critical Heritage* (London: Routledge & Kegan Paul, 1968), pp. 87–105.

SECONDARY SOURCES

Adburgham, Alison, *Shopping in Style: London from the Restoration to Edwardian Elegance* (London: Thames and Hudson, 1979).

Silver Fork Society: Fashionable Life and Literature from 1814 to 1840 (London: Constable, 1983).

Alexander, Sarah C., 'A Tale of Two Dandies: Gore, Dickens and the "Social-Fork" Novel', *Women's Writing*, 16, no. 2 (Aug. 2009), pp. 283–300.

Allan, David, *A Nation of Readers: The Lending Library in Georgian England* (London: The British Library, 2008).

Alter, Robert, *Imagined Cities: Urban Experience and the Language of the Novel* (New Haven: Yale University Press, 2005).

Anderson, Benedict, *Imagined Communities: Reflections on the Origin and Spread of Nationalism* (1983; rev. edn London, New York: Verso, 1991).

Armstrong, Nancy, *Desire and Domestic Fiction: A Political History of the Novel* (Oxford University Press, 1987).

Arvan-Andrews, Elaine, 'The "Lure of the Fabulous": Gift-Book Beauties and Charlotte Brontë's Early Heroines', *Women's Writing*, 16, no. 2 (Aug. 2009), pp. 263–82.

Aspinall, Arthur, *Lord Brougham and the Whig Party* (1927; rev. edn Manchester University Press, 1939).

Politics and the Press, c. 1780–1850 (London: Home & Van Thal, 1949).

Aspinall, Arthur (ed.), *Three Early Nineteenth Century Diaries* (London: Williams and Norgate, 1952).

Asquith, Ivon, 'Advertising and the Press in the Late Eighteenth and Early Nineteenth Centuries: James Perhy and the Morning Chronicle 1790–1821', *Historical Journal*, 18, no. 4 (1975), pp. 703–24.

Bakhtin, Mikhail, 'Discourse in the Novel' (1934–5), in Michael Holquist (ed.), trans. Caryl Emerson and Michael Holquist, *The Dialogic Imagination: Four Essays* (Austin: University of Texas Press, 1981), pp. 259–422.

'Forms of Time and of the Chronotope in the Novel: Notes Towards a Historical Poetics', in Michael Holquist (ed.), trans. Caryl Emerson and

Michael Holquist, *The Dialogic Imagination: Four Essays* (Austin: University of Texas Press, 1981), pp. 84–258.

Bann, Stephen, *Romanticism and the Rise of History* (New York: Twayne, 1995).

'The Victim as Spectacle: Paul Delaroche's "Lady Jane Grey" and "Mademoiselle Anaïs"', in Stephen Bann and Linda Whiteley (eds.), *Painting History: Delaroche and Lady Jane Grey* (London: National Gallery Company, distributed by Yale University Press, 2010), pp. 35–45.

Barchas, Janine, *Graphic Design, Print Culture, and the Eighteenth-Century Novel* (Cambridge University Press, 2003).

'Mrs. Gaskell's *North and South*: Austen's Early Legacy', *Persuasions*, 30 (2009), pp. 53–66.

Barker, Hannah, *Newspapers, Politics, and Public Opinion in Eighteenth Century England* (Oxford: Clarendon, 1998).

Barrell, John, *Painting and the Politics of Culture: New Essays on British Art, 1700–1850* (Oxford University Press, 1992).

The Political Theory of Painting from Reynolds to Hazlitt: 'The Body of the Public' (New Haven: Yale University Press, 1986).

Battaglia, Beatrice and Diego Saglia, *Re-Drawing Austen: Picturesque Travels in Austen-Land* (Napoli: Ligouri, *c.* 2004).

Baudrillard, Jean, *For a Critique of the Political Economy of the Sign*, trans. Charles Levin (New York: Telos Press, 1981).

Bautz, Annika, *The Reception of Jane Austen and Walter Scott* (London and New York: Continuum, 2007).

Beales, Derek, 'The Idea of Reform in British Politics, 1829–1850', in T. W. C. Blanning and Peter Wende (eds.), *Reform in Great Britain and Germany, 1750–1850* (Oxford University Press, for the British Academy, 1999), pp. 159–74.

Behrendt, Stephen C. (ed.), *Romanticism, Radicalism, and the Press* (Detroit: Wayne State University Press, 1997).

Bell, A., *Sydney Smith* (Oxford: Clarendon Press, 1980).

Benchimol, Alex, 'William Cobbett's Geography of Cultural Resistance in *Rural Rides*', *Nineteenth-Century Contexts*, 26, no. 3 (Sept. 2004), pp. 257–72.

Benedict, Barbara M., 'Sensibility by the Numbers: Austen's Work as Regency Popular Fiction', in Deidre Lynch (ed.), *Janeites: Austen's Disciples and Devotees* (Princeton University Press, 2000), pp. 63–86.

Benjamin, Walter, *The Arcades Project*, trans. Howard Eiland and Kevin McLaughlin (Cambridge, MA: Harvard University Press, 1999).

Illuminations ed. Hannah Arendt, trans. Harry Zohn (New York: Schocken, 1968).

Bjornson, Richard, 'Cognitive Mapping and the Understanding of Literature', *SubStance*, 30 (1981), pp. 51–62.

Black, Jeremy, *The English Press in the Eighteenth Century* (Philadelphia: University of Pennsylvania Press, 1987).

The English Press, 1621–1861 (Stroud: Sutton Publishing, 2001).

Blain, Virginia, Patricia Clements and Isobel Grundy (eds.), *The Feminist Companion to Literature in English* (London: B. T. Batsford, 1990).

Blake, Robert, *Disraeli* (New York: St. Martin's Press, 1967).

Boase, G. C., 'Bury, Lady Charlotte Susan Maria (1775–1861)', rev. Pam Perkins, *Oxford Dictionary of National Biography* (Oxford University Press, 2004). www.oxforddnb.com.ezproxy.libraries.claremont.edu/view/article/4147

Bourdieu, Pierre, 'The Market of Symbolic Goods', in Randal Johnson (ed.), *The Field of Cultural Production* (New York: Columbia University Press, 1993), pp. 112–41.

Bourne, H. R. Fox, *English Newspapers: Chapters in the History of Journalism*, 2 vols. (1887; rev. edn New York: Russell & Russell, 1966).

Bourne, K., *Palmerston: The Early Years* (London: Allen Lane, 1982).

Boyce, George, James Curran and Pauline Wingate (eds.), *Newspaper History: From the Seventeenth Century to the Present Day* (London: Constable, 1978).

Brake, Laurel, *Subjugated Knowledges: Journalism, Gender and Literature in the Nineteenth Century* (Basingstoke: Palgrave Macmillan, 1994).

Brantlinger, Patrick, *Fictions of State: Culture and Credit in Britain, 1694–1994* (Ithaca and London: Cornell University Press, 1996).

Rule of Darkness: British Literature and Imperialism, 1830–1914 (Ithaca and London: Cornell University Press, 1988).

Breward, Christopher, *Fashioning London: Clothing and the Modern Metropolis* (New York: Berg, 2004).

Briggs, Asa, 'Middle-Class Consciousness in English Politics, 1780–1846', *Past and Present*, 9, no.1 (1956), pp. 65–74.

Brightfield, Byron, *Theodore Hook and His Novels* (Cambridge, MA: Harvard University Press, 1928).

Brock, Michael, *The Great Reform Act* (London: Hutchinson University Library, 1973).

Brooks, Peter, *Reading for the Plot: Design and Intention in Narrative* (New York: Vintage, 1985).

Brown, Andrew, 'Lytton, Edward George Earle Lytton Bulwer, 1st Baron Lytton (1803–1873)', *Oxford Dictionary of National Biography* (Oxford University Press, 2004). www.oxforddnb.com.ezproxy.libraries.claremont.edu/view/article/17314

Brown, Bruce Alan and Paulette Letailleur, 'Favart (i)', Grove Music Online. Oxford Music Online: www.oxfordmusiconline.com.ezproxy.libraries.claremont.edu/subscriber/article/grove/music/42563pg1.

Brown, Richard, *Economic Revolutions in Britain 1750–1850: Prometheus Unbound?* (Cambridge University Press, 1992).

Brown, Susan, Patricia Clements and Isobel Grundy (eds.), 'Marguerite Gardiner, Countess of Blessington: Life', screen within *Orlando: Women's Writing in the British Isles from the Beginnings to the Present*. Cambridge University Press Online, 2006. http://orlando.cambridge.org

'Rosina Bulwer Lytton, Baroness Lytton: Life', screen within *Orlando: Women's Writing in the British Isles from the Beginnings to the Present.* Cambridge University Press Online, 2006. http://orlando.cambridge.org.

'Lady Charlotte Bury: Life', screen within *Orlando: Women's Writing in the British Isles from the Beginnings to the Present.* Cambridge University Press Online, 2006. http://orlando.cambridge.org.

'Emily Eden: Life', screen within *Orlando: Women's Writing in the British Isles from the Beginnings to the Present.* Cambridge University Press Online, 2006. http://orlando.cambridge.org.

'Catherine Gore: Life', screen within *Orlando: Women's Writing in the British Isles from the Beginnings to the Present.* Cambridge University Press Online, 2006. http://orlando.cambridge.org.

'L. E. L.: Life', screen within *Orlando: Women's Writing in the British Isles from the Beginnings to the Present.* Cambridge University Press Online, 2006. http://orlando.cambridge.org.

'Caroline Norton: Life', screen within *Orlando: Women's Writing in the British Isles from the Beginnings to the Present.* Cambridge University Press Online, 2006. http://orlando.cambridge.org.

'Sydney Owenson, Lady Morgan: Life', screen within *Orlando: Women's Writing in the British Isles from the Beginnings to the Present.* Cambridge University Press Online, 2006. http://orlando.cambridge.org.

'Caroline Scott: Life', screen within *Orlando: Women's Writing in the British Isles from the Beginnings to the Present.* Cambridge University Press Online, 2006. http://orlando.cambridge.org.

Browning, Dominique, review of *The Three Weissmanns of Westport* (New York: Farrar, Straus and Giroux, 2010), in 'A Different Kind of Love Triangle', in 'The Sunday Book Review', *The New York Times*, 11 Feb. 2010.

Burgess, Miranda J., *British Fiction and the Production of Social Order, 1740–1830* (Cambridge University Press, 2000).

Bush, M. L., *The English Aristocracy: A Comparative Synthesis* (Manchester University Press, 1984).

Bushnell, Howard, *Maria Malibran: A Biography of the Singer* (University Park and London: Pennsylvania State University Press, 1979).

Butler, Marilyn, 'Culture's Medium: The Role of the Review', in Stuart Curran (ed.), *The Cambridge Companion to British Romanticism* (Cambridge University Press, 1993), pp. 120–47.

Jane Austen and the War of Ideas (Oxford: Clarendon Press, 1975).

Romantics, Rebels and Reactionaries (Oxford University Press, 1981).

Byron, Glennis, 'Landon, Letitia Elizabeth (1802–1838)', *Oxford Dictionary of National Biography* (Oxford University Press, 2004). www.oxforddnb.com. ezproxy.libraries.claremont.edu/view/article/15978.

Cahill, Gilbert A., *The Great Reform Bill, 1832: Liberal or Conservative?* (Lexington, MA: Heath, 1969).

Campbell, Colin, *The Romantic Ethic and the Spirit of Modern Consumerism* (Oxford: Blackwell, 1987).

'The Romantic Ethic and the Spirit of Modern Consumerism: Reflections on the Reception of a Thesis Concerning the Origin of the Continuing Desire for Goods', in Susan M. Pearce (ed.), *Experiencing Material Culture in the Western World* (London and Washington, DC: Leicester University Press, 1992), pp. 36–48.

Cannadine, David, *Aspects of Aristocracy: Grandeur and Decline in Modern Britain* (London and New York: Penguin Books, 1995).

The Decline and Fall of the British Aristocracy (New York: Random House, 1999).

Lords and Landlords: The Aristocracy and the Towns, 1774–1967 (London and Washington, DC: Leicester University Press, 1980).

The Rise and Fall of Class in Britain (New York: Columbia University Press, 1999).

Carpenter, Kirsty, *The Novels of Madame de Souza in Social and Political Perspective* (Oxford: Peter Lang, 2007).

Casey, Ellen Miller, 'Silver-Forks and the Commodity Text: Lady Morgan and *The Athenæum*', *Women's Writing*, 16, no. 2 (Aug. 2009), pp. 253–62.

Chancellor, E. Beresford, *Life in Regency and Early Victorian Times: An Account of the Days of Brummel and D'Orsay, 1800 to 1850* (London: B. T. Batsford, 1926).

Chandler, James, *England in 1819* (University of Chicago Press, 1998).

'Hallam, Tennyson, and the Poetry of Sensation: Aestheticist Allegories of a Counter Public Sphere', *Studies in Romanticism*, 33, no. 4 (Winter 1994), pp. 527–37.

Chandler, James and Kevin Gilmartin (eds.), *The Romantic Metropolis: The Urban Scene of British Culture, 1780–1840* (Cambridge University Press, 2006).

Child, Harold, 'Lesser Novelists', A.W. Ward and A.R. Waller (eds.), *The Cambridge History of English and American Literature*, 15 vols. (New York: G. P. Putnam's Sons; Cambridge University Press, 1916), XII, i, pp. 272–9.

Christensen, Jerome, *Romanticism at the End of History* (Baltimore: Johns Hopkins University Press, 2000).

Cohen, Margaret, *The Sentimental Education of the Novel* (Princeton University Press, 1999).

Cohen, Michèle, *Fashioning Masculinity: National Identity and Language in the Eighteenth Century* (London and New York: Routledge, 1996).

'"Manners" Make the Man: Politeness, Chivalry, and the Construction of Masculinity, 1750–1830', *Journal of British Studies*, 44 (Apr. 2005), pp. 312–29.

Colclough, Stephen, *Consuming Texts: Readers and Reading Communities, 1695–1870* (Basingstoke: Palgrave, 2007).

Colley, Linda, *Britons: Forging the Nation 1707–1837* (New Haven: Yale University Press, 1992).

Comment, Bernard, *The Panorama* (London: Reaktion Books, 1999).

Cook, Chris, *The Routledge Companion to Britain in the Nineteenth Century, 1815–1914* (London and New York: Routledge, 2005).

Copeland, Edward, 'The Austens and the Elliots: A Consumer's Guide to *Persuasion*', in Juliet McMaster and Bruce Stovel (eds.), *Jane Austen's Business: Her World and Her Profession* (Basingstoke: Macmillan Press, 1996), pp. 136–53.

'Crossing Oxford Street: Silver Fork Geopolitics', *Eighteenth-Century Life*, 25 (Spring 2001), pp. 116–34.

'Opera and the Great Reform Act: Silver Fork Fiction, 1822–1842', *Romanticism on the Net*, no. 34–5 (2004).

Women Writing about Money: Women's Fiction in England, 1790 to 1820 (Cambridge University Press, 1995).

Cowen, Ruth, *Relish: The Extraordinary Life of Alexis Soyer, Victorian Celebrity Chef* (London: Weidenfeld & Nicolson, 2006).

Cronin, Richard, *Romantic Victorians: English Literature, 1824–1840* (Basingstoke: Palgrave, 2002).

Cunningham, Hugh, *The Challenge of Democracy, Britain 1832–1918* (London: Longman, 2001).

Cunnington, Phillis and Alan Mansfield, *English Costume for Sports and Outdoor Recreation* (London: Adam & Charles Black, 1969).

Curran, Stuart, 'Women Readers, Women Writers', in Stuart Curran (ed.), *The Cambridge Companion to British Romanticism* (Cambridge University Press, 1993), pp. 177–95.

David, Deirdre (ed.), *The Cambridge Companion to the Victorian Novel* (Cambridge University Press, 2001).

De Certeau, Michel, 'Practices of Space', in Marshall Blonsky (ed.), *On Signs* (Baltimore: Johns Hopkins University Press, 1985), pp. 122–45.

De Groot, Jerome, *The Historical Novel* (London and New York: Routledge, 2010).

Denlinger, Elizabeth Campbell, *Before Victoria: Extraordinary Women of the British Romantic Era* (New York: New York Public Library/Columbia University Press, 2005).

Deutsch, David, *The Fabric of Reality* (London: Penguin, 1977).

Donald, Diana, *The Age of Caricature* (New Haven: Yale University Press, 1996).

Donald, James, *Imagining the Modern City* (London: The Athlone Press, 1999).

Sentimental Education: Schooling, Popular Culture, and the Regulation of Liberty (London: Verso, 1992).

Dubow, Jessica, 'Outside of Place and Other than Optical: Walter Benjamin and the Geography of Critical Thought', *Journal of Visual Culture*, 3, no. 3 (Dec. 2004), pp. 259–74.

During, Simon, 'Regency London', in James Chandler (ed.), *The Cambridge History of English Romantic Literature* (Cambridge University Press, 2009), pp. 335–54.

Eccleshall, Robert, 'English Conservatism as Ideology', *Political Studies*, 25, no. 1 (1977), pp. 62–83.

Entwistle, Joanne, *The Fashioned Body: Fashion, Dress and Modern Social Theory* (Cambridge: Polity Press, 2000).

Erickson, Lee, *The Economy of Literary Form: English Literature and the Industrialization of Publishing, 1800–1850* (Baltimore: Johns Hopkins University Press, 1996).

Evans, Eric J., *Britain before the Reform Act: Politics and Society, 1815–1832* (London: Longman, 1989).

The Forging of the Modern State: Early Industrial Britain, 1783–1870, (1983; rev. edn London: Longman, 1996).

The Great Reform Act of 1832 (London and New York: Routledge, 1994).

Parliamentary Reform, c. 1770–1918 (London: Longman, 2000).

Everett, Barbara, 'The Last Turn: Henry James and the Spirits of the English Country House', *Times Literary Supplement* (23–30 Dec. 2005), pp. 16–18.

Everett, Nigel, *The Tory View of Landscape* (New Haven and London: Yale University Press, 1994).

Evers, Charlotte and Dave Welbourne, *Britain 1783–1851: From Disaster to Triumph?* (London: John Murray, 2003).

Farrell, John P, 'Toward a New History of Fiction: The Wolff Collection and the Example of Mrs. Gore', *Library Chronicle of the University of Texas at Austin*, 37 (1986), pp. 28–37.

Favret, Mary, 'A Home for Art: Painting, Poetry and Domestic Interiors', in Mary A. Favret and Nicola Watson (eds.), *At the Limits of Romanticism: Essays in Cultural, Feminist, and Materialist Criticism* (Bloomington: Indiana University Press, 1994), pp. 59–82.

Fay, Elizabeth, 'Portrait Galleries, Representative History, and Hazlitt's Spirit of the Age', *Nineteenth-Century Contexts*, 24 (2002), pp. 155–61.

Felluga, Dino, '"With a Most Voiceless Thought": Byron and the Radicalism of Textual Culture', *European Romantic Review*, 11, no. 2 (Spring 2000), pp. 150–67.

Ferris, Ina, *The Achievement of Literary Authority: Gender, History, and the Waverley Novels* (Ithaca and London: Cornell University Press, 1991).

Flanders, Judith, *Consuming Passions: Leisure and Pleasure in Victorian Britain* (London: Harper Perennial, 2007).

Flint, Kate, *The Woman Reader, 1837–1914* (Oxford: Clarendon Press, 1993).

Ford, Trowbridge H., 'Political Coverage in *The Times*, 1811–41: The Role of Barnes and Brougham', *Bulletin of the Institute of Historical Research*, 59, no. 139 (1986), pp. 91–107.

Foucault, Michel, 'Body/Power', in C. Gordon (ed.), *Power/Knowledge: Selected Interviews and Other Writings 1972–1977* (Brighton: Harvester, 1980), pp. 55–62.

Fox, Celina, *Graphic Journalism in England during the 1830s and 1840s*, 'Thesis submitted to the Faculty of Modern History in the University of Oxford for the Degree of Doctor of Philosophy, Trinity Term, 1974' (New York & London: Garland Publishing, 1988).

Fox, Celina (ed.), *London – World City, 1800–1840* (New Haven and London: Yale University Press, 1992).

France, Peter, *Politeness and Its Discontents: Problems in French Classical Culture* (Cambridge University Press, 1992).

Fulford, Tim and Peter J. Kitson (eds.), *Romanticism and Colonialism: Writing and Empire, 1780–1830* (Cambridge University Press, 1998).

Gagnier, Regenia, *Idylls of the Marketplace* (Stanford University Press, 1986).

'Money, the Economy, and Social Class', in Patrick Brantlinger and William B. Thesing (eds.), *A Companion to the Victorian Novel* (Oxford: Blackwell, 2002), pp. 48–66.

Galperin, William, 'Austen's Earliest Readers and the Rise of the Janeites', in Deidre Lynch (ed.) *Janeites: Austen's Disciples and Devotees* (Princeton University Press, 2000), pp. 87–114.

Gamer, Michael, 'Maria Edgeworth and the Romance of Real Life', *NOVEL: A Forum on Fiction*, 34, no. 2 (Spring 2001), pp. 231–66.

Garrard, John, *Democratisation in Britain: Elites, Civil Society and Reform since 1800* (Basingstoke: Palgrave, 2002).

Garside, P. D., J. E. Belanger and S. A. Ragaz (eds.), *British Fiction, 1800–1829: A Database of Production, Circulation and Reception*, designer A. A. Mandal. www.british-fiction.cf.ac.uk.

Gash, Norman, *Aristocracy and People: Britain 1815–1865* (Bungay, Suffolk: Edward Arnold, 1979).

Politics in the Age of Peel: A Study in the Technique of Parliamentary Representation, 1830–1850 (London: Longmans, 1953).

Gillett, Paula, *The Victorian Painter's World* (Gloucester: Alan Sutton, 1990).

Gillingham, Lauren, 'History Suits the Dandy: Catherine Gore's Cecil Novels', *Women's Writing*, 16, no. 2 (Aug. 2009), pp. 218–36.

Gilmartin, Kevin, '"Hazlitt's Visionary London', in Heather Glen and Paul Hamilton (eds.), *Repossessing the Romantic Past* (Cambridge University Press, 2006), pp. 40–62.

Print Politics: The Press and Radical Opposition in Early Nineteenth-Century England (Cambridge University Press, 1996).

Gilroy, Amanda, review 'New Millennial Austens', *NOVEL: A Forum on Fiction*, 36, no. 1 (Autumn 2002), pp. 119–25.

Gilroy, Amanda and Wil Verhoeven, 'Introduction', *NOVEL: A Forum on Fiction*, 34, no. 2 (Spring 2001), pp. 147–62.

Gilson, David, 'Jane Austen, the Aristocracy, and T. H. Lister', *The Jane Austen Society: Report for 2002* (Chawton: The Jane Austen Society, 2002), pp. 56–65.

'Jane Austen, the Aristocracy and T. H. Lister : A Supplement', *The Jane Austen Society: Report for 2003* (Chawton: The Jane Austen Society, 2003), pp. 39–41.

Gores, Steven J., *Psychosocial Spaces: Verbal and Visual Readings of British Culture, 1750–1820* (Detroit: Wayne State University Press, 2000).

Gravil, Richard (ed.), *Master Narratives: Tellers and Telling in the English Novel* (Aldershot: Ashgate, 2001).

Greaves, Margaret, *Regency Patron: Sir George Beaumont* (London: Methuen, 1966).

Greenberg, Michael, 'Freelance', *Times Literary Supplement* (5 June 2009), p. 16.

Greene, D. J., 'Jane Austen and the Peerage', *Publications of the Modern Language Association of America*, 68 (1953), pp. 1017–31.

Greenslade, William, 'The Power of Advertising: Chad Newsome and the Meaning of Paris in *The Ambassadors*', *ELH*, 49, no. 1 (Spring 1982), pp. 99–122.

Griffiths, Dennis (ed.), *The Encyclopedia of the British Press, 1422–1992* (Basingstoke: Macmillan, 1992).

Habermas, Jürgen, *The Structural Transformation of the Public Sphere: An Inquiry into a Category of Bourgeois Society*, trans. Thomas Burger with Frederick Lawrence (Cambridge, MA: MIT Press, 1991).

Hall, Stuart, 'Fantasy, Identity, Politics', in Erica Carter, James Donald and Judith Squires (eds.), *Cultural Remix: Theories of Politics and the Popular* (London: Lawrence & Wishart, 1995), pp. 63–9.

Hamilton, James, *London Lights: The Minds that Moved the City that Shook the World, 1805–1851* (London: John Murray, 2007).

Harper, Graeme, 'Hook, Theodore Edward (1788–1841)', *Oxford Dictionary of National Biography* (Oxford University Press, 2004). www.oxforddnb.com. ezproxy.libraries.claremont.edu/view/article/13686.

Harris, Bob, *Politics and the Rise of the Press: Britain and France, 1626–1800* (New York: Routledge, 1996).

Harris, Jocelyn, 'Jane Austen, Jane Fairfax, and Jane Eyre', *Persuasions*, 29 (2008), pp. 99–109.

Jane Austen's Art of Memory (Cambridge University Press, 1989).

A Revolution Almost Beyond Expression (Newark: University of Delaware Press, 2007).

Haug, Wolfgang Fritz, *Commodity Aesthetics, Ideology and Culture* (New York: International General, 1987).

Hayden, John O., *The Romantic Reviewers, 1802–1824* (University of Chicago Press, 1968).

Hemingway, Andrew, *Landscape Imagery and Urban Culture in Early Nineteenth-Century Britain* (Cambridge University Press, 1992).

Hessell, Nikki, 'News and Newspapers: Readers of the Daily Press in Jane Austen's Novels', *Persuasions*, 31 (2009), pp. 248–54.

Hibbard, Andrea, '*Vivian Grey* and the Silver-Fork Etiquette of Authorship', *Genre*, 32 (Winter 1999), pp. 249–66.

Hibbert, Christopher, *Disraeli: A Personal History* (London: Harper, 2004).

Hides, Sean, 'The Geology of Material Culture and Cultural Identity', in Susan M. Pearce (ed.), *Experiencing Material Culture in the Western World* (London and Washington, DC: Leicester University Press, 1997), pp. 11–35.

Hill, Brian, *The Early Parties and Politics in Britain, 1688–1832* (Basingstoke: Macmillan, 1996).

Hilton, Boyd, *A Mad, Bad, and Dangerous People? England 1783–1846* (Oxford: Clarendon Press, 2006).

Hitchcock, Tim and Michèle Cohen, *English Masculinities, 1660–1800* (London: Longman, 1999).

Hobhouse, Hermione, *A History of Regent Street* (London: Macdonald and Jane's, 1975).

Hogan, Charles Beecher, 'Jane Austen and Her Early Public', *Review of English Studies*, n. s., 1 (1950), pp. 39–54.

Howard, Philip, '*We Thundered Out* – ': *200 years of The Times, 1785–1985* (London: Times Books, 1985).

Howgego, James, *Printed Maps of London, circa 1553–1850* (London: Dawson, 1978).

Hughes, Winifred, 'Elegies for the Regency: Catherine Gore's Dandy Novels', *Nineteenth-Century Literature*, 50, no. 2 (Sept. 1995), pp. 189–209.

'Gore, Catherine Grace Frances (1799/1800–1861)', *Oxford Dictionary of National Biography* (Oxford University Press, 2004). www.oxforddnb.com. ezproxy.libraries.claremont.edu/view/article/11091

'Mindless Millinery: Catherine Gore and the Silver Fork Heroine', *Dickens Studies Annual*, 25 (1996), pp. 159–76.

'Silver Fork Writers and Readers: Social Context', *NOVEL: A Forum on Fiction*, 25, no. 3 (Spring 1992), pp. 328–47.

Humphreys, A. L., *Crockford's, or The Goddess of Chance in St. James's Street 1828–1844* (London: Hutchinson, 1953).

Hunt, Lynn, *Politics, Culture, and Class in the French Revolution* (Berkeley, CA: University of California Press, 1984).

Hunt, Margaret, *The Middling Sort: Commerce, Gender, and the Family in England, 1680–1780* (Berkeley, CA: University of California Press, 1996).

Hunter, J. Paul, '"News, and New Things": Contemporaneity and the Early English Novel', *Critical Inquiry*, 14 (Spring 1988), pp. 493–515.

Hyde, Ralph, *The A to Z of Victorian London* (London Topographical Society, 1987).

Gilded Scenes and Shining Prospects: Panoramic Views of British Towns, 1575–1900 (New Haven: Yale Center for British Art, 1985).

Iacuzzi, Alfred, *The European Vogue of Favart: The Diffusion of the Opéra-Comique* (New York: Publications of the Institute of French Studies, Inc., 1932).

Inglis, Fred, *A Short History of Celebrity* (Princeton University Press, 2010).

Iser, Wolfgang, *The Implied Reader: Patterns of Communication in Prose Fiction from Bunyan to Beckett* (Baltimore and London: Johns Hopkins University Press, 1974).

Jack, Ian, *English Literature 1815–1832, Oxford History of English Literature*, XII (Oxford: Clarendon Press, 1963).

James, Henry, *The Portrait of a Lady* (Boston, New York: Houghton, Mifflin and Company, 1882 [1881]).

James, Lawrence, *The Middle Class: A History* (London: Little, Brown, 2006).

Jameson, Frederic, *The Political Unconscious: Narrative as a Socially Symbolic Act* (London and New York: Routledge, 1989).

Jauss, Hans Robert, *Toward an Aesthetic of Reception*, trans. Timothy Bahti (Brighton: Harvester Press, 1982).

Johnson, Claudia, *Jane Austen: Women, Politics and the Novel* (University of Chicago Press, 1988).

'"Let Me Make the Novels of a Country": Barbauld's "The British Novelists" (1810/1820)', *NOVEL: A Forum on Fiction*, 34, no. 2 (Spring, 2001), pp. 163–79.

Johnson, Randal, 'Editor's Introduction' to Pierre Bourdieu, *The Field of Cultural Production* (New York: Columbia University Press, 1993).

Jones, Aled, *Powers of the Press: Newspapers, Power and the Public in Nineteenth-Century England* (London: Scolar Press, 1996).

Jupp, Peter, *British Politics on the Eve of Reform: The Duke of Wellington's Administration 1828–30* (New York: St. Martin's Press, 1998).

Karlinsky, Simon, 'Russian Comic Opera in the Age of Catherine the Great', *19th-Century Music*, 7 (1984), pp. 318–25.

Keates, J. S., *Understanding Maps*, 2nd edn (London: Longman, 1996).

Keen, Paul (ed.), *Revolutions in Romantic Literature: An Anthology of Print Culture 1780–1832* (Peterborough, ON: Broadview Press, 2004).

Kelly, Gary, *English Fiction of the Romantic Period, 1789–1830* (London and New York: Longman, 1989).

'Romantic Fiction', in Stuart Curran (ed.), *The Cambridge Companion to British Romanticism* (Cambridge University Press, 1993), pp. 196–215.

Kendra, April, 'Gendering the Silver Fork: Catherine Gore and the Society Novel', *Women's Writing, 1747–1848*, 11, no. 1 (2004), pp. 25–38.

'Silver-Forks and Double Standards', *Women's Fiction*, 16, no. 2 (Aug. 2009), pp. 191–217.

'"You, Madam, Are No Jane Austen": Mrs. Gore and the Anxiety of Influence', *Nineteenth-Century Gender Studies*, 3, no. 2 (Summer 2007). www.ncgs-journal.com/issue32/kendra.htm.

Kendra, April and Winifred Hughes, 'Silver-Fork Writers and Readers: Social Contexts of a Best Seller', *NOVEL: A Forum on Fiction*, 25, no. 3 (1992), pp. 328–47.

Kent, David A. and D. R. Ewen, *Romantic Parodies, 1797–1831* (London and Toronto: Associated University Press, 1992).

Kierkuć-Bieliński, Jerzy, *George Scharf: From Regency Street to the Modern Metropolis* (London: Soane Gallery, 2009).

King, Andrew and John Plunkett (eds.), *Victorian Print Media: A Reader* (Oxford University Press, 2005).

Klancher, John, *The Making of English Reading Audiences, 1790–1832* (Madison: University of Wisconsin Press, 1987).

'Romantic Criticism and the Meanings of the French Revolution', *Studies in Romanticism*, 28 (Fall 1989), pp. 463–91.

Klein, Lawrence E., *Shaftesbury and the Culture of Politeness: Moral Discourse and Cultural Politics in Early Eighteenth-Century England* (Cambridge University Press, 1994).

Knott, John, *Popular Opposition to the 1834 Poor Law* (London: Croom Helm, 1986).

Koss, Stephen E., *The Rise and Fall of the Political Press in Britain*, 1 (Chapel Hill: University of North Carolina Press, 1981).

Lamington, Lord, *In the Days of the Dandies* (Edinburgh and London: William Blackwood and Sons, 1890).

Landon, Mike, 'The Death of L. E. L. – A Retrospective Inquest', *Women's Writing*, 16, no. 3 (Dec. 2009), pp. 445–51.

Langford, Paul, 'The English as Reformers: Foreign Visitors' Impressions, 1750–1850', in T. W. C. Blanning and Peter Wende (eds.), *Reform in Great Britain and Germany, 1750–1850* (Oxford University Press, for the British Academy, 1999), pp. 101–19.

Lapp, Robert, 'Romanticism Repackaged: The New Faces of "Old Man" Coleridge in *Fraser's Magazine*, 1830–35', *European Romantic Review*, 11, no. 2 (Spring 2000), pp. 235–47.

Laxton, Paul and Joseph Wisdom, *The A to Z of Regency London* (London Topographical Society, 1985).

Leary, Patrick, '"Fraser's Magazine" and the Literary Life, 1830–47', *Victorian Periodicals Review*, 27, no. 2 (Summer 1994), pp. 105–26.

Lee, Alan J., *The Origins of the Popular Press in England, 1855–1914* (London: Croom Helm, 1976).

Lefebvre, Henri, *Writing on Cities*, eds. Eleonore Kofman and Elizabeth Lebas (Oxford: Blackwell, 1996).

Linley, Margaret, 'A Centre that Would Not Hold: Annuals and Cultural Democracy', in Laurel Brake, Bill Bell and David Finkelstein (eds.), *Nineteenth-Century Media and the Construction of Identities* (Basingstoke: Palgrave, 2000), pp. 54–76.

Liu, Alan, 'The Power of Formalism: The New Historicism', *ELH*, 56, no. 4 (Winter 1989), pp. 721–71.

Llewellyn, Alexander, *The Decade of Reform, the 1830s* (Newton Abbot: David and Charles, 1972).

Loughlin-Chow, M. Clare, 'Bowdler, Henrietta Maria (1750–1830)', *Oxford Dictionary of National Biography* (Oxford University Press, 2004). www.oxforddnb.com.ezproxy.libraries.claremont.edu/view/article/3028

Lynch, Deidre, 'At Home with Jane Austen', in Deidre Lynch and William B. Warner (eds.), *Cultural Institutions of the Novel* (Durham, NC and London: Duke University Press, 1996), pp. 159–92.

'Counter Publics: Shopping and Women's Sociability', in Gillian Russell and Clara Tuite (eds.), *Romantic Sociability: Social Networks and Literary Culture in Britain, 1770–1840* (Cambridge University Press, 2002), pp. 211–36.

'Domesticating Fictions and Nationalizing Women: Edmund Burke, Property, and the Reproduction of Englishness', in Alan Richardson and

Sonia Hofkosh (eds.), *Romanticism, Race, and Imperial Culture, 1790–1834* (Bloomington and Indianapolis: Indiana University Press, 1996), pp. 40–71.

The Economy of Character: Novels, Market Culture, and the Business of Inner Meaning (Chicago and London: University of Chicago Press, 1998).

'Introduction' in Lynch (ed.), *Janeites: Austen's Disciples and Devotees* (Princeton University Press, 2000).

Lynch, Deidre and William B. Warner (eds.), 'Introduction: The Transport of the Novel', *Cultural Institutions of the Novel* (Durham, NC and London: Duke University Press, 1996), pp. 1–10.

McCann, Andrew, *Cultural Politics in the 1790s: Literature, Radicalism and the Public Sphere* (Basingstoke: Macmillan Press, 1999).

MacCarthy, Fiona, *Last Curtsey: The End of the Debutantes* (London: Faber and Faber, 2006).

McDowell, Colin (ed.), *Literary Companion to Fashion* (London: Sinclair-Stevenson, 1995).

McGann, Jerome, 'The Failures of Romanticism', in Tilottama Rajan and Julia M. Wright (eds.), *Romanticism, History, and the Possibilities of Genre: Re-Forming Literature 1789–1837* (Cambridge University Press, 1998), pp. 270–87.

McKendrick, Neil, 'The Consumer Revolution of Eighteenth-Century England', in Neil McKendrick, John Brewer and J. H. Plumb (eds.), *The Birth of a Consumer Society* (Bloomington: Indiana University Press, 1982).

Mackenzie, Gordon, *Marylebone: Great City North of Oxford Street* (London and Basingstoke: Macmillan, 1972).

MacLean, Gerald, Donna Landry and Joseph P. Ward (eds.), *The Country and the City Revisited: England and the Politics of Culture, 1550–1850* (Cambridge University Press, 1999).

McNeil, Peter and Giorgio Riello, , 'The Art and Science of Walking: Gender, Space and the Fashionable Body in the Long Eighteenth Century', *Fashion Theory*, 9, no. 2 (2005), pp. 175–204.

Magnusson, Paul, *Reading Public Romanticism* (Princeton University Press, 1998).

Mahawatte, Royce, '"Life that Is Not Clad in the Same Coat-Tails and Flounces": The Silver-Fork Novel, George Eliot and the Fear of the Material', *Women's Fiction*, 16, no. 2 (Aug. 2009), pp. 323–44.

Maidment, Brian E., '"Penny" Wise, "Penny" Foolish?: Popular Periodicals and the "March of Intellect" in the 1820s and 1830s', in Laurel Brake, Bill Bell and David Finkelstein (eds.), *Nineteenth-Century Media and the Construction of Identities* (Basingstoke: Palgrave, 2000), pp. 104–21.

Major, Emma, 'The Politics of Sociability: Public Dimensions of the Bluestocking Millennium', *Huntington Library Quarterly*, 65, no. 1/2 (2002), pp. 175–92.

Makdisi, Saree, *Romantic Imperialism: Universal Empire and the Culture of Modernity* (Cambridge University Press, 1998).

Mandal, Anthony, *Jane Austen and the Popular Novel: The Determined Author* (Basingstoke: Palgrave, 2007).

Mandler, Peter, *Aristocratic Government in the Age of Reform: Whigs and Liberals, 1830–1852* (Oxford: Clarendon Press, 1990).

Martin, Henri-Jean, *The History and Power of Writing*, trans. Lydia G. Cochrane (University of Chicago Press, 1994).

Mason, Nicholas, '"The Quack Has Become God": Puffery, Print, and the "Death" of Literature in Romantic-Era Britain', *Nineteenth-Century Literature*, 60, no. 1 (June 2005), pp. 1–31.

Matthew, H. C. G., 'Gladstone, William Ewart (1809–1898)', *Oxford Dictionary of National Biography* (Oxford University Press, 2004). www.oxforddnb.com.ezproxy.libraries.claremont.edu/view/article/10787.

Mee, Jon, '"Severe Contentions of Friendship": Barbauld, Conversation, and Dispute', in Heather Glen and Paul Hamilton (eds.), *Repossessing the Romantic Past* (Cambridge University Press, 2006), pp. 21–39.

Meisel, Martin, *Realizations: Narrative, Pictorial, and Theatrical Arts in Nineteenth-Century England* (Princeton University Press, 1983).

Mellor, Anne K., *Mothers of the Nation: Women's Political Writing in England, 1780–1830* (Blomington and Indianapolis: University of Indiana Press, 2000).

Michie, Elsie B., 'Frances Trollope's *One Fault* and the Evolution of the Novel', *Women's Writing*, 18, no. 2 (May 2011), pp. 167–81.

Miles, Robert, 'What is a Romantic Novel?', *NOVEL: A Forum on Fiction*, 34, no. 2 (Spring 2001), pp. 180–201.

Miller, J. Hillis, 'Afterword' to Signet edition of Charles Dickens' *Our Mutual Friend* (New York, 1964).

Mitchell, L. G., *Lord Melbourne, 1779–1848* (Oxford University Press, 1997).

The Whig World, 1760–1837 (London: Hambledon Continuum, 2005).

'The Whigs, the People, and Reform', in T. W. C. Blanning and Peter Wende (eds.), *Reform in Great Britain and Germany, 1750–1850* (Oxford University Press, for the British Academy, 1999), pp. 25–41.

Moers, Ellen, *The Dandy: from Brummell to Beerbohm*, 1st edn 1960 (Lincoln, NE and London: University of Nebraska Press, 1978).

Mole, Tom (ed.), *Romanticism and Celebrity Culture, 1750–1850* (Cambridge University Press, 2009).

Molloy, J. Fitzgerald, *The Most Gorgeous Lady Blessington*, 2 vols. (London: Downey & Co., 1896).

Monypenny, W. F. and G. E. Buckle, *The Life of Benjamin Disraeli, Earl of Beaconsfield*, 2 vols., rev. edn (London: John Murray, 1929).

Moretti, Franco, *Atlas of the European Novel, 1800–1900* (London and New York: Verso, 1998).

Morison, Stanley, *The English Newspaper: Some Account of the Physical Development of Journals Printed in London Between 1622 and the Present Day* (Cambridge University Press, 1932).

Morrow, John, *Young England: The New Generation* (London and New York: Leicester University Press, 1999).

Mulrooney, Jonathan, 'Reading the Romantic-Period Daily News', *Nineteenth-Century Contexts*, 24, no. 4 (Dec. 2002), pp. 351–77.

Mulvihill, James, 'Publicizing Royal Scandal: Nathaniel Jefferys and the "Delicate Investigation" (1806)', *Nineteenth-Century Contexts*, 26, no. 3 (Sept. 2004), pp. 237–56.

Murray, Venetia, *High Society: A Social History of the Regency Period, 1788–1830* (London: Viking, 1998).

Neadic, Stana, 'Romanticism and the Urge to Consume in the First Half of the Nineteenth Century', in Maxine Berg and Helen Clifford (eds.), *Consumers and Luxury: Consumer Culture in Europe 1650–1850* (Manchester University Press, 1999), pp. 208–27.

Negt, Oskar and Alexander Kluge, *Public Sphere and Experience: Toward an Analysis of the Bourgeois and Proletarian Public Sphere*, trans. Peter Labanyi, Jamie Owen Daniel and Assenka Oksiloff (Minneapolis and London: University of Minnesota Press, 1993).

Neill, Edward, *The Politics of Jane Austen* (Basingstoke: Macmillan Press, 1999).

Newbould, Ian, *Whiggery and Reform, 1830–41* (Stanford University Press, 1990).

Newman, Rebecca Edwards, '"Prosecuting the *Onus Criminus*": Early Criticism of the Novel in *Fraser's Magazine*', *Victorian Periodicals Review*, 35, no. 4 (Winter 2002), pp. 401–19.

Nicolay, Claire, 'Delightful Coxcombs to Industrious Men: Fashionable Politics and Performance in *Cecil* and *Pendennis*', *Victorian Literature and Culture*, 30, no. 1 (2002), pp. 289–304.

'The "Fatal Attractions" of "Serious Things": Regency Politics and Performance in Baudelaire's *Le Spleen de Paris*', *European Romantic Review*, 11, no. 3 (Summer 2000), pp. 322–47.

Nord, Deborah Epstein, *Walking the Streets: Women, Representation, and the City* (London and Ithaca, NY: Cornell University Press, 1995).

O'Cinneide, Muireann, *Aristocratic Women and the Literary Nation, 1832–1867* (Basingstoke: Palgrave Macmillan, 2008).

O'Gorman, Frank, *The Long Eighteenth Century: British Political and Social History, 1688–1832* (London: Arnold, 1997).

Oettermann, Stephan, *The Panorama: History of a Mass Medium*, trans. Deborah Lucas Schneider (New York: Zone Books, 1997).

Oxford English Dictionary, 3rd edition (Oxford University Press, 2012).

Parker, Mark, *Literary Magazines and British Romanticism* (Cambridge University Press, 2000).

Parrinder, Patrick, *Nation and Novel: The English Novel from its Origins to the Present Day* (Oxford University Press, 2006).

Pearce, Edward, *Reform! The Fight for the 1832 Reform Act* (London: Jonathan Cape, 2003).

Pearce, Susan M., 'Foreword: Words and Things', *Experiencing Material Culture in the Western World* (London and Washington, DC: Leicester University Press, 1997), pp. 1–10.

Perrin, Noel, *Dr Bowdler's Legacy: A History of Expurgated Books in England and America*, 3rd edn (New York: Atheneum, 1969).

Phillips, J. F. C., *Shepherd's London* (London: Cassell, 1976).

Poovey, Mary, *The History of the Modern Fact: Problems of Knowledge in the Sciences of Wealth and Society* (University of Chicago Press, 1998).

　Making a Social Body: British Cultural Formation, 1830–1864 (University of Chicago Press, 1995).

　Uneven Developments: The Ideological Work of Gender in Mid-Victorian England (University of Chicago Press, 1988).

Pound, R. J., 'Grant, Charles Jameson', *Oxford Dictionary of National Biography* (Oxford University Press, 2004). www.oxforddnb.com.ezproxy.libraries. claremont.edu/view/article/66121.

Pragnell, Hubert J., *The London Panoramas of Robert Barker and Thomas Girtin* (London Topographical Society, 1968).

Price, Leah, 'Reader's Block: Response', *Victorian Studies*, 46, no. 2 (Winter 2004), pp. 231–42.

Pykett, Lyn, 'A Woman's Business: Women and Writing, 1830–80', in Marion Shaw (ed.), *An Introduction to Women's Writing: From the Middle Ages to the Present Day* (London: Prentice, 1998), pp. 149–76.

Rauch, Alan, *Useful Knowledge: The Victorians, Morality, and the March of Intellect* (Durham, NC: Duke University Press, 2001).

Raven, James, *The Business of Books: Booksellers and the English Book Trade 1450–1850* (New Haven: Yale University Press, 2007).

　Judging New Wealth: Popular Publishing and Responses to Commerce in England, 1750–1800 (Oxford: Clarendon, 1992).

Rea, Robert, *The English Press in Politics* (Lincoln, NE: University of Nebraska Press, 1963).

Redfield, Marc, *Politics of Aesthetics: Nationalism, Gender, Romanticism* (Stanford University Press, 2003).

Reeve, Robin Martin, *The Industrial Revolution, 1750 to 1850* (University of London Press, 1971).

Rendell, Jane, 'London's Italian Opera House: Exchanging Looks', *Visual Culture in Britain*, 1, no. 2 (2000), pp. 1–23.

Rich, Adrienne, 'Notes towards a Politics of Location', in *Blood, Bread, and Poetry: Selected Prose, 1975–1985* (New York: W. W. Norton, 1986), pp. 210–31.

Richards, Thomas, *The Commodity Culture of Victorian England: Advertising and Spectacle, 1851–1914* (Stanford University Press, 1990).

Richardson, Alan, *Literature, Education, and Romanticism: Reading as Social Practice, 1780–1832* (Cambridge University Press, 1994).

Richmond, Charles and Paul Smith (eds.), *The Self-Fashioning of Disraeli, 1818–1851* (Cambridge University Press, 1998).

Roberts, Warren, *Jane Austen and the French Revolution*, reprint of 1979 Macmillan edn (London: Athlone, 1995).

Robinson, Alan, *Imagining London, 1770–1900* (Basingstoke: Palgrave Macmillan, 2004).

Robinson, Lillian S., 'On Reading Trash' in *Sex, Class, and Culture* (Bloomington: Indiana University Press, 1978), pp. 200–22.

Roper, Derek, *Reviewing before the Edinburgh, 1788–1802* (London: Methuen, 1978).

Rosa, Matthew Whiting, *The Silver-Fork School: Novels of Fashion Preceding Vanity Fair* (New York: Columbia University Press, 1936).

Rosenfeld, Sybil, 'Jane Austen and Private Theatricals', *Essays and Studies*, 15 (1962), pp. 40–51.

    Temples of Thespis: Some Private Theatres and Theatricals in England and Wales, 1700–1820 (London: The Society for Theatre Research, 1978).

Rovee, Christopher, *Imagining the Gallery: The Social Body of British Romanticism* (Stanford University Press, 2006).

Rowland, William G., Jr, *Literature and the Marketplace: Romantic Writers and Their Audiences in Great Britain and the United States* (Lincoln: University of Nebraska Press, 1996).

Royle, Edward, *Revolutionary Britannia? Reflections on the Threat of Revolution in Britain, 1789–1848* (Manchester University Press, 2000).

Royle, Edward and James Walvin, *English Radicals and Reformers, 1760–1848* (Brighton: Harvester Press, 1982).

Russell, Gillian, *Women, Sociability and Theatre in Georgian London* (Cambridge University Press, 2007).

Russell, Gillian and Clara Tuite, *Romantic Sensibility: Social Networks and Literary Culture in Britain, 1770–1840* (Cambridge University Press, 2002).

Sadleir, Michael, *Blessington-D'Orsay: A Masquerade* (London: Constable & Co., 1933).

    Bulwer and His Wife: A Panorama, 1803–1836 (London: Constable & Co., 1933).

    The Strange Life of Lady Blessington (New York: Farrar, Straus, and Company, 1947).

St Clair, William, *The Reading Nation in the Romantic Period* (Cambridge University Press, 2004).

Sales, Roger, *Jane Austen and Representations of Regency England* (London and New York: Routledge, 1994).

Salmon, Richard, *Henry James and the Culture of Publicity* (Cambridge University Press, 1997).

    'The Secret of the Spectacle: Epistemology and Commodity Display in *The Ambassadors*', *The Henry James Review*, 14, no. 1 (Winter 1993), pp. 43–54.

    '"A Simulacrum of Power": Intimacy and Abstraction in the Rhetoric of the New Journalism', in Laurel Brake, Bill Bell and David Finkelstein (eds.), *Nineteenth-Century Media and the Construction of Identities* (Basingstoke: Palgrave, 2000), pp. 27–39.

Saville, John, *The Consolidation of the Capitalist State, 1800–1850* (London and Boulder, CO: Pluto Press, 1994).

Scheumaker, Helen, '"This Lock You See": Nineteenth-Century Hair Work as the Commodified Self', *Fashion Theory*, 1, no. 4 (Dec. 1997), pp. 421–46.

Schor, Naomi, *Reading in Detail: Aesthetics and the Feminine* (New York: Methuen, 1987).

Scott-Baumann, Michael, *Reforming Britain, 1815–50* (London: Hodder Murray, 2006).

Selway, N. C., *The Regency Road: The Coaching Prints of James Pollard* (London: Faber and Faber, 1957).

Shields, Rob, *Places on the Margin: Alternative Geographies of Modernity* (London and New York: Routledge, 1991).

Siskin, Clifford, 'Epilogue', in Deidre Lynch and William B. Warner (eds.), *Cultural Institutions of the Novel* (Durham, NC and London: Duke University Press, 1996), pp. 423–40.

'Novels and Systems', *NOVEL: A Forum on Fiction*, 34, no. 2 (Spring 2001), pp. 203–15.

'VR Machine: Romanticism and the Physical', *European Romantic Review*, 12, no. 2 (Spring 2001), pp. 158–64.

The Work of Writing: Literature and Social Change in Britain, 1700–1830 (Baltimore: Johns Hopkins University Press, 1998).

Smallwood, Christine, 'Review of Joanna Smith Rakoff, *A Fortunate Age* (New York: Scribner, 2009)', *London Review of Books* (11 Feb. 2010), pp. 29–30.

Smart, William, *Economic Annals of the Nineteenth Century, 1821–1830*, 2 vols. (London: Macmillan and Co., 1917).

Smith, Neil and Cindi Katz, 'Grounding Metaphor: Towards a Spatialized Politics', in Michael Keith and Steve Pile (eds.), *Place and the Politics of Identity* (London and New York: Routledge, 1993), pp. 67–83.

Smith, Paul, *Disraeli: A Brief Life*, 1st edn 1996 (Cambridge University Press, 1999).

Smith, Simon C., *British Imperialism, 1750–1970* (Cambridge University Press, 1998).

Soja, Edward, *Postmodern Geographies: The Reassertion of Space in Critical Social Theory* (London and New York: Verso, 1989).

Solkin, David, *Painting Out of the Ordinary: Modernity and the Art of Everyday Life in Early Nineteenth-Century Britain* (New Haven and London: Yale University Press, 2008).

Southam, B. C. (ed.), *Jane Austen: The Critical Heritage* (London: Routledge & Kegan Paul, 1968).

Jane Austen: A Student's Guide to the Later Manuscript Works (London: Concord Books, 2007).

Southgate, Donald, *The Passing of the Whigs, 1832–1886* (London: Macmillan, 1965).

Stewart, Robert, *Henry Brougham, 1778–1868: His Public Career* (London: The Bodley Head, 1985).

Strachan, John, *Advertising and Satirical Culture in the Romantic Period* (Cambridge University Press, 2007).

Sturrock, June, '*Emma* in the 1860s: Austen, Yonge, Oliphant, Eliot', *Women's Writing*, 17, no. 2 (Aug. 2010), pp. 324–42.

Sussman, Charlotte, *Consuming Anxieties: Consumer Protest, Gender and British Slavery, 1713–1833* (Stanford University Press, 2000).

Sutherland, John, 'Foreword: The Underread', in Barbara Leah Harman and Susan Meyer (eds.), *The New Nineteenth Century: Feminist Readings of Underread Victorian Fiction* (New York: Garland Publishing, 1996), pp. xi–xxv.

'Henry Colburn, Publisher', *Publishing History*, 19 (1986), pp. 59–84.

Sutherland, Kathryn, '"Events ... Have Made Us a World of Readers": Reader Relations 1780–1830', in David B. Pirie (ed.), *The Romantic Period* (London: Penguin, 1994), pp. 1–48.

Jane Austen's Textual Lives: From Aeschylus to Bollywood (Oxford University Press, 2005).

'*Jane Eyre's* Literary History: The Case for *Mansfield Park*', *ELH*, 59, no. 2 (Summer 1992), pp. 409–40.

Swartz, David, *Culture of Power: The Sociology of Pierre Bourdieu* (University of Chicago Press, 1997).

Sweetman, John, 'Brudenell, James Thomas, Seventh Earl of Cardigan (1797–1868)', *Oxford Dictionary of National Biography* (Oxford University Press, 2004). www.oxforddnb.com.ezproxy.libraries.claremont.edu/view/article/3765

Tandon, Bharat, *Jane Austen and the Morality of Conversation* (London: Anthem Press, 2003).

The Tate Gallery, *Illustrated Catalogue of Acquisitions* (London: Tate Gallery, 1988), pp. 74–5.

Thompson, E. P., *The Making of the English Working Class* (London: V. Gollancz, 1963).

Thompson, F. M. L., *English Landed Society in the Nineteenth Century* (London: Routledge & Kegan Paul, 1963).

'Moving Frontiers and the Fortunes of the Aristocratic Town House 1830–1930', *The London Journal*, 20, no. 1 (1995), pp. 67–78.

The Rise of Respectable Society: A Social History of Victorian Britain, 1830–1900 (Cambridge, MA: Harvard University Press, 1988).

Thompson, J. B., *Ideology and Modern Culture: Critical Social Theory in the Era of Mass Communication* (Cambridge: Polity, 1990).

Tillotson, Kathleen, *Novels of the Eighteen-Forties* (Oxford University Press, 1954).

Tillyard, Stella, *Aristocrats: Caroline, Emily, Louisa and Sarah Lennox, 1740–1832* (New York: Farrar, Straus, and Giroux, 2000).

Tobin, Beth Fowkes, *Superintending the Poor: Charitable Ladies and Paternal Landlords in British Fiction, 1770–1860* (New Haven and London: Yale University Press, 1993).

Todd, Janet, 'Jane Austen and the Professional Wife', in Heather Glen and Paul Hamilton (eds.), *Repossessing the Romantic Past* (Cambridge University Press, 2006), pp. 203–25.

Towse, Clive, 'Ward, Robert Plumer (1765–1846)', *Oxford Dictionary of National Biography* (Oxford University Press, 2004). www.oxforddnb.com.ezproxy.libraries.claremont.edu/view/article/28703.

Tristram, Philippa, 'Jane Austen and the Changing Face of England', in Dana Arnold (ed.), *The Georgian Country House: Architecture, Landscape and Society* (Stroud: Sutton Publishing, 1998), pp. 139–51.

Trumpener, Katie, 'The Virago Jane Austen', in Deidre Lynch (ed.), *Janeites: Austen's Disciples and Devotees* (Princeton University Press, 2000), pp. 140–65.

Tuite, Clara, 'Domestic Retrenchment and Imperial Expansion', in You-me Park and Rajeswari Sunder Rajan (eds.), *The Postcolonial Jane Austen* (London: Routledge, 2000), pp. 98–122.

  Romantic Austen: Sexual Politics and the Literary Canon (Cambridge University Press, 2002).

Turner, Michael J., *British Politics in an Age of Reform* (Manchester University Press, 1999).

Vernon, John, *Money and Fiction: Literary Realism in the Nineteenth and Early Twentieth Centuries* (Ithaca and London: Cornell University Press, 1984).

Vickery, Amanda, *The Gentleman's Daughter: Women's Lives in Georgian England* (New Haven: Yale University Press, 1999).

Waddy, H. T., *The Devonshire Club – and 'Crockford's'* (London: Eveleigh Nash, 1919).

Wagner, Tamara, *Financial Speculation in Victorian Fiction: Plotting Money and the Novel Genre, 1815–1901* (Columbus: Ohio State University Press, 2010).

  'Introduction: From Satirized Silver Cutlery to the Allure of the Anti-Domestic in Nineteenth-Century Women's Writing: Silver-Fork Fiction and Its Literary Legacies', *Women's Writing*, 16, no. 2 (Aug. 2009), pp. 181–90.

  'Silver-Fork Legacies: Sensationalizing Fashionable Fiction', *Women's Writing*, 16, no. 2 (Aug. 2009), pp. 301–22.

Wahrman, Dror, *Imagining the Middle Class: The Political Representation of Class in Britain, c. 1780–1840* (Cambridge University Press, 1995).

Walker, Martin, *Powers of the Press: The World's Great Newspapers* (London: Quartet, 1982).

Wall, Cynthia, 'Gendering Rooms: Domestic Architecture and Literary Acts', *Eighteenth-Century Fiction*, 5, no. 4 (July 1993), pp. 349–72.

Warner, Michael, 'The Mass Public and the Mass Subject', in Bruce Robbins (ed.), *The Phantom Public Sphere* (Minneapolis: University of Minnesota Press, 1993), pp. 234–56.

Watt, James, *Contesting the Gothic: Fiction, Genre and Cultural Conflict, 1764–1832* (Cambridge University Press, 1999).

Weinreb, Ben and Christopher Hibbert, *The London Encyclopaedia* (London: Macmillan, 1983).

Wendorf, Richard, *After Sir Joshua: Essays on British Art and Cultural History* (New Haven: Yale University Press, 2005).

Wernick, Andrew, 'The Work of Art as Gift and Commodity', in Susan M. Pearce (ed.), *Experiencing Modern Culture in the Western World* (London and Washington, DC: Leicester University Press, 1997), pp. 174–95.

White, Jerry, *London in the Nineteenth Century* (London: Jonathan Cape, 2007).

Whitfield, Peter, *London: A Life in Maps* (London: The British Library, 2006).

Wicke, Jennifer A., *Advertising Fictions: Literature, Advertisement, and Social Reading* (New York: Columbia University Press, 1988).

Williams, Raymond, *The Country and the City*, 1st edn 1973 (London: The Hogarth Press, 1985).

The Long Revolution (New York: Penguin, 1961).

'The Press and Popular Culture: An Historical Perspective', in George Boyce, James Curran and Pauline Wingate (eds.), *Newspaper History: From the Seventeenth Century to the Present Day* (London: Constable, 1978), pp. 41–50.

Wilson, Ben, *Decency and Disorder: The Age of Cant, 1789–1837* (London: Faber and Faber, 2007).

Wilson, Cheryl A., 'Almack's and the Silver-Fork Novel', *Women's Writing*, 16, no. 2 (Aug. 2009), pp. 237–52.

Winkenweder, Brian, 'The Newspaper as Nationalist Icon, or How to Paint "Imagined Communities"', *Limina: A Journal of Historical and Cultural Studies*, 14 (2008), pp. 85–96.

Woof, Robert, 'Haydon, Benjamin Robert (1786–1846)', *Oxford Dictionary of National Biography* (Oxford University Press, 2004). www.oxforddnb.com. ezproxy.libraries.claremont.edu/view/article/12750.

Zevin, Alexander, 'Panoramic Literature in Nineteenth-Century Paris: Robert Macaire as a Type of Everyday', http://dl.lib.brown.edu/paris/Zevin.html

Index

CAMBRIDGE STUDIES IN
NINETEENTH-CENTURY LITERATURE AND CULTURE

General editor
GILLIAN BEER, *University of Cambridge*

Titles published